CULTURES OF VIOLENCE

Manchester University Press

CULTURES OF VIOLENCE

Lynching and racial killing in South Africa and the American South

Ivan Evans

Manchester University Press

Manchester and New York

distributed in the United States exclusively by Palgrave Macmillan

Published by Manchester University Press
Oxford Road, Manchester M13 9NR, UK
and Room 400, 175 Fifth Avenue, New York, NY 10010, USA
www.manchesteruniversitypress.co.uk

Distributed in the United States exclusively by
Palgrave Macmillan, 175 Fifth Avenue, New York,
NY 10010, USA

Distributed exclusively in Canada by
UBC Press, University of British Columbia, 2029 West Mall,
Vancouver, BC, Canada V6T 1Z2

British Library Cataloguing-in-Publication Data
A catalogue record for this book is available from the British Library

Library of Congress Cataloging-in-Publication Data applied for

ISBN 978 0 7190 7904 7 *hardback*

First published 2009

18 17 16 15 14 13 12 11 10 09   10 9 8 7 6 5 4 3 2 1

Typeset by Special Edition Pre-press Services
www.special-edition.co.uk
Printed in Great Britain
by CPI Antony Rowe, Chippenham, Wiltshire

Contents

Preface

Having lived in South Africa and the United States for lengthy periods, I have often wondered about what my graduate students like to call "the lived experience of race." Because the word "segregation" was used to describe the new system of race relations that took hold in both countries in the first half of the twentieth century, an inescapable aura of sameness seemed to hang over much of the literature on this period. South Africa and the American South did indeed share much in common in these years. The same litany of cruel and dehumanizing devices – disenfranchisement, coerced labor, residential segregation, segregated labor unions, separate and inferior education – clearly dominated the separate histories of the two countries. Indeed, while reading up on the hardships that blacks in South Africa and African Americans endured, the literature seemed to blur, a sensation that intensified when attention focused on labor tenants in the agricultural sectors. There are indeed sound reasons why much of the literature tends to emphasize the commonalities that have made the two racial orders such enduring objects of comparative analysis. Still, the structural, cultural and political differences between them were also large and significant. South Africa's centralized state contrasted with the federal system in the United States. For example, gold mining, South Africa's dominant sector at the turn of the last century, established distinctive dynamics that differed from those that agrarian elites imposed in the South. Racial paternalism persisted longer in South Africa than in the South, especially where regional obeisance to "King Cotton" swamped all relations between African Americans and whites. What significance, I wondered, did these and other differences have for our understanding of the racial state, the sociological entity I intended to examine?

The more I pondered this question, the more my attention came to focus on the phenomenon of extra-legal racial violence. It was not surprising that both contexts sported high levels of formal repression that was carried out by various law-enforcement authorities. For this is what white supremacy meant – a system of racial domination that was backed up and implemented by formal state institutions. Where, I wondered, did extra-legal racial violence fit in?

Like formal repression, extra-legal racial violence – or more precisely for this study, white on black violence – is an unavoidable and ubiquitous theme in South African and Southern history. Slavery and colonial conquest had provided ample opportunity for whites to inflict atrocities on blacks and routinize force and coercion. In ways that I set out to chronicle, this element of racial mastery had clearly carried over into the two systems of segregation that emerged once slavery and colonial conquest ended. Soon, however, I was less interested in the persistence of extra-legal violence in the two segregationist orders. Instead, I was increasingly struck by a tell-ing difference in the *style* of that violence: in contrast to the thousands of lynchings that erupted across the South even before the Civil War ended, all the evidence with which I was familiar indicated that whites in South Africa never resorted to this macabre practice. This is the striking contrast that I examine in this book. The formulation of this basic contrast changed as the study unfolded. All of the refinements that I made to this basic contrast involved more careful specifications of the forms that racial violence assumed in South Africa, there being little to add to or modify in the voluminous and frequently excellent literature on lynching in the American South.

With regard to the South, therefore, this book contends that lynching was ubiquitous and that it indeed became the iconic expression of white supremacy in the region. Various chapters pay attention to the precise con-ditions that yielded variations in the intensity of lynching, encouraging the practice in some parts but restraining it elsewhere in the South. It also con-tends that lynchings were conducted in different ways that are sociologically significant. It is therefore noteworthy that some lynchings were carried out by two or three men who acted furtively and for private motives. On other occasions, large mobs that sometimes numbered in the tens of thousands and included men, women and children would gather in the open to wreak racial vengeance that was manifestly communal and defiantly symbolic. With their faces uncovered, men in these mobs would ritually mutilate the body of a still-living African American before killing him with ropes, fire and bullets under conditions that can only be described as festive. The persistence of such practices, the variety of motives and mob sizes and, most importantly, the widespread tolerance of lynching in Southern communities justify the conclusion that the South developed a distinctive *lynch culture*. Lynching was therefore an organic and durable expression of Southern-style segrega-tion. The practice took root in the 1860s, reached its high point around the First World War and gradually declined until it eventually ceased, at least as a sociological emblem of the region, in the 1950s. The region's lynch culture set it apart not only from racial domination in South Africa but also from all other industrializing nations in the world.

Blacks in South Africa did not have to contend with the macabre practice of lynching. The book discusses several incidents when whites formed mobs and threatened to lynch blacks but invariably failed to do so. Still, extra-legal violence against blacks in South Africa was also extensive. A careful study of the secondary and archival literature on South African historiography sharpened the distinction between private and communal forms of racial violence: whereas extra-legal communal violence against blacks was essentially irrelevant in South Africa, private violence remained at extraordinarily high levels throughout the twentieth century. I argue that the rapid establishment and dominance of a centralized state bureaucracy in South Africa, one of the master trends of the country's twentieth-century history, determined this pattern. In contrast to the lynch culture that emerged in the American South, South Africa developed a *bureaucratic culture* that all but shut the door on white mobbism and restricted whites only to private forms of extra-legal violence which, moreover, the courts regularly punished, but not seriously enough to stamp out the practice. The result, for blacks, was a society that was mercilessly free of the horrors of mob lynchings but taut with the reality of violence from two deadly sources: armed officials and individual white civilians.

Writing a book that explores the distinction between the Southern lynch culture and the bureaucratic culture of racial violence in South Africa took longer than expected. I am very much in the debt of many relatives, friends and colleagues, and I am happy to finally thank them. First and foremost, the book would not have seen the light of day without the support of my wife, Catherine, and two sons, Alexandre and Dylan. I gratefully thank them for providing me with the support I often desperately needed. In retrospect, I cannot thank Catherine enough, too, for the many suggestions she offered about substance and style. I accepted every one of them and am particularly grateful for the vigilant eye she maintains for hyperbole.

Colleagues in the department of Sociology at the University of California San Diego (UCSD) played an important role in helping me conduct the necessary research and also helped refine many of my tentative arguments. Making full use of their temporary power as Chair of the Department, Andrew Scull and Richard Madsen made telephone calls and moved my departmental obligations around to facilitate applications for leave. I am immensely grateful for the free time their exertions made possible. I would like to thank two colleagues in particular for taking an active interest in and contributing so positively to my work. Harvey Goldman offered his usual insightful commentary and first-rate recommendations. Several key suggestions he made have been grafted onto the spine of this book's comparative argument. I am equally grateful for his moral support and constant encouragement. Gershon Shafir also offered important methodological advice on how to frame the comparisons I was interested in. His adeptness at extracting broad comparisons helped me to advance my argument in bolder terms, and the book is all the better for that. I would also like to thank Bennetta Jules-Rosette, Africa's gatekeeper here at UCSD. Her unstinting support and extraordinary energy in promoting anything that bears even remotely on Africa nurtures a supportive intellectual climate that eased the pressure of writing this book. Two other colleagues, John Skrentny and Jeff Haydu, also kindly read drafts of chapters and offered helpful advice. Paul Frymer offered useful information while he was a member of the Department. I should also thank my university for a faculty research grant that made my research trip to South Africa possible. The bulk of the costs of the research trip, however, were borne by the Fulbright-Hays Faculty Research Award that I gratefully received from the Department of Education in the USA.

Staff at various libraries and, in South Africa, also at the State Archives, provided phenomenal assistance. I got to know well the succession of UCSD librarians who labored on my unceasing requests for inter-library loan material from halfway across the world. Librarians in charge of the Carter-Karis Collection at Northwestern University provided prompt assistance that yielded indispensable information. Mostly, however, my thanks go to the courteous and professional librarians and archivists who assisted me in South Africa. Carole Archibald and Michelle Pickover in the William Cullen Library at the University of the Witwatersrand are surely worth their weight in gold. Librarians at the University of South Africa were also extremely helpful – and once even tracked me down as I traveled in South Africa to let me know where else I might search for hard-to-find material. Officials at the National Archives and Records Service in South Africa, especially in the Transvaal and Cape Repositories in Pretoria and Cape Town respectively, were especially important and helpful. They worked hard to ensure that I found what I came looking for.

My sincerest thanks go to Janis Grobbelaar, a dear friend and now head of the Sociology Department at the University of Pretoria. Janis hosted me for four months while I was in Pretoria and, as usual, unstintingly extended to me the hospitality and warmth that are the hallmarks of her friendship. I cannot thank her enough for all her support, both recent and past. I am grateful to her, too, for arranging the talk I presented to her colleagues. I learned much from some of the supportive skepticism I encountered, especially with regard to the nature of Afrikaner theology. Jeff Lever offered his usual brief but telling correctives. Two skeptical remarks (about the limited nature of government intervention in South Africa circa 1910 and the TRC-like nature of the Kerner Commission of 1968 in the USA) sent me scurrying back to my notes. Charles van Onselen, also at the University of Pretoria, provided excellent advice about the relative merits of depth versus coverage when doing comparative research. I often returned to the useful notes I took when we once spoke over the phone.

Many colleagues at other universities, and one other great but now departed friend, also contributed to this book, sometimes unwittingly. From amongst this rather large number, and for different reasons, I would like to thank the following in no particular order: Julia Adams; Ann Orloff; Elizabeth Clemens; George Steinmetz; Ed Kiser; Ed Telles; Jonathan Markovitz; Howard Winant; Fred Cooper; Gay Seidman; Dunbar Moodie; Elrena van der Spuy; Dirk Van Zyl Smit; Tessa Lever; and Jonathan Crush. Several might not recall the important assistance they provided, but I certainly do. Perhaps the very first comment and support for this project came from participants at the NEWSA (New South Africa) conference in Burlington, Vermont, in 2004. Special thanks go to Clifton Crais, Pamela Scully, William Beinart and Saul Dubow. Two undergraduate students – Heather Hughes and Daniel Pechstedt – also deserve mention and thanks for working on the manuscript when it was in much more primitive form.

All of the above persons might recognize that the book is a far cry from the ambitious project I outlined in my earliest conversations. I hope they are not disappointed that I chose to remain relatively sane by not pursuing the comparison beyond the 1940s. Notwithstanding the gratitude above, I hasten to lay absolute claim to all shortcomings that this book may contain. Those shortcomings would have been all the greater without the expert assistance of Emma Brennan and Rachel Armstrong at the Manchester University Press. Fortunately, Corinne Orde caught and corrected many grammatical and stylistic errors in the manuscript.

Finally, I would like to dedicate this book to my wife, Catherine, and to my mother, Aida.

1

Introduction

South Africa and the United States of America, two countries with notorious histories of racial violence, attempted to formally deal with their violent pasts at roughly the same time. Eight years after Apartheid had formally ended and seven years after the Promotion of National Unity and Reconciliation Act of 1995 brought the body to life, the Truth and Reconciliation Commission (TRC) delivered its final report in 2002. The extensive report laid bare the sordid details of the violence that had been committed in the name of Apartheid and called on the new democratic government to make restitutions for the pain and hardship inflicted on thousands of Apartheid's black victims. Two years later, on 17 June 2005, the US Senate approved Resolution 39, formally apologizing for the body's failure to enact a federal anti-lynching law in the course of the twentieth century. According to the two senators who sponsored the resolution, the idea of a formal apology arose after they had read *Without Sanctuary: Lynching Photography in America*, a graphic and disturbing pictorial history by James Allen.[1]

The TRC and Senate Resolution 39 were part of efforts to "bring closure" to the painful racial past, but they did so in very different ways. The TRC was a formal state body, established and fully funded by the post-Apartheid state. Its report also marked the culmination of a massive investigation modeled on the lines of a criminal court inquiry that succeeded in sending to jail a number of violent perpetrators. Its work embroiled millions of South Africans in its remarkably transparent and comprehensive procedures. In contrast, the passage of Resolution 39 was a perfunctory affair, the brainchild of two individuals, Mary Landrieu (Democrat, Louisiana) and George Allen (Republican, Virginia), who took it upon themselves to pilot a resolution through the workings of the Senate. Only a handful of senators were present when Resolution 39 was read; if a roll call had been taken, it would have recorded that two senators from Mississippi, the state that yielded the most lynchings in the South, were not even present when the vote was taken. "The moment lacked the drama of the fiery Senate filibusters that blocked the legislation three times in the past century."[2] The irrelevance of Resolution 39 seems to confirm Elliot Gorn's lament that "Increasingly, Americans are a people without history ... which means ... a people reluctant to engage difficult ethical issues."[3]

The TRC and Resolution 39 were two very different ways of dealing with the painful past. If the TRC signaled the full involvement of the state in dealing with the violent past, Resolution 39 was a telling reminder of the indifference with which the US government dealt with the summary killing of African Americans in the first half of the twentieth century. The TRC and Resolution 39 therefore provide a useful starting point for a comparative study of racial violence in South Africa and the United States because they highlight the different roles that the state played in that violence.

The extensive work of the TRC in post-Apartheid South Africa serves as a metaphor for the systemic and vanguard role that the state played in forging and maintaining the racial order over the course of the twentieth century. From the outset of its emergence in 1910, South Africa's unitary state set out to promote the interests of its white citizens. Drawing on a racially discriminatory constitution, state managers after 1910 elaborated an official policy of "segregation" that authorized them to manage the field of "race relations." Interposing itself between black and white subjects, the state claimed the monopoly over the means of racial violence and undertook explicitly discriminatory legislation that an expanding array of oppressive institutions would enforce over the next eight decades. As in all such monopolies, state control was never so effective or total to preclude unofficial white violence against blacks.

Unofficial violence was particularly high in the white rural areas and the gold mining industry, where *individual* whites were notorious for launching brutal and lethal attacks on unarmed blacks. However, it was only under exceptional circumstances that white citizens staged *collective* attacks against blacks. Collective violence against blacks was not unknown, but it occurred infrequently and usually in moments of extreme intra-white violence, such as in the course of the Anglo-Boer War, the armed Rebellion of 1914 and the violent strike of 1922, prompting historians to recently abandon the idea that these events amounted to "white men's conflicts" in which blacks played little or no role.[4] Still, however much they were involved in internecine white violence, blacks were neither the primary protagonists nor the targets of the various conflicts that tested the foundations of the emerging state. Moreover, violent upheavals amongst whites alarmed state managers who feared that blacks might capitalize on white disunity and encourage them to challenge white supremacy. The subsidence of these intra-white wars, rebellions and strikes in the interWar years (1918–39) therefore prompted the state to intervene ever more extensively and deeply into society by assuming greater controls over all facets of blacks' lives. The result was the consolidation of a tradition of elaborate and extensive state intervention in the twentieth century.[5] The TRC remained true to this tradition of forthright state intervention into South African society. True to form, this state-supported enterprise managed to attach names and faces to the quotidian destruction of black life in a way that made it difficult for whites to deny their responsibility for racial violence.[6]

Resolution 39, in contrast, illustrates the halting and ambiguous, but always complicit, role that the state played in racial violence in the American South. Although it addressed one of the most repugnant episodes in American history, the resolution failed utterly to capture the national imagination. Mentioned only briefly in the national media, it failed to ignite a popular discussion about, let alone a national apology for, the horrors of lynching in twentieth-century America. Furthermore, it addressed only the Senate's "failure to act," omitting the role that the other branches of government played in the segregationist era. Most importantly, the resolution could not do what the TRC had so visibly done in its quest for racial reconciliation: it could not name names and hold specific individuals accountable for the extra-legal killing of the 4,742 lynch victims that the resolution alludes to. For almost all Americans who read reports of the resolution in their local newspapers, the victims remained as nameless and the perpetrators as furtive as they had been in the first half of the twentieth century. Who precisely was responsible for the "festival of violence" against blacks in the South?

In the same breath that it faulted the Senate for not passing anti-lynching legislation and for disregarding "repeated requests" by civil rights groups and several Presidents, the resolution also noted that the House of Representatives had managed to approve three "strong anti-lynching measures" between 1920 and 1940. In this way, the resolution alludes to the theory of divided government, suggesting that the fractured nature of the federal state complicated the task of racial justice. The light that Resolution 39 shone on lynching was shallow and confusing, mirroring the episodic attention that the state as a whole had earlier devoted to the summary killing of African Americans in the segregationist South. Perhaps the most telling aspect of the resolution, moreover, was its preoccupation with the Senate's "failure to enact anti-lynching legislation." This somewhat guarded language reinforced the image of a passive and Byzantine American state, hamstrung not by a systemic racism that implicated the state in racial lynching but by a fig leaf – the formal complexities of the federal system.

The ubiquity of racial violence in both South Africa and the American South has not escaped the attention of comparativist scholars, of course. But the literature shares a common deficiency. Virtually all of it focuses on formal structures and state policies. Accordingly, the literature is largely silent about the role that different forms of *extra-legal* violence played in the genesis and perpetuation of the two racial orders. To date, no major comparative work has considered interpersonal violence as a distinctive component of the broad field of "racial repression." The comparative literature therefore imparts a good idea about the role that state bodies played in establishing segregation but virtually nothing about the extra-legal, unofficial violence that also shaped the two racial orders. This silence is surprising because unofficial violence was extensive in both contexts. Distinguishing unofficial violence from "repression" therefore directs attention away from the activities of formal bodies and highlights the violence that ordinary white citizens inflicted on blacks. By focusing on unofficial violence in the early stages of segregation in both countries,[7] this study hopes to stimulate questions about a neglected phenomenon that tells us much about the development of distinctive forms and "styles" of white supremacy.

Private and communal violence

Unofficial violence assumes a variety of forms. Donald Horowitz, for example, distinguishes eight possible distinct incarnations consisting of violent protests, pogroms, feuds, lynchings, genocides, terrorist attacks, gang assaults and ethnic fights and notes, moreover, that various permutations of these give rise to "hybrid forms" of extra-legal violence.[8] This study, however, is almost exclusively concerned with interpersonal forms of extra-legal violence. More precisely, it is concerned with lynching.

Lynching was the iconic form of racial violence in the American South and the most emotionally fraught development in racial segregation after the Civil War (see table opposite). Lynching pervades the history of the New South and has generated a vast and still expanding scholarship devoted to the institution.[9] In contrast, lynching was virtually absent in South Africa. The word was occasionally used in South Africa after 1910, usually by whites to warn what *might* happen in the absence of stern laws and sterner policemen. In South Africa, one source notes, "the banding together of groups of whites in small towns and villages to engage in frenzied attacks, involving violent and obscene rituals, upon defenseless Africans ... was almost non-existent."[10]

Why was extra-legal racial violence fundamental to segregation in the American South but of minor importance in South Africa? In response to this broad question, the book distinguishes between two cultures of violence: a *bureaucratic tradition* of racial violence in South Africa and a *lynch culture* in the American South. It argues that a tradition of bureaucratic paternalism in South Africa suppressed communal forms of extra-legal violence and tolerated only private violence against blacks. In South Africa, virtually all lethal unofficial violence took the form of common murder. In contrast, a full-blown lynch culture tolerated all forms of racial violence. Racial violence in the South was limited only by the imagination of white killers and incorporated everything from murder to communal (or "spectacle") lynchings. Focusing on the first half of the twentieth century, the book explores the contrast between these two cultures of violence through the prism of three institutions that were central to both cultures of violence: the racially repressive labor market, theological justifications of white supremacy, and the legal system.

Explaining why interpersonal racial violence in South Africa was limited to private violence whereas communal racial violence was widespread across the American South is therefore the principal focus of the book. Like other comparative studies of the two countries, this study also draws attention to

White and colored persons lynched in the United States, 1889–1918*

Year	Total	White	Colored
1889	175	80	95
1890	91	3	88
1891	194	67	127
1892	226	71	155
1893	153	39	114
1894	182	54	128
1895	178	68	110
1896	125	46	79
1897	162	38	124
1898	127	24	103
1899	109	22	87
1900	101	12	89
1901	135	27	108
1902	94	10	84
1903	104	17	87
1904	86	7	79
1905	65	5	60
1906	68	4	64
1907	62	3	59
1908	100	8	92
1909	89	14	75
1910	90	10	80
1911	71	8	63
1912	64	3	61
1913	48	1	47
1914	54	5	49
1915	96	43	53
1916	58	7	51
1917	50	2	48
1918	67	4	63
	3,224	702	2,522

*Excluding victims of the Atlanta, Ga. (1906), and East St Louis, Ill. (1917), riots.
Source: National Association for the Advancement of Colored People, *Thirty Years of Lunching in the United States, 1889–1913* (Negro Universities Press, 1969), Appendix 1.

the many similarities between the American South and South Africa with regard to white supremacy. However, the organizing question of the study emphasizes their differences: why was communal violence so fundamental to the making of segregation in the American South but almost entirely unknown in South Africa? In the process of illuminating this issue, the study casts light on a broader complex of social, political, and cultural practices that led to the development of distinctive "styles" of white supremacy. Focusing on unofficial violence is therefore useful, not only because it sheds light on a neglected phenomenon in the comparative literature but also because it demonstrates that distinct patterns of extra-legal violence require the involvement and support of a broad array of institutions and dispositions in society.

A distinction that William Fitzhugh Brundage underscores in his acclaimed book, *Lynching in the New South: Georgia and Virginia 1890–1930,* provides a key to understanding the difference between the American South and South Africa. Based on the analysis of more than 600 lynchings, Brundage's book devotes sustained attention to the difference between "private" and "communal" lynchings. This analytical distinction clarifies the unique element and the central puzzle of this comparative study. [11]

At the most obvious level, the distinction between private and communal lynching is one of form and scale. *Private lynchings* were extra-legal murders that whites often carried out furtively. The victims of private lynchings would usually be discovered hanging from trees or bridges or shot to death on lonely roads; or they might be killed in the presence of a few witnesses. In all of these instances, individual white citizens usually acted alone and resorted to summary physical violence to discipline or kill specific blacks who offended them. Still, even a hanged corpse was not *prima facie* proof that a lynching and not just a "murder" had taken place. In 1909, when the National Association for the Advancement of Colored People (NAACP) launched its campaign to secure a federal law that specifically criminalized lynching, the legal route that the organization chose compelled it to offer a definition that would clearly distinguish "lynching" from "murder." [12] In South Africa, a specific legal response to lynching was unnecessary because lynchings did not occur. White South Africans certainly murdered blacks in large numbers as the twentieth century proceeded. But the furtive nature of these extra-legal killings meant that it was not always easy to clearly distinguish private lynching from common murder. The use of ropes to hang victims and other forms of killing was rare in South Africa, where the great majority of racial murders were secured with guns or fists. South Africa's criminal code accordingly disaggregated all murder into various classes, such as culpable homicide, manslaughter, and murder in the first, second and third degrees. [13]

In contrast to private lynchings, *communal lynchings* were dramatically different affairs that dispensed with the problem of definitional precision. Communal lynchings in the South occurred in the public sphere, were attended by groups that could be as small as 25 or as large as 25,000, and were frequently announced ahead of time in newspapers, from the pulpit, and by word of mouth. Local luminaries and law enforcement officials brazenly comported themselves at the head of the crowd, while prominent officials, including state governors and US senators, openly championed the cause of violent mobs. In many cases, photographs were made of the event, converted into postcards and sold in local stores. Communal lynchings accounted for approximately one-third of all known lynchings between 1890 and 1930. However, the image of large crowds standing before a dangling black body cast a long shadow and strongly influenced the analysis of lynching in the New South.[14]

In South Africa, however, communal lynching was entirely unknown. It also seems to have been unthinkable. The collective killing of blacks did occur in South Africa, but it assumed the form of "massacres" perpetrated by law enforcement agencies. Police and army units acting under standing orders regularly mowed down unarmed Africans who protested against various aspects of government policy or opposed the administrative regulations that mushroomed from 1920 onwards. Typified by the infamous Bulhoek massacre in 1921 and underscored by numerous lesser and unsung massacres in the urban and rural areas, a tradition of bureaucratic violence became the signature of segregation in South Africa.[15] Still, state officials who frequently used "excessive violence" against unarmed and anonymous Africans differed sharply from the men who summoned festive white citizens to commit extra-legal violence against specific victims in the New South.

Beyond the issue of form and scale, however, private and communal lynchings are also distinguished by another important difference – the extensive use of symbolic or ritual violence in communal lynching. Private lynchings and more prosaic forms of racial murder in the South were generally summary affairs in which rituals were either entirely absent or only of minor importance. Men who committed private lynchings may have desecrated the victim's body, but the rapidity or furtiveness of the killing limited the symbolic impact of such gratuitous violence. The same cannot be said of communal lynching, which was dominated from beginning to end by symbolic functions that loomed larger and reverberated longer than the actual death of the victim. More often than not, the lynch victim would be disfigured before, during and after his death, and the remains of the body were often carved up and sold as mementos. Together with its highly public nature, the extensive use of ritual torture in communal lynching commands attention. Whereas private lynchings symbolized the prowess that individual white men enjoyed over all African Americans, communal lynching in the New South symbolized the collective domination of one racial group over another. The American novelist Ralph Ellison once described communal lynching as "a ritual drama that was usually enacted ... in an atmosphere of high excitement and led by a masked celebrant dressed in a garish costume who manipulated the numinous objects (lynch ropes, the

American flag, shotgun, gasoline and whiskey jugs) associated with the rite as he inspired and instructed the actors in their gory task."[16] The reference to masks and garish costumes is unnecessarily restrictive, however. To the contrary, one of the most arresting aspects of communal lynching was the brazen "confessional" spirit that lynch mobs confidently exuded in public spaces. Indeed, it is the *absence* of masks that stands out. Invariably claiming that they were defending white women from "the black-beast rapist," white Southerners approached the task of public murder with astonishing equanimity, confident that neither secular authorities nor their Christian God would take offense at their deeds.

Communal lynchings were in fact redolent of Christian themes that echoed the evangelical Protestantism that dominated the South. For white Southerners, Old Testament conceptions of a wrathful and interventionist God and readings of the Bible that extolled excessive punishment as Christian virtues squared only too well with the racial hierarchy and punitive vengeance that emerged on the heels of slavery, Civil War, and the reviled period of Reconstruction. Communal lynchings involved symbols and rituals that bear a strong resemblance to human sacrifice in what anthropologists once called "primitive societies." Human sacrifice in those ancient civilizations symbolically reinforced two sorts of relationships: those between sacrificers and their gods and the links that bonded people together.[17] As both act and symbol, communal lynching in the New South reinforced these same relationships in ways that private lynching could not.

The absence of communal lynching in South Africa therefore contrasts strikingly with the fearsome but festive spectacle lynchings that regularly marked white supremacy in the American South. The distinction between private and communal lynching therefore isolates a phenomenon – communal lynchings perpetrated by ordinary citizens – that usefully distinguishes extra-legal racial violence in the two racial orders. Why, then, did ordinary white citizens play such prominent roles in inflicting "punishment" on African Americans? Why was lethal interpersonal violence so fundamental to race relations in the South but much less so in South Africa?

More than anything, lynching testifies to white Southerners' belief that they possessed the right to murder African Americans in civil society with or without the assistance of law enforcement officials. This assumption is manifest in communal lynchings but is also inscribed in thousands of private lynchings, the vast majority of which were never so much as investigated.[18] At first sight, it may seem obvious to attribute the prominent role that lynching played in the New South to the earlier institution of chattel slavery. Southern slavery, after all, vastly exceeded the forms of coerced, or "indentured" labor that persisted in a few Boer-dominated regions of South Africa well into the late 1800s, decades after British reformers in the Cape Colony had abolished the institution in the 1830s.[19] Perhaps whites in the Reconstruction South, being accustomed within their own lifetime to the inherent violence of racial slavery, simply carried over into the postbellum years the rights that whites possessed to punish their slaves at will.

There is no doubt that slavery and the inhumane culture it spawned contributed to the cavalier killing of African Americans in the New South. However, this "crossover theory" of racial violence has to contend with two important caveats. Firstly, prior to the Civil War, almost all lynch victims were *white* men. Yet of the 3,703 persons lynched between 1889 and 1930, fully eighty-five per cent were African American.[20] Secondly, it was in fact *not* customary for whites to arbitrarily kill or even punish slaves who belonged to other slave owners. Such a deadly license would have conflicted with the economic foundations of slavery, challenged the patriarchal powers of slave owners, and bestowed on plain whites powers of life and death that contradicted their impoverished and highly dependent position in slave society.[21] There was, in short, no slave-era "tradition" that supported the indiscriminate lynching of African Americans. Indeed, as Eugene Genovese has shown, slaves who were accused of raping white women were sometimes charged and acquitted in the antebellum courts of the South.[22] Yet a tradition of lynching African Americans arose almost instantaneously once the Civil War (1861–65) ended. Lethal interpersonal violence against African Americans would become such an ingrained feature of Southern society and so important to white men that duty-minded sheriffs, jailers and mayors risked, and occasionally lost, their lives when they attempted to thwart lynch mobs. Whites' "right to lynch" pervaded the New South and hovered like an absent presence over the individual and communal encounters between blacks and whites. That the lynch threat hung heavy even in those counties where black men were never lynched confirms that the New South developed what William D. Carrigan describes as a "lynch culture."[23]

In contrast, no white constituency ever emerged to defend the extra-legal killing of blacks in South Africa. Whites occasionally made dark threats about "taking the law into our hands,"but such talk was bravado, the predictably arrogant fulminations of white supremacy. The word "lynch" expressed the ire of a letter writer with a grudge against the liberal civil servants who staffed the state after 1910. Only occasionally did disgruntled whites coalesce into a mob steadfast in its purpose to make good on threats about killings blacks. And even when such mobs did assemble, the damage they caused fell far short of the astounding destructiveness that Southern lynch mobs were capable of. The clearest exception to this general conclusion occurred in 1922 when, in the course of the white mine workers' strike known as the Rand Revolt, striking white mine workers carried out an unprovoked massacre which left scores of Africans dead. This atrocity closely resembled the "Red Summer" race riots that erupted in several major American cities in 1919.[24] The 1922 massacre in South Africa was without doubt the tragic outcome of communal white violence. Race riots, however, are at the margins of this study, which keeps the focus on "interpersonal" forms of racial violence, and especially on lynching and murder. Race riots are characterized by unfocused attacks on whole communities; they may be massively destructive but are also relatively infrequent. In contrast, lynch mobs and vigilante movements are distinguished by the "punishment" of particular individuals who are used as symbolic stand-ins for the community they are seen to represent. In contrast, lynchings in the New South were "orderly" affairs, which, at their peak, numbered more than 230 in 1898 alone.[25] Lynchings are therefore very different sociological phenomena: as we see in this study, they operate according to different logics, yield different outcomes, and perform functions that are not present in "race riots" such as those that erupted in Atlanta in 1906 and in Johannesburg in 1922.[26]

Yet white South Africans who rarely resorted to communal violence in the public sphere nevertheless murdered blacks in large numbers in private spaces. While white citizens also killed Africans in the urban areas, the most dangerous threats to Africans were on the gold mines and in the white rural areas. At first, violent white mine workers posed the greatest danger to the lives of Africans. This reputation shifted to the *platteland* from the 1920s onward, when farmers frequently resorted to violence and terror to control and punish African farm labor. Scores of murders in rural communities made their way to the courts and were often, if only briefly, reported in newspapers. Some of these cases are lodged in archival files bearing titles such as "Shooting of Natives" or "Assaults Against Natives." While some of these murders may arguably be characterized as "private lynchings," it is more accurate to refer to them as "murder." Accordingly, the dominant pattern of unofficial violence in South Africa may best described as "private violence" interspersed with only occasional episodes of communal violence.

Unofficial violence in the comparative literature

Scholars have long been aware that South Africa and the American South "form a kind of commentary on each other," to borrow a phrase from Clifford Geertz.[27] James Campbell observed in 1998 that comparisons of South Africa and the United States today amount to "a virtual sub-field": "the literature of comparative history has been swelled by a stream of books and articles comparing and contrasting South Africa and the United States. Slavery, segregation, sharecropping, racial ideology, black politics, the relationship of state and capital, the frontier experience, even the historical profession itself have all come under comparative scrutiny."[28] Curiously, unofficial violence remains an unexplored phenomenon, despite the explicit concern with racial repression within this "sub-field." In sharp contrast, the history of lynching in the South already appears to be more than just a sub-field; as articles and books continue to appear, the subject may well have developed into a distinct field unto itself. The intense focus on lynching in the New South, however, has not as yet made an impact on the comparative literature on South African and US history.

None of the four major comparative books that anchor the "sub-field" pauses to explore in any significant detail the role that unofficial violence played in the establishment of white supremacy in the first half of the twentieth century. The silence about unofficial violence is evident in the first of these, *White Supremacy* (1981) by George Fredrickson. More concerned with the differences than the similarities, *White Supremacy* could easily have accommodated a sustained concentration on the relative importance of unofficial violence in the two emerging racial orders. Instead, this pioneering book makes only passing reference to the issue in the American South, noting that lynching "continued to play an important role as a device for intimidating blacks and shoring up the color line" even after Jim Crow laws had been set in place. Apart from attributing lynching to whites' "pathological Negrophobia," Fredrickson advances an institutional explanation for lynching: "a persistent insecurity about the effectiveness of white domination" and "a lack of faith in the full adequacy of legal or institutional controls over blacks." In South Africa, in contrast, "the element of direct regimentation and effective police power built into the segregation–apartheid system made it possible for South African whites to trust the authorities to do their repressive violence for them."[29]

Stanley Greenberg alludes even more briefly to unofficial violence in his pioneering study, *Race and State in Capitalist Development*, and then only to extra-legal violence in the South. Primarily concerned to explain the rise and fall ("intensification" and "relaxation") of the racial orders, Greenberg's focus is exclusively on the formal institutions of racial domination, which, he argued, were rooted in the level of capitalist development. The racial orders emerged in the early stages of capitalist development when dominant classes ("market actors") were too weak to attract adequate supplies of cheap unskilled labor. Dominant classes therefore turned to formal state power to meet their labor needs and so instigated the panoply of measures and practices that came to define racial segregation. In the later stages of capitalist development, however, dominant actors gradually lost their interests in cheap labor. Increasingly willing to rely on market forces to generate skilled labor, they eventually "abandoned" the muscular state forms they had earlier constructed. Greenberg touches on the unofficial violence that brought down Reconstruction in the South and initiated the "period of intensification." He notes that "black voters were kept from the polls by widespread riots, shootings and fraud," but does not refer at all to unofficial violence in the development of the South African economy. Greenberg's attention remains resolutely on the elaboration and erosion of formal state bodies.[30]

Unofficial violence features somewhat more prominently in Anthony Marx's tightly written explanation for the emergence of formal systems of racial domination in South Africa and the United States but not in Brazil. Elaborating on an earlier observation by George Fredrickson, Marx's *Making Race and Nation* centers on the violent divisions that bedeviled the unity of the dominant white populations. In the wake of the two "civil wars" in South Africa and the United States (Marx defines the Anglo-Boer as a civil war), the victors were confronted with recalcitrant co-ethnics in both contexts. In the United States, the Northern Army had to contend with white Southerners who refused to accept racial reforms, while British imperialists in South Africa encountered a similar antipathy amongst Afrikaners who refused to extend the vote to Africans. Segregation emerged as a compromise in each country – a modernized system of race relations adapted to the political and economic needs of whites in Greenberg's "period of racial intensification." Like Greenberg, Marx recognizes the scale of racial terror that erupted in the South but does not comment on unofficial violence in South Africa. His fleeting comments on Southern violence are nevertheless instructive. He notes that Southern whites' near-universal opposition to Reconstruction unified "whites as whites" and cut across class lines, ensuring that "both capital and white workers participated" in regular racial atrocities against African Americans. He also remarks on the complicity of the state, noting that "elected and other officials turned a blind eye" to the "hoodlums" and "lynch mobs" who sowed extraordinary terror amongst emancipated African Americans. Apart from noting that unofficial violence played a key political role in subordinating class differences to a white racial identity and successfully terminated Reconstruction, Marx does not investigate racial violence in the segregation era, complementing a similar silence about racial violence in South Africa in the inter-War years. Marx implies that the active cooperation and subsequent attempts at voluntary "fusion" between English-speaking whites and Afrikaners signaled a "racial consensus" that dispensed with the need for an insurgent campaign of racial terror by the defeated Afrikaners. Because unofficial violence did not play an overt political role in South Africa, Marx proceeds to ignore it.[31]

If the major works that anchor the "sub-field" of comparative studies on South Africa and the United States have not examined unofficial violence at any great length, they are also united by a common assessment: if only by implication, they agree that unofficial violence was more overt, more central to political developments and greater in scale in the United States than in South Africa. After undertaking a tour of the Southern states, Maurice Evans, a prominent South African liberal and champion of segregation, concluded that the "physical security" of blacks in South Africa was much greater than it was for African Americans. Evans' book, *Black and White in the Southern States*, appeared in 1915, just three years before the lynching of African Americans reached its historic zenith in the South. Evans attributed the greater "physical security" of blacks in South Africa to the lower level of economic competition between black and white workers in South Africa.[32]

In *The Highest Stage of White Supremacy*, John Cell supported Evans' assessment that lower levels of racial violence in South Africa stemmed from overtly discriminatory laws that were "much less ambiguous" than in the South. Cell emphasized the moderating influence of paternalism in South Africa. Whereas Southern racism was "blunt," the racism of Afrikaners mirrored that of South Africa's English-speaking whites, a liberal constituency who "ordinarily spoke in more paternal voices."[33] This assessment has generally been borne out by more recent research by scholars such as Charles van Onselen, Helen Bradford, and Ian Ochiltree. For example, Ian Ochiltree observes that in South Africa "paternalism [lingered] in the intimacy of the relationship between sharecropper and landlord" in the inter-War years and was only extirpated after the Second World War once social relations in the agrarian economy became overwhelmingly "monetized." In contrast, slave-era paternalism perished almost immediately once planters in the American South hitched their fortunes to "King Cotton" and labor tenancy.[34]

The predominant view in the comparative literature, including this study, thus supports the basic argument that Fredrickson advanced in *White Supremacy*: unofficial violence was central to the establishment and maintenance of segregation in the American South, but of lesser importance in South Africa in the inter-War years. However, a number of recent studies have either directly or obliquely challenged Fredrickson's thesis. Essays by the comparativist historians John Higginson and Christopher Strobel present the most pointed objection.[35] Focusing on atrocities that Boer komandos committed against Africans they encountered in the course of the Anglo-Boer War (1899–1901) and the 1914 Afrikaner rebellion, Higginson and Strobel take Fredrickson to task for claiming that unofficial violence did "not figure prominently" in South Africa. In a series of articles, Higginson and Strobel have rescued from oblivion the outrages that Boers committed against unarmed Africans, partly to regain the control they had lost over Africans and partly to strike out against the growing impoverishment of Afrikaners before and after unification in 1910. In a reply to this criticism, Fredrickson concedes that he "overstated" his case and that *White Supremacy* "neglected" unofficial violence. At the same time, he correctly underscores a critical distinction between unofficial violence in South Africa and the New South. "The extra-legal violence in South Africa," he writes, "did not assume [a] public and ritualistic character because whites had more trust in the ability of the constituted authorities to deal with what were perceived to be serious threats to white domination."[36]

Fredrickson could have made a further, equally telling, point in his own defense. The South African atrocities that Higginson and Strobel explore all occurred in the context of debilitating moments of war and actual rebellion. Higginson and Strobel therefore convincingly show that Boer atrocities against blacks during and immediately after the Anglo-Boer War mirrored similar Reconstruction-era outrages that lynch mobs and riotous white Southerners perpetrated against emancipated African Americans. But Higginson and Strobel do not account for an important difference: the horrific *persistence* of communal atrocities in the New South and their *evaporation* in South Africa even before 1910. Several appalling atrocities that Boers committed against blacks during the Anglo-Boer War do not constitute a "lynch culture"; nor did they inaugurate one after the War, as was the case in the South. These divergent patterns undermine the case that Higginson and Strobel make for similarities in patterns of racial violence.

Indirect criticism of Fredrickson's thesis also appears in a number of recent works by South Africans writing on racial violence after the unification of modern South Africa in 1910. These studies do not overturn Fredrickson's claim that extra-legal violence was less malignant in South Africa than in the New South. Still, they have the considerable merit of shining a bright light on the private violence that the "sub-field" of comparative studies so badly neglects. Martin Murray's examination of the "reign of terror" that white farmers maintained over rural Africans perhaps comes closest to assimilating unofficial violence in the two racial orders. His description of farm violence in the Orange Free State would be at home in many a study of agrarian violence in the American South. Arguing that "the law alone was simply too elastic and too ineffectual" to contend with African challenges to the authority and property of rural landowners, Murray demonstrates that "violence was an instrument of terror" that "served to intimidate the propertyless [i.e. Africans] into submission to the will of the propertied, to assert through superior physical strength the prevailing 'rules of the game' and to sow terror amongst the labouring poor." He concludes that "a symbiosis between the law and vigilantism" enabled farmers to discipline Africans they suspected of minor acts of "resistance" such as petty thievery with "floggings, beatings and even killings."[37] In the course of his study of the death penalty in South Africa, Robert Turrell likewise exposes the lethal violence that prevailed in the white farming areas and the unwillingness of the courts to impose commensurately serious sentences on white killers, a theme that pervades segregation in the South.[38] The respective work of scholars such as Murray and Turrell therefore make a strong case for the argument that white mobbism and the ability of white citizens to establish a "reign of terror" over Africans were perhaps as characteristic of South Africa after 1910 as it was of the American South from approximately 1890 onwards.

Two studies of "white riots" also corroborate this claim. Sheila Smith McKoy's cultural comparison of riots by whites, however, is principally concerned to expose white lawlessness and hypocrisy and not to root them in common socio-historical contexts. Her study is undermined by a comparison of events that occurred under dramatically different circumstances (during Reconstruction in the South and in the 1990s in South Africa). The similarities she identifies in the murderous riot that Southern Redeemers staged in Wilmington, NC, in 1898 and the violent fiasco of Afrikaner vigilantes who, one century later, sought to stymie the emergence of democracy by staging a violent putsch in the Boputhatswana "Homeland" in 1994 therefore does not shed much light on the role that unofficial violence played in the formative stages of segregation.[39]

On the other hand, Jeremy Krikler's study of the racial massacre that white miners in Johannesburg committed during the debilitating strike they staged in 1922 offers insightful commentary on the symmetry of urban "race riots" in South Africa and the United States. Krikler demonstrates that analogous conditions in each context heightened the material and racial insecurities of working-class white communities immediately after the First World War. Common precipitating factors such as racial competition for jobs, housing and higher wages in both contexts sparked rumors that prompted whites to view blacks as scapegoats. The parallels that Krikler carefully draws between the "Red Summer" riots that swept several American cities in 1919 and the 1922 race riot in South Africa that dispatched dozens of innocent blacks are therefore instructive and expose important similarities in the etiology of communal white violence against blacks in both racial orders.[40]

It is highly unlikely that future research will refute George Fredrickson's observation that segregation in the American South sported much higher levels of racial violence than in South Africa claim. Taking off from Fredrickson's observation, this study sets out to explain why South Africa's *bureaucratic culture* tolerated only private forms of racial violence while both private and communal forms of racial violence flourished in the encompassing *lynch culture* that emerged in the New South.

Central themes and organization of this study

This study does not purport to provide a comprehensive comparison of all forms of unofficial violence. More modestly, its principal goal is to account for the contrast between the lynch culture of the New South and the bureaucratic culture that prevailed in South Africa in the inter-War years. The study hinges around three central claims. Firstly, it contends that employers were primarily responsible for shaping the scale and form of racial violence in the two racial orders. By extension, white workers played a secondary role in defining the pattern of racial violence in each context. Secondly, it demonstrates how different legal systems reinforced the emergence of the two cultures of racial violence. Thirdly, looking beyond structural and institutional explanations, it contends that different religious traditions legitimized the two regimes of racial violence, providing a sense of moral vindication to the Southern lynch culture and the bureaucratic tradition of racial violence that predominated in South Africa. These themes are briefly explored below.

Employers, white workers and racial violence

The rapid emergence of a lynch culture dramatized the uncontested hegemony of farmers, the ex-slave owners who would become the commercial farmers of the New South. The end of the Civil War destroyed slavery and brought turmoil into the world of a class accustomed to complete control over a captive labor force. Bent on establishing the highly coercive system of sharecropping, farmers gave focus to the general refusal of almost all white Southerners to accept the freedom of African Americans, especially since many African Americans occupied seats in state, county and municipal government and were therefore in a position to promote Reconstruction-era racial reforms. Ex-slave-owners played the vanguard role in fomenting an ideological climate that legitimized all forms of violence and successfully brought Reconstruction to a close. Thereafter, farmers "redefined labor rights and property laws to favor planters; law enforcement agencies pointedly excluded blacks; and elaborate election laws whittled away at black voting rights."[41] Racial violence and lynching had emerged in the course of a political campaign against Reconstruction. When Reconstruction ended in 1876, farmers ensured that lynching developed into a diffuse instrument to subjugate African American freedmen. Later, they supported racial terror as instrument for maintaining segregation. Without serious rivals to contest their specific commitment to and dependence on sharecropping, commercial farmers used their regional influence and authority within state governments to institutionalize a violently repressive labor market. Simultaneously, they also secured the active support of white workers.

Southern white workers shared equally the racist assumptions and stereotypes that took hold in the postbellum South. They were caught in a crippling position. Generally averse to radical ideologies and suspicious of labor movements, white workers were poorly positioned to improve their living standards, which were frequently not appreciably better than those of African Americans. But too racist to ally with black workers, they tended to support the very employers who kept them pinned down at the lower reaches of the agrarian-dominated economy. White workers therefore obsessed about their whiteness and supported all attempts to "keep the black man down"– including racial violence and suffrage restrictions that also disqualified large numbers of the regions' "poor whites."[42] Elites and white plebeians therefore coalesced in common support of the emerging lynch culture in the New South, but for different reasons. White workers looked upon racial violence as a mechanism for intimidating black rivals and asserting their whiteness in Southern society. They therefore collaborated with employers who buttressed their class hegemony by dividing the working class, partly by fomenting a permissive lynch culture. Diffuse support for lynching therefore obscures the primary responsibility that employers, particularly farmers, bore for transforming the political terror of the Reconstruction era into a generalized mechanism of racial terror in the New South.

Whereas the monocrop economy of the South facilitated a lynch culture, economic diversity in South Africa impeded the emergence of a uniform regime of coercive controls. Unlike in the monocrop New South, cheap black labor in South Africa was a rivalrous and highly divisive commodity that pitted the three great sectors – mining, agriculture and manufacturing industry – against one other.[43] Unable to resolve the escalating competition for cheap labor, employers turned to the state to devise a uniform "racial policy" and implement controls on black workers that corresponded to the varying nature of work in the mining, farming and industrial centers. An increasingly complex bureaucratic framework centered on the "pass system" grew steadily from 1910 onward, gradually authorizing the state to manage the movement, employment and accommodation of Africans across the country. This development reinforced the state's monopoly over the means of racial violence and rendered it both unnecessary and counter-productive for employers to resort to communal violence as an essential instrument for controlling black workers. This statist orientation also shaped white workers' response to blacks.

In South Africa, white workers did not look upon cheap black workers as the immediate and most proximate enemy in a racially structured labor market. Instead, they formed increasingly combative labor movements to oppose the "symbiotic union of state and [mining] capital" after 1910.[44] Skilled workers – who were almost exclusively British – were essentially indifferent to the black unskilled workers they supervised, a class that was incapable of threatening the position of the "labor aristocracy" above them. Unsurprisingly, competition with black workers for unskilled jobs was most threatening to the predominantly Afrikaner stratum of "poor whites." Still – and notwithstanding the racial massacre they conducted in the course of the Rand Revolt – Afrikaner workers were arguably no more violent towards African workers than other white South Africans. White workers in South Africa resembled Southern white workers in this regard: each group merely participated in the levels and type of violence that prevailed in the respective racial orders. However, two factors characterized the racial politics of white plebeians in South Africa, distinguishing them from the white working class in the South.

First, white labor in South Africa displayed little reluctance to challenge the hegemony of employers and went so far as to stage a violent insurrection that was partly inspired by the successful Bolshevik revolution in Russia.[45] South Africa's white workers developed militant, socialist-influenced unions to boost wages and vigorously challenged the "native labor policy" that was so crucial to the owners of the gold mining industry, the country's largest employer.

Second, racist white workers were also essentially indifferent to African workers: they neither looked upon African workers as allies in their battles against employers nor identified them as the cause of their material insecurity. Such indifference contrasted significantly with the racism of Southern white workers who, goaded by the "divide and rule" stratagems of employers, remained perennially haunted by a "fear of displacement" by more vulnerable African American workers.[46] White workers in South Africa responded to a "fear of displacement" with militant labor movements, demanding formal incorporation into the emerging machinery of industrial reconciliation and policies that boosted their employment, education and wages on explicitly racial grounds. Thus, like employers who demanded state intervention to directly shape South Africa's emerging labor market, white workers also enlisted the state to acknowledge and formally provide the racial and class privileges they demanded. This orientation diminished the importance of interpersonal racial violence for white workers. Instead, it linked white proletarian politics to statist expectations that held official institutions responsible for controlling the field of "race relations."

Racial violence and religion

To explain how white people understood the racial violence they routinely committed and supported, it is particularly appropriate to draw attention to the meanings that whites attached to racial violence because white Southerners and the Afrikaners who championed the harshest forms of segregation in South Africa were both religious communities with strong streaks of Calvinist Protestantism.[47] Both communities had entertained the idea that they were God's "chosen people" in the period before civil war erupted in their respective countries . However, it was only after military defeat in the Civil War and the Anglo-Boer War that these ideas congealed into "Lost Cause" religions bristling with what David Goldfield calls a "God-haunted" sense of ethnic and regional exclusivity.[48] In both contexts, religion played central, but also very different roles in sanctifying racial violence.

After the American Civil War, evangelical Protestants – the largest and most influential religious denomination in a region that was almost exclusively Protestant – immediately embraced "Lost Cause" explanations that sacralized the South's defeat at the hands of a Northern army they viewed as morally inferior. Protestant leaders subsequently nurtured a distinctive "Southern religious identity" that was dominated by a soul-saving evangelism, a suspicion of the Social Gospel and a pronounced conservative disinclination to confront, let alone transform, the racial and class politics of the New South.[49] Instead, Southern Protestantism placed a heavy premium on the "conversion experience" and the "rapture" that signified the individual's full submission to God. Southern Protestantism stoked the emerging lynch culture and gave moral support to the emerging and cancerous view that portrayed black males as "black-beast rapists" who should be expunged from white society. Not all white Protestant organizations and leaders supported lynching. However, despite the singularly dire threat that white mobs posed to human life, clerical repudiations of lynching remained unorganized and fitfully dispersed across hundreds of small churches in the New South. At the very least, Southern Protestantism provided the tacit moral compass that enabled ordinary white men from all classes and professions in Southern society to participate in the lynch culture. By framing lynching as a virtuous defense of women and the "Southern way of life," evangelical Protestantism upheld the subordination of women to men and attributed the poverty of poor whites not to employers or the asymmetries of capitalism but to the moral failings of individuals. This deeply conservative theology – in which the triple evils of "sex, sin and segregation" were inextricably blended – ultimately sacralized lynching, a practice that several scholars have described as ritual human sacrifice. African Americans, in contrast, almost immediately grasped what whites could not see: the "strange fruit" that swung from Southern trees mirrored the ritual killing of Christ.[50]

Afrikaners after 1910 also developed a "Religion of the Lost Cause" to swallow the bitter pill of defeat at the hands of a reviled liberal enemy.[51] A notable feature of the "Afrikaner civil religion" that emerged in the period, however, was the marginal attention it devoted to Africans. Unlike white Southerners, who immediately framed segregation as a religious crusade against the multiple threats that African Americans were said to embody, Afrikaners' theological and political interests in Africans not only developed gradually but also remained well within the parameters of a paternalist theological framework that repudiated racial violence throughout and even beyond the inter-War years. While Southern Protestants refrained from challenging employers by championing the social cause of the region's "poor whites," Afrikaner churches showed no such timidity. Afrikaner churches energetically embraced a vigorous Social Gospel that embroiled them directly in the social and political tumult of the day. Taking charge of a combative republican and anti-imperial cause, the Dutch Reformed Church (DRC) quickly transformed itself into a self-styled *volkskerk* around the time of the First World War and set out to rescue "poor whites," thereby aligning itself with Afrikaner workers' struggles against the alliance between the mining industry and the state. The *volkskerk's* muscular advocacy of poor white social movements distinguishes Afrikaner Protestantism from the cautious approach that Protestant churches adopted towards the Social Gospel in the New South. The Afrikaner churches did more than lavish attention on the material plight of Afrikaner workers: their goal was nothing less than gaining control over the state. The Church therefore "entered into politics" after the First World War, when many DRC ministers won seats in Parliament.

The upshot of these developments was a theology that echoed the liberal aversion to the crudest forms of racial violence and reinforced the statist ideology that marked state formation in South Africa. In the United States, Protestants in the North and South divided over the issue of slavery and remained organizationally distinct thereafter, permitting Southern Protestant theologians to champion the region's lynch culture. In South Africa's centralized state after 1910, the DRC actively sought to cooperate with black and white Christians in the "Benevolent Empire," a loose association of liberal paternalists committed to missionary work amongst the black majority. This ecumenical movement was an important moment in the evolution of the DRC. Cooperation with the Benevolent Empire placed pressure on the DRC to either accept a racial paternalism that hinted at the gradual "equalization" of blacks and whites in some distant future or justify the church's customary preference for racial segregation. Although Afrikaner church leaders resolved the church's dilemma by elaborating an Apartheid theology that promised intensified segregation, their association with the Benevolent Empire also left its mark: at no point prior to the 1950s did the DRC portray violence as a positive force.

Racial violence and the legal system

Racial violence could not have taken root if law enforcement agencies such as the police, sheriffs and the army – and in South Africa, the quasi-military corps of civilian "Native administrators" and other labor control specialists – had carried out their formal obligation to "protect and serve" the general public. Legal institutions in both contexts must therefore be held complicit in the extra-legal killing of blacks. However, the two legal systems performed this common function in very different ways.

A lynch culture in the New South could not have been so rapidly institutionalized without the great and prior importance that Southerners attached to "popular justice," an ideology with roots in "the Southern code of honor."

The central pillar of the code of honor was the notion of "respect," or more accurately, "respect from others." In terms of this feudal code, honorable men and women developed and defended their reputations in the public sphere and so judged themselves according to the respect that others showed for their social standing. Slavery sustained these creeds, manifested, for example, in the slave owner's right to punish "disrespectful" slaves with the degree of summary violence he deemed appropriate. Members of the plantocracy took pride in ritualized combat such as duels while plebeian whites also earned a fearsome reputation for unchecked violence in brawls. "An eye for an eye," the basic tenet of *lex talionis,* became the most common medium for resolving disputes between friends and enemies alike, seriously undermining the legitimacy of the courts as the proper forum for resolving disputes.[52] The correlation of an obsessive concern with "honor" amongst whites was the image of blacks as irredeemably "dishonorable" and inferior. Because the glorification of motherhood and feminine virtue was essential to the code of honor, white men claimed unchecked authority and power to lynch "the black-beast rapist" in the name of defending the "honor" of white women and children. White Southerners believed that slavery had checked the dangerous pathologies that were inherent to African Americans and that emancipation had subsequently disgorged these threats into white society. Once whites portrayed African American freedmen as congenitally crime-prone and a permanent hypersexual menace to all white women and children, "popular justice" in the New South increasingly came to mean summary violence against "the black-beast rapist" – an incantation without rival in its capacity to mobilize white mobs and legitimize lynching as an extension of the law.

When the North abandoned Reconstruction, the incorporation of a racialized *lex talionis* introduced a profound ambiguity into the administration of justice in the South. Southern courts were placed in what the anthropologist Max Gluckman describes as an "intercalary position," suspended between the formal system of courts and the practice of popular justice.[53] Raising the banner of "states rights," white Southerners exploited and openly mocked the federal system. Local court officials invariably resolved the tension between federal and state jurisdictions by supporting popular justice, refusing to indict lynchers or find them guilty despite incontrovertible evidence placed before the court. At the same time, the sheer existence of federal laws and constitutional rights emboldened African Americans to seek justice in the courts. Once the NAACP (founded in 1909) resolved to transform the South by shattering racial segregation in the US Supreme Court, a federal system that permitted Southern states to elevate "states rights" above the constitution seemed to threaten the "Solid South." Despite the anxieties it occasionally caused amongst white Southerners, however, the Supreme Court failed to act decisively against popular justice.

The legal system had contradictory effects on racial violence in South Africa: it simultaneously tolerated and constrained extra-legal racial violence. Constitutional segregation essentially required white citizens to surrender to the state their capacity to summarily inflict violence against the black majority, failing which the courts would punish violent whites. Successive governments upheld this orientation within the law whenever the potential for serious collective violence arose in the streets. In contrast, the country's courts dealt lightly with "Shooting of Natives" cases and other forms of serious non-lethal assaults of blacks. The position that the courts adopted was in part the outcome of the highly centralized state system created in 1910, which provided minimal opportunity for judicial review. An arrangement that required the courts to merely implement the will of an all-white parliament effectively hamstrung the country's judges, most of whom were stalwarts of the liberal establishment and firmly committed to legal formalism, a legal doctrine that enjoins judges to enforce the letter of the law. However, jurists who were committed to legal formalism regularly resorted to racial discourse to hand down trivial sentences on violent whites, especially the rising number of *platteland* Afrikaners who killed blacks, and levied much harsher sentences on blacks who dared to assault whites. Nevertheless, by comparison with the legal system in the American South, South African courts were much more likely to prosecute violent whites and deal somewhat impartially with Africans charged with assaulting, murdering or raping whites. Despite broad similarities in the maladministration of racial justice, South African courts were much more committed to formal court procedures than their Southern counterparts.

This, however, is not saying much, for the very laws that the courts sought to impartially implement were expressly biased against blacks and designed to maintain white supremacy. Moreover, a focus on the legal institutions that resolved cases dealing with blacks and whites conceals the full extent to which the judicial system was complicit in systemic racial violence. The integration of racial repression into the routinized administration and government of the country inflicted death and hardship on blacks – outcomes which mobs of white lynchers achieved in the American South.

The book is structured around an examination of these three themes. It begins, however, by comparing the respective roles that rape panics played in the construction of racial segregation in South Africa and in the American South. Although similar in content, rape panics in fact sharply illuminated the contrasting logics that culminated in the emergence of a lynch culture in the American South and a bureaucratic culture of violence in South Africa. An examination of rape allegations therefore foregrounds how anxieties about gender and sexuality were inseverably intertwined with the class, legal and religious determinants of the two forms of racial violence that this book explores.

Caveats

Comparative history is filled with pitfalls.[54] Before commencing, it is well to be candid about three particular issues dealing with comparative research on the two racial orders: the units of analysis, the archival sources and the forms of racial violence.

Units of analysis

South Africa is a country while "the South," whatever else it may be, is a region – and a famously complicated one at that. Moreover, the highly centralized nature of the racial state in South Africa has honed the country's historiography, encouraging scholars to assume that the unity they perceive at the center overshadows regional variations in the country's politics. Regional variations are recognized, but they are not a central feature of theory or empirical research.[55] To date, the paucity of detailed research on unofficial racial violence in South Africa is reflected in the absence of research that self-consciously correlates patterns of violence with variations in specific variables such as the nature of production in a region, prevailing racial demographic ratios, the impact of ecological changes, the role of local courts, etc. Unable to benefit from such studies, this study limits itself to existing sources that are biased towards urban regions and especially to those located in the industrial areas of the Transvaal. At the same time, to the extent that it adduces examples and dynamics in the smaller towns and rural areas of the country, it offers a broader picture than those which John Cell and George Fredrickson paint. For example, Fredrickson's *White Supremacy* is presented as a study of South Africa but deals almost exclusively with dynamics in the Cape Colony leading up to the consolidation of the modern South African state in 1910.

Analogously, the federal architecture of the US state is a dominating presence in studies of the South. Regional specificity – including, of course, a *consciousness* of the South's "distinctiveness" – is the spine of "Southern culture" as well of academic research. Adding to the inescapable influence of regional distinctiveness, furthermore, are the multiple political, economic, demographic and cultural variations within the region, which, for example, make Florida such a different place from a Black Belt state such as Alabama. Similarly, a multicultural and cosmopolitan city such as New Orleans contrasted starkly with Birmingham, a bi-racial fortress of reactionary politics. Many differences are so salient that some scholars deny that "the South" is a meaningful analytical category. These observations are certainly valid and I have attempted to accommodate them. For example, John Cell's comparative book more or less abstracts "the South" from its embattled moorings within the US federal system. In contrast, this study argues that unofficial violence in the South may also be thought of as a direct response to white Southerners' deep distrust of an "alien" federal legal system. Precisely because a "regime of courts and parties" held the United States together, as Stephen Skorownek argues, whites countered the legal system by developing an alternative, racially determined brand of "popular justice." It should be noted that such a development is obscured in John Cell's *The Highest Stage of White Supremacy*, a pioneering book that uses "the South" as a synecdoche for national racial developments in the United States. The present study contends that the regional divide *within* the American state system was central to the evolution and use of unofficial violence in the New South.

Intra-regional differences do indeed make "the South" a vexingly complex research setting. Nevertheless, there are grounds for approaching "the South" as a complex but composite entity. Because white supremacy established a distinguishing degree of commonality across the region, race was the glue that held together the juggernaut of "the South." This commonality makes it possible to view racial violence as a distinctive crosscutting phenomenon, notwithstanding important differences that characterize the region. Devoted to just two states, Brundage's analysis of more than three hundred cases of lynching and near-lynching underscores the forbidding variations that are the pitfall of so many studies of "the South." Nevertheless, communal lynchings *did* occur across all the Southern states and did so at much higher levels than in the Northern and Western states. For example, although the practice was both more entrenched and virulent in Black Belt states such as Mississippi, Alabama and Georgia, communal lynchings also took place in Virginia, the Southern state most known for a liberal-paternalist approach to the management of race relations.[56] (Chapter 3 examines the reasons why lynch patterns in Virginia and Black Belt states diverged so significantly.) At the same time, a sensitivity to differences among states should not detract from the pertinent fact: Virginia, the most liberal state in the New South, *did* sport a "pattern" of lynching that was higher than non-Southern states. Thus, even Virginia's relatively weak lynch tradition justifies the claim that the South as a whole shared a "lynch culture."

Archival sources

The use of archival sources for the South African case but not for the South introduces an obvious disparity in the examination of the two contexts.[57] I settled for this approach when I commenced this study several years ago. At the time, I reasoned that it was justifiable to rely only on South African archival sources given the enormous discrepancy in the volume and intensity

of research on extra-legal violence in South Africa and the South. The handful of available studies of unofficial violence in South Africa is dwarfed by
the mountains of material devoted to the topic in the United States. For
example, nothing in the South African literature comes anywhere close to
just one of these sources, William Brundage's *Lynching in the New South*,
to take just one of many full-length studies devoted to lynching. Brundage's
meticulous analysis enables him to draw numerous conclusions about, for
example, the conditions that promoted or inhibited lynching; the distinctive
requirements that yielded different types of lynch mobs; differences in the
geographical intensity of lynching (sometimes even within a single county);
and the correlations between lynching, economic patterns, social class and
gender. The absence of a commensurate body of secondary work on racial
violence in South Africa necessitated the use of archival sources. Still, concentrating archival sources on just one of two research settings suggests
an obvious need for caution. In their respective works, Shula Marks and
John Breuilly correctly warn against the biases that such a disparity inevitably introduces in comparative studies.[58] Only a steady accumulation of
archival research on racial violence in South Africa can whittle away at this
imbalance. Hopefully, this study will contribute towards this effort.

Forms of racial violence

By concentrating on lethal interpersonal violence that whites inflicted on
blacks, this study abbreviates the range of violence that sustained white
supremacy.[59] This is particularly true for the American case. Despite the
hundreds of examples in the work of such superb scholars as Leon Litwack,
Steven Hahn and William Brundage, no one text could do justice to the
gory cornucopia that white Southerners bequeathed to American history
and culture – hence, perhaps, the recent growth of single-case studies of
lynching. Moreover, racial violence was but part of a broader subculture
of violence in the South, reflecting Southerners' tolerance for resorting to
violence in a variety of contexts in which race was not a salient factor.[60] Yet,
even this subculture of violence was subsumed under an overarching American ethic that legitimized a broad panorama of violence, as Ronald Takaki
argues in his book, *Regeneration Through Violence*.[61] Richard Hofstadter
observed that almost all of this violence occurred between citizens and communities in society and was only rarely directed against elites. America's
pattern of ubiquitous but "conservative" violence departed from the European tradition in which citizens often used violence to challenge or topple
ruling regimes. Lynching is therefore a small subset of the broad and violent
American pattern that Hofstadter delineates: "The United States has been
able to endure an extraordinary volume of violence without developing a
revolutionary tradition ..."[62]

William Beinart also points to the breadth of violence in his evaluation
of "political and collective violence" in South Africa.[63] Nineteenth-century
settler violence against indigenous Africans, though never unrestrained,

also formed part of a larger pattern of colonial rule in which formal state bodies dismantled the "traditional" African polities with combinations of state power and the strategic use of outright terror. Violence reverberated not only in the material organization of African society but also in the consciousness of subjugated populations. Frans Fanon therefore conceived of the colonial state as the "bringer of violence into the home and into the mind of the native ." In the course of evaluating how such patterns influenced twentieth-century South Africa, Beinart observes that violence was endemic in "a wide range of social phenomena from high rates of family violence to high rates of murder, judicial hanging and road accidents."[64] Any study that concentrates on lynching and murder inevitably underplays the Hydra-headed nature of the violence that sustained white supremacy in both racial orders. This study could perhaps have said more about the myriad, subtler forms of unofficial violence that degraded blacks. I have tried to compensate for this shortcoming by referring to the micropolitics of everyday life as "racial etiquette"– the numerous uncodified rules that arose "to define and maintain the social distance necessary to highlight the social superiority of whites in relation to blacks."[65] More could also have been said about the less spectacular violence that whites routinely used to intimidate and brutalize black labor, especially in the countryside. This issue is explored in Chapters 3 and 4, but the treatment is by no means exhaustive.

By focusing on racial killing, finally, this study ignores two other groups that also bore the brunt of white mob violence – indigenous Mexicans and European immigrants who streamed into many Southern states in search of employment in the late 1800s. "For a Mexican living in America from 1882 and 1930," one source notes, "the chance of being a victim of mob violence was equal to those of an African American living in the South." According to Rodolfo Acuna, "Mexicans came to know Euroamerican democracy as 'Linchocracia.'"[66] These claims find ample support in William D. Carrigan and Clive Webb's essay on "the lynching of persons of Mexican origin or descent."[67] Despite strong evidence of similarities between the lynching of African Americans and that of Mexicans, this study maintains an exclusive focus on the "racial," as opposed to the *racialized* lineaments of the two contexts. Mob violence against immigrant whites paled before the horrors that African Americans and Mexicans endured. Still, Italian immigrants were in particular danger of being lynched. Sicilians stood out in the Anglo-Saxon Protestant South by virtue of their Catholic faith, foreign language and unfamiliar customs. They quickly came to occupy an intermediate and vulnerable position in the racial binary that dominated Southern society. Eleven Sicilians were lynched in New Orleans on 14 March 1890 after a court acquitted nine Sicilians who had been arrested on charges of murdering a police officer. In all, 29 Sicilians were summarily dispatched by Southern white mobs between 1886 and 1910.[68]

The distinction that Clive Webb draws between the lynching of Sicilians and that of African Americans – and, by extension, also of Mexicans – is central to the present study. The distinction, moreover, reinforces the central importance that René Girard attaches to the role that victim vulnerability plays in the selection of sacrificial "scapegoats." Out-muscled and too vulnerable to repel white mob violence, African Americans and Mexicans bore the full brunt of mob violence by comparison with Sicilians, who were better placed to mobilize against the scapegoat role. Webb notes that Sicilians were able to draw on "stronger institutional resources than African Americans [and Mexicans]." They benefited especially from the intervention of Italian diplomats, who provided a "'permanent institutional opposition' far beyond the organizational means of African Americans." More effective was the canny decision by the Italian government to mobilize federal authority against uncooperative law enforcement agencies in Louisiana.[69] Within decades, the intermediate racial status of Sicilians gradually dissolved as the postbellum racial binary crystallized. Sicilians in the Southern racial order "became white" – to borrow Noel Ignatiev's term for the analogous experience of Irish immigrants – sometime around the First World War.[70]

Nothing remotely comparable to the assault against Sicilians occurred in South Africa. To the contrary, working-class European immigrants were actively recruited by successive governments and invested with all the privileges of citizenship even when suspicious Afrikaners and snobbish English-speaking whites discriminated against them, as Milton Shain's study of Jewish immigrants illustrates.[71] To a much greater extent than the Sicilian counterparts who protected themselves by lobbying for institutional support from the Italian government and from local authorities in the South, white immigrants in South Africa were almost automatically protected from extra-legal violence. More importantly, they profited directly from concerted state policies to overcome intra-white divisions and black opposition by creating a broad white identity that transcended class and ethnic fissures in the inter-War years. Like the black majority, white immigrants also benefited from the absence of a "lynch culture" in an otherwise still rugged and under-policed country. For these reasons, the Sicilian nightmare in the South did not stalk white immigrants in South Africa's racial order.

All comparative historical studies quickly confront the limitations of space. Experience suggests that this is particularly true for studies that chronicle the differences amongst cases. Hopefully, the chapters that follow will convey the central purpose of this study: to explain why analogous but still divergent patterns of racial violence emerged in the racial orders of South Africa and the American South.

2

"Rape" and violence in the making of segregation

It is not surprising that "the protection of our women" became a prominent mantra of white politics in South Africa and the South in the postbellum period. Because economic, cultural and social relations in both racial orders were inseverably bound up with gender relations, significant changes in race relations simultaneously inflamed deep-seated anxieties concerning the security and status of white women. At the center of these anxieties resided the black male as a sexual predator. Despite their different histories – one a recent slave society, the other a still precarious settler colonial society – this mutual sexual stereotyping expressed the three-fold thrust of white male domination: to gain control over black males, retain access to black women, and inoculate all white women at all times from the black-male-as-rapist. For a time, the victory of the more liberal forces, the Northern and the British armies, raised the disconcerting possibility that blacks would enjoy greater freedoms and protections from formal and informal thralldom. As a result, "sexual panics" and fears of sexual "outrages" emerged immediately after the Civil and Anglo-Boer wars and contributed significantly to racial segregation in both regions.

White men contended that the safety of their women and children were at the center of their hostility against black males. Yet, as was also true for the antebellum period, there was little to no evidence that white women were in any significant sexual danger from blacks in the postbellum era.[1] In the South, Ida B. Wells' pioneering research in the 1890s confirmed that the actual number of cases involving black men who raped white women was extremely low. Officials in South Africa reached a similar conclusion immediately before and after unification in 1910 and wondered about the causes that so agitated the authors of the letters piling up on their desks and appearing in newspapers, all warning of Black Peril. If black men were not assaulting white women, what was the cause of the moral panics that inflamed whites and prompted them to portray black men as "brutes," "beasts" and "savages" in both racial orders?

Conditions in the postbellum period eroded white men's confidence in their ability to control white women and support their families. White unemployment, especially at a time when blacks were increasingly available for recruitment by employers, had more than material ramifications for the white male. By weakening the white male's role as breadwinner, material instability also threatened to weaken the ties of dependency that bound white women. One of the ways in which the growing independence of white women disturbed men was the prospect of inter-racial sex. Despite expressions of horror that attended discussions of inter-racial sex, sufficient evidence in both places suggests that not all white women were willing to accept the full panoply of the moral and racial restraints of "respectable white society." Intimate relations between white women and black men struck at the heart of the "double standard," one of the more pleasurable perks of white masculinity. White men refused to surrender their access to black women, but bridled at the thought of their women in the arms of black lovers. Rumors of "rape" therefore easily served as a bugle call to action.

Establishing the racial order therefore simultaneously incorporated a defense of the patriarchal authority of white men, which, in turn, entailed the protection of the double standard. White men looked upon black men as embodying a two-fold threat to their claims to dominance. Within the labor market, black males, and the lower wages they were prepared to accept, were viewed as competitors for jobs that were held to be in short supply. Within the realm of intimacy, black males were depicted as ogres who dared to inflict themselves on the women and children of white households. As a result, fears of a double displacement – from the economy as well as from the home – lay at the core of the hostility that white males displayed towards black males in the decades after the wars ended.

However, similar stereotypes and neuroses about sex in South Africa and in the South tell only part of the story. More striking than the similar etiology of white masculinist hostilities is the very different ways in which they manifested themselves in the two racial contexts. The central contention of this chapter is that the contrasting expression of white masculinist hostilities is explained by contrasting patterns of state formation in the South Africa and the South.

Sexual anxieties in the South were inextricable from the violence that arose to first destroy Radical Reconstruction and then impose segregation. Fears of rape formed a perennial rationale for the thousands of lynches that took place from the 1890s until the Second World War. Even when demonstratively baseless, allegations of sexual assaults proved to be a blood-boiling ululation. White males, many of whom openly exploited the joys of the double standard, could be quickly roused to ferocious action at the faintest hint of an "outrage" against their white womenfolk. The cleavages that separated poor whites from the affluent plantocracy magically melted away in pursuit of a common quarry. The authority of the law, with its potential to block the popular will, weakened as extra-legal movements arose under the pretext of extending it. More often than not, state officials and politicians were complicit in excusing the violence that erupted in civil society and frequently imparted a veneer of legitimacy to extra-legal mayhem by orchestrating it. Uniformed officers of the law were photographed in the act of lynching their black victims; the deceitful reports of detectives, coroners and county doctors corroborated sometimes patently absurd accounts of the victim's end, and the local judge concurred. Some whites dared to denounce this culture of illegal violence, but not until the 1940s would their voice gain sway. Until then, rape was linked to lynching in the popular white mind and served as the pretext for some of the most appalling acts of extra-legal violence undertaken by ordinary citizens and state officials alike.

In contrast, in South Africa, white sexual anxieties and the "Black Peril" scares that followed rarely erupted into violent attacks on blacks, and when they did, the ensuing disorder paled in comparison to the vengeful savagery that was a commonplace in the South. Furthermore, Black Peril outbreaks were not left to mobs in civil society but were addressed by law enforcement agencies and a state that had no interest at all in tolerating, let alone instigating, any form of civil unrest. As many studies have shown, uncertain political and economic dynamics at the time of unification prompted governments to gain control over "race relations" by strengthening the power of the state. Black Peril was harnessed to this approach to state building. Potentially explosive, Black Peril joined a growing array of reasons for the central state to rationalize "Native Affairs" and formally extend its reach over blacks in the process. Black Peril in South Africa therefore contributed to the search for a coherent policy of segregation, one that would entrust the field of "race relations" to the state. Accordingly, febrile white masculinities were not permitted to descend into orgies of violence against blacks. Instead, the psycho-sexual hostilities of white males were diverted into the more predictable and safer processes used to consolidate the segregationist state.

In short, state formation in South Africa emphasized bureaucratic repression and disparaged private vengeance. In the American South, state formation permitted private vengeance to either fuse with or even displace the instruments of repression. These broad and contrasting patterns account for the truncated impact of Black Peril scares in South Africa and the extraordinarily violent impact that myths about "black rapists" had on the emergence of segregation in the South.

The chapter does not attempt to provide a complete history of rape scares. Instead, focusing on the violence that rape myths inspired, it shows that racial violence in South Africa and the South were conditioned by contrasting patterns of state formation in the aftermath of debilitating wars. The chapter is organized into three sections dealing with the impact of rape scares on state formation. Each section demonstrates that whites in South Africa and the American South, although haunted by similar sexual fears, drew on different traditions and took different paths when the moment to act arrived.

Rape myths as a moral panic

Not only does existing comparative work on South Africa and the American South have little to say about the question of inter-racial violence, it has also managed to skirt more or less entirely the role that sexual discourse played in the formulation and establishment of segregation. This is not to say that scholars have failed to perceive the importance of sexual discourses and social movements in each country. To the contrary, South African scholars have long discussed the odium and fear that whites, especially Afrikaners, have attached to Black Peril. Likewise, confronted with graphic evidence of similar neuroses amongst white Southerners, many students of the South have placed sexual discourse at the center of explanations of "Southern violence." Surprisingly, comparativists have not considered the phenomena jointly, although Black Peril and Southern myths about rape are but variations of the same theme. Both, after all, were manifestations of moral panics amongst whites.

The literature on Black Peril in southern Africa pales in comparison to the scholarly attention devoted to the veritable industry that has emerged to explain the "Southern rape complex." Nevertheless, because they both address the same moral panic, a comparative consideration of these literatures suggests an overlap in explanatory frameworks.

Explanations of moral panics around race fall into three approaches that are distinguished on the basis of the respective emphases they make: psycho-sexual accounts, those that attribute moral panics to some specific economic, social or political anxiety, and those that view moral panics as attempts to forge an internal cohesion within white communities. These approaches are not mutually exclusive and share several common arguments even when they reject claims that are central to contending explanations.

Psycho-sexual theories view moral panics around rape as a form of communal catharsis within the white community. The approach borrows heavily from Freudian theories of sexuality and places great weight on concepts such as repressed or excessive sexuality and projection, concerns that are embedded in the notion of the "double standard." White society, so the argument goes, placed a premium on the patriarchal authority of men and the subservience of their women. The result was a conception of white women as chaste, virtuous and sexually passive. Chivalrous codes in the South and the Victorian outlook of settler societies in late nineteenth-century South Africa embodied this conception of white women. White men sought more satisfactory sexual pleasure from black women and therefore found themselves competing against black males in a war with two fronts: while asserting their own right to have sex with black women, white males had to eliminate the black male's access to white women. Southerners and white settlers also shared the view that blacks were "uncivilized," "primitive" and "barbarous," and hence were less capable of controlling their passions. The same sexual instincts that made black women more attractive sexual partners charged black men with an "excess of desire." The stunted internalized controls in black men demanded the opposite accomplishment in white women. To paraphrase Forrest Wood slightly: "If white women took it upon themselves to express their sexuality fully, the presence of high-powered animalistic [black men] could destroy completely the socio-sexual culture that had evolved over the decades."[2] White males projected their own sexual fantasies onto black women, demanded that white women should repress their own sexual instincts, and so stood on permanent guard against the hypersexed black male. In the resultant superheated sexual culture, the triggering incident that sparked a moral panic also served to depressurize white society, restoring it to its taut but stable condition. Another variation of this approach stresses that rape, especially if the assailant was black, was a violation that could not be mentioned in "respectable" society. Hence, fear of rape was driven inwards into the psychology of whites, producing an amorphous and volatile sense of psychic dread.

A number of sociologists and historians avoid the psycho-sexual approach on the grounds that propositions about "repression," "hypersexuality" and "sexual energies" are inherently impossible to confirm or disprove. Not all claims made within this approach are rejected, however. But even when they accept arguments about the double standard, scholars such as Orlando Patterson express doubt about the primacy of psychological motivations in moral panics.[3]

To avoid these pitfalls, a second approach to rape anxieties points to *specific empirical events* that befall white society. The empirical event that triggered a racial murder could assume a number of forms: a plunge in economic conditions; a rumor about "restlessness" amongst local blacks; or allegations of an "outrage" that a black male was said to have committed against a white female were the sort of specific event that prompted whites to rapidly reassess their security and resort to the extra-legal killing of blacks. Norman Hetherington and Charles van Onselen adopt this approach in their respective accounts of the Black Peril scares that gripped colonial Natal in the 1860s and the Transvaal from 1890 to 1914. In Natal, Etherington observes, exaggerated claims about sexual assaults on white women was the idiom for concerns about ongoing threats to the property and status of white settlers. Etherington concludes that sexual panics arose whenever specific events seemed to imperil Natal's community of far-flung settlers. Likewise, van Onselen's account of the Transvaal rape panic points to successive declines in the material circumstances of middle-class and working-class whites in the fifteen-year period he examines. Van Onselen's focus on economic fluctuations echoes in the work of American sociologists such as Stewart Tolnay and E. M. Beck, who also take pains to attribute moral panics to discrete empirical events. Tolnay and Beck further note the influence of class and timing. Poor whites and local elites were preoccupied with different problems – the former with competition from cheap black labor, the latter with the threatening possibility of solidarity between blacks and poor whites. The convergence of these interests at specific moments established the sociological condition for the emergence of rape panics to sweep across white communities. [4]

The advantage of this approach is simultaneously its weakness. While research on rape panics in South Africa is still in its infancy, American scholars have questioned the tight correlation between sociological conditions and the outbreaks of rape panics in the South. Not all material misfortunes yielded rape panics, and rape panics emerged in the absence of the conditions that Tolnay and Beck posit. For example, one study concluded that news or rumors of a panic in one locality were better able to explain the outbreak of a panic in nearby areas, regardless of prevailing economic circumstances.[5] For the American case at least, the link between empirical misfortunes and rape panics seems too strict to fully account for the amorphous anxiety that marked Southern communities.

The third approach departs from the structuralist moorings of the second approach by emphasizing the role that rape panics played in the *cultural construction of white unity*. In today's language, rape panics contributed to the formation of "whiteness." Whites assumed that they were bound together by common racial and/or cultural patrimonies, an assumption that may have been more deeply rooted in white settler colonies. Whites claimed or simply assumed that these commonalities cleanly distinguished them from non-whites.[6] However, authors in the third approach observe, cleavages of gender, class and religion complicated and often defied claims about the "natural unity" of white society. Rape scares galvanized the internal unity of whites by depoliticizing internal fault lines and creating an illusory unity amongst whites. Much of this approach to the study of rape panics follows from recent developments in cultural theory. In particular, they owe a special debt to the pioneering work of Edward Said's *Orientalism* and Foucault's work on disciplinary regimes centered on the body. The post-structuralist school that has since emerged demonstrates how diverse is the array of influences that are implicated in the formation of subjectivities that ultimately constitute the "unity" of communities, including a sense of bourgeois respectability that was as much prized by whites in settler societies such as ninth-century South Africa as it was in the American South. Discourses of cleanliness, marriage, masculinity, the family, child-rearing, disease and sexual behavior all illuminate the multiple sites involved in the construction of subjectivities, the nature of power and the operation of hegemony. Rape panics contribute powerfully to these projects, deepening the distinction that whites posited between a civilized white "We" and the savage black "Other." Empirical evidence of rape is thus not the primary issue in this approach. According to Elizabeth Hale, African American fear of lynching actually increased in the 1920s and 1930s even as the incidence of lynching decreased, in testimony of the wider circulation of information and body parts of lynched victims as communications media and market relations circulated more in broader swathes of areas in the South.[7] Instead, rape panics are treated as cultural projects that transformed the subjectivities and bolstered the internal unity of white communities.

These three approaches are clearly not mutually exclusive and each contributes to the explanation of rape panics. All accept the importance of sexual rivalry embodied in the double standard, none would deny that rape crises may be triggered by specific events, and all concur that rape panics were at least partly intended to bolster a degree of unity amongst whites by depoliticizing divisive and competitive relations amongst them. All are therefore useful in explaining the rape panics to which South Africa and the South were prone in the early stages of segregation. What these three lack, on the other hand, is further consideration of the relationship between rape panics and state formation.

Moral panics and state formation

The end of Radical Reconstruction and the Anglo-Boer War raised the question of blacks' incorporation into the emerging new states. The segregationist solution that emerged in both orders was very much a matter of structures and institutions. At the same time, these "objective" phenomena were strongly influenced by a sense amongst whites that segregation addressed highly personal concerns of white men and women. The postbellum emergence of stereotypes about black sexuality, vividly captured in the image of the "black-beast rapist," lent order to this pervasive dread. It is significant that this heightened sexual fear emerged on the heels of violent wars. War had dismantled antebellum law-enforcement institutions, destabilized economies on which white men's patriarchal control over their women and households rested, and so called into general question the ability of white men to protect their women and children.[8] Whites' sexualized anxieties in the postbellum years were therefore built into the reconstruction of white supremacy and its most visible manifestation, the segregation state. As elites swooped in to determine the nature and destiny of the emerging state, state formation increasingly acquired a top–down character that threatened to estrange ordinary whites. In this context, widespread paranoia about black rapists crystallized into an idiom for conveying deep-seated personal fears into the formation of segregation, injecting the personal into the structural. Because they expressed a wide array of dissatisfactions, one scholar notes that rape panics were "protean in their causes and effects."[9] Moral panics about rape afforded ordinary white individuals an opportunity to contribute to the emergence of the segregationist state.

Scholars such as Ann Stoler and Jock McColloch have shown that rape panics contributed to the formation of the colonial state in a number of ways.[10] Several of these insights may also be applied to the Southern context. To begin with, rape panics were never only about rape. Beyond the emotion and pain they sensationalized, rape panics were highly *instrumental* phenomena. They fed off and merged with other concerns or controversies in society and established a political terrain that also served as a moral high ground from which whites could make demands on elites and state authorities. For example, rape panics became vehicles for expressing dissatisfaction with "nigger-loving" courts in the South, just as they were always accompanied by demands for improved police protection in South Africa. Most cogently, race panics were vehicles for demanding and maintaining segregation. Rape panics also had distinct *class* etiologies. It is striking that many of the alleged rape victims were drawn from the lower classes.[11]

As Brundage notes for the South, rape was one of only two allegations (murder being the other) that guaranteed a communal lynching when the victim was working class. Whipping up a rape-inspired manhunt attracted the finest burghers to one's cause, a sure-fire way for poor white women to obtain recognition from above of both their whiteness and feminine virtue. Sexual violations of racial taboos were most likely, and therefore also most dangerous at the bottom-most rungs of the social ladder. In South Africa, the galvanizing fear of *verkaffering* (Africanization) that emerged amongst Afrikaners immediately after unification was more than a metaphorical fear of social *gelykstelling* (equality) with blacks: it also amplified fears of biological assimilation into blackness in a few mixed-race slums sprouting up in the country's largest towns. Rape panics were therefore a clarion call to stand firm against the sexual seductions that poverty imposed on the most destitute whites. Rape panics also became opportunities for priests and town planners to pontificate on bourgeois morality and "civilized standards." In the South, white males who raped or enjoyed voluntary sex with black women became violent Ku Klux Klan "regulators" when an allegation of rape against a white woman arose. Almost always directed at the white poor, expressions of revulsion against inter-racial sex encapsulated demands for the drawing of a *cordon sanitaire* between the white and the black communities. Sexual assault was a real danger, and some women were indeed raped. Still, moral panics about rape were always double-edged: they sought to bolster personal morality by securing or consolidating broader patterns of segregation throughout society.

Asserting or restoring the *patriarchal powers of* the white-male-as protector was also central to rape panics, arising as they did around the image of the white-woman-as victim. Rape panics that were ostensibly triggered by the "black-beast rapist" therefore reinforced white women's subordination to white males. The vulnerability of white women became increasingly important in times when women were entering the labor force as wage earners who were potentially independent of male breadwinners. For example, women and children accounted for many "lintheads" in the textile factories of the Black Belt South and so benefited from "welfare capitalism" in mill villages at a time when white farmers were struggling to make ends meet. Likewise, in South Africa, leading men and women in the Afrikaner nationalist movement fretted about adolescent Afrikaner girls who worked as domestic servants in English-speaking white households or, worse, in shops owned by Indians. High unemployment amongst "poor white" males transformed the prospect of independent white female breadwinners into a threat against the system of patriarchy. This prospect added to the premium that whites placed on segregation.[12]

To claim that rape panics largely sprang from amorphous, ill-defined sexual anxieties is not to suggest that black men did not occasionally attack and rape white women. By the sleight of racism's hand, however, one rape committed by a black male outweighed a dozen rapes that white men committed against white women. But, however small the number of black-on-white rapes, rape panics combined the two distinct elements of fear and retribution. On this score, the relationship between rape panics and state formation differs in South Africa and the American South. For notwithstanding the great similarities in the etiology of rape panics in the two racial orders, whites developed very different strategies for surveilling society and punishing the "black-beast rapist." These different outcomes cohere closely with the different patterns of state formation in the two contexts.

State formation in the South was reflected in the ideology of popular justice, signaling whites' reluctance to fully relinquish the means of racial retribution to the state.[13] Accordingly, rape panics in the South almost always generated lynch mobs and the lethal involvement of citizens who viewed vigilantism and summary justice as supplements to the formal law. The open collusion of politicians, including governors and senators who gave defiant interviews in support of lynch mobs, is a reminder of the role the culture of lynching played in suppressing class differences amongst whites and sustaining the ideology of the "Solid South." "The protection of our women" was an irresistible ululation to men across the class divide, authorizing them to coalesce and usurp the state's punitive functions while underscoring women's dependence on men.[14]

In contrast, South Africans, who were more divided by rapidly souring class divisions and an insurgent Afrikaner nationalism that turned to open violence on several occasions after 1910, displayed little inclination for organized collective violence against the evil "black-beast rapist." When they did arise, rape-instigated vigilante movements were furtive and apologetic affairs; they do not once appear to have summarily executed alleged black rapists; and they were quick to dissipate when confronted by the police. White civilians, including elements within the Afrikaner nationalist movement who rejected the legitimacy of the South African state, were too drawn to and dependent on the state to reject its authority to regulate "race relations," the one field that an imparted a broad, if problematic, unity to whites. Discourses of sexuality were never permitted to generate movements that rivaled the state for legitimacy, even when whites claimed that the bodies of their women and children were at stake. In South Africa, therefore, the instrumental motivations that rape panics embodied seem more transparent than in the south, where mobs frequently expressed their satisfaction after taking summary retribution against the "black-beast rapist." In South

Africa, where mobbism was rare, rape panics always seem directed at the state and invariably petered out with whites beseeching local authorities for more police, improved residential amenities and more controls over blacks.

The "Southern rape complex"

In the USA, evidence that sexual assaults by blacks on white women were on the increase in the South was as spurious as in South Africa. When she began assembling data on the frequency and reasons for lynching in the South, Ida B. Wells was astonished to discover that records were kept and propagated "by word of mouth" in a region where both elites and poor whites had a vested interest in subjugating emancipated African Americans. No official investigations were ever made to assess the scale and nature of either the "Southern rape complex" or the lynching that it yielded. Wells' data, the first reliable assessment of the phenomenon, would be systematically updated by studies published by the NCAA from 1912 onwards.[15]

Wells noticed that from 1890 onwards, Southern whites did not wait for details gleaned from the press or trial records before inflicting lethal violence on blacks accused of sexual crimes. Her findings failed to uncover one incident in which a sheer rumor of rape did not yield a lynching but many in which rape allegations surfaced in cases that had nothing to do with sexual assault. Allegations of rape were raised in two-thirds of lynchings, but, because blacks were "lynched for anything or nothing," this was a worthless statistic. One incident she used to illustrate this point – although any number of similar accounts in *Red Record* would serve the same purpose – involved the lynching of an African American man named Smith in Roanoke, Virginia. Whites seized Smith after he was observed in heated conversation with a white woman:

> It was known that the woman refused to accuse Smith of assaulting her, and that his offense consisted in quarreling with her about the change of money in a transaction in which he bought something from her market booth. Both parties lost their temper, and the result was a row from which Smith had to make his escape. At once the old cry was sounded that the woman had been assaulted, and in a few hours all the town was wild with people thirsting for the assailants blood.[16]

Within hours, twenty men marched Smith to the center of Roanoke and hanged him from the branch of a hickory tree on Ninth Avenue in the residential area of the town.

The demise of the hapless "Smith" is emblematic of the fate that overtook thousands of other, even more nameless black men around the same time that whites were forming "vigilante associations" in Johannesburg. Wells admits that she commenced her research expecting to find significant evidence that would corroborate the uproar about black rapes on white females. Ready to reprimand black men for raping white women, she initially believed that lynching was an "unreasoning anger over the terrible crime of rape" and that "the mob was justified in taking his life." She quickly concluded that rape allegations were an expeditious fiction, "an excuse to get rid of Negroes who were acquiring wealth and property and thus keep the race terrorized." Wells concluded that "rape" was a discursive subterfuge, a master narrative that exonerated the summary killing of blacks for any variety of reasons. Black males, she concluded, were caught in a "Southern rape complex" that projected black masculinity as an omnipresent threat to white women and their children, the security of the household, and so by extension, to the dominance of white males. No other factor in Southern life was as effective as the "Southern rape complex" in providing an ever-ready excuse for white men to eliminate the sexual and economic rival that assumed the shape of the emancipated black male.[17]

Just two cases, selected at random from the tragic cornucopia of work on the "Southern rape complex," will serve to underscore the contrast between the violence of white men in South Africa and in the South. This contrast will then be addressed below.

The lynching of Paul Jones (Macon, Georgia, 1919)
Jones, a "suspicious-looking negro," was accused of raping a fifty-year-old widow as she made her way home from church. When news of the alleged assault began to circulate, large numbers of white men began frantically searching for suspicious blacks. Deputy sheriffs captured Jones in a nearby railroad yard, but a mob quickly formed and compelled the officers to take refuge in a railroad car. The county sheriff hurried to the scene and attempted to dissuade the mob from overpowering the law officers and lynching the prisoner. After extended negotiations the sheriff was permitted to take Jones to the home of his victim for identification. The bruised and battered woman, hysterical with fright, identified Jones as her assailant by blood marks that she claimed she had made upon his clothing. Roused by the victim's anguish and her "positive" identification, the mob, which had swelled to more than a thousand, seized Jones, shot him repeatedly, and then dragged him, still-living, several hundred yards before dousing him with gasoline and setting him ablaze. When the fire dwindled down without killing Jones, he was pulled from the pyre, re-saturated with gasoline, and thrown back into the flames until only charred bones remained.[18]

The lynching of Claude Neal (Florida, October 1934)
At noon on Thursday, 18 October 1934, Lola Cannidy left her home to water the family livestock but did not return. Her mutilated body was found the next morning on a wooded hillside near her home. One doctor advised Jackson County sheriff W. F. Chambliss that Lola had been raped. The gravity of the implications prompted the sheriff to seek a second opinion from another physician who concluded that Lola had had sexual intercourse shortly before her death but that she had probably not been raped. The sheriff soon learned that Lola was last seen in the company of Claude Neal,

a black farmhand who lived across the road from the Cannidy home. Neal was arrested and charged with rape and murder, and so began his descent into the blood-soaked pages of Southern history.

To circumvent the inevitable lynch mob, and much to his credit, Chambliss detained Neal not in the Marianna County jail but in the nearby facility in Chipley. Within a few hours, as word of Neal's arrest began to summon up a mob, Chambliss again moved Neal to a jail in Panama City, fifty miles further. Neal would be secretly moved several more times after that, finally ending up in Brewton, Alabama. Although Neal was now in a different state and more than 200 miles away from the scene of the crime, he was still in the South and so still within reach of the enraged men who formed a motorcade and tracked him down in the dead of night to Brewton's small jail. The mob leveled their guns at Neal's jailers, forcing them to surrender their petrified prisoner. A "confession" was allegedly extracted from Neal on the ride back to Marianna. Although he was held captive for two days in an undisclosed location, there was nothing secretive about his impending doom. A newspaper in Dotham, Alabama, published the details of his coming execution, a local radio station broadcast the news even further and word of mouth carried it further still. Newspapers in Jacksonville, Tampa and Montgomery took up the story in support of the advertised lynching. Neal's coming fate was then relayed even further until astonished citizens across the country could read, "Florida to Burn Negro at the Stake." The NAACP and Jessie Daniel Ames of the ASPL even apprised the governor of Florida and President Franklin D. Roosevelt of the injustice being planned.

Walter White, the executive secretary of the NAACP, obtained a verbatim account from an observer who witnessed the lynching:

> After taking the nigger to the woods about four miles from Greenwood, they cut off his penis. He was made to eat it. Then they cut off his testicles and made him eat them and say he liked it. [I gathered that this barbarous act consumed considerable time and that other means of torture were used from time to time on Neal – W.W.]
>
> Then they sliced his sides and stomach with knives and every now and then somebody would cut off a finger or toe. Red hot irons were used on the nigger to burn him from top to bottom. From time to time during the torture a rope would be tied around Neal's neck and he was pulled up over a limb and held there until he almost choked to death when he would be let down and the torture begin all over again. After several hours of this unspeakable torture, "they decided just to kill him."
>
> Neal's body was tied to a rope at the rear of an automobile and dragged over the highway to the Cannidy home. Here a mob estimated to number somewhere between 3000 and 7000 from eleven southern states were excitedly waiting his arrival. When the car that was dragging Neal's body came in front of the Cannidy home, a man who was riding the rear bumper cut the rope.
>
> A woman came out the Cannidy house and drove a butcher knife through is heart. Then the crowd came by and some kicked him and some drove their cars over him.

"Men, women, and children," Walter White continued,

> were numbered in the vast throng that came to witness the lynching. It is
> reported from reliable sources that the little children, some of them mere
> tots, who lived in the Greenwood neighborhood, waited with sharpened
> sticks for the return of Neal's body and that when it rolled in the dust on
> the road that awful night these little children drove their weapons deep
> into the flesh of the dead man. The body, which by this time, was horribly
> mutilated, was taken by the mob to Marianna, a distance of ten or eleven
> miles, where it was hung to a tree on the northeast corner of the courthouse
> square. Pictures were taken of the mutilated form and hundreds of photo-
> graphs were sold for fifty cents each. Scores of citizens viewed the body as
> it hung in the square. The body was perfectly nude until the early morning
> when someone had the decency to hang a burlap sack over the middle of
> the body. The body was cut down about eight-thirty Saturday morning,
> October 27, 1934. Fingers and toes from Neal's body have been exhibited
> as souvenirs in Marianna where one man offered to divide the finger that
> he had with a friend as "a special favor." Another man has one of the fin-
> gers preserved in alcohol.[19]

The lynching of Claude Neal remains one of the best-known examples of a
spectacle lynching.

Neal's murder is notable on several accounts. The allegation of rape, the
sheer savagery of the mob, the known identity of the mob's ringleaders, the
inadequacy of the protection given to Neal while he was incarcerated, the
public space in which the lynching took place and the carnival atmosphere
that attended it were all familiar elements in the South. By the time Neal
was put to death, however, support for mass lynching in the South was on
the wane and Neal's unwarranted death – he was innocent of the crime
– breathed much-needed life into the anti-lynching campaign. Coming as it
did in the tail end of the lynch era, when the weakening of support for lynch
emboldened more whites to speak out against the practice, the resurrection
of all the devices associated with spectacle lynching strongly suggests the
continuing power of the "Southern rape complex."

Rape panics and segregation in South Africa

From 1902 until 1912, a spate of articles and letters in the newspapers and
urgent communications addressed to various state officials announced the
outbreak of a Black Peril scare on the Witwatersrand. Officials within the
colonial administration were baffled. Hasty inquiries were made of magistrates in the Department of Justice, the South African Constabulary and
the Criminal Investigation Department, but no evidence was found of an
alarming upsurge of "assaults" and "outrages" committed against white
women. Still, civic concerns about Black Peril refused to subside. For the
next four years, letters to the press raged about a number of cases in which
Black men were accused or found guilty of attacking white women and
girls. Veiled threats of lynch law surfaced. Letters and articles appeared in

the press openly admiring Sam Lewis who, in full public view and at point-blank range, on Saturday, 17 October 1908, had calmly shot and killed a young African man in the streets of Salisbury, Rhodesia, because he had dared to profess his love for Lewis' daughter. Disturbed at the sheer thought of such an event in South Africa, the Governor-General Herbert Gladstone sought the advice of the country's Supreme Court about an adequate legislative response to Black Peril concerns.[20] Although personally convinced that black rapists posed no particular threat to white women, Gladstone established a formal "Commission on Black Peril" that duly issued a report in 1912.

Yet even before the outbreak of the First World War distracted the nation's attention, the Black Peril phenomenon mysteriously subsided. The withering away of the Black Peril scare around 1912 therefore repeated a pattern that the historians Norman Etherington and Jeremy Martens identified in the rape panic in colonial Natal in the 1860s. Then, too, a rape scare had arisen and retreated for reasons that baffled colonial magistrates and administrators.[21]

An examination of the secondary literature and relevant archival material suggests two important conclusions. Firstly, as in the South, rape scares in South Africa were never supported by empirical evidence. This suggests that the phrase "rape scare" should be treated as a trope for the periodic eruption and evaporation of lynch-minded movements in South Africa. One of the striking features of the Black Peril scare that lasted from 1902 until 1914 was the volume of records that state officials helped to author and which they duly filed away. After compiling and examining tables that correlated sexual assaults cases with race and region, state officials in the Transvaal, from where most claims about "outrages" originated and the epicenter of politics in South Africa, were convinced that the Black Peril scare was a fiction. They could not assert this conclusion quite as baldly, however. The volatile state of politics in the postbellum years compelled a more solicitous approach towards the agitated white citizenry. Although their own empirical data scotched the idea of a Black Peril, state officials set about dealing with the fantasy of black rapists largely as an exercise to legitimate the unsettled young state.

Secondly, Black Peril scares in South Africa had a limited purchase on white males' propensity for violence. No evidence appears to exist in the records consulted to demonstrate that white men took to violently killing blacks suspected of committing sexual assaults on white women. Whites were certain that the actual number of sexual assaults was much higher than statistics claimed. It was widely believed that white women who were raped by blacks were too ashamed to press charges and endure the resultant press and legal inquiries. Allegations and rumors were therefore received as sufficient evidence that assaults had in fact taken place. Yes, despite the circulation of these rumors, white men in South Africa did not form mobs that lynched black males at will.

To grasp the full dimensions of the violence that distinguished "rape panics" in the South, it is instructive to examine in some detail the context and evolution of a rape scare that emerged in Johannesburg in 1912. Black Peril scares in South Africa invariably developed in two stages. First came a persistent stream of letters to the press and government officials in which widely held beliefs and myths about Black Peril were circulated as self-evident truths. Second came the official response of the state, the center-piece of which was the marshalling of empirical evidence about inter-racial sexual assaults as the proper basis on which to found any new changes to the law.

Immediately after the Anglo-Boer, rumors surfaced that blacks were plan-ning to use wartime dislocations to re-take land from Afrikaner farmers.[22] Rumors of land invasions and counter-attacks by farmers circulated widely, injecting a jittery note into relations between Afrikaners and their English conquerors. A specific anxiety about sexual attacks was a prominent dimen-sion of the rumors. The Commissioner of Police would be kept increasingly busy by allegations of the sort that were printed in the *Leader* on 22 Janu-ary 1903. Under the heading "Kaffir Assaults," the newspaper reported: "There have been ugly rumors here [Pretoria] during the past few months of attempted assaults by kafirs on white women." The details were calculated to frighten white readers:

> In one case especially, where a kafir entered the kitchen of a house during the owner's absence, the facts are such that they should be more widely known. The wife, who was in delicate health at the time, was startled by the appearance of a native boy in her kitchen, apparently with aggressive intent. Fortunately, the husband arrived on the scene in time to capture the assailant, but not in time to prevent disastrous effects on the wife's health.

Proceeding from the specific to the general, the article warned of "larger dangers":

> There are rumors, too, of kafirs frequenting houses of low repute kept by alien whites. Taking the two together and reading between the lines, and keeping in memory the fact of the high wages received by the domestic kafir today, the necessity for dealing with crimes of this nature must be apparent to even the most casual observer. In this town especially, where the number of white women and girls has been so largely increased since the British occupation, such an evil must not be allowed to exist for a single day ... If it is necessary that more stringent regulations be made these should at once be passed and put into force.

Almost as an afterthought, the article concluded by observing without com-ment, "A Kafir boy from Marabastad was convicted of rape on a woman, and sentenced to two years' imprisonment and twenty lashes."[23] The lack of comment establishes a seamless whole between the details of an attack on one white woman and the criminal sexuality of an entire community – the essence of Black Peril.

Dozens of newspaper reports and letters to various newspapers and government officials between 1903 and 1907 kept alive the Black Peril issue. Letters to the press were sent off by a diverse array of civic and religious organizations. In addition, speeches in parliament and the Transvaal Provincial Council in 1907 and 1908 stoked the issue. In the Transvaal Provincial Council, J. Hunt addressed to the Minister of Justice the question of "whether, in view of the frequent assaults made by natives on white women and girls, and the alarming cases recently reported on the Witwatersrand where natives [had] entered the sleeping apartments occupied by white women and girls," the courts could be pressed to impose "exemplary sentences whenever convictions [were] obtained." J. Munnik in the Senate, who also demanded stiffer sentences for black assailants, took up the refrain.[24]

A change of tactic seems to have occurred around mid-1907. Instead of simply alerting the authorities to Black Peril, whites began demanding accurate empirical information about the frequency and distribution of assaults on white women. In 1907 the Guild of Loyal Women of South Africa addressed a question to the Attorney General of the Transvaal asking for "the exact statistics of the crimes of assaults and rape committed by black or coloured men on white women and children." The Rand Pioneers (Incorporated) followed suit, attacked what it regarded as "lenient sentences" handed down on guilty assailants, and dismissed available official statistics after considering "the number of instances of crime against women which are generally understood not to reach the ears of the authorities, [and] the difficulties of identifying and bringing to justice the criminals responsible for such revolting atrocities." Citing "recent reports of Outrages by Natives on White Women," the principal of Lovedale College, James Henderson, in November 1908 requested "a return of the number and the locality of the cases dealt with" in each province in the preceding five years."[25] From that month onward, officials in the Department of Justice and the South African Police remarked on a steady stream of letters from a host of different organizations across the country, either alleging "fresh cases of outrages" or requesting information about "trends in the incidence of such cases," or criticizing various aspects of the legal process, and all demanding action of some sort from the state.

The three most popular recommendations was that punishment for "outrages" should be increased, women should be spared the humiliation of appearing in a public court and more police patrols should be established to protect white communities. One organization, the "Districts Bestuur 'Het Volk' Witwatersrand," submitted a resolution in January 1907 "with regard to the prevalence of criminal assaults on white women by natives" and also demanded that "repressive measures ... and penalties be inflicted commensurate with the heinousness of the offense."[26] The telegram that the Guild of Loyal Women of South Africa fired off to the Governor-General cited Rhodesia's death penalty as the appropriate measure in Black Peril cases. The Transvaal Farmers' Association asserted the standard views that sexual assaults were on the increase and that "only a comparatively small percentage of these cases [were] brought into court, owing principally to the dread of publicity and the ordeal of court trial by women of refined and nervous temperament." This knowledge emboldened Africans, who knew that women would not want to "appear in court and make public her misfortune." "Outraged women" should therefore be permitted to give evidence in camera and in the privacy of their home.[27] Calls for improved surveillance of Africans were equally important to the various letter writers and delegations, most of whom asserted that policing measures were either inadequate or non-existent. When the Chamber of Mines announced that imported Chinese males would be quartered close to the mining premises in accordance with its "Chinese labor policy," a spate of letters demanded an immediate pre-emptive beefing up of police patrols in the Johannesburg area.[28]

Calls for stricter punishment, more sympathy for victims of assaults and improved policing strategies enjoyed universal support amongst whites. Other suggestions were more contentious. The request that the death sentence should be imposed on "natives and coloureds" found guilty of either rape or attempted rape appeared regularly in the press. Other recommendations were more extreme. One letter requesting the death sentence for black rapists recommended that "after the execution of the criminal the Chief or head man of the kraal to which the criminal belonged should be advised of the fact" and "the particulars should be printed and read in every compound on the Witwatersrand." Charging that the "Attorney-General [did] not realize the gravity of the situation judging by the inadequate means taken to cope with the evil of outrages by Natives on White Women," the Rand Pioneers pressed for public executions of black assailants to instill the "terror and fear" which the Presbyterian Branch of the Pretoria Mothers' Union had envisaged in a separate letter to the Minister of Justice.[29]

Gladstone was particularly unsympathetic to such recommendations, but spoke for the entire Reconstruction administration when he refused to countenance a request that the death penalty should be made mandatory in Black Peril cases. Gladstone considered the results in Rhodesia to have been disastrous and manifestly heavy with cases of miscarried justice.[30] A distance between increasingly impatient white citizens and government authorities emerged over the "menace" of Black Peril. As a rule, the more senior officials disapproved of the various "recommendations" and "solutions" that members of the public proposed. General James Barry Munnik Hertzog, the Afrikaner war hero during the Anglo-Boer who also served as Minister of Justice from 1910 to 1912, dismissed all talk of public executions or imposing the death sentence on blacks found guilty of rape or attempted rape. But lower down the hierarchy, town councilors and municipal administrators seriously considered at least some of these proposals. For example, the "Rand Pioneers," a white civic body formed to transmit concerns about race relations to government authorities, managed to wrangle a compromise position from city administrators representing Roodepoort-Maraisburg, Springs and Johannesburg in September 1908. Although he rejected public executions as "wholly undesirable," the Johannesburg mayor sought a compromise: "If a native be convicted of rape on a white woman the kraal from whence he comes should be ascertained and he could in my opinion be executed in that kraal. This would ... do away with the objections to public executions in civilised communities and would carry out the desired effect."[31] The Rand Pioneers, however, rejected the mayor's compromise as "unsatisfactory" and hinted darkly of "the grave danger of illegal reprisals" – a veiled threat about extra-legal violence that perhaps won the body a second invitation to send another delegation to meet with municipal associations on the Rand.[32] Whereas municipal officials and their associations waffled, Gladstone emphatically rejected each of these recommendations.

Pressure on government authorities mounted as newspapers published lurid accounts of "outrages" perpetrated by alleged African rapists who were generally described as "brutes." A document titled "Cases of Indecent Assault By Coloured Persons on White Women or Children" summarized twelve court cases in a three-month period in 1908.[33] These cases suggest that there was reason for the residents of Johannesburg to be concerned about the safety of their women and girls from March to May 1908. Yet, notwithstanding the title of the file, the most striking feature of the cases compiled is that six of the twelve cases involved *white* male assailants; Africans were involved in four cases, an Indian in one case, while the racial identity in the case of the attack on the child was not known. This was a familiar double standard in South Africa. Newspaper articles and editorials wrote passionately about "outrages" perpetrated by black males, but said little or nothing about white assailants, even after they had been found guilty in the courts of rape or indecent assaults on white women or girls.[34]

Against a background of white dissatisfaction with the state's official response to Black Peril attacks, a mood of civic impatience and frustration emerged. Yet, whether real or imaginary, sexual assaults by blacks, decried by whites as "the most revolting of violations," did not culminate in the atrocities that were so familiar in the South. Despite threatening allusions to "lynch law" in speeches and newspaper articles, rape panics did not culminate in extra-legal organizations bent on exacting revenge on specifically sexual grounds.

The "Turffontein outrage" of 1912
Several cases of spurious reports concerning white vigilantism may be found in the record. For example, on 28 July 1904, the British Secretary of State cabled Gladstone in Johannesburg in connection with reports that "a Vigilance Committee of whites has been elected and has already lynched a native in that city." After instigating an investigation, Gladstone cabled his reply: "Report of lynching absolutely unfounded and due to discovery of body of native who was clearly proved at inquest to have committed suicide."

Moreover, he was "satisfied that the idea of the existence of a secret society organization to punish natives assaulting white people [was] pure imagination."[35] A handful of newspaper reports in the period 1902–10 alludes to whites who "took matters into their hands" in the wake of reported allegations of Black Peril. The denouement to these cases was invariably uneventful. Evidence of vigilante movements was spotty at best and likely to have suggested the feelings of the newspaper more than actual events. Newspaper articles made much of the use of such language as "Vigilance Society" at a number of neighborhood meetings, imparting an air of menace to such civic gatherings.[36] The best-documented instance of an incipient vigilante movement concerns the "Turffontein outrage" of 1912. This incident provides a good indication not only of the ephemeral nature of a lynch sentiment amongst South African whites but also of the state's resistance to organized extra-legal activity.

On 19 April 1912, W. A. Wyndham, a member of parliament for Turffontein in Johannesburg's southern suburbs, informed the Acting Secretary for Justice of a sexual assault that had occurred in his area of jurisdiction, a "badly lit" working-class district in the southern suburbs of Johannesburg.[37] The police regarded the area as crime-prone and acknowledged that its white inhabitants felt "under siege." The violent rape and subsequent death of a white woman in April 1912 appears to have pushed whites in Turffontein over the edge.

On a warm Saturday night, on 12 April 1912, the woman, the wife of a miner who was at work at the time of the attack, was asleep in bed with her 18-month-old daughter, the youngest of her three children. An African, John Jacobs, slipped in through the open window and attacked the woman, asleep "with the baby in her arms." She was "awakened by feeling her throat gripped tightly" and "although not of powerful build, she strenuously fought her assailant" before losing consciousness. When she awoke, the horrified woman found herself under some trees in a plantation about 150 yards from her house being assaulted by a second African male. One of her breasts "was hanging out and bitten" and her throat "bore the marks of fingers." She again passed out. Meanwhile, the cries of the girl awakened the eldest child, a boy of seven, who alerted the neighbors to his mother's disappearance. Upon the husband's return at 6 a.m., the police were notified of the assault and bloodhounds were set to work. When John Jacobs was arrested several days later, however, it was on the strength of information that Jacobs had given to an acquaintance, Klaas, who had gone over to Jacobs' hut to collect a small debt. According to Klaas, Jacobs confessed "I went into a white woman's room at Turffontein, choked the woman and took her out through the window." Jacobs volunteered similar details to a second man, who subsequently also testified against him.[38] According to this second witness, Jacobs and his accomplice fled when the woman stopped moving, but returned when they saw her sit up. They then fled again. Jacobs was arrested three days after the crime. Jacobs was surprised to learn that the woman had died and that he was charged with murder. The sentence was reduced to assault, however. One month later, he was found guilty and sentenced to three years with hard labor. A letter published in the *Star* spoke for many whites when it ridiculed the sentence for being too light. A flurry of letters to the press and police raged about "trivial sentences" and "inadequate police protection in the Southern Suburbs." The *Leader* announced that "black brutes" had imposed "a reign of terror among the women of Turffontein district" and that "the families of several men who were absent on night shift joined forces for mutual protection, the women being afraid to sleep alone with their children."

In response to extensive press coverage devoted to the case, dog, mounted and foot police patrols were increased and provision was made for 62 more police officers to monitor the area.[39] But the residents of Turffontein were not satisfied with these measures, despite the timeous detention of Jacobs. Nor did the reasonable grounds on which the charge had been reduced from murder assuage them. A cable from the police explained the reduction to the Minister of Justice: "after the outrage the woman was seen walking about ... the doctor gave her three pills to dissolve in water wherewith to douche herself. Instead however the unfortunate woman applied one pill to her uterus direct without first dissolving resulting in blood poisoning on which death followed."[40]

Sometime late in April, a leaflet advertising a meeting called to deal with the assault was distributed by a newly formed organization, the "Southern Suburbs Vigilance Society, Turffontein." According to the leaflet, the Society was formed "with the view of protecting our homes and affording greater security for our wives and families. The residents are called upon to give their whole-hearted support and assistance to carry out [the Society's] work in a thorough manner." Large bold type indicated some of the ways that white households could help:

> All Male Residents over the age of 21 years to enroll his name on the list for patrol duty.
>
> Do not allow natives other than your own servants to sleep on the premises.
>
> Dismiss the adult houseboy if possible and engage picaninies or native women.
>
> Never permit male natives in the bedrooms.
>
> Stop supplying natives with special passes allowing them to remain at large after hours.[41]

The Vigilance Society took to staging raids on nearby African quarters in search of "known criminals." These raids, however, alarmed the local police who "warned these people to behave themselves" because "any transgressions of the law on their part will lead them into serious trouble as Law will be rigidly enforced."[42] Ugly rumors of indiscriminate violence and "organ-ised drives" against Africans surfaced throughout the month of May, irri-tating the local police in the Turffontein district who, notwithstanding the warnings they issued to the Vigilance Society, disclaimed knowledge of the Society's activities in their areas.

On 3 June, the *Cape Times* pressed the Department of Justice to open an inquiry into the matter. According to the *Times*, Vigilance Society "drives" had left victims "horribly mutilated" and two Africans had perished at the hands of the white mob.[43] As evidence, the *Times* described a violent inci-dent that occurred on the night of 31 May. The Society's version of the events was given by one of its members, William Band Goldsmith. On hear-ing that "unauthorised natives" were sleeping in the grounds of the Turf-fontein Racing Club, Goldsmith assembled a party of men and headed for the racing grounds. Armed with the written permission from the manager of Club to conduct a search, they entered the premises together with the Club's caretaker, but failed to find their quarry. According to Goldsmith, the group departed for home without either searching elsewhere or assaulting any Africans that night.

Investigations by the *Times*, which included interviews with members of the Society, revealed a different picture. Once assembled, Goldsmith and his men immediately conducted "pass raids" under the moonlight of "a clear crisp night." At the Racing Club, they found several African men who handed over their documents "with piteous whines and cringes to their fierce, forbidding captors" who proceeded to thrash them. In the words of one vigilante, the Africans were "'tickled with the stick', kicked over the fence and allowed to go." A splinter group of vigilantes then scoured the nearby woods and surprised a group of African men ("boys") suspected of belonging to the notorious Amalaita gang. Chased deeper into the woods, an African man turned on one of his tormentors with a "huge battle axe" before a "well-directed blow under the jaw from a pick-handle laid him low, and probably saved the white man's life." According to the *Times*, "The other boys received a terrible thrashing, and when the vigilantes left the plantation they also left lying amongst the tangled undergrowth, two natives ghastly and blood bespattered, who would not speak for many hours to come."

The police, however, made light of this information and supported Gold-smith's account. The report of, J. S. G. Dougles, the Acting Commissioner of the Police was clearly contradictory, however. Dougles blamed the florid account that appeared in the *Cape Times*: "The whole matter is a storm in a teacup due to wicked lies by men who ought to know better." But Dougles also blamed the secretary of the Turffontein Racing Club for admit-ting members of the Vigilance Society on to the Club's premises. The failure of his report to so much as mention the later attack in the woods and the alacrity with which he accepted exculpatory testimony from Racing Club officials confirms the *Times*' suspicions about the impartiality of the police:

"The attitude of the police is surprising. Their weakness amounts almost to countenancing disorder." For its part, the *Times* failed to uncover evidence concerning the death of two Africans said to have been assaulted by member of the Society.[44] Dougles summoned the editors of the *Sunday Post* and the *Transvaal Leader*, which had also commented negatively on the Society's activities, and warned them about the "very bad effect such articles had on the Natives." Already, "a very strong but erroneous feeling exists among them that the white man is chasing and killing the black."[45]

A number of themes may be extracted from the "Turffontein outrage." To begin with, the incident condenses the standard rhetorical devices that were calculated to inflame racial and masculine passions. Descriptions of the unfortunate white woman, sleeping Madonna-like with her arms protectively enfolding her little child, were calculated to contrast the mother–child–home triad to the "black brutes" encircling the white burgers of Turffontein. Not for nothing did newspapers and official documents refer repeatedly to the fact that the husband was at work at the time of the attack on the "unprotected" family. If the woman was unprotected, the ethics of work and responsibility exonerated the male head of the household gainfully employed in the mining industry. In contrast, her attackers were "black brutes" and "criminals of the loafer-type" who concealed themselves in squalid, crime-prone locations. They ventured forth by night without the "special permits" that permitted them to break the municipal curfew to "lurk in trenches," scheming to terrorize the sleeping citizens of Turffontein. In contrast to the criminal nocturnal activities of John Jacobs and his accomplice – who immediately were held to stand in for the entire population of blacks nearby – the criminal violence of the Vigilance Society was lauded by the white inhabitants of the Turffontein area and tolerated by the law enforcement authorities. Only the *Cape Times* emphasized that Goldsmith's gang had badly assaulted men who had nothing to do with the rape and whose pass documents were actually found to be in order. Police documents do not refer to this fact at all.

Instead of inquiring into the Society's moonlight "drives," the police responded by escalating their surveillance of blacks in the area, explicitly conceding the Society's claims that the movement was an extension and "supplement" to the law, not its antagonist. Men such as Goldsmith envisaged themselves as speaking on behalf of bourgeois respectability, if not actually for the state itself. Because the incident did not enter the court records and the newspapers devoted little time to the backgrounds or the number of the men in the Vigilance Society, the class composition of the body is not clear. One newspaper, the *Post*, claimed that the Vigilance Society was composed of "respectable men who were 'under siege' and woefully neglected by the local police." The *Cape Times* disagreed: "Many people have run away with the idea that the vigilantes are recruited from the elite of the southern suburbs ... In fact they are the laughing stock of the neighbourhood." In fact, the *Post* was more likely to have been correct. The cooperative relationship between the Vigilance Society and the Racing Club, the alacrity with which Dougles exonerated the men of violence, and the speed with which scarce police resources were dispatched to the Turffontein area suggest that the Vigilance Society possessed some social standing in white society. In response to a threatening letter from the South African Police warning against "taking the law into your own hands," a thoroughly intimidated Goldsmith immediately promised to refrain from further "raids."[46]

It is possible, even likely, that other vigilante movements similar to Goldsmith's Vigilance Society emerged in response to Black Peril in this period. If so, they are not recorded in the thick files devoted to "Black Peril" and "Assaults on Women" in the archives. The Southern Suburbs Vigilance Society may therefore be treated as emblematic of the limits within which mobs of white men remained in the course of Black Peril scares. For even if more such movements did arise, it is almost certain that they would have behaved much as Goldsmith's mob did. Violent, arrogant, and aware of a sympathetic response from the local white community, the Vigilance Society stopped well short of the lawless effrontery rampant across the South.

The official response: The Black Peril Commission

The official response to these criticisms was surprisingly muted and considerably more liberal than the views of most white citizens. Many civil servants shared the public's concern. For example, H. J. Trent, a district commandant of the South African Constabulary stationed in Pretoria, sent off a confidential letter to the Resident Magistrate in April 1907 noting that "during the last three months no less than five cases of natives entering the houses of Europeans during the night time with intent to rape inmates" and recommended "the infliction of more severe sentences."[47] Official support for proposals and sentiments of this nature was not lacking. At the same time, it was tempered by an appreciation of a range of other political and legal considerations. These ensured that the Black Peril scare at the time of Union would not result in any dramatic changes.

Of overarching importance was the state's ambivalence towards the field of "race relations" in the Reconstruction period. Two considerations that pulled in somewhat different directions were of particular importance. On the one hand, the Reconstruction administration had no interest in antagonizing defeated Afrikaners by imposing liberal racial policies on the still unconsolidated country. Moreover, three of the four colonial territories – the Transvaal, the Orange Free State and Natal – were already jockeying to block the extension of the Cape's non-racial franchise to the rest of the country. Unsettled tensions in the rural areas of the Transvaal, where attempts by Africans to reclaim land from Boers displaced by the war, presented an immediate and pressing problem. The administration was anxious to resolve these tensions by forestalling African rural resistance, restoring Afrikaners' dominance in the countryside and depoliticizing the still unresolved issue of the "Native franchise." Failure to respond to Black Peril could potentially present the administration as pro-black at the expense of whites' racial sensitivities. The emergence of white vigilante tendencies in the urban areas, especially on the sprawling Witwatersrand, added a note of concern to this consideration.

Rather than compromise the legal system by accommodating violent white vigilante movements, however, liberal administrators latched on to the Black Peril scare and used it to strengthen calls for a comprehensive policy of segregation. As in the colonial era, the Black Peril scare of 1912 would peter out but leave its legacy on the legislative and administrative measures that shaped the segregationist state after the First World War. Throughout the Black Peril scares before and after 1910, British administrators hewed closely to a liberal approach to the problem, demanded convincing evidence, and levied "appropriate sentences" for sexual assault crimes. With whites baying for capital punishment, life imprisonment and "the indeterminate sentence," judges were known to dismiss accused Africans or impose sentences that outraged the white public. In 1906, "A Father" expressed his outrage that a six-month jail sentence was handed down on an African found guilty off "criminally assaulting a white girl of tender years": "Now the question arises: are parents going to remain quiet and see their children outraged by brutes who get what is no punishment to them – imprisonment for six months? ... the British public go crazy because brutes of this kind are lynched for crimes like these in America."[48] Anger rose, too, when judges would base sentences on considerations such as the degree of remorse shown by the accused, whether he had a prior criminal record or the certainty of his intentions. This liberal outlook limited the corrosive impact of Black Peril on the country's legal system. In sharp contrast to the American South, South Africa's legal system militated against a culture of vengeance and denied mob tyranny a purchase within the state.[49]

In response to continuing Black Peril anxieties, in 1912 the government appointed a commission "to inquire into assaults on women."[50] The Report that the commission issued the following year was by no means impartial and echoed many of the racist assumptions and prejudices it harvested from the 281 witnesses who gave evidence before the commission, 231 of whom were white.[51] At the same time, the report neither belabored government authorities for failing to deal with the rape "crisis" nor winked at white vigilantes who took the law into their own hands. Basing its arguments on "empirical trends" that poured cold water on the Black Peril scare, the report framed the rape scare as a consequence of the state's still unsettled "Native policy." Its broad conclusion was that the solution to Black Peril lay in strengthened segregationist measures. In this way, what began as a probe into an intensely personal and inflammatory phenomenon ended up in the final pages of the report as a series of droll administrative changes that formed the stock in trade of prevailing calls for segregationist policies.

The Chair of the Commission, Melius De Villiers, the ex-Chief Justice of the Orange Free State, was alive to the "sensitive nature of the investigation." The report denied that his commission was investigating "Black Peril" and contended that the commission's brief was to examine the plight of all women, black and white alike. But de Villiers' claim is contradicted by the title page of the draft report, which indeed does state "Commission on Black Peril – Galley One." The report distinguished amongst the various racial permutations of inter-racial sex and discussed each racial couplet in turn: "Sexual assaults by White men on White females," "Sexual assaults by Coloured men on Coloured females," "Sexual assaults by White men on Coloured women" and "Assaults upon White women by Coloured men." But the report was primarily exercised by black assaults on white women. For this reason, the dispassionate tone of the report seems all the more understated. [52]

The report adduced the empirical evidence it had obtained from the police and Department of Justice to cautiously dispel Black Peril claims. Empirical counts of various forms of sexual assaults (rape, attempted rape and indecent assault) between 1900 and 1912 suggested that inter-racial sexual assaults were far from common. This was clear from the "Complete Return, For the Union, of Rapes, Attempted Rapes, and Indecent Assaults on Females, for the Ten Years from 1st January, 1901, to 31st December 1910."[53] The return will not be deconstructed here. This chapter is less concerned with making sense of the numerous reported variations in the matter of sexual assaults than with the sheer importance that the state attached to the compilation of such data in the first place. Still, a number of trends are worth emphasizing.

The commissioners drew two broad conclusions. Firstly, sexual assault cases, while always deplorable, were not notably high and were in fact on the low side. Nationwide, the number of assaults by blacks on white women had increased from 11 to 70 between 1901 and 1912: "[T]he heads of the police throughout the Union generally, and more particularly in the Transvaal, are of the opinion that … [the] increase has only been commensurate with the increase of crime generally," which in turn, probably only reflected the growth of the urban population. There was no cause for alarm, let alone panic. Secondly, blacks appeared to receive harsher sentences than whites who were charged with similar crimes. To begin with, 34 blacks were sentenced to between two and ten years for raping white women, whereas only one white male suffered a similar fate for raping a black woman. Of the twelve blacks who were hanged, fully ten were put to death for raping white women. The report noted that the great reluctance of judges to impose the death sentence when no murder accompanied a rape appears to have worked to the advantage of whites: whereas only one white male was executed for rape, twelve blacks were hanged for the same crime (eight of them in the Transvaal). White males, furthermore, were also twice more likely than black males to have the charges dismissed (suggesting that black convictions were in part procured through the institutional bias of the courts and police and are not therefore an indication of criminality). Finally, the most obvious and alarming statistic was not the number of black on white assaults, but the astronomically high number of black on black assaults: in contrast to the 277 white males charged with sexually assaulting black women, a whopping 5,498 blacks were charged with assaulting black women.

A striking aspect of the report is that it did not indulge in speculations about black male hypersexuality but strove, instead, for a balanced tone in accounting for sexual assaults. This attempt at evenhandedness can be seen in the discussion of two counter-balancing reasons the report provided to explain black sexual violence – "tribalism" amongst Africans and question-able moral virtue amongst whites.

Much has been written about the gathering national interest in tribal-ism at the time of the Union, and a number of scholars have pointed out that even in the Cape tribalism had begun to gain ascendancy over the ter-ritory's assimilationist policies.[54] The fountainhead of pro-tribalist policies in modern South Africa was the 1902 Report of the South African Native Affairs Commission (SANAC), which argued that tribalism was and should remain the "natural system" of Africans. De Villiers' report spoke for the vast majority of whites when it portrayed tribalism in positive terms and accorded it a key role in explaining the generally "law abiding character" of Africans in the rural areas:

> Loyalty to the Chief and to the Tribe has always been the mainstream of native morality. The responsibility of the tribe and the family for the offences of its members was a recognized factor, which imposed upon every member of it a personal obligation in the prevention of crime and caused him to be directly interested in the observance of the law.

There was, therefore, nothing biological that predisposed Africans to crime and sexual excesses. Instead, the report identified a certain cultural licen-tiousness in tribal society as a root cause of sexual violence:

> It is stated by witnesses that the raw native is born and brought up in an atmosphere of lust, his thoughts and speech are lewd; the topics of his ordinary conversation from an early age are sexual matters; even in the presence of the other sex his talk in this respect is unrestrained ... persons who do not understand the native language, it is said, can hardly real-ize how low, according to European standards, the state of morality is amongst them.

These views reflected the "cultural relativism" that was on the ascendance at the turn of the century. The report implicated practices such as super-stition and sorcery in sexual assaults: "Kaffir doctors supply potions which have the power to make a female succumb"; "charms are sold which are supposed, and even by the native female herself are believed, to be irresist-ible in making her yield to a man's advances," while "other charms are sup-posed to be of such a nature as to have the effect of procuring an acquittal when the native is brought to trial for sexual assaults or other offences." De

Villiers' commission felt that these elements of tribal culture were deplorable but also relatively harmless – but only if "tribal authority" was strong. They had unfortunately mutated into open threats to whites only because rising numbers of Africans were moving to the urban areas. By eroding black conceptions of morality, urbanization compelled anxious whites to manage the modernizing influences amongst "detribalized natives." Practical administrative measures were therefore required to prevent black urbanization from "contaminating" whites. If the problem was therefore structural, the commission's solution was administrative: the state should segregate white from black in the urban areas and corral the African's traditional lasciviousness where it belonged – in the reserves.

The second aspect of the report's attempts at evenhandedness provides an even more glaring contrast with developments in the American South. In the report's candid view, *white* immorality had a "demoralising effect on natives" and propelled African men into criminal behavior, including sexual assaults on white women. The report trotted out familiar cant to bolster this claim. Pornography, the sale of liquor to Africans and white criminals who consorted with them were roundly deplored. "The baneful traffic in indecent pictures and prints" which had come to light in a number of court cases was condemned because it "served to degrade the white woman ... and must have a pernicious effect in arousing [African men's] passions." Similarly, "the sale of hard liquor" – debilitating cultural and commercial intoxicants which differed entirely from "wholesome ... traditional Native beer" – was another precipitating factor in sexual assaults. These, however, were relatively minor contributions to the "demoralising of natives." Of much greater importance was the disquieting evidence of a fact that was as incontrovertible as it was unpleasant: despite whites' claims about the repugnance and "immorality" of inter-racial sex, a lot of it was clearly taking place, and it was not confined to white men only.

In a manner that seems entirely inconceivable in the American South, De Villiers' report forthrightly established that white men, white women and civil servants were engaging in voluntary inter-racial sex. Publicly implicating white men was not quite as controversial: as with the double standard in the South, it was tacitly accepted that white men frequently had intercourse with black women. Laws in Natal and the Transvaal expressly criminalized intercourse between white women and black men, but not sex between white men and black women. It was widely known that white men across the country made liberal use of the double standard and, as a minister of religion testified before the commission, "It is very seldom a matter of brute force." Numerous court cases amply confirm the scale of inter-racial sex in this period. Newspapers articles, editors, judges and betrayed white spouses decried the problem of concubinage as a steady stream of white men were charged with contravening the immorality laws. Policemen, ex-soldiers, farmers and "criminals in the lower class" all enjoyed sex with African women and regularly fathered children with them.

But publicly implicating white *women* in both the sin and crime of inter-racial sex, as the report did, was another matter. Prostitutes were the major culprits and the easiest to finger. The boom in prostitution immediately after the Anglo-Boer was accompanied by the influx of "foreign professional prostitutes from Europe" who had "allowed and even invited intercourse between themselves and natives." According to the report, this marked "the first beginning of the evil" in the minds of black males: "individuals unable to discriminate between one class of women and another were inclined to gauge the standard of morality of white women by the examples presented under such circumstances, and to fancy that they need only make advances to be accepted by white women generally."

Prostitution was bad enough, but more disturbing was the evidence that "respectable" white women were known to enjoy trysts with black men. "Though the occurrence of these have greatly been exaggerated," consensual sex "would ... naturally affect the mind of the native and make even a deeper impression than in the case of professional prostitutes." Of particular concern to De Villiers was the use of condoms in inter-racial sex. Condoms posed a pernicious paradox. The virtue of condoms was that they at least prevented the birth of "bastards" and so contained the "problem of miscegenation," a problem with disproportionate implications for the whiteness of "poor whites" living cheek by jowl with blacks in working-class neighborhoods. On the other hand, by preventing pregnancies, condoms also *concealed* the scale of "immorality" amongst white women. In this sense, condoms were as conducive to "immorality" as another South African "evil," the pheno-menon of the "houseboy." There was a widespread assumption amongst whites that African men who labored within white households were guilty of improper sexual behavior and assaults against white females. But the commission argued against this assumption and pointed out that the vast majority of African "houseboys" did not exhibit such predatory behavior. To the contrary, the commission mused about the role of *white women* who were placed in such potential intimacy with African males: it illustrated, "in the ... question of the 'house-boy', that, unfortunately, opportunities for intercourse are occasionally permitted to natives so employed, by others than prostitutes." But, unwilling to concede that "normal" white women might willingly enter into such sexual liaisons, the report contended that the white women in such cases were mentally defective and driven astray by "sexual perversions."

Court cases involving white men having sex with black women certainly were greater than those involving white women and black men. But there were enough of the latter to conclude that the phenomenon was not as rare as whites believed. By comparison with the role of women in the South, it is a striking fact that white women in South Africa were prosecuted and brought to the dock to answer for the crime of having had sex with black men. The mere suggestion that white women desired black men was a red flag to Southern males. Men were lynched and newspaper buildings razed to the ground for making the suggestion – Ida B. Wells herself had to flee the South after publishing her opinion on the matter and had to continue her efforts to secure anti-lynching legislation from the North. Yet in 1921, the African nationalist and scholar Sol Plaatje forthrightly discussed consensual inter-racial sex in South Africa in his pamphlet *The Mote and the Beam: An Epic on Sex-Relationships 'twixt White and Black in British South Africa* and came off none the worse for it.[55]

By no means an impartial document, De Villiers' report avoided sensationalism and strained for a detached tone that it backed up with practical recommendations. These recommendations were straightforward and perfunctory, devoid of sensationalist language that might mark them as fundamental demands. The recommendations were of three kinds: Jim Crow-like measures that promoted social segregation; administrative reforms to strengthen the pass system and minor legal reforms to protect white women in court cases involving racial rape.

To enforce social segregation, for example, the report recommended that marriage between "Europeans and aboriginal natives" should be illegalized, in keeping with practice in the Orange Free State and Transvaal; white prostitutes who had sex with blacks should be deported, and the sale of hard liquor to Africans should be illegalized. It also called for a prohibition on African males from doing the "the work of a lady's maid, chambermaid, laundry maid or nursemaid."

Greater weight was given to the *pass laws* and more, generally, to the controls on the mobility of Africans. The commission identified two opportunities for tightening controls over Africans. Firstly, the various pass laws inherited from the pre-Union era should be consolidated, a new set of uniform laws should be extended across the country, and the central government should be vested with overall authority for the application of the various measures. Secondly, the commission viewed residential segregation as a pivotal response to Black Peril. In the urban areas, the growing population of urbanized Africans should be concentrated in segregated municipal locations where they "may dwell under clean, decent and healthy conditions of family and social life." Employers who relied on migrant labor should house their workers in compounds along the model pioneered by the diamond and gold mining industries. Not one of these proposals was new, all having been comprehensively discussed by the Report of the SANAC of 1902.

The proposals to reform the *legal system* are also noteworthy for their restraint. The commission pointedly rejected what it described as "panic legislation" and recommended two mild measures. The qualifications of jurors should be carefully assessed in "mixed cases of sexual assault" to ensure impartial verdicts. Furthermore, judges should protect in two ways the identities of all women who laid charges of sexual assault cases. They could permit evidence to be given *in camera* at preliminary hearings and remove from the court "all persons whose attendance they consider unnecessary." The report consistently rejected suggestions from white witnesses who had demanded racially based sentencing guidelines and other extreme solutions such as castrating or banishing black rapists to a "remote island." (The policeman who made this suggestion had Papua New Guinea in mind.)[56]

Conclusion

The communal lynching of unfortunate African Americans such as Claude Neal and the administrative response to the mob behavior of the Turffontein vigilantes illustrate how similar allegations of rape leveled against blacks culminated in vastly different outcomes in the American South and South Africa. Stewart Tolnay and E. M. Beck argued that communal lynching of the sort that dispatched Claude Neal served four functions, all of which are generally exercised by states armed with the monopoly over the means of violence in society. The "manifest function" of lynching, they write, was the "punishment of specific criminal offenders." Mob violence, however, also served three "latent functions":

> first, to maintain social order over the black population through terrorism;
>
> second, to suppress or eliminate black competitors for economic, political, or social rewards;
>
> third, to stabilize the white class structure and preserve the privileged status of the white aristocracy.[57]

In other words, these functions, which are assessed in subsequent chapters, amount to the usurpation of state authority. Strongly present in the lynch culture of the American South, they were only weakly present in the activities of white vigilante movements in South Africa. Gender relations were certainly fraught with enormous potential for violence in both contexts. White men who were genuinely concerned about the viability of their households and the safety of their women and children inevitably sensed that their authority over women was faltering in uncertain postbellum conditions. The propensity for violence against the perceived "black-beast rapist" was therefore high in both contexts. Yet the outcome was remarkably different: white fears about "the safety of our women" culminated in unrestrained savagery in the South but yielded tentative and tepid movements in South Africa.

Rape-inspired violence in the South illustrates Richard Maxwell Brown's observation that extra-legal violence in the United States has generally served conservative causes with the active support of the working class.[58] The heir of the elite-driven terror that took root in the war against Reconstruction, communal lynching in the United States was a tragic affirmation of this claim. Subsequent chapters detail how agrarian elites successfully orchestrated racial terror to seize state power in the decades after Reconstruction. By exploiting the federal structure of the American state, they successfully shielded and fomented a lynch culture marked by two broad features: a truncated state authority in the area of "race relations" and a virtual *carte blanche* for plebeian whites to violently assert their dominant masculinity by lynching African Americans. In this context, rape panics and the enormous violence they inevitably sparked were diffuse expressions of whites' abilities to directly exercise the four functions that lynching embodied. Indeed, allegations of racial rape served as perhaps the most powerful metaphor for the Southerner's fractious relations with federal authorities. After the Civil War, rape-inspired lynchings in the South generated the only extra-constitutional challenge to the authority of the federal government in the twentieth century.

In contrast, rape-inspired violence in South Africa illustrates the statist trends that shaped the emergence of segregation. All four of the functions that Tolnay and Beck identify above were only hinted at, not trumpeted, in the relatively anemic violence that white South African men inflicted on blacks in response to allegations of racial rape. To the contrary, officials took pains to ensure that the monopoly over the means of violence remained firmly under the control of the state. Rape panics in South Africa were thus no less "protean in their causes and effects" than they were in the South. But state managers in South Africa ensured that these effects were channeled into predictable confines, specifically into policies and administrative changes that were managed by state officials. Hence, state officials were quick to disabuse white men of their claims to lawful authority. Instead, as the report of the commission illustrated, officials deftly transformed white *angst* over Black Peril scares into an opportunity to bolster the emerging policy of segregation.

The communal lynching of Claude Neal illustrates how lethal violence was permitted to remain dispersed in civil society in the South. Likewise, the hasty disappearance of the Turffontein Vigilante Society captures the master trend – prompt state intervention – that invariably abbreviated extra-legal racial violence in South Africa. Explaining this basic difference is the burden of the chapters that follow.

3

Racial violence and black labor in the South

The basic pattern of racial violence in the South was largely determined by the attempts of landowners and commercial farmers to gain mastery over a world turned upside down by the end of slavery. Emancipation raised two dire threats that struck at the heart of the former slave society: the *emergence of a free market in labor* and the *plantocracy's lost grip over land*. Landowners across the South mobilized against these twin threats, employing all mechanisms at their disposal to regain their former dominance. It was transparently clear that the success of this quest was depended on destroying a third dagger that pointed at the heart of the postbellum agrarian class: the *enfranchisement of emancipated slaves*. Reconstruction provided concentrated evidence of the dangers confronting landowners. "Freedmen schools," public education, rising wages in response to labor shortages, emancipated slaves in public office, and "welfare" policies that boosted the independence of African Americans all promised to remake the South in the image of the reviled North. For the majority of white Southerners, such developments were offensive in themselves. But because they harbored such profound implications for the region's political economy, landowners approached them as matters of life and death. After weathering challenges from the Farmers' Alliance and the more threatening Populist movement in the 1880s and 1890s, agrarian elites successfully aligned the vast majority of white Southerners with racial controls that were first and foremost designed to serve the interests of planters.

In so doing, they knitted together the general defense of white supremacy with the defense of their particular interests in a low-wage, labor-repressive economy. By the time the progressive goals of Radical Reconstruction went down in blood, *all* whites were drawn into the new alignment that placed landowners at the head of the task of "redeeming" the South. Unable to resurrect the system of slavery, landowners – the commercial farmers of King Cotton in the New South – resorted to its closest approximation and settled for a system of sharecropping, a suffocating and exploitative arrangement that many scholars, like all sharecroppers, have described as "worse than slavery."[1] This chapter argues that landowners' quest for political and economic control forms the indispensable point of reference for any discussion of extra-legal racial violence, providing the terrain for even plebeian whites to participate in the lynch culture of the New South.

Agrarian dominance and racial violence

By its very nature, the monocrop Black Belt economy amplified landowners' success in restoring their violent control over the South. The fact that all landowners shared identical interests in controlling a vulnerable African American labor force effectively eliminated dissent over the violent methods that planters employed to discipline and intimidate African Americans. Likewise, the absence of significant competition from another economic sector that could force landowners to secure labor by scaling down the sector's commitment to violence deprived the South of an influential moderating voice in race relations, further cementing the plantocracy's reliance on extra economic violence. By the time manufacturing industries took off, a development that George Tindall locates soon after the First World War, planters had already firmly established the essential contours of a racially repressive economy. [2] As Stanley Greenberg and Gavin Wright argue in their respective works, the ascending class of mill owners, urban merchants and the "Big Mules" in the mining sectors therefore found it convenient to simply adapt to the region's racial hierarchy. Although businessmen would be the first to break ranks and distance themselves from the violence on which white supremacy rested, that day was still a long way off. It would take the combined effects of the boll weevil, international competition, the Great Depression, the New Deal and an upsurge of African American mobilization after the Second World War to finally crack the violent order that farmers constructed in the first decades after Reconstruction. Until the Solid South finally buckled under the weight of these transformations, the dominance of a landowning class united in service to King Cotton established the violent system of racial control across the plantation South.

The implications of farmers' quest to regain their dominance were of far-reaching and systemic importance to the region. Postbellum landowners' deep hostility to the emerging free market in labor resulted in concerted attempts to destroy the fledgling rights of African American workers. During Reconstruction, the dominance of farmers was marked by a "mixture of markets, coercion and uncertainty" that had compelled individual labor-hungry farmers to experiment with a variety of mechanisms to attract or retain free African American labor in many parts of the South. [3] While coercion remained a constant in these endeavors, farmers bristled at having to obtain labor by offering cash wages to former slaves, competing with other farmers (and later, with industrialists) by increasing wages, improving tenancy agreements or improving working conditions. Tenancy and share-cropping, and all the asymmetries this dependent relationship embodied, soon emerged as the universally popular alternative to the racial and class indignities that landowners identified with the free labor market which had begun to emerge during Reconstruction.

The turn to violence as the principal means for controlling African American labor was not a sudden development but instead grew seamlessly from the violence used to defeat Reconstruction. The initial assault on emancipated African Americans took the form of "Black Codes," a spate of measures intended to return African Americans to bondage, deny them any civil or political rights, and tie them to individual farmers. Although Congress soon overturned them, the Black Codes were an early indication of landowners' hostility to free labor and anticipated the establishment of the racially repressive controls that emerged in all Southern states before the First World War.[4]

The sheer ability of Southern states to enact the Black Codes points to another critically important consequence of agrarian dominance: namely, their ability to control the various institutions and levels of state government. Sharecropping, the spine of the cotton economy and the long-term successor of the Black Codes, would have been impossible without "control over legislation in the State, and over the police power generally."[5] To reinforce the sharecropping system, post-Reconstruction governments enacted laws that limited land sales and denied credit and marketing opportunities to freedmen; they forced African Americans into the grip of landowners by severely restricting or eliminating poor relief and rations and sought to tax out of existence the new category of labor recruiters that sprang up across the Black Belt in response to postbellum labor shortages. While legal arrangements such as these compelled African Americans to enter into agreements with white farmers, other legal measures sought to cement the power of farmers over a captive population of farm labor. Lien laws were perhaps the most formidable legal weapon that farmers controlled. These laws, which varied only in their severity across different states, underscored the farmer's superordinate position by granting landowners first claim on the cotton crop that was planted, tended and harvested by sharecroppers. Later, additional laws reinforced the farmers' dominant position within the entire economy by elevating the farmer's claim above the claims of local merchants. From the mid-1880s onward, the "false pretenses" law in Alabama criminalized the breach of contracts. The law emerged on the heels of the decision by the US Supreme Court which held that debt peonage violated federal laws. Although Pete Daniels has shown that debt peonage in fact continued to persist well into the next century, the "false pretenses" law added an additional sword above the farm worker's head, ensuring that every contract entered into could potentially deliver him into the convict labor system that flourished across the South.[6]

The success of legal measures enacted in state legislatures depended on their implementation at the local level. The specific labor controls that farmers desired thus became the everyday work of a clutch of agencies at two levels of the civil service. At the level of local government "an amorphous collection of mayors, county officials, sheriffs, justices of the peace, judges and election officials" in effect became "an agent of labor control, or, at the very least, practiced a studied indifference to the impositions on African American labor."[7] Further down the institutional chain, an alliance of plantation owners, constables, and plantation managers enforced the legal fetters that bound African American farm workers. These white Praetorian guards were also positioned to obtain African Americans' submission to the most minor peccadilloes of racial etiquette. In a rural atmosphere where law and custom enjoyed equal force, African Americans lived in a world fraught with danger and lethal threat, there being little they could do to evade the multiple venal "offenses" that inhered in their oppressive environment. African Americans were hounded for being "sassy" and for failing to make good on fictitious "debts," and they were exposed to a limitless cache of false accusations. Since entire localities, counties, and even states were dependent on the success of the cotton crop, all branches of government, administration and civic life could generally be relied on to march in lock step to the dictates of the agrarian class.[8]

Still, despite their sturdy position within the cultural and political economy of Southern states, the various devices above were charged with a certain measure of volatility for two reasons. Firstly, not all African Americans submitted to them without challenge, not even after Reconstruction ended in 1877. Against staggering odds, a few brave souls dared to challenge white supremacy by questioning the accounting methods of farmers, "deserting" employers, migrating to the North or defending land they had acquired, most of it during the Reconstruction years.[9] The ability of African American sharecroppers to vote with their feet and enter into agreements with other landowners points to an important and curious limitation on the power of Southern white landowners. Limited though it was, freedom of movement was an important right that African Americans sought to exercise whenever they could. In contrast to white farmers in South Africa, white landowners in the South never managed to remove this right by enacting laws that limited or outlawed African Americans' right to move about. Instead, as we see below, Southern planters relied on coercion and violence to retain direct control over their African American labor force. Not even the banner of "states rights" guaranteed the legality of racially oppressive measures that sprouted from every level of government. Several rulings at the turn of the twentieth century illustrated that Supreme Court judges in Washington were willing to weaken legal codes in the South, notwithstanding other rulings, such as *Plessey v Ferguson* (1896), that legalized racial segregation. Striking down debt peonage was one such unpleasant reminder to white Southerners of the Supreme Court's occasional perfidy. Likewise, the 1911 Supreme Court ruling that Alabama's "false pretenses" laws were unconstitutional deepened landowners' resolve to hold onto their African American workers with extra-legal violence.[10]

These two caveats – African American resistance and the occasional

unfavorable Supreme Court ruling – underscore the special premium that
Southern planters placed on extra-legal coercion. Unchallenged agrarian
dominance required the massive complicity of the local state in labor policies that were simply illegal or contestable in the courts. At all costs, African
Americans had to be violently dissuaded from challenging the exploitative
relations that bound them to farmers, either by quitting employers or by
going to the courts. Complete submission to the specific powers of landowners and to the general dominance of all whites therefore became two
closely related imperatives. Farmers relied on direct domination and extensive violence to achieve this degree of submission and extra-legal violence
became the final arbiter of race relations across the plantation South.

Such systemic racial violence, however, could not be confined to the narrow domain of labor relations. Racial violence had to be framed in ways
that *all* whites would support. In the agrarian South, this meant bringing on
board the region's vast population of poor whites. Even before Reconstruction ended, landowners grasped that the most effective way to legitimize
their violent domination was to fuse the establishment of sharecropping and
the disfranchisement of African Americans into a single cause. Because "the
question of labor control was inseparable from the question of the African
American franchise,"[11] destroying the African American vote and forging
a racially repressive economy constituted two prongs of the same violent
objective – constructing a white supremacist state marked by the dominance of landowners in a monocrop economy. However, landowners were
remarkably successful in using racial violence to consolidate their dominance over poor whites as well. As befits any hegemonic class, landowners
successfully parlayed their own agrarian interests in a racially repressive
labor market into a "universal" ideology of white supremacy that extended
beyond their farms and attracted the active, even enthusiastic support of
poor whites. Setting the basic template that the capitalists in the iron and
coal sectors would soon emulate, landowners did more than tap into the
abundant wells of racism amongst poor whites – they also *exacerbated* the
racial divide within the region's poor by pitting African American and poor
whites against each other.[12]

The violent world that farmers made largely confronted the emerging
classes within the white population – businessmen in primary and secondary industry and the white working class – as a *fait accompli*. This convergence of interests around a racially repressive labor market in which mob
terror and lethal violence on plantations played such prominent roles was
highly consequential. It meant that nowhere in the political economy of the
South was there a dynamic and influential class prepared to challenge the
world-view of commercial farmers, virtually ensuring that the basic tenets
of the agrarian sector would come to undergird Southern society generally.
By the First World War it was clear that the overwhelming majority of businessmen and white workers supported the version of white supremacy that
farmers demanded. All whites therefore became implicated in the violence

used to forge the "Solid South."[13] Rural Redeemers, urban businessmen, poor whites eking out a debt-ridden existence as croppers and tenants, as well as workers in mill villages and the mining centers of the South, were all, to borrow from a controversial book on an analogous context, "ordinary people" who became "willing executioners" of African Americans.[14]

As in South Africa, businessmen in the New South nominally ascribed to the logic of "free markets," as theorists of the "growth school" would expect, but also found it convenient to profit from the exploitation of unfree labor in the two racial orders.[15] In Greenberg's words, businessmen in primary and secondary industry came to occupy an "ambiguous" force in the establishment of racial domination, not fully identified as co-authors of the racial order but keen to tap into the profits and managerial convenience these measures provided. As Gavin Wright also illustrates, employers in the textile and mining industries therefore accommodated themselves to the racial order by adapting and incorporating segregation into their enterprises. In the cotton mills that dotted the Black Belt, segregation emerged simultaneously with the rise of the textile industry itself. The close integration of the textile industry and agricultural sectors was no doubt inevitable in this context. Mills were located within the cotton-producing areas in the very areas where farmers held sway, ensuring that the culture of the plantation would swamp the emerging textile industry.[16]

Another important arrangement indexed the close integration of mills and plantations: the absence of significant competition between farmers and mill owners for the same labor. Soon after the Civil War, farmers briefly experimented with white immigrant workers, and even took on local white workers, before turning permanently to their traditional source, African American labor. In contrast, virtually from the moment the textile industry emerged after the Civil War, mill owners adopted the opposite strategy and employed white labor exclusively. The mills "recruited labor on the tenant farms and in the hollows and relied increasingly on the labor of children and women."[17] Well into the 1960s, "lintheads" (as white mill workers were called), were exclusively white. The non-competitive relationship between farmers and the textile industry therefore dampened the likelihood of fractious disputes over access to labor and the overall management of race relations. As we see in the next chapter, intense inter-sectoral competition for cheap labor in South Africa reflected the difficulties that white employers faced in fashioning a racially repressive labor market.

The emergence of primary industry centered on coal and iron mining did not seriously challenge the broad and supportive relationship between farmers and mill operators. Workers – African Americans, whites and immigrants newly arrived from Europe – streamed to the coalmines and iron works close to the burgeoning city of Birmingham, creating a multicultural milieu that, to the concern of many Southerners, threatened to undermine the traditional racial hierarchy. But mine owners developed employment strategies that preserved both the racial divide and their power over the emerging proletariat. Mine owners relied on two principal methods to these ends, both of which illustrate their strong relations with state authorities. Firstly, they made liberal use of convict workers, almost all of whom were African American as early as 1877. Lucrative contracts with state and county governments provided thousands of virtually free African American workers who, as we see below, were all too frequently treated as chattel. Employers also used convict labor as a prophylaxis against unionization. Secondly, mine owners were enthusiastic campaigners for laws that criminalized "vagrancy" and hampered the work of labor recruiters. Laws that targeted any individuals who had "no visible means of support" or lived "without employment" yielded a steady supply of African American prisoners for farmers and miners alike.[18]

Mine owners were therefore hardly likely to speak out against policing practices that dispatched African American men to jail for minor "offenses" such as "loitering." Instead, they stoked the white public's obsession with the sexual and criminal "dangers" that African Americans were said to pose, fusing their labor requirements to Jim Crow laws that sought to limit inter-racial solidarity and social contact from 1890 onwards. Mine owners also obtained "anti-enticement" laws that prevented labor agents from recruiting African American workers in mining districts. The existence of anti-enticement laws suggests that state authorities were prepared to regulate the competition for cheap labor between employers in different sectors – a major goal of the pass system that emerged in South Africa. However, anti-enticement measures in the South did not give rise to the extensive gridwork of administrative regulations and bodies that emerged to protect the recruitment of migrant labor in the gold mining industry in South Africa.[19] This important difference between the two systems of racial domination in South Africa and the American South is pursued in the next chapter.

A powerful "property alliance of big planter with business and industry" therefore became a dominant feature of industrialization in the New South.[20] This marriage between businessmen and the racial order was not perfect or free of contradictions. Businessmen were sometimes placed in the awkward position of having to either support the racial order and its numerous racial taboos or rationally pursue profits in defiance of local white sentiment. But whenever they were confronted with a clash between "stability and profit maximization," businessmen in the New South invariably settled the question by prioritizing stability, preferring to comply with the racial hierarchy rather than disrupt their relations with the mass of conservative white Southerners. Prior to the First World War, for example, mill owners sought to employ African Americans as mill workers but immediately confronted a hornet's nest of opposition from white workers who refused to countenance the policy under any circumstances.[21] By coming out in support of a segregated industrial arena and the growth of Jim Crow laws, businessmen added their weight behind a racial order anchored in the racially repressive agrarian sector. The result was the consolidation of an alliance amongst like-minded employers within and across economic sectors that critically impacted white workers by sharply limiting their opportunities for upward mobility.

Lynching and economic diversity

The unchallenged dominance of "King Cotton" established an overlapping of interests and a common identification that had critical implications for the style of racial domination in the South. The absence of significant disputes over the allocation and use of black labor meant that economic homogeneity and lynching were almost certainly positively related. A comparison that William Brundage makes between lynching patterns in Virginia and Georgia, two Southern states with distinct economies, illustrates this point well. In some respects, the two states are a study in contrast. Nevertheless, both sported a tradition of lynching African Americans.[22]

With its cotton economy, the record and pattern of lynching in Georgia were considerably grimmer than in Virginia. The 464 known lynchings that took place in Georgia between 1880 and 1930 made it the second-most lynch-prone state after Texas. Georgia displayed high levels of all forms of extra-legal racial violence. Posses, which were ostensibly formed to capture criminals, ended up lynching at least 52 men, in contrast to a singular instance in which posses lynched their quarry in Virginia. Lynchings that were perpetrated by private mobs also illustrate the malevolent forces at work in the cotton-dependent state of Georgia. Private lynching serves as a "barometer of both public attitudes and towards mob violence and vigilance by law officers." In other words, the greater the support for lynching, the higher the proportion of communal lynching in a particular state. Conversely, weak or declining mass support for lynching was reflected in the increasing number of victims who were lynched under furtive conditions. Communal lynching in Virginia lagged behind private forms of extra-legal violence in the 1880s. The pattern changed in the 1890s when, in response to a groundswell of political challenges to the Democratic Party, whites across all the Southern states publicly assembled in large groups to lynch African Americans. Georgia and Virginia conformed to this trend until 1900. But trends in the two states would thereafter differ sharply. In Virginia, communal lynchings became rare after whites retreated to the earlier tradition of private violence, indicating growing public disapproval of extra-legal violence in the state. In Georgia, however, communal lynchings remained high until the 1920s when they finally began to decrease. Until then, lynching of all types – those carried out by "unknown mobs," "posses, ""terrorist mobs," "private mobs" and "mass mobs" – remained significant in Georgia, contributing to a lynch tradition that was not only more persistent but also more variegated than the pattern in Virginia.[23] Brundage concludes from these trends that circumstances in Virginia yielded only a brief period of public support for lynching, while conditions in Georgia sustained a lynch culture that was almost unrestrained in the methods employed to lynch African Americans.

Brundage insists that sheer economic diversity, considered on its own, does not account for the relative paucity of lynching and the declining support for communal lynching in Virginia. Still, the association between the state's weak lynch tradition and its diversified economy is highly suggestive. Virginia had sported a diverse economy even in the antebellum years. The Old Dominion state subsequently acquired a reputation in the New South for its enterprising embrace of modernity and industrialization, reflected in the emergence of three distinct economic zones within the state. A combination of industrial and transportation activities (rail and ports) prevailed in the *eastern* reaches of the state. The *upper middle* region of the state, the Piedmont counties, sported a diversified agricultural economy that was devoted to grain farming, dairy products, fruits and vegetables. In contrast, counties in the *lower middle* of the state strongly resembled neighboring Black Belt states. Planters in these counties specialized in tobacco, sharecropping and corn, and, like the Black Belt farmers they closely resembled, also relied on sharecropping, intimidation and crop lien laws.

Lynching did occur in the state of Virginia – 85 incidents were recorded statewide between 1880 and 1930. However, a closer examination reveals significant similarities with, and differences from, a Black Belt state such as Georgia. For example, lynching in Virginia reached its peak in the 1890s, just as it did across all Southern states. But this number was driven by a spike in lynching that occurred in the lower middle zone where Black Belt features were concentrated. Lynching actually declined in the eastern and upper central zones of the state in the 1890s, contradicting the upward curve of lynchings in Georgia and the South generally. By 1910, lynchings in Virginia "had become as rare as in Illinois or Arizona."[24] With its developed system of commercial agriculture, transportation and industrial infrastructure, and the high percentage of African Americans in all economic activities, race relations in eastern Virginia differed significantly from counties in the south and southwestern regions. Eastern Virginia, the most developed and economically diverse region of the state, developed a system of race relations that was notably more relaxed and flexible than anywhere else in the state, and stood out favorably from even the least lynch-prone counties in Black Belt states. Furthermore, the ritualized sadism associated with communal lynching was infrequent in Virginia. Although mobs did mutilate the remains of four victims, accounts of the 55 lynchings in eastern Virginia did not mention torture.[25]

Brundage summarizes the complex reasons for the relatively benign management of race relations in Virginia as follows:

> In rough proportion to the degree that a particular region diverged from the plantation South, the likelihood of habitual mob violence in that region shrank. Thus, in large portions of Virginia, as well as parts of North Carolina, Tennessee, and Arkansas, where the evolution of agriculture and of labor and race relations diverged from the plantation South, the devasta-

tion wrought by lynch mobs pales in comparison to that of mobs in the Plantation belt.

With only a small portion of the state devoted to monoculture agricul- ture with all of its attendant evils, Virginia landlords were able to experi- ment with both new crops and new methods of securing labor ... Virginia planters simply devised a system of labor that was exploitative, stable, and lucrative and yet did not rest upon the steady application of coercive methods. They discovered that the lash of wages was at least as effective as time-honored methods of coercive labor.

The private nature of extra-legal racial violence in the upper reaches of Virginia bears a strong similarity to the South African setting, where ritual mass lynching was unknown but the private murder of blacks abounded. It is not accidental, as we see in the next chapter, that the South African economy reflected patterns of economic diversity and diverse labor practices that were not too dissimilar from those in Virginia after 1900.

Racial violence in the monocrop economy

Fully two-thirds of all recorded lynchings in the South assumed the form of private lynching. Thousands of cases were recorded in which the corpses of lynch victims were "discovered" hanging from trees, hidden beneath bushes or alongside quiet county roads, put to death "by persons unknown."[26] The precise circumstances that led to these furtive deaths will never be known, but the fact that almost of the victims were sharecroppers or farm workers supports the link that Walter White established between lynching and the rural workplace.[27]

No doubt, many private lynchings may be attributed to the social stand- ing of lynchers who were not sufficiently reputable or esteemed in local white communities to summon up a mass lynching. "Poor whites," "shift- less" whites, small farmers or white sharecroppers, for example, could not always rely on other whites to come to their aid by forming a posse or supporting a mass lynching. In such cases, the aggrieved white might take matters into his own hands or rely on a close friend or family relatives to secure the death of an offending African American man. It was also likely that the offense that the African American man was accused of fell short of the racial tripwires that reliably yielded communal lynchings. Disagree- ments between sharecropper and landlord, such as those involving wages, rations or prices for the cotton crop, were routine matters that individual farmers were expected to resolve without the electrifying drama of com- munal murder, which was reserved only for serious offenses such as murder, robbery and rape.[28] Constant friction inhered in the relationship between sharecropper and landlord, requiring landlords to exercise vigilant control over African Americans, who naturally resented the ceaseless surveillance. The sharecropper's anger tended to peak on "settlement day," but was by no means confined to the day when exploitation was made most visible.

Suspicious of their sharecroppers, farmers who were primarily concerned with the profitability of their farms constantly scrutinized their laborers because "when he steals, fights, assembles 'unlawfully', plots, marries secretly, indulges in fornication, has illegitimate children, spends his time in gambling, cockfighting or courting, the planter suffers some threat of loss."[29] Much as slave owners had done, individual farmers reserved the right to deal with any of these "transgressions" in the manner they saw fit, introducing an amorphous volatility into workplace disputes that could at any moment erupt into violence.

Private forms of lethal and non-lethal violence were thus endemic across the plantation South. Neither law enforcement authorities nor white public opinion impeded the violent traditions that slavery bequeathed to the region. Whites perceived racial violence as a problem "only when [it] reached epidemic proportions and threatened to lead to an exodus of African American laborers," a concern that became increasingly prominent after the First World War.[30] If institutionalized rural violence underscored the domination of planters, even limited African American mobility reveals that the control that individual farmers enjoyed over their labor was imperfect. Why planters failed to develop an immobilizing grid of pass controls, as employers in South Africa did in the inter-War years, is not entirely clear. It is likely that such measures, had they been attempted after 1900, would have been struck down in federal courts and gone the way of the Black Codes. But it is also likely that pass measures were not attempted for another reason: traditionally hostile to government interference, Southern employers were too jealous of their right to directly control African American workers to invite the intrusion of "big government" into the management of plantation affairs. In the absence of an overarching region-wide system of labor controls, farmers resorted to their own devices to counteract the limited market rights of African Americans.

Neither white workers nor employers ever sought to obtain legislation to buttress racist employment patterns in the mills and mines of the South. The racial reservation of jobs thus never came to enjoy the statutory and administrative entrenchment that it did in South Africa. Southern employers no doubt opposed any "big government" measures that would have compelled them to organize their labor force in particular ways, especially if this meant employing more expensive and less vulnerable white workers. For their part, white workers were too wary of radical ideologies and were too weak, in any case, to compel state legislatures to legally reserve certain occupations for white workers only.[31] On the other hand, the US Supreme Court did not expressly illegalize racial discriminatory practices in the economy. As a result, employers – and white workers, too – could use their social and political clout to restrict blacks' access to certain occupations.[32] In short, the absence of extensive statutory prohibitions on the employment of blacks meant that the task of excluding and controlling blacks in industry fell to whites in civil society.

It was no accident, the historian Frank Tannenberg observed, that lynching reached its zenith in the 1890s, three decades after General Lee's army surrendered at Appomattox. A new generation of freedmen and women refused to live as obsequious slaves and took every opportunity to bolster their freedom with property and education. At the end of the Civil War, African Americans had owned 20,000 farms; the number rose to one million by 1922. African American progress took off just as "the worst depression in American history" coincided with declining cotton prices in the mid-1890s. As large numbers of white farmers sank into the ranks of sharecroppers, African Americans began taking up employment in the steel mines of Birmingham.[33] Tannenberg attributed racial violence to envy and a sense of racial competition amongst "a people sinking into the abyss of poverty." Agreeing with Tannenberg's diagnosis that whites' economic misfortune deepened racial competition and encouraged lynching, Walter White concluded that "lynching has always been the means for protection of profits": "The total of 1780 lynchings during the last decade of the century was, in large measure, the mob's effort to check this rising tide of [African American] economic independence."[34]

Brundage views this as an excessively narrow explanation of lynching, however. In Brundage's assessment, "specific alleged transgressions – rather than inchoate white fears about the economic status of local African Americans – produced lynchings."[35] The problem with Brundage's view, however, is that whites also lynched blacks for the most innocuous and ill-defined "transgressions." For this reason, the distinction that Brundage insists on between "specific alleged transgressions" and "inchoate fears" seems much too rigid. What might have begun with a whipping could easily have concluded in a lynching before a large crowd. The evidence seems conclusive that at least some lynchings and white riots – such as the one that devastated Tulsa, Oklahoma, in May and June of 1921 – were motivated by white resentment against prosperous black individuals and communities.[36] In the racial miasma of the South, whites knew that they could convert "inchoate" fear or anxiety into a "specific alleged transgression" and stand a good chance of summoning either private or popular support for lynching. Brundage is certainly correct that only "specific alleged transgressions" could yield *communal* lynchings. Private lynchings, on the other hand, could emerge from the most innocuous contretemps. Under these conditions, it seems pointless to inflexibly insist that only "specific alleged transgressions" could lead to lynching.

The ubiquitous recourse to violence is significant because nowhere was the dominance of white agrarian interests ever in the slightest dispute anywhere in the New South. That work-related disputes over the most minor incidents could so easily lead to lethal outcomes suggests that the details that triggered conflicts between whites and African American were not the major issue. Any ripple that seemed to disturb the natural order between landlords and their African American tenants and croppers threatened to immediately transcend the workplace, inflaming the tissues that connected plantations, churches, courts, police stations and, frequently – at least in the minds of whites – the bedrooms of white homes as well. For example, when whites in Talbot County, Georgia, sensed disquiet amongst their African American croppers in June 1909, they did not respond by fastening on to any specific act of insouciance by a particular black offender. In a lynching that also reflected their principled suspicion and resentment of the few African Americans who held title deeds to land, whites in Talbot County latched – without so much as a shred of evidence – on to the household of William Carreker, an African American man who owned the land he farmed and lived on. White farmers concluded that the note of disquiet they sensed amongst local African Americans was somehow linked to the arrival of an elderly blind preacher taken in by William Carreker.

Led by William Leonard, a prominent farmer who easily convinced other white planters that the "voodoo preacher" intended to provoke an "insurrection" amongst African Americans, a group of whites surrounded Carreker's house and demanded that he turn over the preacher for a whipping that would force him to vacate the county. Carreker refused and a group of white men soon encircled his house. A shotgun blast emanated from Carreker's house and Leonard dropped dead. Both the group of whites and the two African American men fled the scene. White men from across and beyond Talb County streamed to Carreker's farm in preparation for the expected double lynching. The sheriff deputized a posse of fifty men to conduct the search, but hundreds of men also formed small posses that scoured the county. The blind man was soon discovered, with his head smashed in and bullets pumped into his body before it had been tossed from a bridge (thereafter known as Blind Man's Bridge). Two days later, Carreker surrendered to a white man he knew and was placed in jail by the sheriff, setting the context for the inevitable jail storming. The mob circumvented the sheriff's reluctance to release Carreker with a cunning ruse. One of the deputized men awoke the sheriff claiming that a witness to Leonard's murder had been captured and the keys to the jail were therefore required to detain him. Trapped by the request and unwilling to take on the mob that he knew must have assembled outside the jail, the sheriff complied. Carreker was hanged from a telephone pole across from the courthouse. A newspaper noted, "It was all done quietly and in perfect order." The obvious pride in the professionalism of the lynch mob that this observation contained echoed the many editorials and reports that commented with disdain on the way mobs could sometimes bungle a lynching. Newspapers occasionally raised doubts about the civic spirit amongst whites when faggots failed to burn properly or ropes or branches snapped, or when riotous crowds sometimes fired at the body but felled "innocent" white bystanders instead. "Clean" lynchings such as that of Carreker were good for cementing the self-image of impoverished towns and counties that languished on the margins of local and national attention. The lynching of Carreker also underscores how thin the distinction between "inchoate fears" and "specific alleged transgression" could be.[37]

The violent aura of labor relations in the rural economy cannot be considered separately from the debt peonage system that existed throughout the plantation South. Like the pass laws in South Africa, this Southern institution was intended to control cheap African American labor. But to a degree that far outstripped similar developments in South Africa, debt peonage was closely associated with ordinary violence in two ways. Firstly, it was an inherently violent institution because it legalized the involuntary servitude of African Americans (and some whites). Secondly, it provided ample opportunity for whites to inflict physical violence on African Americans mired in the thrall of brutal landowners.[38] In the South, violence stood alongside debt and coercion, legally the only two essential components of peonage, to form a trinity of controls that bonded African Americans to individual white farmers. As late as the 1920s, landowners and storekeepers who resolutely used violence to extract their "just dues" from African Americans were genuinely astonished to learn that debt peonage was in fact illegal. Their ignorance was not entirely their fault. Although the first legal test case of peonage was brought before the Supreme Court in 1901, it was only in 1942 that the Supreme Court brought decades of prevarication, legal hairsplitting and public indifference to an end by outlawing all forms of debt peonage.[39]

Debt peonage had to contend with two threats: the worker's death, which terminated the source of profits, and freedom of movement, which might remove African Americans from the clutches of the white farmer. Pete Daniels' socio-legal study of debt peonage includes cases in which peons were indeed worked to death. The central problem, however, was how to prevent African Americans from moving beyond the reach of their "creditors." Employers in South Africa in the inter-War years dealt with this problem by developing an increasingly restrictive "pass system" to immobilize African Americans in white farming areas. Such a system never arose in the South and farmers resorted to debt peonage as its closest approximation. Legalizing peonage, as Florida did, had the considerable advantage of enjoining the courts and police in tracing and disciplining African Americans who escaped or defaulted on their debts. Still, white farmers did not leave it to these institutions to retrieve peons who went missing. Armed with weapons and hounds, they hunted down escaped peons themselves and meted out punishments that frequently led to the death of escapees. It was not an uncommon sight in Florida to encounter hunting parties near train and bus stations in the hope of seizing escaped peons. While local sheriffs assisted in the private forays of such "man hunters," farmers did not view their presence as essential.[40]

Daniels provides ample evidence in his classic study of debt peonage in Florida to show that plantations resembled what Irving Goffman called "total institutions."[41] As late as 1921, federal agents who were investigating rumors of debt peonage on a farm in Jasper County, Georgia, unwittingly revealed a tale not only of mass murder but of actual slavery. Their investigations ultimately revealed that a white farmer named John S. Williams and his sons had regularly obtained labor by paying the fines of African American convicts in the local jail. On the eve of the Civil War, the cost of slaves has risen to approximately $1,000 and reached $1,500 in some parts of the South. In the early 1920s, however, it cost Williams no more than $5 to purchase a peon from the local jail. The police asked no questions when the Williams men did not return the convicts, nor even when they turned up to secure more convicts. As the investigation proceeded, John Williams and his sons became anxious. To thwart the federal investigators, they began killing the convicts on their farms to prevent federal agents from questioning them. Evidence at the subsequent court case led the police to many bodies buried on Williams' farm after survivors recounted harrowing tales of inexplicable whippings and fatal shootings. Williams, who was astonished to hear that debt peonage was illegal and claimed that every farmer in the county relied on the practice, became "the first Southern man since 1877 to be indicted for the first-degree murder of an African American," ensuring that he also became the first white man in the South to be found guilty of the charge. In May 1921, the Williams' untroubled confidence that no judge would imprison any white man for murdering any number of African Americans was brought up short when the presiding judge imposed a life sentence, making Williams the first Southerner to receive the sentence for murdering an African American. In another sense, however, the conclusion of the trial remained true to Southern creeds by sparing Williams from the death sentence.[42]

A case of communal violence: The lynching of Sam Hose

The rural workplace presented a fertile context for violence to serve multiple purposes. In the majority of cases, disagreements between African American laborers and white landlords took the form of private violence that either remained confined to the farm setting or transpired under a veil of secrecy. As the killing of peons by the Williams men above illustrates, the absence of ritual was characteristic of these private murders. However, interpersonal violence was so endemic and essential to racial relations in the South that it required the smallest of sparks for a work-related contretemps to flare up and embroil white society generally. But for a communal lynching to occur, "specific alleged transgressions" comprising allegations of murder, assault and rape committed against whites were required. Newspaper reports of such lynchings rarely bothered to inquire into the exact circumstances that summoned large numbers of whites to witness a ritual execution in public. Indeed, at such moments newspapers became a critical part of the technology of racial violence. Journalists uncritically accepted and disseminated allegations of African American guilt, larded the initial fiction with incendiary claims and calls to action and left no stone unturned to connect the incident, whatever it may have been, to imperiled "white womanhood." Unlike in South Africa, where murder always led to court proceedings, no formal inquiries were made into even the most spectacular cases of violence in the New South, and so no paper trail of relatively impartial evidence was created in the vast majority of lynch incidents.

The incident that led to the lynching of Sam Hose began with a minor dispute over money in April 1899. Sam Hose had sought the permission of his employer, a farmer named Alfred Cranston, to return home to visit his ailing mother and asked for an advance on his wages to this end. Cranston refused and tempers flared on both sides. Cranston drew a weapon and Hose flung the axe with which he had been chopping wood, mortally wounding Cranston before fleeing the farm. News of the killing spread like wildfire across neighboring farms, growing increasingly fictional and sensational with each retelling. Within days, newspaper accounts presented Hose as a murderous brute who had sneaked up on an unsuspecting Cranston innocently enjoying his dinner. Hose was said to have split Cranston's head with an axe, repeatedly attacked the stricken man before forcing Mrs Cranston to lead him from room to room as he plundered her house. Journalistic norms evaporated entirely at such moments, and Hose was next accused of raping Mrs Cranston, infecting her with venereal disease in the process. The "crazed" Hose was also reported to have inflicted life-threatening injuries on the woman's baby by flinging it to the ground. Subsequent articles, devoured far beyond Coweta County, soon reported that a clutch of assorted unsolved criminal atrocities, including murders, rapes and other suspicious activities, were actually the handiwork of Sam Hose. There was little wonder, the *Kissimmee Valley Gazette* in Florida noted, why whites in "the entire state of Georgia have waited with impatience for the moment when the negro would pay the penalty for his fiendish deeds."[43] Two thousand spectators turned up for the lynching near the town of Newman, Georgia. Before he was doused with oil and set alight, a newspaper in Massachusetts reported, "the negro was deprived of his ears, fingers and genital parts." The report continued:

> He pleaded pitifully for his life while the mutilation was going on, but stood the ordeal of fire with surprising fortitude. Before his body was cool it was cut to pieces, the bones were crushed into small bits ... The negro's heart was cut into several pieces, as was also his liver ... Small pieces of bones [were sold] for 25 cents, and a bit of the liver cooked sold for 10 cents.[44]

"Even the tree upon which the wretch met his fate," Stewart Tolnay and Elwood Beck write, "was torn up and disposed of as souvenirs."[45] Like all communal lynchings, the escalation of a simple dispute between employer and employee into fever-pitched collective mayhem was stoked by the combination of unconscionable charges. On its own, each charge of murder, rape and abuse of a white baby would have secured Host's demise. In combination, they were a deadly trifecta, guaranteed to uncork limitless cruelty amongst whites.

In the course of his interrogation, Hose was said to have admitted to the murder of Cranston in exchange for $20 from a African American priest, "Lige" Strickland. Hose's tormentors were aware that the desperate man had told a number of lies in an effort to escape death, but accepted Strickland's guilt without question. One day after Hose's lynching, the nearby community of Palmetto, Georgia, was treated to a second lynching. Strickland refused to confess to any involvement in Holt's deeds. The mob ignored the interventions of Strickland's employer, a former state senator "and one of the most distinguished citizens of Coweta county." Strickland's ears and one finger were hacked off before he was lynched on the limb of a persimmon tree. The mob next set out for another "negro who had been heard to say his race should be avenged, and at last account it was still spreading terror and death among the African Americans, while a similar mob in South Carolina has inaugurated a like campaign." In the unlikely event that African Americans in Georgia, indeed across the South, had somehow failed to observe how a simple request for an advance on wages could spiral into such protracted communal violence, a placard with the following words was attached to Strickland's body: "We must protect our ladies. Beware all darkies! You will be treated the same way."[46]

Cracks in the Solid South

Despite broad white support for segregation and the paeans that were sung to the idea of "the Solid South," the emerging industrial arena was marked by an open secret: within the bounds of the segregated order, employers used every opportunity to hold down white wages and hobble unionization. This strategy exerted enormous pressure on the living standards of poor whites. While some scholars argue that white wages were sometimes higher than black wages, others point out that the difference was negligible; white wages in the South, in any case, were amongst the lowest in the country.[47] Yet plain whites in the South proved remarkably amenable to cooperation with the very employers who pinioned them to the lowest reaches of Southern society, perilously close, white workers worried, to the condition of blacks. The paucity of employment alternatives and proximity to the social condition of blacks thus became the defining feature of life for poor whites in the New South.

Poor whites had valorized whiteness in the slave era for an important reason: other than skin color, little else distinguished the lot of whites from black slaves. Above all other meanings, David Roediger notes, whiteness for antebellum poor whites symbolized "freedom," the antithesis of the slave's essence.[48] In the postbellum era, poor whites remained as penurious and vulnerable as they had been prior to the war when had they subsisted in a variety marginal occupations: as laborers in the turpentine camps in the "piney backwoods" or "river rats," and "tackies" eking out a Spartan existence near river banks and salt marshes. Shields McIlvane wrote of the class of "dregs and driftwood" in Mississippi in the first quarter of the twentieth century, "Living on the level of the blacks, doing the same work, being treated in much the same way by the landlord, the poor-white tenant has felt even more degraded than he did during slavery times; for then he could stay in the backlands away from humiliation ... They are poor white trash afloat."[49] For the majority of poor whites, mobility meant moving up from cropper to tenant, a pattern reflected in the declining proportion of black tenants in the first three decades after 1900. Poor whites were better off than the majority of blacks only to the extent that tenant farming was preferable to sharecropping chiefly because it permitted the tenant greater freedom but not necessarily greater profits. As impoverished, malnourished and illiterate as blacks, and sporting similarly large numbers of ill-clothed children, white tenants labored under the crop lien and "advances" system much as sharecroppers did.[50]

Why such impoverished whites resisted a class alliance with African Americans and identified with miserly employers is therefore a question that continues to fascinate scholars of the New South. Two broad schools have arisen to account for this development. Continuing a tradition begun by W. E. B. Du Bois, the first emphasizes the psychological, social and cultural benefits that poor whites derived from inclusion into a racial oligarchy. Du Bois contended that poor whites failed to benefit materially in the postbellum era and, to supplement their low wages, settled for a "public and psychological wage" – that is, the simple recognition from employers that poor whites were in fact not black. Du Bois leaves no doubt that white struggles to win the "psychological wage" were fatally flawed from the outset, the high cost of victory being tantamount to defeat. The formal recognition that skin color entitled whites to more considerate treatment implanted a "permanent wedge between white and black workers" and deepened their dependence on profit-driven elites. Du Bois' brief comments about "the public and psychological wages of whiteness" serve as the fountainhead for the "whiteness studies" school that took off after the publication of David Roediger's *The Wages of Whiteness*. Like Du Bois, Roediger concludes that the pursuit of the "psychological wage" prevented poor whites from embracing the common interests they shared with blacks.[51]

The second approach argues that poor whites *did* gain materially, if marginally, in exchange for their identification with and support for employers. In this view, the "psycho-cultural" premises on which the "wages of whiteness" thesis rests merely updates the Marxist claim that racism represents the "false consciousness" of the white working class. For scholars such as Michelle Brittain, it is unsurprising that, given their penuriousness and powerlessness in the low-wage economy, white workers spurned a class alliance with blacks and forged non-combative relations with powerful employers instead. Brittain argues that Southern poor whites, who had *always* "received intangible compensation merely for the color of their skin," did in fact manipulate their claims to whiteness in ways that benefited them materially and deepened a class distinction between black and white workers. Race ensured that "whiteness actually determined the ability *to become* working class in the New South," as the all-white employment policy in the textile industry illustrates. Incorporation into the ranks of the labor force of the textile industry represented a step up the ladder of mobility in the New South, a progression that was all but denied to blacks. Furthermore, white workers considered themselves fortunate to obtain mill employment because of the paternalist "welfare benefits" that came with the job. In the 1920s, for example, it was not unusual for a mill town to sport a community center, an indoor pool and a movie theater. The abyss of rural poverty, Michelle Brittain writes, "made it seem as if the notoriously low-wage industries that came to dominate the New South really were serving the interests of farmers-turned-workers."[52]

These two schools are not mutually exclusive. Nevertheless, the evidence in favor of the "materialist" school is thin and unconvincing, a point that even Brittain acknowledges. W. E. B. Du Bois' explanation is therefore all the more compelling because his original "psychological" account does not, in fact, discount the minuscule "material" benefits that poor whites enjoyed. He was insistent, however, that psychological benefits dwarfed the material rewards that flowed from collaboration with employers. Observing that poor whites were mired in fear and suspicion, he posed and answered a key question: What were poor whites so scared of that prompted them to embrace rapacious employers?

> Of what? Of many things, but usually of losing their jobs, being declassed, degraded, or actually disgraced; of losing their hopes, their savings, their plans for the children; of the actual pangs of hunger, of dirt, or crime. And of all of this, most ubiquitous in modern industrial society is that fear of unemployment.

Weighed down by a crushing combination of economic fears and ceaseless anxiety about their "social degradation" in the racial order, poor whites looked at blacks and became "writhing, yelling, cruel-eyed demons."[53]

The demise of the Populist movement and racial violence

Virulent racism was not the only response of poor whites to emancipated blacks, their perceived competitors in the emerging industrial arena of the New South. Poor whites had been initially open to cooperating with blacks in the inter-racial Populist movement of the 1880s and 1890s. Plebeian racism distilled and reached its apogee only *after* these initial attempts failed. Like the asymmetrical pact that white workers formed with employers, the consolidation of racial violence amongst the ranks of the white poor was in many ways a direct consequence of the defeat of the Populist movement.

For a brief but critical decade in the 1880s and 1890s, the inter-racial Populist movement presented a real threat to the dominance of Bourbon Democrats in the South. Ravaged by the same changes that threw thousands of farmers and tenants into debt – plummeting commodity prices, international competition made possible by expanding railroad and shipping routes, rising farm costs, high railroad transport costs in the South and high interest rates – black and white farmers in the South and Midwest responded by organizing farmers' associations (the "Grange" movement) in the 1870s. In 1889–90, a number of "poor people's movements" – the Northern Alliance, Southern Alliance, Colored Farmers' Alliance, Knights of Labor, Farmers' Mutual Benefit Association and the Union Labor Party – came together to form the Populist Party.[54] A vibrant third party was injected onto the national stage.

Populist demands included the unlimited coinage of silver, a graduated income tax, government ownership of the railroads, the direct election of US senators, and reforms to bolster debt-ridden farmers and place agriculture on the same footing as northeastern industry. A major goal was to free the South from the electoral fraud that Bourbons used to stay in power. The party went on to contest national elections in 1892, when it won several victories, and again in 1896. By this later date, however, the Republican Party had already appropriated several Populist platforms, leading to the "fusion" of the two parties in many states. With the movement weakened and torn apart over the "fusion" issue, Bourbon Democrats successfully capitalized on the splintered Populist Party. Supported chiefly by reactionary Bourbon Democrats," the Democratic machine also resorted to extensive violence to nip the third party in the bud, shooting Populist leaders and driving their supporters from the polls.[55]

Before it disappeared, however, the Populist Party severely unsettled Southern Democrats. In 1892 in Louisiana, for example, an upswell of Populist mobilization delayed the Party's attempts to implement literacy and property qualifications that struck African Americans and some poor whites from the rolls.[56] Populists supported African Americans' attempts to register for the vote and fanned across counties, encouraging them to register. Populists electrified many Southerners – but probably alienated many more – by permitting women to address public meetings and speak in favor of women's right to vote. Populists also took up causes such as educational reform and supported attempts to allocate more funds to the poor and to African Americans. Progressive politics of this nature greatly alarmed Democrats. According to Morgan Kousser, Southern Democrats feared that these developments foretold a nightmare scenario in which the Republican Party – or worse, the new Populist Party – might yet snatch political power from reactionary Bourbons.[57] Hence the all-out campaign that Democrats launched in 1896 to steal the vote and inflict a reign of terror wherever they suspected support for the Populist cause.

The defeat of the Populist movement in the late 1890s confronted poor whites with an historic choice. White workers could either re-construct an inter-racial alliance that would force employers to the bargaining table or cooperate with employers in exchange for concessions. The first option was a lost cause. *Hors de combat* and demoralized by the routing of the Populist movement, white workers knew that a more radical incarnation would not emerge from the detritus of the inter-racial movement. The vast majority therefore turned their backs on the politics of militant confrontation, bringing Populism to such a decisive halt that, in the words of one scholar, "the People's party of the 1890s appeared and then passed into oblivion in the winking of an eye."[58] Populism turned out to be the last hurrah of radical white politics in the South. By and large, white workers thereafter pursued their interests by seeking a racial alliance with employers. So resolute were they in this quest that, for at least seven decades after Populism was gutted in the 1890s, race would trump class.[59] White workers therefore submitted to the construction of the "Solid South."

Poor whites in the first half of the twentieth century supported all devices that singled out African Americans for discriminatory treatment. They supported the disfranchisement of African Americans as well as the codification of Jim Crow laws that meticulously extended segregation into the emerging industrial and urban centers of the South. [60] Jim Crow laws primarily sought to restrict intermarriage and prevent inter-racial activity in commercial enterprises where black and white clientele were likely to interact on a daily basis. Poor whites therefore benefited from laws that trumpeted the prima facie superiority of skin color at the bottom of the social hierarchy, where common poverty often blurred the distinction between blacks and equally poor whites. Plebeian white support for segregation did not falter even when racially restrictive measures harmed poor whites themselves.

The most prominent example of the latter involved the various disfranchisement policies that all Southern states adopted. For example, Glenn Feldman ably refutes the claim that poor whites in Alabama allied themselves with African Americans to oppose disfranchisement, a view held by such eminent historians as C. Vann Woodward, J. Morgan Kousser and Michael Perman. Feldman shows that poor whites were keenly aware that suffrage requirements intended to hobble blacks also harbored the same danger for Alabama's poorest whites. Still, they set aside their anxieties about suffrage restrictions in exchange for vague guarantees at the state convention held in 1901. The final constitution they actively supported contained "five disfranchising mechanisms with no corresponding loopholes for poor whites ... All five could be equally applicable to blacks and poor whites." Feldman shows that the effects were immediate, the statewide tally of registered white voters in Mississippi falling by 41,329 in 1903 despite the growth in the white population. In 1890, 120,000 whites were registered to vote in Alabama; by 1892, only 68,000 voters were left on the rolls. Disfranchised poor whites accounted for the overwhelming bulk of the lost voters.[61]

For Du Bois, such evidence eloquently reveals the depth of poor whites' desperate search for allies. The bargain that poor whites struck with employers hinged on Jim Crow laws, which addressed only social issues. Because they did not intrude on the vital matter of jobs, wages and employment policies, Jim Crow laws did little to address the extensive poverty that marked the life of poor whites. Jim Crow laws, it should be noted, had nothing in common with the "job color bars" that emerged to protect white employees in South Africa. "Job color bars" in South Africa reserved entire occupations for whites only and formally introduced segregation and racial domination into the very organization of work. (See the next chapter). Nothing remotely similar emerged in any of the Southern states, where Jim Crow laws were in fact the *pinnacle* of racially explicit legislation. Whereas Jim Crow laws were extensive and even meticulous, Idus Newby observes, the economic dimensions of white supremacy "were never so rigidly defined; nor were they the subject of inclusive legislation." The result was that "there remained significant areas of inter-racial competition for the unskilled and semiskilled jobs Plain Folk could fill."[62] Although her "split labor market theory" unconvincingly attributes calls for industrial segregation to white workers themselves and not to employers, Edna Bonacich correctly concludes that the white working class in this period was perennially haunted by a "fear of displacement in the economy."[63] Similar anxieties emerged amongst white workers in South Africa as well. In South Africa, however, white workers parlayed their "fear of displacement" into extensive legislative activity, contributing to a number of laws that sought to insulate struggling, mostly Afrikaner communities from competition with cheap black labor. In contrast, introducing and enforcing industrial segregation in the South was left almost exclusively to informal institutions such as "custom" and "racial etiquette," practically inviting racial hostility against blacks.

Proponents of the "American exceptionalism" thesis long ago pointed out that the combined hostility of state functionaries and capitalists towards organized labor distinguished state formation in the US from European developments.[64] Across the US, "Repression, rather than conciliation, was the method chosen by most American government officials to deal with large strikes and with rising labor militancy."[65] Wherever support from the local gendarmerie was in short supply, Gerald Friedman notes, "businessmen filled the gap with private force, including lynch mobs, armed Pinkerton guards, and quasi-public bodies like the Pennsylvania Coal and Iron Police."[66] (The strike-breaking company of Bergoff Brothers and Waddell boasted that it could provide ten thousand strike breakers within seventy-two hours, a service that not even the federal government could match).[67] The onslaught against unionism was also taken up by the legal system, which waged a war against the "vague terror … [of] … socialism" by securing numerous injunctions against strikes. Injunctions gathered steam "like a rolling snowball" after 1880, until they were "at the disposal of the employer almost upon request."[68] For their part, many state leaders in the New South took the view that government was "the decisive and powerful ally of corporate interests." They repeatedly made state armories available to employers and turned a blind eye to the thuggish violence of state officials and private "detective agencies." The result, as Philip Taft and Philip Ross conclude, was that "the United States had the bloodiest and most violent labor history of any industrial nation in the world."[69]

In addition to hiring cheap black convicts to undermine white wages, industrial employers in the South also used black workers as strike breakers. "Mill owners shamefully encouraged the mill hands' hatred of the Negro and manipulated that hatred to their own ends. They preferred ... to cultivate the racial phobias of white operatives and to exploit their fears of competition from blacks," Melton McLauren writes. Alan Stokes' assessment of the mills applies with equal force to the mining centers: the racially divisive policies of industrialists "yielded considerable benefit to the owners, including possibly lower labor costs."[70] White workers, of course, were well aware of these intentions and some of their leaders sought to resist by forging inter-racial unions. In many industries across the South – the bituminous coalfields of Alabama and West Virginia, the timber mills of eastern Texas and Louisiana, the waterfronts on the Gulf Coast, and the mining fields of Texas and Appalachia – white workers did attempt to collaborate across racial lines to challenge employers. But, too weak organizationally and too compromised by racism to long endure the perils of inter-racial fraternity in the segregated South, they abandoned these attempts by 1910.[71]

Numerous studies of Southern labor movements, including the more recent crop of labor studies that rejects the image of the instinctively racist and strike-shy white worker in the New South, therefore all reach the same conclusion: inter-racial unions either collapsed or evolved into separate racial unions, with white unions echoing much of the racism of employers. Indeed, many white workers found the divide-and-rule strategy of paternalist employers reassuring: "It advanced the idea of an Anglo-Saxon kinship between management and labor" even if it "also reminded white workers that the kinship did not allow them to challenge the owners' authority."[72] For their part, black unions warily studied invitations to join forces with white unionists they suspected of using them.[73] By 1896, too, blacks had grown weary of the growing number of Populists who "fused" with Republicans. Bishop Henry McNeal Turner exhorted fellow African Americans to cast a protest vote for the Democratic Party in that year's presidential election. "What time has the fool Negro to bother with the gold or silver side either, while he is lynched, burnt, flayed and imprisoned, etc., two-thirds of the time for nothing?"[74]

Southern white workers therefore paid an historic price for turning their backs on solidarity with blacks, arguably the most effective tool at their disposal for imposing their demands on employers. Fobbed off by employers and unable to turn state power to their specific ends, poor whites clung to the customary foundations of white supremacy, chiefly by maintaining a prickly vigilance over the few prerogatives they enjoyed over blacks. "This effort to keep white group solidarity led to mob law," W. E. B. Du Bois wrote in 1925: "Every white man became a recognized official to keep negroes 'in their places'. Negro baiting and even lynching became a form of amusement."[75]

The gutting of the Populist challenge was thus of extraordinary importance for the trajectory of racial violence in the South. The abrupt cessation of a radical movement that could have limited grinding exploitation in the region severely disabled poor whites. For the latter, a racial alliance with callous employers appeared to be a more attractive alternative to "equality" with blacks in radical but doomed labor movements. The most punishing consequences of Populism's demise were therefore borne not by whites but by African Americans. By triggering a racial concordat between white employers and poor whites, the defeat of Populism democratized a culture of violence that elites had earlier pioneered to overthrow Reconstruction. After 1900, a dynamism was set in motion authorizing poor whites to defend the "Solid South" by violently turning against African Americans. Membership has its privileges. For poor whites, lynching was a privilege that had been denied to them in the antebellum era. In the new South, lynching afforded poor whites with a spectacular opportunity to prove that they belonged to the ruling race.

Plebeian violence

When white workers in South Africa complained that employing blacks deprived them of jobs, they almost always channeled their anger through political parties and unions. In contrast, white workers in the New South were much more likely to launch attacks against blacks themselves. In May 1899, for example, white workers at Kincaid Manufacturing Company in Griffin, Georgia, launched an unprovoked attack against three black men employed as menial workers in the factory. A mob of thirty men seized them from their homes one night and severely flogged them. The local newspaper reported that the victims' "only offense seems to have been working at the mill" and the flogging was intended to force mill owners to cease hiring blacks. Black workers were threatened with violence the next day, forcing most of them to immediately quit; later, a well-known black man "who had the respect of all law-abiding whites" was also seized from his home and severely assaulted. Anonymous letters from a group styling itself the "Laborers' Union Band" were sent to the superintendent and owner of the mill demanding that no blacks should be hired, which prompted the mayor of Griffin to call out the militia to protect mill officials and the mill itself. Having frightened off black workers in the cotton mills, "The band then turned its attention to [other] employers of negroes in Griffin and warned them to dispense with colored labor and secure white men in their place." A notice appeared in town declaring: "no negro will be allowed to ask for employment at certain manufactories, and in fact should not have any employment that comes in competition with white labor."[76] White mill workers staged several such successful strikes across the plantation South, ensuring that mill work remained a white preserve well into the twentieth century.

White workers knew that such assaults against blacks could be represented as a defense of white supremacy and white womanhood. Actual or threatened violence against blacks therefore became a card that white workers used against their employers, forcing them to reconsider the hiring of black employees. An early attempt to employ blacks in the textile industry epitomizes this racial conflict. In 1899, the owners of the Oxford Knitting Mills in Barnesville, Georgia, sought to introduce three black workers into the mill. For several months before that, the three men had been employed on the premises of the mill, to the dissatisfaction of white mill workers. No incidents had arisen, however, because "the work is said to be of a nature that a white man should not be required to do." The decision to move the men into the factory, where they would work alongside white women, was received as an intolerable violation of racial custom. In protest, the white women went on strike and forced the mill to close. In response, the president of the mill caved in to the women's demands and dismissed all black employees. But the incident had threatened racial etiquette within the working class and aroused wider racial animosities amongst whites. Anonymous posters appeared in town warning blacks against returning to the mill and, to drive the point home, local blacks were randomly assaulted in a series of violent attacks.[77]

A strike by white workers at the Fulton Bag and Cotton Mills in 1897 followed a similar pattern and illustrates the nature of industrial segregation in the South. In an attempt to overcome a shortage of workers, Jacob Elsas, president of the mill, attempted to employ twenty-five black women as folders in his mill. Sensitive to local racial etiquette, Elsas prudently ensured that all norms of segregation would be preserved. The black women were not only employed in a segregated compartment of the mill but were also confined to a separate floor. No black men were to be employed. Elsas communicated these arrangements to the white women ahead of time and, to prevent any trouble, ensured that the black women arrived at the mill well ahead of their white counterparts. The white women were unmoved by these precautions. With the support of the white male employees, they brought the factory to a standstill by noon.

The arrangements that Elsas had made suggests that he approached the issue in purely racial terms. By this reckoning, spatial segregation within the mill would suffice to mollify his white employees. White mill workers, however, also saw the issue in economic terms and did not pause to extricate the two. Although they looked upon spatial segregation within the mill as a non-negotiable demand, for them the issue was not merely one of racial etiquette, it was also one of jobs: in their view, any job given to a black employee was a job denied to a white. This economic view was buttressed by an important aspect of racial wages in the New South, according to Gavin Wright. The dominance of a low-wage agricultural economy at the turn of the nineteenth century virtually guaranteed that white and black wages would be not only low but identical in many cases.[78]

Mill workers were thus not exclusively concerned with wage levels – specifically, that black workers would underbid them in the labor market – and may have been more concerned with sheer access to employment. Whether black and white females were consigned to separate floors in the mill was thus not the only issue. As one of the striking women bitterly observed, "It is all piece work and so far as we were informed all would be paid the same price. There was no question of difference in wages in the case."[79] The Fulton strike received wide support across the South and newspapers ran articles roundly condemning the mill owners for tampering with racial etiquette and especially for subjecting white women to intolerable "racial equality." Faced with this region-wide hostility and alarmed by calls for boycotts against the Fulton mill, the mill owners gave up, handing the striking white workers a "swift and complete" victory by promising to never again employ any blacks in the mill.[80] The virtually complete exclusion of blacks from the early days of the textile industry underscores Michelle Brittain's observation that whiteness yielded at least some material benefits: "not only did race determine occupation, but in time occupation played a determining role in defining race."[81]

As with other white Southerners, it required little for poor whites to participate in or initiate violence against blacks. William Brundage recounts an incident that led to the lynching of four black miners at the hands of white miners in Clifton Forge, Allegheny County, Virginia, in 1891. The four were part of a group of six black miners who spent the day drinking, shopping and carousing in Clifton Forge. Their boisterous behavior attracted the attention of a police officer, who attempted to arrest them. The miners refused to be taken, however, and began the return journey to the nearby coal mines. Meanwhile, the police officer, feeling "humiliated," formed a posse that took off after the departing men. A gun battle ensued and two members of the posse were seriously wounded, one of them mortally. News of the violent encounter raced back to Clifton Forge, and armed white men poured into the woods where they eventually captured four of the black miners and held them in the town jail. A mob of white men soon broke into the jail, and three of the prisoners – one Miller, John Scott, and William Scott – were dragged into the woods. The men were permitted to say their final prayers before being lynched and shot hundreds of times. The fourth prisoner, Bob Burton, holed up in his cell with a shattered leg, was next taken from his cell, strung up alongside his swaying companions and his body also filled with leadshot.[82] Idus Newby also recounts an incident in which a white mill worker in Salisbury, North Carolina, led a mob of thirty white co-workers who broke into the local jail and lynched a black mill employee, George Hall, who was suspected of "killing a white family."[83]

That lynching served as a broad affirmation of plebeian whiteness is clear in the correlations that William Brundage establishes between social class and types of lynching. Variations in types of lynching, Brundage argues, were linked to three forms of honor amongst whites: individual, social and communal "honor." Like all Southern men, poor white men were permitted to violently retaliate against any black who affronted their *individual honor*; like wealthier white citizens, poor white men were therefore as likely to impulsively murder blacks for the most trivial reasons. But his low social standing meant that a poor white man could not easily summon a large mob to publicly lynch a black man. Poor whites were accordingly more likely to settle affronts against individual honor with private lynchings that are often difficult to cleanly distinguish from common murder.

The limitations of low status, however, were offset by a deadly option that enabled poor whites to transmute a private lynching into a communal affair. It was possible for poor whites to escalate any encounter into a matter of *social honor* – that is, into an issue involving family, property and womanly virtue – and so significantly increase the likelihood of a mob execution. Yet, even in such cases, poor whites could not assume the full support of the white community and so were likely to resort to what Brundage classifies as a lynching by a "terrorist mob" such as the one that executed Will Jones, a black tenant farmer in Schley County, Georgia, in 1922. A friend of Jones had provoked white outrage by offering a white woman a ride in his car. When rumors circulated that whites planned to whip the man, Will Jones made it clear that he would protect his friend. In this case, a terrorist mob attacked Jones in his home at night, sparking a gunfight that wounded Jones and several of the attackers. Jones was eventually captured and shot to death.[84] Terrorist mob executions of this sort were most likely when the social standing of the affronted white party was judged to be low. This meant that terrorist mobs did not always enjoy the support of a town's leadings citizens from the 1920s onwards when newspapers began to castigate mobs for furtive executions and even called for or endorsed prosecutions in such cases. The usual response, however, was to avoid commenting on terrorist violence. Leadings citizens "accepted that a violation of white honor might demand extra-legal punishment but felt no responsibility to administer the punishment as a community."[85]

In contrast, they actively gave their support to poor whites when transgressions against racial etiquette impinged on *communal honor*. All whites looked upon transgressions of racial etiquette as a fundamental assault on communal honor that imperiled white supremacy itself. Hence, nothing reassured poor whites more of their racial standing than their ability to ignite a spectacle lynching that attracted the broad approbation and participation of all whites. However, only a select number of offenses – rape, murder and violent resistance to law enforcement agencies – could instantaneously slice through the complications of class to galvanize universal approbation and support for lynching.[86] Even the most innocuous challenge to the police set off the "John Brown syndrome," triggering wildly exaggerated rumors that portrayed all whites as actual or imminent victims of black immorality and criminality. In 1915, Daniel Barber resisted the local sheriff's attempt to arrest him on charges of bootlegging near Monticello, Georgia. Even after Barber was successfully arrested, accounts of his effrontery spread and whipped up a storm of white outrage. Two hundred whites rushed into the jail, removed Barber from his cell and prepared to hang him from a nearby tree. As often happened, the lynch mob clearly intended Barber's demise at the end of a rope to be received as a warning to all blacks. To broadcast the warning, Barber's son and two married daughters were also rounded up and brought to the scene. One by one, each family member was hanged while Barber was forced to watch before he, too, became one of the South's "strange fruit."[87]

Communal lynchings such as this were public manifestations of a major Southern accomplishment – employing racial violence to dilute class distinctions amongst whites. A common enterprise – hunting down, arresting, and jeering before ritually killing a black transgressor – reinforced common interests in white supremacy and concealed the asymmetrical relations that distinguished poor and affluent whites. Communal lynchings therefore functioned much as New South boosterism did. Both proclaimed to high- and low-born whites alike: "we are all in this together." As C. Vann Woodward observed well before the "whiteness studies" focused on the precarious nature of plebeian white identity in the "Solid South," "Boasts of white solidarity ... were often loudest in the presence of division."[88]

Poor whites were keenly aware that allegations of sexual attacks by blacks were virtually guaranteed to defeat objections to a proposed lynching. Moreover, glowing descriptions of the moral character of alleged rape victims bestowed a degree of social recognition and honor on poor white females that was usually lavished on affluent women only. Poor whites therefore had every incentive – and many opportunities – to link any affront by blacks to the "blackest of crimes." Poor white anxieties about inter-racial sex were the subtext of virtually all aspects of their relations with black men. The sexualization and criminalization of racial confrontations was made transparently clear in the case of the "Scottsboro Boys" in 1931–32. The origins of the celebrated trial that riveted the nation lay in a quarrel that broke out between two groups of white and black "hobos" on a freight train on 25 March 1931 near Paint Rock, Alabama. One of the white youths, returning from a trip to Huntsville where they had unsuccessfully looked for jobs in the cotton mills of Chattanooga, stepped on the hand of a black man named Haywood Patterson. A scuffle ensued. After they were forced off the train, the white men had the train stopped and the black men arrested for assault. It was at this point that two white women who were also on the train entered the drama. Although they were not part of the initial fight between the men, Ruby Bates and Victoria Price, who were dressed in men's attire, agreed to testify that the nine black men had raped them.[89]

Bates claimed that three of the men had raped her, while Price, a local prostitute, testified that six of the men had raped her. The women's motive was to escape prosecution for vagrancy and violating the Mann Act, which outlawed the crossing of state lines for "immoral purposes." According to their trumped-up testimony, "We was just poor working girls. We had got laid off at Margaret Mills and there weren't no work here in town so we caught a freight to Chattanooga to look for work ... [T]hey held us down and took turns ravishing us. I hope they all burn for what they did to me."[90] The rumor of rape raced from the city into the countryside. A mob said to be thousands strong and drawn from all social strata in surrounding areas quickly formed outside the jail. A band festively played "There'll be a Hot Time In The Old Town Tonight" while an all-white jury was assembled. Only the intervention of the National Guard spared the men from summary death. Within three weeks of the alleged rapes, eight of the nine black youths were convicted by an all-white jury and sentenced to death, despite a mountain of evidence proving that sexual assaults had not taken place, including numerous contradictions in the evidence given by Price and Bates and a medical report that ruled out rape.

The "Scottsboro Boys" escaped both extra-legal and legal lynching largely because communists in the International Labor Defense rushed to their assistance and turned their impending doom into a national debate. The case vividly underscored the ease with which even "shiftless" itinerant whites, a suspect category in most parts of the rural South, could convert a minor encounter into a rape incident worthy of a lynching involving the best of Alabama's burghers.[91] Dramatic and public affairs, communal lynching unleashed a common bloodlust that united men, women and children and enabled "lintheads, 'Big Mules' and 'tackies'" to suspend such vexing issues as wages, unions, prices at the commissary and perceived deficits of social status.

Indeed, lynching enabled white workers who regularly suffered violence at the hands of militias, state troops and "detective agencies" to themselves transmogrify into quasi-legal killers in the service of white supremacy. In the course of a strike on 19 December 1921, Fred Rouse, a black worker, was brought in as part of a contingent of scab workers to break a strike by white workers at Amour and Company in Dallas, Texas. When the striking miners accosted him as he crossed a picket line, Rouse drew a gun and wounded two striking brothers. The picket line instantly evolved, first into a posse that tracked down Rouse and then into a mob that "beat Rouse with iron boards ripped from a street-car window." Rouse was not expected to live when he was brought to the local hospital. Within hours a polite but insistent mob of unmasked men appeared at the hospital. They extracted the barely conscious Rouse from his bed, hanged him from a tree in the center of town and pointedly placed the gun he had used beneath the dangling body.[92]

The prospect of lynching a black men also brought excitement into the lives of people whose different socio-economic status was circumscribed by the common monotony of small-town Southern life. The prelude to a "triple lynching" provided an opportunity for cross-class male bonding in Kirvin, Texas, on 6 May 1922. "The lynchings followed one of the most thrilling man hunts in the history of these parts," a newspaper report proclaimed. "Farmers and business men of three counties joined together to comb every inch of the territory" before lynching "Shap" Curry, Mose Jones and John Cornish in the town square at dawn. Suspected of "the usual crime" – the rape of a white woman – the three men were horribly mutilated ("no organ of the negroes was allowed to remain protruding") and then, still alive, the men were "roasted in a bonfire that was kept going for six hours."[93] "Almost all Maryville [Missouri] – 3,000 strong – ... turned out for the feast of blood" when an unnamed black man, again suspected of "the usual crime," was incinerated in an African American church in January 1931.[94] In October of 1933, the *New York Times* printed an account of a communal lynching in which "ordinary men, farmers and townsmen" in Princess Anne, Maryland, orchestrated the lynching of a black accused of "the usual crime." The account drew attention to the motley composition of the mob: "In the wildest lynching orgy the state has ever witnessed, a frenzied mob of 3,000 men, women and children, sneering at guns and teargas, overpowered 50 state troopers" before dragging the corpse of their lynch victim through the streets.[95]

Lynching, in fact, provided "ordinary men" with the rare opportunity to threaten local elites and law enforcement officials who might move to apprehend them. Duty-minded officials were threatened, ruthlessly beaten and occasionally shot to death if they too ardently barred white mobs from their black quarry. Such attention to duty frustrated a large mob in Sherman, Texas, in 1930. To seize the black prisoner, the mob entirely destroyed the Grayson County Courthouse. Similarly, 300 men in El Campo, Texas, attempted to simultaneously lynch no fewer than "five Negro men and four Negro women" who had been detained for questioning in the murder of a white man. When State Rangers herded the suspects into a café owned by a white man, the mob burned the building to the ground.[96] A graphic illustration of the rapid inversion of power between sheriff and white civilians took place in Lima, Texas, in 1916. Despite its best efforts, a mob failed to induce Sheriff Sherman Ely to reveal where he had hidden a black prisoner detained for questioning in a rape. "The mob seized the Sheriff, stripped him of his clothes, kicked, beat and cut him, dragged him to the principal street corner of this town and tied a noose around his neck threatening to hang him to a trolley pole ..." For heroic but unrecorded reasons, the sheriff refused and the mob dispersed.[97] The mayor of Omaha, Alabama, was not as fortunate. The mayor was himself lynched in September 1919 for attempting to prevent the lynching of a black prisoner.[98]

Such brazenness is all the more noteworthy because Southerners placed a premium on the region's law-abiding, authority-respecting and property-protecting reputation.[99] The determination to lynch frequently dissolved all distinctions of class and status amongst whites. A well-regarded employer who was prepared to vouchsafe for the victim's "character" sometimes saved blacks on the verge of being lynched.[100] On other occasions, men who ordinarily submitted to the authority of local police and employers declined to do so when a lynching was in the offing. Assuming the status usually accorded to elites squarely placed ordinary whites within the circle of whiteness.

Conclusion

Lynching bore a strong relationship to the monocrop economy and weakened wherever economic diversity prevailed. This pattern reflects the ability of planters to transform the initial pattern of political terror they had fomented to destroy Reconstruction into a broad campaign to subjugate freedmen to the oppressive regimens of labor tenancy. Competition between African American and poor whites for employment also increased as the South slowly began to industrialize. After Bourbon Democrats violently dismantled the Populist movement, depriving poor whites of their only potent weapon against landowners and employers in industry, extra-legal violence against African Americans became important to the "plain folk" of the New South. Unable to extract adequate benefits from employers, poor whites asserted their whiteness by endorsing not only segregation but also the emerging tradition of racial lynching.

By and large, class distinctions and the perceived seriousness of the offense that African Americans were alleged to have committed largely determined whether racial violence would yield either private or communal forms of lynching. At the same time, white civil society provided ample leeway for whites from all classes to override these determinants. In the miasma of segregation in the New South, the distinction that William Brundage establishes between "specific alleged transgressions" and outright caprice frequently evaporated. Thus, even the most trivial work-related disputes between whites and African Americans were capable of escalating well beyond private violence on quiet Southern farms into a carnival of communal violence that temporarily bonded all whites together and, not incidentally, also reinforced the hegemony of the agrarian class.

4

Racial violence and state intervention in the South African economy

> The white group in South Africa can say, with Louis XIV of France, "*l'état c'est moi*"! — R. F. Hoernlé[1]

In the aftermath of the Anglo-Boer War, whites in South Africa pursued two strategies that distinguished state formation from the path followed in the USA. They constructed a centralized state and authorized state officials to intervene extensively into the economy. With the American Civil War foremost in mind, British and Afrikaner representatives at the negotiations leading to post-war unification explicitly rejected a federal system. Federalism, they reasoned, would exacerbate intra-white conflict, a prospect that the presence of the large black majority in South Africa rendered decidedly dangerous. Once liberals in the Cape Province dropped their proposal to extend the non-racial franchise to Africans in the other three provinces, the passage to a centralized, Westminster-style state was cleared.[2] It is significant that the state's "Native policy" at this time was informed by the ideology of benevolent paternalism and that the upper reaches of the civil service were dominated by liberal administrators. These men were wary of black opposition and were ideologically opposed to the sorts of overtly repressive controls that South Africa's farmers and white workers increasingly favored. In sharp contrast to state authorities in the American South, the South African civil service declined to surrender authority to violent white citizens. Indeed, to the chagrin of farmers in particular, senior administrators even hesitated to utilize the full range of the powers they lawfully possessed to control Africans.

Whites immediately set about expanding the role that the state would play in imposing order on a contested and violent industrial economy. However, mine owners, farmers and manufacturers pressed competing agendas on the state. They therefore injected discord into the state's search for a coherent "Native policy." Still, all employers depended on state controls to secure and control their black labor. Divided though they were, they were all nevertheless locked into the orbit of the state. Employers' statism – that is, their support for and dependence on an interventionist state – impacted racial violence in a critical way.

On the one hand, employers entrusted the business of controlling black workers to the state. They therefore yielded to paternalist sentiments within successive governments in the inter-War years, all of which rejected the extensive use of violence against blacks. Statism in South Africa therefore precluded a tradition of collective violence against blacks because this function remained firmly in the hands of paternalist state officials. On the other hand, state authorities themselves shared the racist presumptions of the day, including the broad view that paternalism justified the judicious use of physical force by individual employers to discipline blacks and "teach them a lesson" – as long as such violence did not lead to organized counter-violence by blacks. The combination of trends that precluded communal violence but encouraged private violence against blacks establishes the master difference between the South African and Southern economies with respect to the role of racial violence. This pattern meant that, although Southern-style lynchings did not take place in South Africa, the work place nevertheless remained a violent and dangerous arena for South Africa's black workers.

State control over white labor contributed to this same trend. Chapter 3 showed that the racism of the emerging white proletariat in the postbellum South entailed a sometimes vitriolic enmity towards blacks that a desultory bi-racial movement failed to stanch. White workers in South Africa were no less racist and a great deal more averse to the prospect of inter-racial unions. Still, one of the most striking contrasts between the two racial orders is that white South African workers did not translate their "fear of displacement" by cheaper black workers into organized violence against blacks.[3] Instead, South Africa's white workers embraced an aggressive unionism that held *employers* – not Africans – directly accountable for their woes. South Africa's white workers were keenly aware that social segregation of the sort that Jim Crow laws enshrined in the American South would not guarantee their status as members of a privileged racial elite. What distinguished white workers in South Africa was their demand for explicit legal guarantees that would boost their material position and catapult them above black workers. To this end, white workers channeled their "fear of displacement" into militant and combative labor movements that violently challenged the employment policies of mine owners and the legitimacy of the state. They demanded to be included in the statist pacts that employers and state authorities forged in the two decades after unification. White workers presented the state with its greatest threat in the first half of the twentieth century, but, no less than employers, they too rallied to the ideology of statism.

In response to mounting pressure from employers and white workers, successive governments from 1910 onward embarked on a campaign to modernize and boost the interventionist powers of the state. They did this chiefly by empowering the state to control the turbulent industrial arena and the field known as "Native Affairs," both of which were still ambiguous and uncertain in the decade after 1910. The combined drift of these trends reinforced a state-oriented perspective within the white population generally. In South Africa, all roads led to the central state. Employers turned to the state to administer a labor allocation system sufficiently flexible to meet their competing labor demands; white workers pressured the state to actively eliminate the "poor white problem"; and the segregationist state garnered greater powers for itself to modernize and strengthen the racial order. The early consolidation of a broadly statist ideology and the establishment of an interventionist state are central to the *differentiae specificae* of racial violence in South Africa: the absence of communal violence amidst high levels of private violence against blacks.

Economic diversity and structural violence in the South African economy

It was argued in Chapter 3 that variations in patterns of lynching in the New South were related to an important difference between monocrop and diversified economies. Extra-legal violence was highest and communal lynchings were more likely to occur in the monocrop economies of states such as Georgia and Mississippi. But in the diversified economy of Virginia, lynchings were not only much less frequent but also more likely to take the form of private violence perpetrated by small groups of men to settle minor affronts to personal honor. Wherever manufacturing industry and a reliance on skilled black and white labor prevailed in Virginia, for example, employers were much more reluctant to support the summary killing of valuable employees. The early disappearance of communal lynchings in these areas reflected the absence of the conditions that promoted a societal consensus over the most public and gruesome forms of racial killing.[4]

Developments in South Africa support the argument that racial violence was at least partly conditioned by the complexity of the economy. In contrast to the relatively straightforward political and economic dominance of farmers in Black Belt states, a complicated constellation of class and ethnic tensions drove state formation in South Africa. From its outset in 1910, the South African state displayed a degree of structural differentiation that contrasted with the long-term dominance of monocrop production in the South. As a result, farmers, urban employers and mine owners developed important differences over a range of issues such as taxation, subsidies and infrastructural requirements. However, the most divisive issue in the decades immediately after 1910 centered on increasingly acrimonious competition over access to cheap black labor.

White employers felt that South Africa possessed vast reservoirs of cheap black labor. Unfortunately, this labor was still tied to the land as peasant producers in the "tribal areas." Industrialization in a context of so-called "labor shortages" gave rise to two major questions that shaped the emergence of South Africa's coercive labor control system. Firstly, how should "tribal members" be dislodged and converted into cheap labor in the developing capitalist economy? Secondly, how should employers share access to this bonanza? These two questions injected discord into relations amongst employers, undermining concerted efforts to unify Afrikaners and English-speaking whites by dispelling the bitter aftertaste of the Anglo-Boer war. The prospect of cheap black labor therefore became an increasingly rivalrous commodity in the two decades after 1910. However, whites who were deeply divided by fractious disputes over black labor were also reflexively united by a fear of black opposition. Peasant unrest in the "tribal areas," the beginnings of moblization amongst farm workers in the white rural areas and the emergence of strikes by black workers kept this fear simmering.[5] Unable to coordinate their labor demands on their own, whites quickly agreed to transfer to the state the task of shaping an appropriate labor control system. This bedrock consensus underlay the broad support that all whites gave to the emerging policy known as "segregation."[6]

Economic diversity at the outset of capitalist development in South Africa therefore generated two important outcomes: it undermined the emergence of a uniform labor regime across the economy and fully implicated the state in establishing and maintaining not one, but several divergent racially coercive labor regimes across the economy. Two factors were particularly salient in preventing whites from rallying around a uniform system of repressive controls.

Firstly, employers in the three sectors relied on *different kinds of cheap black labor*. In South Africa, as in other industrializing colonial contexts, the integration of pre-capitalist and capitalist economies yielded a complex class structure with a range of labor forms. "Cheap labor" in South Africa therefore assumed a complex variety of forms, but for the purposes of this study, may be reduced to three ideal types: migrant labor, labor tenants and wage workers. Generating and managing these three forms of labor required contrasting policies that pitted employers against one another. Unable to sort out their differences on their own, employers looked to the state to devise a practical solution for regulating access to cheap labor.

Secondly, employers in the three major sectors also relied on different strategies for *securing the labor effort of their black workers*.[7] Apart from the handful of Africans who possessed the vote in the Cape, all Africans were disfranchised and, in theory, were therefore equally vulnerable to the incentives, inducements and coercion that whites used to obtain their labor. In practice, however, the nature of production in the three sectors differed significantly. As a result, employers in the mining, farming and industrial sectors championed competing policies for obtaining labor and linked these to different strategies for extracting labor from their black employees. The result was that coercive devices that worked in one sector did not work in another. This outcome of capitalist development contrasts significantly with patterns in the American South, where the smothering dominance of agrarian interests facilitated a durable consensus over the role of violence in reproducing and disciplining cheap black labor. Violence was therefore a "one size fits all" solution to the problems of securing and controlling cheap black labor in the Southern plantation economy. The early complexity of the South African economy yielded a different dynamic, as we see below. Copious studies have explored the competing labor policies that shaped state policy in the inter-War years, and only a brief summary is necessary here.[8]

Mine owners were principally concerned with inducing black workers into oscillating between mining areas and the reserves, and linked the industry's fortunes to migrant male labor, "tribal reserves," and pass documents to control the mobility and employment of migrant workers. To buttress the migrant labor system, the mines championed the policy of setting aside "Native reserves" which, theoretically, would subsidize the reproduction of the migrant worker's family. Mine owners therefore sought to enlarge the initial size of the reserves established in accordance with the Natives Land Act of 1913. They also looked to formal bodies to recruit, regulate and discipline their black workers.[9] To implement the pass laws and discipline black mine workers, the Chamber of Mines relied on cooperation amongst its own inspectorate, the South African Police, and the clutch of "Native administrators" who supervised the pass system. To control workers on the mines, the Chamber instituted a quasi-formal "induna" ("bossboy") system for surveilling migrant workers in company-built hostels, infusing "tribal" structures into the bureaucratic system developed to manage black workers. Finally, as we see below, the mines developed a reputation for tolerating the physical violence that white workers used to uphold racial etiquette in the mining areas. Unprovoked thrashings and attacks with bare hands, sometimes resulting in fatalities, became a staple of the black worker's underground experience.

Farmers were primarily dependent on black labor tenants. Sharecropping or "farming on the halves" dominated the sector, providing the only means by which the majority of mostly Afrikaner farmers were able to remain afloat. Only a small number of wealthy farmers – the so-called "progressive," invariably English-speaking landowners – were in a position to engage wage laborers. Alongside labor tenants and the small number of wage laborers, a large community of independent African peasants managed to subsist on land they either owned or rented from white absentee landlords. This peasantry was therefore in a position to avoid working for labor-hungry white farmers. Farmers demanded legislation that would convert independent black peasants into labor tenants and prevent them from moving freely within and outside the rural areas. As in the American South, labor tenancy directly exposed black workers and their families to the control of farmers, and commercial farming became notorious for institutionalizing high levels of physical violence against blacks in the *platteland* (the white rural areas). Cut off from public scrutiny and keenly aware that they were dependent on a labor force they regarded as "primitive tribal people," farmers were notorious for resorting to physical violence to uphold the compliance and obsequiousness of rural blacks. In addition to relying on the pass laws – which were administered by formal state institutions – individual farmers also set considerable store on their right to personally control black workers; for example, farmers ensured that the "whipping clause" that had existed in the days of the Transvaal Republic was incorporated into farm labor legislation in the twentieth century. More so than in the other two sectors, extensive physical violence became a hallmark of agricultural employment.

Urban industrialists also supported the pass system. Like all white South Africans, they demanded racial segregation and accepted the policy of "territorial segregation" embodied in the creation of reserves for Africans in 1913. Unlike mine owners and farmers, however, they were much less attached to extra-economic controls that impeded the movement of cheap black labor into the Union's towns. Instead, urban employers were distinguished by their reliance on an urbanized labor force and a willingness to accept blacks as a permanent and irreversible presence in the country's urban areas. They denounced the punishing regime in the rural areas and lobbied for tepid versions of the pass laws. Urban employers therefore emerged as the champions of a weak "liberalism" in South Africa. When strikes and a militant African nationalism politics emerged in the urban areas immediately after the First World War, urban employers pressed the state to address the material needs of the growing population of blacks in the Union's urban areas. While mine owners and farmers adhered inflexibly to static and apocryphal "tribal" conceptions of Africans, industrialists were compelled to confront the declining purchase of "tribal" discourse in the Union's bustling urban areas and the unmistakable signs of industrial mobilization in the Union's larger cities. At precisely the same time that the strike by white mine workers in 1922 apprised the state of the virtues of a depoliticized white labor movement, African struggles in the mines, factories and segregated townships prompted urban employers to contemplate the same proposition for black workers. Even as they accommodated themselves to the racially restrictive measures that mine owners and farmers pressed on successive governments, urban employers explored modern forms of governance for controlling the increasingly restive black proletariat.[10]

White employers in South Africa therefore shared a definite consensus over a racially repressive labor market but differed over the nature of the controls required to incorporate blacks into the economy. Viewing one another as rivals in the quest for cheap labor, each sought to limit the other's access to black labor. Mine owners and farmers favored policies that pointed the state in different directions: one to the bureaucratic management of the migrant labor system, the other to labor tenancy arrangements that subordinated black workers to the direct control of farmers. Urban employers added to this tension by developing an antipathy to draconian labor controls that might restrict the size and skill levels of the urban black labor force. They therefore maintained a measured distance from the tribal discourse that saturated mine owners' policies and, with even greater clarity, rejected the coercive regimes that defined tenancy in the agrarian sector.[11] In South Africa, a broad white consensus over segregation therefore also encompassed significant tensions over the way Africans would be incorporated into the capitalist economy.

Unable to impose a uniform regimen on all Africans, successive governments in the two decades after unification sought to develop a labor allocation system that would balance the three-cornered conflict over the organization of the labor market.[12] Reflecting the dominance of the mining sector, the first measure that anchored the framework was the Native Labor Regulation Act of 1911. As its preamble plainly stated, the Act sought to "ensure as far as possible a more equal division between conflicting industrial mining and agricultural interests in different parts of the Union ..."[13] The second major measure that fleshed out the labor allocation system was the Natives (Urban Areas) Act of 1923. This complex piece of legislation sought to stabilize the urban labor force by calibrating the growth of urban black communities to the provision of basic residential services in the segregated "urban Native locations" that the Act provided for. The final cornerstone of the labor allocation system was the 1932 Native Servants Contract Act. The primary purpose of this oppressive piece of legislation was to rationalize and protect labor tenancy in agriculture, but it also contained provisions to gradually phase out this system.

This brief survey cannot capture the mounting complexity of the labor allocation (or "pass") system that came into being in the inter-War years. Nevertheless, it underscores the divergent interests and policies that prevented white employers from coalescing around a single strategy for dealing with Africans, prompting employers to accept a massive state presence in the economy. Regardless of the variable strength of their commitment to this basic principle, whites in South Africa supported policies that deeply embroiled state authorities in all facets of the labor market. The result was the early emergence of a bureaucratic culture that limited the institutionalization of Southern-style personal violence and systematically amplified the "structural violence" of the state in South Africa.

Structural violence and state formation in the South African economy

Johan Galtung coined the phrase "structural violence" to direct attention away from dramatic forms of "manifest" violence. Galtung notes that manifest violence is attention-grabbing because perpetrators usually intentionally cause the harm they inflict on others, whereas structural violence is distinguished by its taken-for-granted character. Galtung's distinction between manifest and structural violence is of particular importance to the pattern of violence in South Africa. "Ethical systems directed against *intended* violence," Galtung warns, "will easily fail to capture structural violence in their nets – and may hence be catching the small fry and letting the big fish loose." Galtung also suggests that social orders in which manifest violence is rampant are more rigid and less able to limit the spread of violence throughout society. In contrast, social orders in which structural violence predominates are distinguished by their greater ability to "compartmentalize" manifest violence – that is, to confine it to particular spheres. They are also better equipped to explore alternatives to high levels of spectacular violence. Levels of personal violence may actually be high wherever structural violence prevails as the signature form of violence, but this condition may be also obscured. Because it permits regimes some degree of flexibility as well as a capacity to engage in "legitimation excercises," structural violence frequently leads to patterns ("successions of periods of absence and presence of [manifest] violence") which conceal the ubiquity of violence.[14] State formation encouraged such a pattern in South Africa's administered economy. Three motifs stand out within this pattern.

Firstly, structural violence became a civil religion in South Africa. Statism encouraged amongst whites the impression that the wide-ranging violence used to institutionalize segregation was no more than "policy" and quotidian "administration." Structural violence frequently appears benign, remote and unintentional.[15] The Native Land Act of 1913, the measure responsible for transforming thirteen per cent of South Africa into "tribal reserves," exemplifies the logic of structural violence. Native administrators routinely acknowledged the Land Act as the "cornerstone of Native administration" and the paternalist policies they implemented in the reserves. In fact, the Act marked a fundamental assault on Africans. The measure destroyed Africans' access to land outside the reserves, led to the summary ejection of thousands of Africans and the subsequent ejection of hundreds of thousands more, and guaranteed a crisis of landlessness and grinding poverty which, by design, would force males into the migrant labor system. Reserves that were already unable to support the African population in the 1920s became the matrix of untold hardships that included malnutrition, climbing infant mortality rates, violent disputes over access to scarce land, the extraction of able-bodied men from the peasant economy, the dilution of family systems and the "double oppression" of women left behind by migrant male family members.[16] Structural violence of this nature was the spine of white prosperity in South Africa – yet it was largely invisible to whites, who persisted, for example, in portraying the reserves as a bucolic paradise.[17] Indeed, structural violence enabled the white administrative corps responsible for governing the reserves to actually *reverse* the causal dynamic of immiseration in the reserves. For example, Native administrators attributed the deteriorating physical and human condition of the reserves to the "inefficient farming methods" of subsistence agriculture and not, as Africans volubly protested, to the unsustainably high population densities which the Act itself created. The callous but unintentional inversion of the causes of African hardship in the reserves suggests the powerful ideological and cultural forces that arise to legitimate structural violence and help to explain its "invisibility."[18]

Secondly, the predominance of structural violence in South Africa overshadowed the persistence of direct personal violence throughout the South African economy. One of the most pervasive myths in the segregation years therefore portrayed whites who brutalized blacks as "a few bad apples" who departed from the norms of Western civility, including those that mandated the "just treatment of the Native." The phrase "a few bad apples" was routinely applied to citizens and state officials alike, effectively masking the extent to which personal violence was an ineradicable feature of both white civil society and the official bureaucracy. Personal violence tended to be extraordinarily high wherever white superordinates were able to exert direct control over Africans, which explains why physical violence was endemic to mine shafts and *platteland* areas. White men, whether as employers or supervisors, were not alone in looking upon personal violence against blacks as germane to their dominant masculinity. Whenever formal constraints are weak, Galtung notes, structural violence readily provides a cover for personal violence.[19] It therefore comes as no surprise that brutal police and authoritarian Native administrators regularly discounted their own paternalist creeds and either condoned or made light of the private violence that white civilians committed against Africans. In the end, structural violence encouraged ordinary civilians to game the system and inflict personal violence on vulnerable subordinates, knowing that their actions were likely to be either excused or only lightly punished.[20]

Thirdly, the extensive institutionalization of structural violence in South Africa left its mark on the racial order in a critical way: it ensured that white citizens would not inflict *collective* violence on black individuals. In ways that were impossible in the American South, the liberals who ran the segregationist state were careful to codify the use of violence against blacks and entrust this function to law enforcement authorities such as the police, Native administrators and the army. This arrangement was regularly breached in practice in the mining and farming sectors in particular, accounting for the voluminous records devoted to "the shooting of Natives." Nevertheless, these liberals paid more than lip service to standard settler colonial cant about "the just treatment of Natives." To the intense ire of farmers in the 1920s and 1930s, state authorities, especially the more senior personnel in the Native Affairs Department and the Department of Justice, often repudiated their own powers to administer those labor controls which they viewed as excessively "oppressive." This tendency was most pronounced in the control of African farm labor. For example, administrative officials chose to occasionally prosecute brutal farmers while doing little to prevent African tenants from "deserting" one farmer for another or from departing the rural areas entirely, either for the mines or, increasingly as the years wore on, for the relatively benign conditions and greater freedoms of the urban areas.[21]

Official ambivalence over the opressive measures they controlled limited the role that violence played in the economy. Although they often tolerated private violence within the workplace, administrators and law enforcement authorities also ensured that patterns of brutality would not evolve into a lynch culture that whites could celebrate at will in the public space.

Racial violence in the mining industry

Dependent on revenues from gold mining, successive governments did their best to collaborate with the Chamber of Mines by establishing policies that mine owners viewed as vital to the industry's profitability. The Chamber of Mines, for its part, "both feared intervention and understood that it could not survive without it." With the state willing to offer its services in return for gold-generated revenues, the Chamber of Mines entered into a "symbiotic union" with the state, the only body capable of protecting its labor sources and greasing the wheels of the migrant labor system.[22]

Close collaboration with the state and a reliance on official administrative and law enforcement bodies became central to the industry's development. Mine owners were therefore able to distance themselves from the coercive "bureaucratic"management of the migrant labor system. Migrant workers were housed in austere, all-male hostels that were segregated along "tribal" lines while "indunas" (African "headboys") were employed as subaltern assistants to white authorities on the mine. African workers remained under white supervision in every aspect of the mine's operations. Isolating black workers in "tribal" hostels complemented the isolating effects of the reserves themselves and ensured that black and white workers would never socialize under any conditions. Black and white workers were also separated by prevailing cultural distinctions that reinforced racial segregation. African workers were migrant workers who either had already established families on land in the reserves or looked forward to one day doing so. Few Africans spoke English or Afrikaans and the vast majority of whites did not speak any African language. A pidgin language therefore emerged to facilitate the giving and taking of instructions and so reinforced the social alienation of black and white workers. Religious differences also established a formidable divide between the two working classes, contributing to a cultural divide that was vastly greater than the chasm that existed in the post-bellum South.[23]

These factors accentuated the indentured and transient nature of migrant labor. Almost from the outset, therefore, migrant labor was larded with a cultural freight that whites reflexively understood as illuminating the "fundamental" difference between white "civilization" and African "tribalism." White mine workers never attempted to organize black workers and, with little thought to the matter, assumed, as legislation formally declared, that the term "employee" applied exclusively to "civilized" (white) labor. In contrast, African miners were formally distinguished as "mine workers." Racialized union rights turned on this semantic difference, since only "employees" possessed the right to bargain, and from 1924 onward, to form registered trade unions.[24] White workers, employers and state authorities were divided over many issues in the decades after union, but not over the subordinate position they believed Africans should occupy in the evolving industrial economy: all agreed that black workers had no political rights, no rights to collective bargaining and, because they derived income in the form of agricultural production in the reserves, also that they deserved a lower cash wage than white workers.[25]

Work on the mines provided ample opportunity for white supervisors to maltreat and brutalize black workers. Historians of the industry have demonstrated that violence against blacks was so pervasive that it amounted to an essential "rite of passage" that confirmed the masculinity of white workers. One study of violence on the mines notes that relations between white and black workers were "intrinsically violent" even before the First World War. The first formal investigation into violence on the mines, the 1913 Crown Mines Inquiry commission, revealed an engrained pattern of violence against black workers, who complained that "assaults" stemmed from the most minor lapse and sometimes for no reason at all. Workers reported that they were subjected to the full panoply of violence that "ranged from racist caprice to an elaborate sadism."[26] A black miner, Amos Bam, recounted to the Commission how he had been forced to stand on one leg while a white supervisor beat him with a plank soaked in water: "he'd beat till he stops when he feels like it and I wouldn't beat him back but then when I work and get used to the place, he asks me to put some planks in water so as to beat others – but when I arrived I was beaten as well." Three black miners employed by the Welgedacht Exploration Company reported that a white supervisor had "beaten them with a whip made of fuse rope while they were at their work tramming underground."[27]

As a rule, sheer proximity between black and white employees explained the frequency of assaults. Assaults were likely in places where contact was greatest in the mineshaft – such as in narrow tunnels and the areas where workers waited to embark on the cages that ferried them to and from the mine surface – and rare in areas where workers toiled with the least amount of supervision. The latter jobs were held by men with the greatest seniority and pay, meaning that the bulk of the violence that was the black worker's daily fare involved the newest and youngest recruits. Still, even senior mine workers reported that they were not spared from unpredictable assaults.[28]

Fatal assaults on Africans appear to have been extremely unusual, however. From his own archival research on racial violence on the gold mines, Keith Breckenridge concludes that lethal beatings most likely did not exceed "more than one every year."[29] Although no statistics about fatal assaults were uncovered, at least one such case occurred in 1926 on the Langlaagte mine. The prosaic tones of the formal document offer no clue to as to the frequency of such deaths. Titled "Assault on Native Jelliconise:

No. 371899/3766, Langlaagte Consolidated," a letter that an inspector in the NAD (Native Affairs Department) sent to the General manager of the Native Recruiting Agency (NRC) noted: "With reference to the above case brought to my notice by your Mr Gedye, I have the honor to inform you that I find that on the death of the native, after conviction and sentence of his assailant, the papers were sent to the Attorney-General who, however, declined to re-open the case" – strongly suggesting, in other words, that the NRC had sought to have the conviction against the white assailant reviewed and overturned.[30] In another case involving a fatality, the courts ruled, that "the native died, not as a result of the assault but from heat apoplexy." Mine authorities used the finding to justify the decision not to censure or dismiss the white assailant.[31]

Mining authorities were well aware of the scale of assaults on black workers but routinely came down on the side of white assailants. Blacks bold enough to report acts of violence were sometimes beaten by mining authorities themselves. The Chairman of the Crown Mines, for example, did not bother to dispute the violent aura that suffused the underground labor process. Speaking as a witness before the Crown Mines Inquiry of 1913, appointed to investigate allegations of violence on the Crown Mines, the Chairman of the mine, Samuel Evans, instead pointed to the functional benefits of underground violence. Beatings, he argued, instilled prompt compliance with instructions in a dangerous environment and "the prevention of serious accidents was dependent on such discipline."[32] In 1914, a white shift boss named John Barker severely beat "a native" with his fists and a wrench after being accidentally burned with an underground lamp. Although Barker admitted that "the burning of his hand was an accident and also confessed to having been warned several times about the ill-treating of natives," the manager of the East Rand Premier Mine recorded that Barker had reacted to "an incident of gross provocation by the boy." In this case, the Director of Native Labor rejected the manager's report and prosecuted Barker, securing a sentence of £10 or one month with hard labor.[33] In another of numerous similar cases in the archives on "assaults on mine Natives," a manager who had been fined £25 for assaulting "William 3607/422607" had his fine paid by the mine in an agreement stipulating that the payment was "not an admission for liability."[34]

Numerous assault cases were dismissed in courts after mine representatives testified that African complainants had "provoked" the incident.[35] According to R.W. Norden, an inspector for the NAD, "the department was aware that assaults on natives by miners [were] continuously happening on all mines along the Reef" and felt that, "notwithstanding evidence from compound managers to the contrary ... it [was] desirable as far as possible to test each case before a magistrate." In 1909, the department took the opinion that cases of assaults on black workers "were not unduly numerous in proportion to similar cases of assault on other communities in South Africa and elsewhere." But by 1920, the department had grown sufficiently wary of mining authorities' accounts of violence to circulate to inspectors and labor recruiters a continuously updated "Departmental Black List" of violent white miners it deemed "incorrigible."[36]

The complicity of management in the subterranean culture of violence was not surprising: violence was accepted as long as it did not debilitate the production process. And blacks, unlike the gathering storm of white labor unrest in the years after 1910, were still decades away from acquiring the capacity to disrupt the industry. More importantly, the times were not propitious for mine management to challenge a prerogative that white workers took for granted. As strikes by white workers in 1907, 1913, 1914 and 1922 underscored, relations between white workers and mine owners at the time of Union were gradually deteriorating around the issue of unemployment. In this increasingly volatile context, assaults on black workers were either dismissed as a non-issue or tolerated by mining authorities. Moreover, NAD officials charged with supervising the well-being of African mine workers were increasingly supportive of the industry. In a letter he sent to the Secretary for Native in October 1926, H. G. Falwasser, the Acting Director of Native Labor defended the decision by mine authorities to cease the practice of automatically dismissing whites who were convicted for assaulting blacks:

> At that time [c.1909] it used to be the practice for the Mines to summarily dismiss men convicted of assault, and, while such a cause gave great offense to the Unions who regarded it as amounting to a double punishment, it did not have the desired effect for the reason that skilled miners had no difficulty in finding employment on other Mines. In many cases assaults are due to momentary outbursts of temper or special provocation and a hard and fast rule of discharging in every case would savour of injustice ... Short of "blacklisting," to which there are serious objections, there is no means of preventing the re-employment of a man so discharged and I think that the matter should be left to the discretion of the management subject to the right of this Department to make special representations if unrest or dissatisfaction is likely to result from the continued employment of a convicted European on a particular mine.[37]

In practice, this meant that the department would not intervene, even when whites convicted of aggravated assault were retained in positions of direct authority over Africans. The case that initiated the correspondence into this issue provides further evidence of the cooperative relationship between the state and the industry. Although an African had been fatally assaulted, the courts reduced the charge against the two assailants, C.J. Smit and an African "boss-boy," from aggravated assault to "a case of common assault." Smit was spared the "double punishment" and fined £3. However, in keeping with its zero-tolerance of violence by blacks, the "boss-boy" was fined £3 and discharged to boot.[38]

Personal violence was a ubiquitous and degrading fixture of the black worker's underground experience, and there is little doubt that white workers well understood the connection between the caprice of personal violence and the structure of racial domination. Despite their own conflicts with mine owners, they grasped that "they functioned as representatives of an informal racial power within mine management."[39] The violence they deployed to assert their masculine identities and racial authority, after all, flowed from and buttressed similar themes that were inherent to a state bent on incorporating black males into the gendered and racial institutions that comprised the migrant labor system.

However, Dunbar Moodie suggests that interpersonal racial violence on the mines is only "partially explained by general cultural factors such as masculinity or race, social factors such as corporal punishment in schools, political factors such as state support for whites, or spatial factors such as working underground." For Moodie, the primary culprit lay in the organization of production relations on the mines and specifically in the "maximum average wage system" that emerged in 1913. In response to the precarious profits of "low grade" mines, mining companies agreed to hold down wages by suppressing inter-mine competition for "ultraexploitable" black labor.[40] However, placing a low ceiling on black wages also meant that mining authorities could not use the "carrot" of monetary rewards (or encourage the "game" that Michael Burawoy calls "making out") to boost the productivity of workers. Under pressure to maintain productivity, white workers resorted to the "stick" of violence to control the workers they supervised even when widespread violence failed to achieve its aims: "Efficient and non-violent production incentives were sacrificed on the alter of low wages."[41]

Confronted with physical beatings on a daily basis, black workers resisted by dissuading men in the reserves from seeking employment on the mines. A shortfall of 1,000 black workers at the Crown Mines alone led to the Chamber of Mines to appoint the Crown Mines Inquiry in 1913. Evidence from black workers in the course of the Inquiry revealed for the first time the scale and humiliation of underground interpersonal violence. On 6 July, just days after the inquiry ended, black workers staged a serious strike for higher wages that spread across the Reef mining area. Although police and army units quickly put down the strike, the episode revealed the threat that an ultra-low wage system posed to the mining industry and, by implication, to the state as well. However, the maximum average wage system was too vital to the low-grade mines to be modified, and the system remained in effect until the 1960s. Until that time, Moodie concludes, the sheer organization of the labor process was the principal matrix of interpersonal violence on South Africa's mines.

It is quite conceivable that a sustained pattern of racial violence on the mines could have escalated into a pattern of unrestrained murder. It is therefore important to explain why a tradition of quotidian violence by white workers did not escalate into a pattern of lethal assaults against vulnerable black subordinates. Two reasons explain the limits within which racial violence in the mining industry usually operated. One has already been suggested above: mine owners would not have tolerated a scale of white violence that interfered with the stability and profitability of the industry. Secondly, given the centripetal forces that pulled the *Weltanschauung* and material ambitions of all whites towards the state, what the state was prepared to tolerate clearly mattered a great deal. It is significant, therefore, that the state did not countenance systematic breaches of the legal and informal codes that limited violence to non-lethal attacks against black employees. Had the state not exercised a restraining influence, the possibility of quotidian violence evolving into Southern-style violence would have been significantly enhanced – not only within the mining industry, but across the country generally. The discussion below illustrates how these two factors worked to prevent popular racial violence from congealing into the system of "repressive justice" that prevailed across the South.

White workers and communal violence

The routinization of structural violence and the "containerization" of private violence account for almost all racial violence in South Africa. John Galtung notes that under the right conditions, however, civilians who regularly commit private violence are likely to coalesce into mobs and intentionally inflict death on members of the "outside group." This is often the case in "race riots," but the violence that occurs during riots differs from the interpersonal violence with which this study is mostly concerned. "In a lynching," one scholar notes, "there is an identity between precipitating agent and target that typically does not prevail in a riot."[42] Riots, in other words, are not intended to punish specific victims for specific offenses. Although they are not formless outbursts of inchoate passions as sociologists once argued, race riots derive their deadly power from the combination of "spontaneity" and "instrumental elements." The unscripted logic of race riots therefore permits even peaceable citizens to participate in collective attacks and "make a holiday of killing."[43] This is indeed what happened in the course of a massive strike by white mine workers in 1922.

The strike is remembered for the extraordinary violence the South African Party (SAP) government used to quell the uprising and as a critical event that directly reshaped the alignment of forces within the state. More than 250 white strikers were killed and more than 1,000 wounded before the strike was quelled. The strike led to the unseating of the SAP government in the election of 1924 and the formation of the Pact Government, an electoral alliance between the National Party and the Labor Party. Until recently, these epochal events completely overshadowed the massacre of blacks by white civilians.

Because communal racial violence was not a prominent feature of racial domination in South Africa, the racial massacre that occurred in 1922 stands out as a unique episode in which white workers successfully launched a lethal communal assault on blacks. In the course of their storied challenge to the mining industry in March 1922, white workers hunted down and murdered dozens of unarmed black bystanders in the streets of Johannesburg. Jeremy Krikler, to date the only scholar to dwell on this extraordinary event, observes that the massacre shares close parallels with the "Red Summer" race riots that erupted across US cities after the First World War.[44] Well after the strike had commenced, a number of white strikers turned on nearby black mine workers, igniting a fortuitous fracas that rapidly evolved into a cold-blooded massacre. As soon as the first killing of black innocents was underway, groups of strikers fanned out into the city, cold-bloodedly executing black passersby who strayed into view. After shooting blacks they encountered in the white quarters of the city, groups of strikers gunned down more victims in the black locations of Western Native Township, New Clare Township and Sophiatown, as well as in the racially mixed working-class neighborhoods of Vrededorp and Ferreirastown. Much of the racial killing took place in full view of white crowds that gathered to witness the violence. The number of casualties would almost certainly have been much higher had the police not come to the defense of African mine workers trapped in a mining compound that the strikers had put under siege. The twenty blacks who died on 7 and 8 March alone exceeded the numbers of blacks killed during Chicago's "Red Summer" race riot of 1919. In all, the total count of blacks who were murdered "approximated the number [47] of Jews murdered in the Kishinev pogrom of 1903."[45]

The similarities between these events and the urban "race riots" in America are indeed striking. Like the Red Summer riots of 1919, the 1922 massacre in South Africa occurred in a moment of acute stress and significant social change. Scholars of the Red Summer riots identify disruptive adjustments such as a heightened racial competition for housing and jobs immediately after the First World War as the immediate trigger that unleashed the violence. Likewise, the massacre in 1922 also erupted at the outset of a bitter strike against mine owners; it also occurred against a background of growing African urbanization, a shortage of housing for both whites and black workers, and an accelerating fear amongst Afrikaners that racially mixed residential areas would lead to the biological and cultural "degradation" – or *verkaffering* ("kafferization") – of poor Afrikaners. In both racial orders, which were already fraught with racial antagonism and suspicion, fast-moving rumors were critical in creating "a sense of generalized belief" that concentrated hostility on vulnerable black scapegoats.[46] Krikler therefore describes the riot of 1922 as a "socio-psychological phenomenon" triggered by "an intense fear that gripped white working class communities that they were about to be subjected to a general attack or rising by Africans."[47] By inducing feelings of what Donald Horowitz describes as "arousal, rage, outrage, or wrath," the rumor of an African uprising provided a "keenly felt sense of justification" that enabled whites to discard customary constraints against extra-legal murder.[48] Similar "Black Peril" rumors had also raced through working neighborhoods in the Red Summer of 1919 and, as in

South Africa, had also stimulated a sense of murderous self-defense amongst white mobs.

Yet it is precisely on this score that the lethal riot of 1922 also illustrates the contrast between racial violence in South Africa and the South. From beginning to end, white rioters in the Red Summer riots identified the black community as the object of their communal rage. In the events of 1922, however, white strikers did not set out to confront blacks. Nor did the racial attack, when it was concluded, bring the strike to the end. Blacks were attacked well *after* the strike had commenced, confirming the conventional arguments that the strike was not sparked by racial hostility against black workers. Moreover, once the army and police promptly terminated the racial massacre, the white strikers again refocused their resources and anger on the issue that had initiated the strike and remained the *casus belli* through its end: popular white anger against the "symbiotic" alliance between the SAP government and mining capital.[49] Two factors are particularly germane to the mass killing of Africans by mobs of white civilians.

First is the radical ideology that propelled "poor whites" in South Africa to view the state–employer alliance as the primary enemy of labor. This outlook distinguishes white South African workers from their counterparts in the New South. White workers in the American South were not passive agents who meekly endured their poverty. However, they reserved their greatest efforts to extract concessions that deeply reinforced their subordination to paternalist employers. At most, one sympathetic study of Alabama's textile workers concludes, paternalism "delivered small concessions in the form of welfare-like services and the recognition of whiteness."[50] In South Africa, white workers were much more secure about their "whiteness": the constitution of 1910, after all, formally conferred on them much of the "psychological wage" that plain whites in the South had to struggle for. White workers in South Africa were also more physically secure. Whereas "the right to form a union" is a storied part of America's violent labor history, the theme finds no counterpart in South Africa's industrial arena. White workers in South Africa did not experience the lethal violence that "detective agencies" (violent professional strike-breaking companies) regularly inflicted on labor movements in the US, although white trade unions in South Africa were formally recognized only in 1924. South African white workers were therefore concerned with more than the "psychological wage of whiteness" and "the right to form a union." What they demanded was the *material* substance of white supremacy. This demand ensured that white plebeian politics were much more confrontational and radical in South Africa.

What white workers demanded were "job color bars" that would formally spare them from having to compete with cheaper black workers for a range of jobs in the mining industry. A formal policy of job color bars has no parallel in the Southern economy, where employers would never have acceded to statutes, or even informal agreements, compelling them to employ whites over cheaper black workers. In contrast, job color bars were of fundamental importance to the "civilized labor policy" demanded by white workers after the First World War. Poor whites looked upon job color bars as the antidote to their "fear of displacement" by cheaper black workers. For Afrikaner workers and work seekers in particular, statutory protection against racial competition was an indispensable weapon in their struggles to bring the "poor white problem" to an end. Largely reassured about their formal classification as members of the ruling racial elite, whiteness, white workers saw in job color bars the *material* promises of racial citizenship in the racial state. With the support of the SAP government, however, mine owners rejected white workers' demands for an expansion of the job color bars. Instead, the Chamber of Mines proposed a "native labor policy" that would have reduced – but *not* abolished – the range of jobs covered by the job color bars. The 1922 strike was triggered by this disagreement over the range of jobs that should be covered by the job color bars.[51]

For white workers, cheaper black competitors in the labor market were not the principal threat to the material basis of whiteness. Of much greater importance was the "symbiotic union" between the Chamber of Mines and the SAP government. Workers who were reflexively racist therefore singled out white employers as their strategic enemy. White workers therefore planned and staged a tumultuous armed insurrection that was intended to extract greater material and statutory guarantees from the alliance between state and capital. White workers accordingly manned the barricades and bravely died in throngs during the 1922 strike in order to transform the racial order into a racialized workers' republic – although race was *not* the animating force of their rebellion. (Hence the banner they raised, "White workers of the world unite. You have nothing to lose but your chains.") That is, radical white insurrectionaries did not target blacks. While the subsequent massacre of unarmed blacks was indisputably an organic offshoot of white proletarian racism, Krikler correctly insists that the incident was brief, unexpected, and incidental to the thrust of the strike. Moreover, no further collective attacks against blacks were made, either later in the strike or in subsequent decades. White workers in South Africa did not develop a "tradition" of communal racial violence such as emerged in the American South.

The second point that flows from the mass killing of Africans by mobs of white civilians is the *state's* aversion to public violence. The persistent fear that Africans might stage counter-attacks touched on one of the Smuts government's greatest fears in the volatile decade after unification. Canny strikers had also sought to capitalize on the swirl of rumors about a violent African retaliation by offering to patrol the streets together with the police. This attempt at rapprochement with the uniformed foe, still possible in the early stages of the strike, was significant. It reflected an attempt to overcome and replace the class hostilities that were tearing white South Africans apart with a rekindled sense of racial community. The police, however, rebuffed the white workers' offer to help monitor Africans. Instead, police and army units raced to the assistance of Africans trapped in a compound that white workers had put under violent siege. Instead of excusing or aiding white attackers, Smuts' government charged at least one striker with murdering Africans in the course of the rebellion. Eight months after the strike ended, on 17 November 1922, Carel Stassen was duly hanged for murdering two African men during the convulsion of 1922.[52]

This response was less categorical than it sounds, for Stassen was by no means the only striker to have publicly executed blacks in cold blood. Nevertheless, Stassen's execution sent a clear symbolic message. By symbolically asserting its authority over a mobilized white citizenry, the state declared that it would not confound the distinction between private and communal violence: private violence by whites was tolerable as long as it was "containerized," but communal violence that threatened to engulf all of society in a racial war was not.

Agrarian violence

Just as the northern Army had permitted Southern Redeemers to regain control over the American South, a victorious Britain also struck an agreement that restored Boers to dominance in the agrarian economy immediately after the Anglo-Boer War. Bent on achieving political and economic stability as soon as possible, Britain almost immediately pursued policies that effectively returned blacks to the mercy of demoralized and vengeful Boers. Racial violence in the agrarian sector was shaped by these two forces: the construction of a racially paternalist state and the immediate restoration of Boer landlords, the country's future commercial farmers.

In the course of the war, Boer kommandos had resorted to a policy of massacring Africans, either because they suspected them of aiding the imperial enemy or to seize their livestock. Many kommando atrocities resembled white collective violence in the South in the Reconstruction period. It seems reasonable to expect, therefore, that collective violence by Afrikaners should have persisted and perhaps even escalated once Britain reneged on its vague promises to "liberate" blacks and took up the cause of assisting Boers instead. John Higginson, the only comparativist to explicitly compare Reconstruction-era racial violence in the two countries, points to the similar violent outcomes in the two postbellum racial orders:

> The 1873 Colfax War in Grant Parish, Louisiana, the 1876 Hamburg Riot or War in Edgefield County, South Carolina, the 1899 insurrection in Wilmington, North Carolina in the United States, and also the 1914 Rebellion in South Africa fit this pattern. The state stamped out these fitful and sporadic rebellions with half-hearted measures but failed to punish rebellious white landowners in any meaningful way... As a result, disgruntled whites retained their sense of grievance against the state and, more importantly, their capacity for violence.[53]

The parallel is suggestive but also misleading. Collective racial violence escalated and reached a frenzied peak in the two decades after Reconstruction in the American South and persisted with declining intensity for three decades after the First World War. In South Africa, collective racial violence dissipated during reconstruction and was virtually unknown after 1910. Conforming to the national pattern in South Africa, not even disgruntled and armed Afrikaner farmers caught in the post-war grips of a mounting "shortage" of cheap labor returned to the familiar kommando tradition to violently hammer home their renewed but still tenuous dominance over Africans. At the same time, Afrikaner farmers struggling for survival on the *platteland* would indeed go on to play the most prominent role in private violence. This section is therefore concerned with these two trends: the rapid extinction of collective racial violence and the escalation of private violence in South Africa's postbellum agrarian sector.

Boer atrocities do indeed bear a strong resemblance to the mob violence that dispatched hundreds of African Americans during Southern Reconstruction. Boers' capacity for cold-blooded racial murder was without doubt the bloody fruit of decades of frontier racism, wars that dispossessed Africans of their land and the inability of penurious Boer "republics" to impose orderly control over black "tribes." When nomadic bands of Boers departed the Cape colony, one source notes, they left behind the slave-holding past but took with them "the presumptions that would govern race relations and farm labor."[54] A sense of personal mastery over Africans was an inevitable pillar of the Boer patriarchs who controlled the wobbly "Boer republics" in the late 1800s. Bernard Mbenga's study of flogging practices in the Saulspoort area suggests that ritual violence was not used sparingly to impose control over Africans. As a young farmer and devout Christian, Paul Kruger, the future president of the Transvaal Republic, liberally whipped Africans who refused to render him forced labor. Several chiefs were publicly whipped for various acts of non-compliance between 1840 and 1870, suggesting that the violent abuse and debasement of commoners must have been vastly greater.[55]

Kommandos were also an emotional Boer symbol of alternative authority to British rule so that British victory in the Anglo-Boer war effectively brought the kommando age to a close.[56] However, kommando atrocities during the Anglo-Boer war were also a response to the nature of the war itself. The British army responded to Boer guerilla tactics by forcing Boer women and children, as well as local African communities, into concentration camps and interspersed numerous blockades across the Transvaal and the OFS, effectively severing central command over the Boer military forces. The result was the genesis of more or less independent guerilla bands of Boers who, furthermore, had to battle high attrition rates throughout the conflict. Small groups of Boer guerillas were forced to maneuver amongst and extract food supplies from Africans who not only overwhelmingly supported the British enemy but also made use of wartime conditions to wreak small measures of revenge against Boers who had taken over their lands.[57] It was in these specifically war-time conditions that Boer kommandos resorted to atrocities and ritual violence.

In May 1901, for example, two Boer members of a kommando led by Field Cornet Thys Pretorius dragged an African man named Krooles from his hut near Doornfontein, accused him of spying for the British Army and shot him dead in the presence of his family. A twelve-year-old boy named Ruta suffered the same fate at the hands of the same kommando near Pretoria in May 1901, as did another youth and two men in Vlakplaats in October 1901. In a memorandum dated 13 February 1902, Major H. Walton reported an incident in which a number of British soldiers escorted a convoy comprising an English doctor and eight Africans into a Boer camp at Modderfontein Ridge, presumably to provide medical and other assistance to the Boers after they had surrendered. Instead, the Boers attacked the convoy, killing the doctor and all eight Africans. Walker reported that "every single native was shot in cold blood" and "they were actually dodging about among the Tommies to avoid the Boers." Walton claimed that evidence placed "Smuts, the Staats-Procureur" at the scene, which, if true, implicated the future Prime Minister in "a slaughter that was not inconsiderable and one of the most dastardly wholesale heartless affairs I have ever heard of."[58]

Some Boer atrocities were as gruesome as anything perpetrated in the course of Southerners' uprising against Reconstruction. Late in 1900, for example, a Boer *kommando* captured several wagons and their African drivers:

> A native driver of one of the wagons appears to have been rolled up in a buck-sail by two men called Willem Barnard and Jan Van Rensburg; bags of oats were piled on the top of the sail, these were then sprinkled with paraffin, and the whole set on fire.

The same memorandum reported that Boers had murdered an additional 37 Africans near Kimberley and 23 more in Orange River Colony in the preceding few months, although it did not describe the circumstances of these killings.[59] On 5 June 1902, 13 Africans on a farm near Kana accosted a group of Boer men they accused of stock theft. In response, Field Cornet Michael du Plessis ordered his men to open fire, killing 7 Africans on the spot.[60] Numerous files report the brazen killing of unarmed Africans all across the Transvaal and OFS. "On the night of 1st October 1901, a party of Boers surrounded the house, and called on the kaffirs to come out … they killed 4 of the natives in or about the house" before asking one of the survivors "when the English were going to leave the country." Yet, when Boers caught two British soldiers and one African "scout" named Klaas on 10 December 1910 in the Clanwillima District, they released the two white men and executed the African. Upon searching for Klaas' remains, British troops found the bodies of four more Africans, all shot through the head.[61]

Of the nine black corpses discovered by a British unit on the Magaliesberg mountains, "Ears, tongues and genitals had been cut off." The remains of nine black bodies that a British unit discovered on the Magaliesburg mountains also bore marks of ritual desecration, conveying a clear symbolic warning to other Africans to stay out of "the white man's war." Five of the men had been paid scouts of the British army while the other four were suspected of providing intelligence to the British. Numerous blacks were executed on suspicion of being "spies," sometimes as a prelude to the seizure of the victims' stock.

Blacks often retaliated against Boer atrocities, although it is unclear how widespread their actions were. What is clear, however, is Britain's concern that war-time violence might persist into the Reconstruction years. At a time when peace with Afrikaners was high on Britain's agenda, Milner's Reconstruction administration therefore clamped down on African attacks against whites. The case of Chief Hans Masibi illustrates that Milner was anxious to avoid further racial violence of any sort after the war. From the spotty records that remain of this case, it appears that Hans Masibi had claimed at some point during the War that "the Boers had killed some of his tribesmen" and "as a retaliatory measure ... ordered his men to kill any burghers whenever they could be found." Nine of his men subsequently ambushed and killed three Boers. The men were arrested and at a trial held after the War were sentenced to death for the cold-blooded triple murder. A letter writer to a local newspaper objected to the sentence and came to Masibi's defense with the argument that "during the late war there was a contemporaneous state of war between the Boers and several native tribes."

In response to the letter, J.C Lyttleton, an official in the Governor's Office, wrote the Lieutenant-General, Sir Henry Rildyard, urging him to reject the letter writer's appeal for leniency on the grounds that Boers and Africans had in fact not been in a "state of war." In Lyttleton's opinion, the death sentence should have been passed on Masibi alone because he had "practically commissioned the murders." Yet Lyttleton remained uneasy with even this recommendation. He warned:

> the Government might carefully take into consideration the impression which will probably be created in the native mind if the death sentence is carried out ... Is it not almost inevitable that the natives will consider it an act of revenge on the part of the Boer Government? All that they will see is that for five years after the murders were committed, during which time the English administered the country, no action was taken to punish the perpetrators of the crime, while directly the Boers came to power the matter is at once taken up and nine men hanged.

Lyttleton's anxieties about the stability of the Reconstruction authority and the legitimacy of the law "in the native mind" saved the men's lives, their sentence being commuted to imprisonment for life.[62]

The restoration of Boer landholders: Labor tenancy and violence

The fortunes of Afrikaners underwent a dramatic and swift reversal from Empire's victim to Empire's partner within the space of a decade after 1901. For Boers, there would no Freedmen's Bureau to revile, no blacks to violently unseat from power and no racially egalitarian laws to rage against. Beginning with the terms of the peace treaty signed in Vereeniging in 1901 to the historic compromise in 1910 that left intact the tiny sliver of African voters in the Cape but denied political rights to all other Africans, Afrikaners fared immensely better than their defeated counterparts in the American South.[63]

Agricultural policy after unification initially aimed to keep as many white farmers on the land as possible. Rather than permit market forces to weed out the least productive farmers or exert pressure on conservative farmers to modernize their farms, the Department of Agriculture continued the Reconstruction strategy of providing extensive state support for agriculture.[64] To the relief of the majority of farmers, this meant immediate support for the sharecropping system. As in the South, sharecropping in South Africa became the farmer's bridge into the modern economy.

Meanwhile, however, Africans who had managed to evade dispossession continued to exist as a free peasantry. This black "squatter peasantry," as it was known, engaged in subsistence agriculture and had responded with notable success to the growing market for food that the mineral revolution stimulated in the late 1800s. In large measure, the history of capitalist farming in South Africa is the story of Afrikaners' desire to extend labor tenancy while destroying the independent peasantry. Twentieth-century agrarian demands may broadly be summarized as a two-step process. Firstly, the majority of farmers demanded measures that would forcibly eliminate "squatter peasants" and convert them into labor tenants on white farms. Secondly, farmers sought state assistance to gradually wean themselves off labor tenancy and make the transition to wage labor on terms that suited individual farmers.[65]

This second theme points to an important difference between South Africa and the American South with respect to the status of labor tenancy. In the US, Southern farmers hitched their fortunes to the long-term preservation of labor tenancy: for them, labor tenancy *was* the solution to their inability make the costly transition to mechanized production and wage-based labor. Preserving tenancy by all means at their disposal therefore became the conservative foundation of the region. State governments and white citizens closed ranks in defense of the institution until the system collapsed in the 1930s. In South Africa, labor tenancy did not set the standard by which the agrarian sector measured its prospects; neither did government officials ever fully approve of the practice. Farmers and state policy looked upon labor tenancy as a "halfway measure" in a process that should culminate, sooner rather than later, in full-blown capitalist practices. Thus, even farmers for whom labor tenancy was an indispensable lifeline were oriented towards a capitalist future in which mechanization, greater productivity and cash wages would prevail. The small number of capitalist farmers who were known as "progressive farmers" already upheld these goals. In contrast, planters in the American South sought to permanently inoculate labor tenants from the vagaries of "free markets." They resorted to peonage, debt slavery and Ku Klux Klan forms of terror to immobilize tenants on farms and prevent them from freely moving about. In South Africa, we see below, labor tenancy arrangements were calibrated to the growth of the capitalist economy in ways that diminished farmers' reliance on the sort of totalitarian controls that took firm root in the American South. In many cases, furthermore, a degree of paternalism also softened the relationship between white landowners and black tenants in South Africa.

Afrikaner farmers strongly identified with coercive labor practices from the outset, and their demands would set them apart as the most reactionary constituency of white politics. In defiance of the promise contained in the Native Land Act to increase the acreage of the reserves (the promised land known as "scheduled reserves"), farmers strenuously resisted such ideas and derailed the work of the Beaumont Commission (1916) appointed to fulfill the task. Instead, farmers took every opportunity to destroy "squatter peasants," expand the labor tenant system and delay the transition to wage labor. Across the Transvaal, Orange Free State and Natal, farmers who wished to expand the acreage of cultivated land or, less commonly, switch to paid labor began evicting peasant households "squatting" on land, setting adrift thousands of Africans who wandered about in search of employment in the farming areas and nearby towns. Farmers seized or bought for a song the crops, stock and implements of displaced tenants; frequently, they permitted Africans to retain these if they agreed to provide unpaid labor for a longer period than before. Lamenting the lengthening tenure of his servitude in the 1920s, a labor tenant in the Orange Free State concluded: "We are working for *boroko* [nothing]."[66]

The agrarian sector stood out within this period for the extent of direct control that farmers enjoyed over their black workers. In terms of the Native Servants Contract Act of 1932, for example, the "unit of labor" was defined as the labor tenant's entire household so that the tenant's children and women were also required to labor without remuneration. Like the tenant, they were subject to discipline by the farmer, a prerogative that the "whipping clause" of the same act also formalized.[67] Underwritten by formal legislation and implemented by a professional civil service scattered across an array of government bodies, institutional violence of this nature escalated after unification to yield an ever-tightening skein of laws, regulations and agencies to limit the mobility and liberties of blacks.

However, liberals within and outside the state, as well as the small class of "progressive farmers," repeatedly disparaged the "feudal" and oppressive character of tenancy arrangements.[68] Unsurprisingly, most disputes between black tenants and white landowners centered around the terms of tenancy agreements such as the length of the working day, the right not to work on Sundays and, most incendiary of all according to Charles van Onselen, the rights of whites to thrash the children of tenants.[69] Abetting the culture of violence in the countryside were the remoteness of the *platteland* and the isolation of African families dispersed across large farms. Unable and unwilling to attract Africans with adequate wages, many farmers, such as the maize and potato farmers in the Bethal area and the sugarcane farmers of Natal, emulated the mines by erecting prisons ("compounds") to house workers who tended to bolt the farm at the first opportunity. The notorious Bethel district in the eastern Transvaal was an early pioneer in this practice. Here tenants and convict workers were locked up at night in austere compounds and monitored by African "boss boys" equipped with whips. To prevent flight (farmers called it "desertion"), farmers often confiscated the worker's clothes and replaced them with sacks with armholes cut out. Bethal's inmate-workers were fed a diet that rarely deviated from simple servings of *mielie* (maize) meal. Only in the 1920s, when the Industrial and Commercial Workers' Union (ICU) began to mobilize in the countryside, would African farm workers come to possess an organization to protest the daily debasement and "shooting of Natives" in farming districts.[70]

Frequent interactions between black and white in rural areas always held the potential that subordinate blacks might mistake signs of easygoing affability in whites. As in the South, blacks were frequently bewildered by the rapidity with which a white farmer could turn to unexplained violence. No less than in the South, race relations on the *platteland* were governed by a rigid racial etiquette that blacks transgressed at their peril. Isolated farmers who ruled their farms with an iron fist were prone to rumors about "Native uprisings." Always false, wild rumors may have peaked at particular times, such as when the ICU held a meeting in an area, but never disappeared from the racial miasma that informed farmers' dealings with their workers.[71] As prone to rumors about "uprisings" as white farmers were in the American South, white farmers sought to stave off the threat with perpetual vigilance and so demanded obsequious deference from black bodies, the paradoxical source of both fear and prosperity in the rural areas.

Tenancy agreements, the imposition of various taxes on Africans and the expulsion provisions of the Land Act ensured that the decks were firmly stacked against blacks in the white farming areas. Under these conditions, several scholars have argued that ties of paternalism afforded blacks significant protection against harsh treatment by farmers. In his examination of the rural economy on the eve of the First World War, Tim Keegan argues that paternalism lingered on as a "a compromise, a modus vivendi, that enabled masters and servants, landlords and tenants on the farms to sustain working relationships." Helen Bradford offers a similar summation of race relations in the white framing areas in the 1920s and 1930s, noting that a "stunted ethic of paternalism" mitigated the aura of thralldom on the *platteland*. In his detailed chronicle of farm life in the southwestern Transvaal, Charles van Onselen also offers an account of "paternalism" between blacks and whites.

Kas Maine, the hero of van Onselen's book, recalled numerous occasions of mutual cooperation and even camaraderie amongst black tenants and white farmers in this region of the Transvaal. Helen Bradford and Rob Morrell have also pointed out that *baaskap* (white supremacy) in white farming areas was not so total that it prevented farmers and their black tenants from devising paternalist arrangements that addressed their respective concerns. Farmers demanded productive and deferential workers while labor tenants insisted on adequate land they could work for themselves and, perhaps less emphatically, also a modicum of respect from whites who were typically crude racists.[72]

However, others doubt whether occasional displays of humanity and generosity from whites deserve the appellation "paternalism." After all, the term implies a definite degree of reciprocal obligation between a stern but kindly father figure and subordinates who are often described as "quasi-kin" in the literature on paternalism. The evidence for paternalist bonds of this sort in rural South Africa is extremely sparse, however. Ian Ochiltree is probably correct in describing the asymmetries that bound farm workers to white landowners in South Africa as a "weak paternalism" that cushioned relations between racist farmers and vulnerable blacks.[73] Another practice may also have softened the economic and social relations between white landowners and black tenants. In the American South, tenants were frequently permitted to grow nothing other than cotton on their portion of a white farmer's land. This policy effectively deprived tenants of edible products and ensured that all their transactions with farmers and local storekeepers were monetized. In South Africa, labor tenants generally cultivated wheat and maize and were free to plant other vegetables to sustain their households. Furthermore, transactions between white landowners and black tenants were very often conducted in kind, so that "skilled rural craft-workers such as stonemasons, thatchers and wool-shearers" and even wage farm laborers "were often remunerated in beer, cattle, meat or sheep rather than in cash." Together with "the timely exercise of the 'gift' for purposes of social control," this practice played a decisive role in preserving "paternalism" in rural race relations and also the sense that, at least to some degree, white landowners were responsible for the well-being of their labor force.[74] The persistence of pre-capitalist social relations also preserved an informal sense of mutual identification between tenants and white landlords, both of whom struggled with increasing desperation to hold on to their farming operations as the modernization of the industry steadily increased.[75]

The tenuous existence of many white farmers also encouraged another practice that was not found in the South. Instead of violently immobilizing tenants on their farms, white farmers initially welcomed the opportunity their tenants took to seek wage employment in the mines in the off-season. Farmers signed the tenants' "work pass" (permitting blacks to exit the rural district) knowing that tenants returned to the rural economy with much-needed cash, the lifeblood of the small rural stores that many farmers maintained on their farms.[76] White farmers in South Africa were therefore much less chary than Southern planters of black farmworkers' mobility and so signed the "trek pass." For their part, black farm workers invariably returned to the white farm because tenancy was the only way to retain some degree of access to land. Farmers grew hostile to requests for "trek passes" once tenants increasingly secured permanent jobs in urban industry. Even then, however, white farmers did not escalate the coercion and physical violence that were ubiquitous in the rural areas into anything approaching Southern-style violence. As a result, "The highveld saw no lynch mobs, and no equivalent of the Klan."[77] To the contrary, labor "shortages" often empowered tenants to some degree. In 1934, for example, when farmers in the Lydenburg district in the eastern Transvaal attempted to intimidate unreliable tenants by evicting them, they set off reprisals from Africans who simply secured more favorable tenancy agreements with neighboring farmers. By 1930, a report by the Department of Agriculture observed that it was "practically impossible to obtain a permanent labor supply unless the native is given land and grazing."[78]

Similar disputes, especially the "desertion" of tenants, were the bane of planters and the cause of numerous lynchings in the American South. In South Africa, however, farmers turned to the state for support and volubly complained when government officials hesitated or simply refused to implement various pass control provisions under the Master and Servants Act, the Native Service Contract Act and the Urban Areas Act. Their grievances declined only after 1948, when addressing "the farm labor problem" became a first-order priority for the Apartheid government.[79] Throughout the inter-War period, a "weak paternalism" in the rural areas helped stay the hands of farmers who were marinated in racist ideology and confident in their capacity to violate black bodies – and get away with it.

Private violence on white farms

The evidence is overwhelming that government support for labor tenancy in the inter-War years was at best half-hearted and generally unsympathetic to what officials disparaged as "kaffir farming." As a result, many farmers held a low opinion about the reputed majesty of the law and a lower one of the Native administrators and police whose task it was to enforce labor controls. Meanwhile, hundreds of small *boere* after the First World War lost the increasingly desperate struggle to hold on to their farms. In rising numbers, they sold their land for whatever they could get. Many simply abandoned the land. All joined the swelling ranks of "poor whites" in the urban areas. In light of the desperate conditions in white agriculture, it is perhaps remarkable that white farmers existing on the knife-edge of bankruptcy did not embrace the Southern solution in which mobs of armed white men liberally meted out "communal justice" against vulnerable but uncooperative blacks on their land.

Britain's restoration of Afrikaner landowners preserved the tradition of personal violence that Boer men took for granted in their dealings with *kaffirs*. The growth of farm violence after 1910 therefore attests to the individual farmer's growing control over black workers.[80] But such physical violence is also evidence that Africans resisted white control, ensuring that farmers never achieved the dominance they viewed as essential to labor relations on their farms. Tenants mutilated stock, pilfered whatever they could, defended their households against unwarranted intrusion and abuse by farmers, burned barns and homes, and occasionally even murdered the *baas*.[81] Most importantly, tenants bargained hard for access to land because with land came some measure of independence. In exchange, they endured the tyranny of racist and violent landowners. State officials and administrators never approved of this violence. Instead, they drew unflattering comparisons between the "backwardness" of labor tenancy and the gentler conditions that "progressive farmers" relied on to attract and retain farm labor.[82]

Still, as the chapter on the South African legal system argues, liberals in the state could not bring themselves to decisively terminate rural violence by throwing the book at violent farmers. Trivial sentences for abusing and murdering blacks, the failure to prosecute and the unwillingness to convict violent landowners all confirmed with depressing regularity, as every black farm worker knew, that no government would take seriously the institutionalized violence that prevailed in the rural areas. In combination, the secluded nature and the regularity of private farm violence help to account for the paucity of records documenting violence in the farming areas. Violence was sufficiently real and frequent to deter vulnerable blacks from going to the courts. Usually stopping short of fatalities, assaultive violence became an ingrained feature of farm life that "weak paternalism" failed to quell.[83] A few examples will suffice to impart the nature and scale of private violence in the white rural areas.

One such instance, dubbed the "the Reitz case," took place in July of 1932 in the town of Reitz in the Orange Free State. The case, involving an assault by a white farmer on a black worker who asked for his wages, affords a revealing glimpse of the ordeals that Africans faced:

> The farmer refused to pay, and, on the native repeating his request, for payment for what was owing to him the following morning, the [farmer] struck him in the face with his fist, kicked him and hit with a *sjambok* [whip]. The native ran away; the farmer, on horseback, overtook him, tied a *riem* [leather rope] around his neck and dragged him home, the horse cantering all the way. The complainant was then chained to a cartwheel and beaten with a stirrup leather, and left chained up. Later he was again beaten and was finally released at sundown, having being beaten three times with a *sjambok* and leather belt.[84]

Evidence of similar brutality also surfaced in "the Standerton flogging case" in 1924 after a farmer flogged to death an African girl of sixteen

whom he accused of stealing items from his household. The case generated
a number of articles and letters in the newspapers that decried the cruelty
of "some Europeans" and roundly condemned the white jury that acquitted
the farmer.[85]

Many cases confirm that farmers violently assaulted and murdered farm
workers for the most trivial reasons and often for no discernable reason at
all. Petrus Johannes Heckroodt, a farmer near Kimberly, for example, saw
a farm hand named Japie "standing near his sister." He called out to Japie,
who did not reply, whereupon Heckroodt shot and killed him. Heckroodt
explained that he fired "because he thought the native was going to stab or
assault his sister." Heckroodt was pronounced not guilty.[86] Workers suspected of shirking or pilfering small amounts of money or items on farms
were thrashed to the point of death, beaten with poles and, like the unfortunate "Alfred" who complained that he was too sick to work, even shot
to death.[87] One farmer, C. J. Kruger, obtained an acquittal in court when
he explained why he had shot and killed Dewet Tsaoi. Kruger had beaten
Tsaoi's wife for "climbing through a fence" on the farm. Tsaoi remonstrated
and was promptly dismissed from service and told to fetch his "trek pass."
When Tsaoi duly returned, Kruger shot him and kicked him as he lay on
the ground. "Baas, you have finished me" escaped his lips before he died.
Kruger received a suspended sentence.

V. Webb, the manager of a farm near Maritzburg, could give the court
no reason for "shooting a Native" in October 1936. Witnesses reported
that "Webb did not say anything and did not seem annoyed." Justice
Landown sentenced him to 15 months with hard labor. Another farmer
similarly offered no reason for assaulting a fifteen-year-old youth, placing a
noose around his neck and tying him to a truck on a farm near Worcester
in the western Cape.[88] Farmers across the country regularly adduced stock
theft as a reason for killing blacks, a response that was common to remote
stock farming across the world.[89] On the other hand, Bernard Buthelezi, an
African teacher near Ladysmith, learned first-hand that even the most minor
breach of etiquette could generate explosive violence from prickly farmers.
Accosted by four white men on a rural road, Buthelezi made the mistake of
greeting the men in English and not in Zulu, as the men had expected him
to. Buthelezi was severely beaten with rocks and a bicycle chain.[90]

Martin Murray examined an outbreak of "Native shootings" cases in
the Orange Free State countryside between 1917 and 1924 and detected a
pattern. The first shootings in 1917 appeared to be "isolated and random
events," but "by mid-1918, the first flush of seemingly random acts of violence had ballooned into a 'reign of terror' that lasted until 1922. After a
temporary lull, this indiscriminate violence erupted once again in 1924 and
only gradually subsided over the next few years." Murray attributes this
pattern to white farmers' attempts to fuse their personal mastery over rural
Africans to emerging forms of capitalist production in agriculture. "The
spate of shootings, physical assaults and other forms of violence symbol-

ized the outward signs of capital's parasitic, frenzied feeding on all non-capitalist relations that impeded its advance." Murray concludes that "the O.F.S. 'reign of terror' was an integral part of the so-called 'primitive accumulation' of capital in agriculture."[91]

In 1935, the *Cape Times* surveyed a decade-long flood of complaints emanating from the country's farming areas and concluded that "Native shooting" cases were a "shameful throw-back to an age of savagery" that "blackened South Africa's name in the eyes of the world." With more hope than reason, the editor declared that "The time has passed when an illiterate farmer in the back-blocks could beat a native into insensibility and escape all but the congratulations of his neighbors":

> To-day such assaults as those which we reported from Lichtenburg a day or so ago are debited against the South African people as a unit. The accused in this Lichtenburg case was a European farmer charged on four counts of flogging his native servants. The first victim, a 60 year old man, was tied up and thrashed with a sjambok ... The second victim was a Native woman ... The doctor found her body covered with bruises and weals 'too numerous to mention' ... Giving evidence, the accused pleaded guilty under provocation, explaining that the natives had been 'cheeky' ... The magistrate imposed fines totaling £15, or an average of £3.15s a flogging ... Any country magistrate can tell stories of platteland farmers who, summoned for a brutal assault on a native, come to court naively expecting to be congratulated by the magistrate for administering a well-deserved chastisement!"[92]

Six years later a state prosecutor also reviewed the flood of farm violence but managed to arrive at a very different conclusion. As he told the court, he was "sick and tired of hearing cases in which natives alleged assault against farmers and the police who arrested them." The police, he contended, "were only doing their job".[93]

Contrary to the "pattern" that Murray detected, levels of farm violence appear to have remained high throughout the 1920s and 1930s, the constant harvest of a racial etiquette that demanded complete deference to even the smallest of white children on farms. Murray's diagnosis suggests that farm violence should have decreased once "bourgeois law" developed to fully encompass class relations in the countryside. To the contrary, the development of capitalist agriculture under the Apartheid regime was accompanied by an explosive *increase* in both official and private violence in the farming areas from 1948 onward.[94]

"Near lynchings" and state intervention: A case of communal violence

The cases above are representative of the private violence that was taken for granted in the white rural areas. Whereas violence of this nature was legion, cases of communal violence were rare. Regardless of the nature of the triggering offence, whites' attempts to escalate private violence into communal

lynching invariably seemed to fizzle in South Africa. Failed lynchings conformed to a predictable sequence. Whites would form mobs and attack the
symbols and property associated with "cheeky" blacks, who usually fled
to escape harm. At some point, usually very quickly, the forces of law and
order intervened and interposed themselves between the white mob and the
black quarry. Intimidated by the police in every case, the mob dispersed and
the incident died down. Helen Bradford's study of "lynch law and laborers"
in the Umvoti region in Natal exemplifies the logic of this pattern of collective mobilization, which ensured that not even the most racist *platteland*
areas would generate Ku Klux Klan-style spectacle violence.

In the 1920s, Umvoti's white labor-hungry farmers were trigger-happy
and in a state of high anxiety, particularly incensed at tenants who were
responding in droves to the inflammatory rhetoric of the ICU. Their rage
burst into the open in March 1928 when Zabuloni Gwaza, freshly released
from jail for desecrating headstones in a graveyard for white policemen,
waited no more than four days before resuming his nocturnal assaults, this
time damaging two Voortrekker graves. This symbolic violation of dead
whites who were ensconced in land that once belonged to Africans uncorked
in farmers a fury that Gwaza's immediate re-arrest could not calm. In 1927
and 1928, wattle prices had slumped precipitously, farmers lost a lucrative
lumber contract to the mines, the summer rains had failed and foreclosures
loomed as banks began to call in loans. Moreover, "All around them, black
resistance seemed to be spreading unchecked while the state was in disarray.
In Estcourt, white police were refusing to execute summary ejection orders
[on black tenants]. In Mooi River, resistance to eviction culminated in a
series of bloody confrontations between constables and crowds of Africans.
And in Umvoti itself, an outbreak of midnight stock maiming extended the
scope of tenants' challenge to landlords' property."[95] Jolted by Gwaza's act
of supreme bravado, white farmers resorted to the *kommando* tradition
on 1 March 1928. British subjects and Boers who may have fought against
each other in the Anglo-Boer War (but were subsequently brought closer by
joint membership in the Umvoti Mounted Rifles, a reserve unit of the South
African Army) joined forces and launched a violent attack on the ICU. A
five-day rampage ensued. Signs of what Wilbur Cash called the "primitive
frenzy" of Southern lynch mobs suddenly erupted:

> Incensed whites armed with shotguns twice stormed the prison, and
> grappled with the police outside the very door of Gwaza's cell. At noon,
> as bells tolled, businesses closed, and both blacks and whites poured into
> town, farmers attended an impassioned anti-ICU meeting. Shortly thereaf-
> ter, hundreds of Africans successfully forestalled a raid on the Union office.
> But in the later afternoon about seventy whites surged past the police
> guarding the office, smashed up the interior and made a huge bonfire of
> all documents and furniture … members of the mob 'started to drive the
> Natives towards the Hills.' Several black/white clashes erupted, and the
> ICU branch secretary was hounded and thrashed in a mielie field. Finally

at about 8 pm, as police reinforcements streamed in to patrol the district
with their machine guns, eight cars packed with Greytown men pulled up
outside the ICU office in the neighboring village of Kranskop. Here they
triumphantly fired all the contents, and scoured a nearby farm for the ICU
secretary.

Rumors that Africans planned to "massacre the whites" and destroy
their property prompted the Minister of Defense to telegraph to the Prime
Minister, warning that unless mob violence was speedily terminated "native
reprisals by members of the ICU may result firing cane wattles etcetera."
Prompt police intervention brought the mayhem to an immediate end.

The storming of a jail was highly unusual in South Africa, a riveting
departure from the usual deference that white civilians displayed towards
law enforcement authorities. Moreover, the event occurred in the context of
peace, unlike the racial killings that insurrectionary conditions encouraged
in the course of the 1922 strike by mine workers. A mob assault on the very
embodiment of state authority is therefore a telling comment on the pent-up
rage of white farmers who felt short-changed, even punished, by a pusillani-
mous labor control apparatus. As in the South, the composition of the mob
illuminates the functional role that ritual violence played in cementing unity
amongst whites. "Wealthy English businessmen," "struggling Afrikaner
farmers" and "penurious clerks" closed ranks in defense of Umvoti's threatened racial order. Communal violence in Umvoti bolstered a white identity that seemed threatened in two fronts: from below, by African unionists
and tenants who flouted white authority; and from above, by a state con-
fusedly searching for a "just balance" between the liberal and authoritarian
approaches to the "Native Question."

Indeed, this dramatic episode of retributive justice contains all the
elements of Southern-style, communal "popular justice" – save for one fact:
a lynching did not in fact occur. The mob also failed to murder the unfortunate Union secretary once it ran him down in a recondite maize field.
Instead, enraged white farmers settled for a beating – a decidedly unlikely
turn of events in the American South. Two salient factors therefore stand
out: the intervention of the police and the self-restraint of murderously angry
white civilians. Bradford's three-fold explanation for the role of the police
illuminates the specificities of the South African racial order. Firstly, the
Labor Party, the National Party's junior coalition partner in the Pact government that lasted from 1924 to 1928, would not countenance a violent
offensive against trade unionists, white or black. Senior government officials therefore instructed the local police to forthwith terminate the violence
against the ICU. Just as importantly, secondly, the Pact government had
inherited a civil service that remained hostile to the "primitive" labor tenant
system and to the harsher controls that Umvoti's farmers were demanding. Magistrates therefore did not want to endorse violent measures that
propped up an unpopular and "backward" practice. The official response,

finally, was also conditioned by the pervasive fear of African retaliation. Like the police who placed themselves in the line of fire to prevent white strikers from massacring African miners in the Rand revolt, Umvoti's local police took a stand against white mobbism to allay the much more terrifying prospect of African resistance.[96]

In the end, the official conclusion of the mayhem in Umvoti mirrored the larger contradictions of the liberal segregationist state. A handful of white rioters were arrested and the violence did not reoccur. Several white rioters were taken to court, where they received fines of £5 (which could be paid off in 10 shilling installments). On the other hand, the law also reasserted itself against Africans, many of whom angrily mocked the light sentences and the court's obvious sympathy for Umvoti's riotous whites. The same magistrate who fined the white rioters also declared: "[because]farmers cannot get Natives who fail to fulfill their contracts moved off their land ... the aggrieved parties are the whites: they have applied to the Law for a remedy and the law has failed utterly to help them. If ... they adopt primitive measures for redress can anyone blame them?"[97]

Extensive research on the agrarian sector has sharply illuminated a state of affairs that Africans, state authorities, and even white farmers' associations in the 1920s and 1930s viewed as lamentably self-evident: labor tenancy and brutal violence were joined at the hip. By its very nature, labor tenancy imposed a striking symmetry in patterns of farm violence in South Africa and the American South. "Progressive" commercial farmers rarely complained of labor shortages and their wage workers were much less likely to report the litany of hardships that attended the tenant's existence. In both the American South and South Africa, farmers imposed debilitating fines and "fees" on tenants that effectively institutionalized debt peonage and abused their powers by rigging the prices they paid for tenants' crops.[98] Integrating convict labor and the attendant policing methods into rural labor supplies, furthermore, underscores farmers' access to local state authorities in both racial orders.[99] Callous and direct, racial violence by farmers and their operatives was built into the marrow of farm life wherever labor tenancy prevailed.

White farmers in South Africa therefore committed many murders that meet William Brundage's definition of "private lynching." Farmers knew that the courts were not likely to turn a blind eye to such murders. They therefore either attempted to conceal these killings or concocted stories to win the sympathy of judges and juries who were culled from the local population. Despite farmers' misgivings about the administration of labor controls, they did not attempt to usurp the state by brazenly killing blacks in public. This unwillingness sharply circumscribed the rituals that were indispensable to communal lynchings in the American South. The Umvoti incident, for example, captures the same escalating drama which, in the South, summoned large crowds to participate in the inevitable destruction of a black body. Assembling a caravan of killers, forming a "laager" in the city center, hunting down the quarry, destroying the symbols of the ICU, and asserting the "popular will" by laying armed siege to a jail cell with the intended victim within arm's length, for example, were South-like rituals that also bolstered the unity of whites in the Umvoti district. But there the communal violence stopped.

In the management of "race relations," white employers and white workers were content to celebrate the state as the embodiment of the "popular will" and so contented themselves with inflicting a reign of private violence on African subordinates. If the macabre rituals that distinguished communal lynching in the New South were absent in South Africa, racial violence was nevertheless surrounded by a different set of rituals that lionized the supremacy of the racial state. The pomp and ceremony of the all-white parliament, ubiquitous signs that segregated "Europeans" and "Non-Europeans"; "Native Courts" that concealed white violence under the cloak of "tribal justice"; "job color bars" that legally assigned blacks to the lowest-paying jobs; and a "whipping clause" that lawfully authorized white farmers to thrash even the children of their labor tenants – these were some of the quiet emblems and institutional logic of "structural violence" in the South African economy.

5

Racial violence and religion in the New South

> The most vicious oppressors of the Negro today are probably in church. — Martin Luther King, Jr.[1]

There are solid reasons for inquiring into the relationship between lynching and religion in the South. To begin with, leading spokespersons and religious leaders in the South themselves asserted that Southern identities and Southern uniqueness were rooted in a religious understanding of history. Legions of scholars have subsequently demonstrated the central role that religious beliefs and church membership played in the emergence of the "Solid South." If religion informed all aspects of Southern society, then it is surely plausible that lynching was as much reinforced by religious sensibilities as by any of the region's other institutions. Lynching, in other words, was not an aberration from but an organic outgrowth of the theological framework of Southern Protestantism that emerged in the New South where "Protestant Evangelicalism [had] long been the largest Christian tradition, its most prominent and dominant religious form."[2] Yet, even if the connections between Southern Protestant theology and lynching remained unrecognized at the time, the empirical details of numerous communal lynchings suggest that whites intuitively grasped lynching as a religious, spiritual and ritual affair. This claim is less compelling in the case of private lynchings, many of which were indistinguishable from common murder. Communal lynchings, on the other hand, were redolent of religious ritual, and Orlando Patterson is not alone in describing communal lynching as a "blood sacrifice" that echoed the crucifixion of Jesus Christ.[3]

The insight that communal lynching was a religiously framed blood sacrifice corroborates the observations of many African American scholars and artists over the course of the twentieth century. Paul Lawrence Dunbar, Charles Chestnutt, W. E. B. Du Bois, Langston Hughes, Gwendolyn Brooks, James Baldwin, William Melvin Kelly and John Edgar Wideman – to name just a few – all made lynching a prominent motif in their writings. For most of these authors, the connections amongst Christ's death, communal lynching and Southern segregation seemed obvious, even banal. As the African American poet Gwendolyn Brooks wrote in her poem, "The Chicago Defender Sends a Man to Little Rock" (1957):

> In Little Rock the people sing
> Sunday hymns like anything,
> Through Sunday pomp and polishing.
>
> [...]
>
> I saw a bleeding brownish boy.
>
> The lariat lynch-wish I deplored.
>
> The loveliest lynchee was our Lord.[4]

The recent writings of two scholars in particular, Orlando Patterson and Donald Mathews, mark a return to the essential insight that there was something deeply religious – something *Christian* – at work in the act of lynching, and that the victim's demise was a tragic echo of Christ's own death.

However, neither Patterson nor Mathews adequately connects this insight to another vital aspect of Southern Protestantism – the truncated version of the Social Gospel that emerged in the segregation era. Yet a consideration of this version of the Social Gospel is vital to understanding why racial lynching could proliferate in a such a self-consciously Christian social order. Likewise, an appreciation of the role of Social Gospelism is also essential for understanding why a racist Protestantism among Afrikaners in South Africa steadfastly *rejected* a theology of "blood sacrifice."

The "Anglo-Saxon evangelical faith" of segregationists in the American South led them to firmly reject the aggressive statism that Afrikaner theologians developed in the early twentieth century. Evangelicals in the South recoiled from political upheaval after 1900 and denounced social movements that challenged the dominance of the region's elites. Instead, they spurned "handouts" and urged white workers to progress by dint of hard and honest individual labor. Without the sort of overtly discriminatory benefits that sought to elevate white workers above their black counterparts in South Africa, white workers and religious leaders in the South firmed up the racial divide by vigilantly patrolling the encompassing field of "race relations" in civil society. Widespread white poverty continually threatened to expose the fallacies on which the Solid South rested, however. In this context, religious discourse played a crucial role in shoring up claims that whites were superior to blacks.

Even so, many white religious leaders bravely spoke out against the gathering assault on African Americans. The Populist movement became a defiant inter-racial repudiation of white supremacy and a bi-racial Pentecostal movement even managed to persist well into the 1920s. These examples of racial tolerance suggest that the evangelical movement still exuded at least some of the insurgent politics that marked the movement's emergence at the end of the eighteenth century when evangelicals – then still a fringe movement – had originated and worshipped in bi-racial churches. For all practical purposes, however, the authority-challenging thrust of the evangelical movement would not survive three major nineteenth-century developments: the gradual institutionalization and increasing conservatism of all evangelical churches from the 1840s onwards; the breakaway of African Americans from bi-racial churches after the Civil War, a move that left impoverished whites ripe for picking by reactionary elites; and the Democrat Party's success in violently defeating first Reconstruction and then the Populist movement. These epochal developments swamped the moderate white evangelicals such as those who joined the bi-racial Pentecostal movement in the 1910s and 1920s or spoke out against racial oppression as a matter of Christian conscience. For the vast majority of Southerners in white churches, endless sermonizing about segregation's secular and religious foundations acquired a facticity that daily life in the Solid South unfailingly upheld. They therefore sensed, or knew, that there was something about their religion that afforded all whites, even the poorest amongst them, an always-ready rationale to sacralize the ritual killing of vulnerable blacks. They understood that "holiness and the demonic are kin."[5]

The ambiguities of evangelical Protestantism in the nineteenth century

It was by no means pre-ordained that evangelical Protestantism would play such a critical role in reinforcing either segregation or the racial violence that became endemic in the New South. This development in fact departed from the outlook of the evangelical movement that spread outwards from its home in the northeast colonies in the late eighteenth century and quickly made its way across the Southern states. The evangelical movement stimulated a highly emotional approach to worship that often inspired congregations to weep and ecstatically convulse as preachers delivered sermons bearing titles such as "Sinners in the Hands of an Angry God," a landmark sermon delivered by Jonathan Edwards, the prominent Calvinist Congregational minister from Enfield, Connecticut. By emphasizing the need for an unmediated and personal embrace of a God who was more wrathful than forgiving, the First Great Awakening underscored the moment of conversion as the centerpiece of a theology that underscored religion as an experiential phenomenon. A movement that transcended "local and particular allegiances" and supplanted the traditional importance of ancestry, learning and wealth also invigorated democratic impulses based on common experience and so played an important role in "molding the separate colonies into a united nation."[6]

The Second Great Awakening (1800–30) deepened these democratic developments. Exuberantly postmillennial, this Awakening was marked by a strong commitment to social activism to cleanse the world of its ills in preparation for Christ's promised return. The revival spawned numerous grassroots religious associations, "multiplied local congregations and overflowed into a veritable phalanx of evangelical organizations" that helped to stabilize a dynamic post-revolutionary society.[7] Methodists and Baptists, followed closely by Presbyterians, rapidly outgrew their fringe status within American Christianity, eclipsing the established Anglican Church to become the largest denominations by 1820. The swiftness of this change was most striking in the Southern states. Here, so entrenched did this "radical experiment with religious liberty" become that, already by 1830, it is possible to distinguish a distinct Southern religious tradition that hinged around a "revivalistic evangelical Protestantism."[8]

The roots of this tradition actually lay in the First Awakening, which had coincided with the "upsurge of African [slave] importations, the beginning of net population growth for African-born slaves, and the birth of Afro-American culture." Religious changes that underscored the increasing importance of democratic grassroots civil associations therefore intersected with racial changes that deepened the unfreedom of African Americans. This development accordingly posed something of a moral conundrum for the growing evangelical movement. The earliest response of white evangelicals was to open the church doors to black slaves, often in defiance of wary slave owners. Baptists and Methodists believed in monogenesis – the belief that all human beings derive from a single pair of ancestors. They therefore evangelised in bi-racial churches, inaugurating a tradition of joint worship that lasted throughout the antebellum period. African Americans requited this Christian initiative in full measure. Slaves were attracted by the message of an all-powerful God who rewarded the faithful with benevolence and the promise of joyous life in the hereafter. Moreover, echoes of their own vibrant African religious traditions were visibly present, indeed central to the preaching style of evangelicals. Evangelicals replaced the staid and formulaic recitation of prayer and quietly reasoned sermons that prevailed in Episcopal churches with energetic exhortations that thrived on the equally loud and fervent responses of congregation members. These performances "bore a comfortable resemblance to African possession"; similarly, the subdivision of the Christian god into a holy Trinity was easily incorporated into African spiritual concepts that distinguished amongst ancestral gods, nature gods and an omnipotent creator god. Immersing converts in water, the emblematic experience of the Baptist church, washed away an unpleasant past and marked a joyful rebirth in ways that reverberated with the water rites in traditional African religions and hinted at the unfettered community that slavery denied in this life. African concepts of humanity and equality also echoed in the use of appellations such as "brother" and "sister" without regard to race, a practice that embodied both a critique of the present and the promise of Godly fellowship in the hereafter.[9] Unsurprisingly, the evangelical churches therefore became the first refuge for African slaves and African American families. The result, as contemporary scholars have shown, was the emergence of black and white evangelical traditions that were inextricably bound by a multitude of overlapping outlooks and practices that made "'Southern religion" a "bi-racial and bicultural phenomenon."[10]

However, African Americans "got religion" in growing numbers just as white evangelicals reappraised their outsider status in Southern society. As the first three decades of the nineteenth century wore on, white evangelicals capitalized on their spiritual dominance and searched for greater "respectability" and acceptance from the region's slave-owning elites. After several decades of phenomenal growth, Baptist and Methodist churches scaled back their itinerant camps in favor of building more churches and – to counter the erratic learning of the many autodidacts who "went into preaching" – seminaries as well. By 1830, both churches "bristled with the beginnings of denominational apparatus."[11] Although evangelicals had earlier bucked the slave-owning culture by organizing bi-racial churches and spoke out against slavery, they had not actively organized against slavery itself. Instead, they straddled the divide between an otherwordly Christian populism and the harsh realities of slavery by attempting to "remain apolitical." This position became unsustainable as the evangelical churches gravitated to the forefront of Southern culture and the most respectable members of the slave-owning elite and urban society filled the pews. By the time the Second Awakening came to a close around 1830, the three major evangelical churches – Baptists, Methodists and Presbyterians – had essentially come out in favor of slavery just as the tide against the peculiar institution began to gather steam in the North, where Protestants were active in the abolition movement. Simmering disquiet between Northern and Southern views over slavery came to a head when Southern Baptists broke away to form a Southern Baptist Convention in 1845. Methodists followed suit later that year. More given to internal fissure, Presbyterians dodged the inevitable until 1861, when regional rancor over slavery, secession, and the war finally superseded the "Old School" and "New School" theological disputes and split the church into two camps.[12] Although short-lived, the proclamation and militarized existence of a Confederate States of America immediately imposed an overarching unity on the three major evangelical denominations, galvanizing the region's claims to cultural distinctiveness.[13] It helped, too, that "Methodists, Baptists, Presbyterians, and many members of smaller denominations saw in each other far more similarities than differences ... They all shared the same beliefs. This common ground helped make the moral attitudes of Southern evangelicalism the accepted morality of the region."[14]

The antebellum legacy of the Southern evangelical churches was thus ambiguous. On the one hand, the early history of the evangelical churches was shaped by an insurgent, counter-cultural role and a willingness to challenge prevailing racial, class and gender codes. The churches introduced a bi-racial strain that served as a living refutation of the dehumanization and "social death" that were inherent to slavery. This bi-racial culture never succeeded in making itself felt outside the confines of church walls; nevertheless, its persistence until the Civil War provided white moderates and black ministers with a beleaguered cultural space that served as a reminder of the common humanity that united the free and the enslaved. Likewise, the evangelical churches rescued the mass of Southern worshippers from the straitlaced refinements of the region's Episcopalian elite and welcomed them into a genuinely grassroots, "log-cabin" religious movement that squared better with the country's republican ideals. Women, too, were accorded greater voice and authority in the evangelical churches. Some churches for example permitted voting rights for women, and even for slaves, in matters relating to the election of church officers.[15] These enlightened practices stand out as beacons of tolerance in a rigid and oppressive social system.

But the insurgent thrust that evangelicals brought to the region could not survive the increasingly supportive relations between an upwardly mobile evangelical leadership and the entrenched regional plantocracy in the second half of the nineteenth century. Cordial relations between the two in the post-Civil War years became so strong that historians today debate only the scale, but not the essential fact, of the churches' complicity in supporting a war that was fought to prolong slavery before rushing to establish a violent system of segregation. Having converted to the view that "slavery had Jehovah's blessing," conservative evangelicals became seceding evangelicals, the mournful authors of a "religion of the Lost Cause" in the New South.[16] In a sharp contrast to its incarnation as a relatively enlightened and countercultural upstart at the turn of the eighteenth century, the main thrust of the evangelical movement one century later was to either sanction or tolerate the violent subjugation and disfranchisement of African Americans. In response to another revival – the Third Great Awakening – that arose in the second half of the nineteenth century, Southern evangelicals cohered around a dyspeptic view of the strong Social Gospelism that the same revival stoked in the North. Preferring to concentrate on reforms that stopped short of challenging the power of the region's agrarian elites and the small but growing class of industrial employers, Southern theologians – when they did rouse themselves to engage their social and political environment – united around "blue law" issues such as alcoholism, marital infidelity and smoking.[17]

The bi-racial movement did not disappear entirely; indeed, it was briefly revived by the Third Awakening. But bi-racialism emerged transformed and weakened by the traumas and aftermath of civil war. Bi-racialism was now confined to a small Holiness movement that amplified both the experiential and apolitical approach to religion. To the vividness of the "first baptism" (conversion), the holiness movement added a "second baptism" that marked a process of either gradual or instant "sanctification" in which God's presence within the soul of the convert became permanent. Partially an offshoot of Methodism, the Holiness movement evolved into a plethora of Pentecostal sects after the famous 1906 "Azusa Street revival" in Los Angeles when worshippers claimed to have miraculously given praise to the Lord in foreign tongues. "Speaking in tongues" added another regimen to the shouting and physical ecstasy that made camp meetings in the South such lively affairs. But these communal expressions of spiritual transportation were no substitute for the organizational work that was required to nurture a beleaguered and waning bi-racial tradition. The Holiness and Pentecostal movements approached faith exclusively as a matter of internal experience that was almost entirely severed from the everyday world. The result was a bi-racial movement that, at most, engaged racism across the country only sporadically, and only obliquely at that. By the First World War, racial divisions emerged and Pentecostals across the country retreated into segregated organizations. In the South, too, bi-racialism in the Pentecostal movement wilted as white supremacy became entrenched, but not before it had contributed to a violently oppressive and exploitative social order that thrived on political passivity and mocked the very notion that blacks and whites were equals, even in spiritual affairs.[18]

"Independent African churches" and the end of bi-racial churches

The second development that paved the way for a rapprochement between the "apolitical" evangelical churches and a violent class of planters and urban employers in the New South sprang from the eruption of independent African American churches during Reconstruction. More than any other factor, the headlong exodus of African Americans from the antebellum churches brought bi-racialism in Southern churches to an end. The movement was swift and categorical. Fully two-thirds of African Americans left the Baptist, Methodist, Presbyterian and other churches by the end of 1866; in 1871, another surge of departing freedmen, mostly Methodists, also severed their links with the antebellum church, leaving behind only a fraction of freedmen in the now fully white evangelical churches.[19] The exodus was undoubtedly a response to the continuing dominance of white ministers who refused to alter antebellum practices such as segregating the pews or delivering sermons that enjoined freemen to accept the "kindly protection of their former master." But the movement primarily expressed the desire of African Americans to worship separately from whites, to give free rein to their own interpretations of the Bible and to indulge in worshipping styles that served as repositories of their African cultural patrimony.

The "independent African churches" became the first free institution that African Americans formed in the United States. No aspect of the freedman's life – social, cultural and political – could fail to pass through the church. Churches provided the first space for socializing and courtship and for reuniting family members dispersed by slave owners. Ministers enthusiastically turned their modest churches into debating chambers that rang with freewheeling debates about the war and later, with rising exasperation, about the waning and eventual betrayal of Reconstruction. Churches disseminated information about wages, working conditions and the systems of labor contracts that emerged after 1865, providing African Americans with the prototype of trade unions that white workers would establish only in the 1880s and 1890s. For the Freedmen's Bureau, the independent churches were the point of entry into black communities. Churches became the hub around which schools and all educational reforms revolved. A deluge of African American missionaries from the North looked upon the defeated South as a liberated vineyard of the Lord and naturally took up shop in the ebullient rash of new churches. These Northern clergy were soon repelled by the discovery of "primitive" worship styles amongst their intensely religious Southern kin – the convulsions, voluble back-and-forth exhortations between preacher and congregation, and mysterious "voodoo" practices. Still, they broadened black Southerners' horizons and optimism by connecting them to the fabled cities of the North.[20] Disputes over issues such as the purchasing of property to build churches, the role of women in leadership positions and the admissibility of various forms of "African" religion greatly complicated religious unity across the multitude of churches and associations that sprang up in the 1860s and 1870s. Still, the mass exodus from bi-racial churches was in fact a powerful revival experience that consolidated the unrivalled grip that churches exercised over the individual lives and the collective spirit of African American communities across the South.

Inevitably, however, the exodus also fueled the emergence of segregation. Scholars rightly distinguish between the racist motivations that underlay whites' support for segregation and the "positive" grounds on which freedmen demanded and voluntarily established independent separate churches for themselves. These contrasting motivations were reflected in the segregated theologies that arose as soon as the Civil war ended. Partly relieved and partly aggrieved by the flight of black souls from their churches, white evangelicals coalesced around the mournful lamentations of Lost Cause religion and found in various sources – the Bible, emerging Social Darwinism and their own practical knowledge of "the nigger" – ample reason to bind African Americans to the regimens of a second serfdom. Scientific racism had been "anathema to the theologically orthodox" during slavery. Emancipation and the problem of controlling blacks who were armed with the vote and reinforced by the Fourteenth and Fifteenth Amendments quickly made the heresy *de rigueur*.[21]

In contrast, the theology of African American evangelicals never strayed from its original incarnation as a celebration of liberation and a sense of recovered community. Undergirding these themes was an almost palpable optimism that suffused postbellum hymns:

> Jesus break slav'ry chain, Lord
> Break slav'ry chain Lord,
> Break slave'ry chain Lord,
> Da Heben gwinter be my home.[22]

Released from the oversight of white ministers, charismatic African American religious leaders rejoiced in subversive Old Testament themes such as the Israelites' exodus from Egypt, but were drawn even more to the New Testament and its image of a loving God of forgiveness and endless forbearance.

African American theology saw in Jesus Christ an innocent fellow-sufferer sacrificed on the altar of freedom. Accordingly, the Lord's allegiances could not be in doubt in the embattled South, a former slave observed: "Lincoln died for we, Christ died for we, and me believe him de same mans."[23]

If the exodus from bi-racial churches was the wellspring from which the beloved community would spring, it also unwittingly contributed to the "festival of violence" that was about to descend on African Americans in the postbellum South. The exodus effectively deprived whites of an alternative socio-ethical vision that could have dulled whites' support for racial terror. White clergymen often raised their opposition to lynching, assassinations and mob killings. But even the most paternalist of these men were ardent segregationists and so were much too compromised to serve as an inspiring and alternative moral center. In the antebellum era, African Americans had played a direct and important role in shaping religious community and scholars such as Winthrop Jordan, Eugene Genovese, Donald Mathews, Katherine Dvorak and others stress the fraternal ties that a common Christianity fostered between blacks and whites in this period.[24] For example, the Armenian view that required individuals to open themselves and actively receive salvation applied to all people, black or white, free or unfree. It also entitled, indeed required, all individuals to spread God's word by preaching and converting individuals wherever they could be found, regardless of either the preacher's or the convert's race. Within the associational form of religion that prevailed in the evangelical South, lay egalitarianism enabled African American slaves to encode within their sermons Biblical messages and imagery that underscored the essential humanity that bound all people together. Before segregation emerged to rigidly racialize space, antebellum practices around essential religious rituals such as commensalism (sharing food at a common table, or receiving Communion in church) also brought black and white into close contact. Commensalism, which Katherine Dvorak extends to the sharing of a common sermon, was certainly attenuated by hierarchical arrangements that placed white elites ahead of plebeian whites and both ahead of the slaves who were consigned to the rear of churches. Seating arrangements in antebellum churches therefore reinforced the slave and class hierarchies of the region. But because the antebellum sermon "was received simultaneously by all present regardless of spiritual or social status, race, or condition of servitude," commensality also preserved the "egalitarian Christian creed of southern revivalism."[25]

Blacks and whites who jointly participated in the bi-racial churches certainly drew different conclusions from the same sermons and even extracted different lessons from the very experience of joint worship.[26] Nevertheless, bi-racial churches and the leveling implications of evangelic Armenianism encouraged a degree of fraternity that did in fact cut across the racial divide.

This tempering element of common humanity all but disappeared from the Southern religious landscape after 1865. Breakaway African American churches provided white ministers with a pretext for supporting segregated churches. As a minister wrote in 1866, most whites "can't accept the idea that we should take part in the intellectual as well as moral culture of this now most unfortunate race." He suggested that the problem of managing freed slaves should be handed over to the Northerners who had liberated them.[27] All too frequently, the sense of a shared humanity was replaced by invective ministers who, armed with sometimes brilliantly poisonous pens, rejoiced in demonizing African Americans and expressly denying their humanity. The distance between hateful pen and burning faggot was short and often seamless. By opening the moral floodgates in this manner, the authors of Lost Causism enabled unrestrained savagery to masquerade as upright Christian duty.[28]

The eruption of independent churches had more than socio-ethical implications for the tenor of race relations. The exodus further tightened the embrace between white evangelicals and a bloody-minded plantocracy because, without exception, freedmen immediately aligned their new churches with the successive battles against Reconstruction and Bourbon domination. The theological embrace of Reconstruction was particularly unrestrained: "In black churches, associations, and convention meetings, stump speeches for Republican candidates rang out as fervently as evangelical themes." Leading theologians set the example by running for office themselves. One historian counts no fewer than 237 black ministers who successfully ran for and held public office in local, state and national elections during Reconstruction.[29]

The vanguard role that these enterprising men played is suggested by the efforts of activists such as James Simms, a "minister-missionary" who entered politics in Georgia. Simms managed to purchase his freedom on the eve of the Civil War and departed for Boston. He returned to Georgia an ordained minister and was soon working for the Freedmans Bureau, the American Baptist Home Society and the Union League (formed during the war to promote the Republican Party and Reconstruction policies). Simms successfully ran for election to the Georgia House of Representatives before Klan activity drove him from the county. He later became the only black district judge in Reconstruction-era Georgia, the editor of the *Freedman's Standard* and testified before Congress on race relations in his state. In this period, Simms observed, ministers "had to leave their flock and legitimate field of labor to enter the arena of politics to secure right and justice for their people." Some, like Richard Burke, died for their "religio-political" work. Burke, a minister, teacher and Union League organizer, served in the Georgia's House of Representatives from 1868 to 1870 until Klan members murdered him. His former owner gave evidence before the hearings into the Klan's activities confirmed that, through his extensive political involvements, Burke had "made himself obnoxious to a certain class of young men." The strenuous organization and sacrifice of Simms and Burke illustrate the near-complete fusion of religion and pro-Reconstruction politics.[30]

White evangelicals instinctively recoiled from this development. They categorically refused to interact with their black counterparts on the grounds that equality violated the divinely sanctioned racial hierarchy. With unsurpassing hypocrisy, they accused black ministers of "meddling" in politics. They ridiculed black theologians as "religious fanatics and political scoundrels" who had steeped themselves in the "science of party politics." Under the tutelage of their Northern supporters, these "dupes" had learned to carry "the radical platform concealed among the leaves of the Bible" and would now settle for nothing less than "the gospel according to Radicalism," another term for "negro domination." In North Carolina, Presbyterians railed "in the name of the Church of God, against ministers who turn politicians being regarded as representatives of the clergy in any sense" and attributed the sudden appearance of politicized religion amongst African Americans to the "cunning of Satan, as represented by his agents in the Gorilla convention." The upshot of scores of similar, hate-filled assessments across the South was clear: the duty of white Christians was to defend their Lord by resurrecting white supremacy. Any white minister who "does not feel and *manifest* an interest in political affairs in the present crisis," a Presbyterian theologian from South Carolina summarized in 1867, was "recreant to his duty" – the italicized word being readily understood as a theological endorsement of the beginnings of anti-Reconstruction violence in the state.[31] By the time the South was Redeemed, monogenesis, once an axiomatic truth for white evangelists, belonged to an all but forgotten past. By the 1870s, polygenesis and scientific racism were everywhere ascendant in Southern intellectual circles. Spawned equally by the white laity and clergymen, the offspring of spurious science and biblical misreadings was a permissive culture that proclaimed or at least tolerated the essential virtue of racial violence.

The challenge of evangelical Populism

These views did not go unchallenged. Redeemers had hardly succeeded in extruding Reconstruction governments from the various states when the specter of Populism arose to challenge the Democratic Party. For a brief but decisive decade that effectively ended in the late 1890s, Populism presented the region with a challenge that profoundly rattled the configuration of postbellum power relations. Very nearly a national movement, Populism primarily targeted Bourbon Democrats, whose industrial, agricultural, banking, and railroad policies rested on *laissez faire* prescriptions that gave them overwhelming power over the country's working poor. In the agrarian South, agricultural issues, followed by struggles over the nascent industrial economy, enjoyed greatest currency amongst the poor. Tom Watson, a leading Populist in Georgia in the 1890s (before he become a rabid segregationist after 1904), managed to forge a viable working relationship between "Northern Progressivism and Southern Agrarianism" that vaulted Populism onto the national stage in the elections of 1894 and 1896.[32]

African Americans had terminated ecclesiastical bi-racialism by immediately fleeing *en masse* from white-controlled bi-racial churches. Bi-racialism in the emerging New South *economy*, however, was another matter. In economic matters, African Americans gladly turned to the emerging Populist movement. In so doing, they threw their weight into a bi-racial movement that was insurrectionary yet also deeply conservative, a movement that never successfully resolved the combination of the region's traditional racism with the inter-racial sentiments that evolved in the 1880s and 1990s. Nevertheless, Populism did spawn an inclusionary political culture and presented poor whites with strategic options that elevated class unity above the region's customary racial divisions. Populism's collapse therefore removed a bulwark that had checked the racism of plebeian whites, weakening further this diminished and vulnerable class even as employers fanned the flames of racial division by turning job competition into racial resentment.

Religion played a central role in these developments. The broad struggle against Reconstruction had welded white evangelicals to the restored plantocracy at the top of the Southern hierarchy, fusing together their mutual support for segregation. An analogous movement emerged at the lower rungs of Southern society. Here, however, the sundering of the inter-racial Populist alliance cleaved poor whites from blacks, setting in place a vital precondition for the emergence of a cross-class, intra-racial unity amongst poor whites and elites. The majority of Southern Populists were also members of the evangelical movement and fervently believed that their movement manifested "the Christian religion in concentrated form."[33] Simultaneously evangelical and militant, Populists who shared an essentially religious view of society readily conceived of their battles against reactionary Bourbon Democrats as also a struggle against immoral avarice and an un-Christian indifference towards "the little man." For them, eminently secular grievances such as the crop lien system, landlessness and tenancy, paltry wages and the absence (or debilitations) of credit were also inextricably affairs of their evangelical faith. Sizable numbers of ordained ministers in the Baptist, Methodist and Presbyterian churches left the ministry and devoted themselves to Populist reforms because the organized churches had failed to support poverty-stricken farmers and the emerging class of wage workers. Many, such as the Bible-quoting activists that Keith King examined in his study of Texas Populists, were convinced that evidence of individual immorality such as laziness and alcoholism were but symptoms of a much larger evil, corporate greed, and the inhumanity it bred.

> As a result, evangelical ideas about politics, democracy, economics, and relationships of class, race, and gender not only shaped Populists' blueprint for reform but, more important, motivated Populists duty to God above duty to party and at times even to race in order to restore what they understood to be America's God-given system of economic liberalism and politi-

cal freedom ... [Populists] wove their political and economic reforms into a grand cosmic narrative pitting the forces of God and democracy against those of Satan and tyranny. As they did so ... they recruited new Populist converts with revivalistic intensity, and they sought political reform with a fervor usually reserved for seeking salvation from sin.[34]

Dr Cyrus Thompson, a Methodist lay leader in North Carolina, married anti-Catholicism to his scathing opposition to capitalism: "just as the church may lose the spirit of its head and accept the lordship of Constantine or Mammon ... so a republic may be robbed of the fruits of democracy and its citizens ... become slaves of increasing aggregations of wealth and power."[35] Yet evangelical Populism never successfully overcame the foundations of a conservative agricultural society in which conservative evangelicalism and widespread racism were part of the cultural ether. While the very idea of a militant evangelical Populism challenges John Lee Amy's claim that evangelical churches were trapped in "cultural captivity" and mired in the region's conservative mores, the characterization is a reminder of the multiple conservative influences that evangelical Populists absorbed and exuded. For example, elements of Populism also drew from the same evangelical creeds that stressed individual salvation, community discipline and racial separation. Christian religious and moral values were a requirement for admission. Those who wished to join the movement first had to declare their belief in the existence of God and be of "good moral character." In North Carolina, a known moonshiner was denied membership because he was judged to have "willfully and persistently" violated state laws. An application from a man in Tennessee was also refused because he allegedly mistreated his wife.[36] Populism was insurrectionary in some ways, but it was by no means revolutionary. To the contrary, Populism "sacralized the status quo." Opinion therefore divides over the degree to which Populism was a genuine inter-racial phenomenon.[37]

Republicans and Populists managed to cobble together a working alliance that yielded encouraging electoral results in many Southern states. Many of these electoral victories would have been impossible without the stolid and massive support that African Americans gave to Populist and Republican candidates. But the differences between radical Populists and the more moderate Republicans over "free silver" and other issues could not be contained. In the presidential elections of 1896, the Democratic Party took up several positions that the People's Party had advocated, diminishing the distance between the two parties. William Jennings Bryan delivered his "Cross of Gold" speech, a stirring pietistic masterpiece, at the Democratic Party convention of 1896. The spellbinding address merged the sufferings of Christ on the cross, "the farmer who goes forth in the morning and toils all day" and "the miners who go down a thousand feet into the earth." Bryan echoed Populists' opposition to the gold standard and won the support of small farmers and the poor (who looked to "free silver" and "bimetalism" policies to increase the money supply and help pay off their debts). As more and more Republicans made overtures to Democrats, key Populist leaders also broke rank. When talk of "fusion" between the People's Party and the Democratic Party gave rise to actual alliances in different states, most radical Populists, including the vast majority of African Americans, felt bitterly betrayed. They punished the People's Party by joining the Republican Party *en masse*. Indeed, the scale of African Americans' departure rivalled the exodus that had destroyed bi-racial churches in the four years after 1866.[38]

The inter-racial populist movement had run its course. Irreparably splintered and crippled, the Populist Party effectively merged with the Republican Party in the 1908 presidential election but lingered on as a separate organization until it ebbed into irrelevance within a few years. The demise of a movement that had once stood like a David against the Goliaths of the South removed the only redoubt that could have staved off "Bourbon rule."

The Democratic Party moved in for the kill as soon as the People's Party began to buckle. In state after state, Democrats launched "a full-scaled white supremacy campaign ... aimed at intimidating blacks and uniting white voters behind loyalty to race and manhood." The Party declared open season on Populists, and its rank and file responded. In state after state, Populists faced threats of death; armed thugs in red shirts stood guard at voting places as law enforcement authorities looked on; assassinations of known Populists spiked. Not satisfied with intimidating potential voters, the Party's goon squads turned on African Americans in public office, killing many and driving even more into flight. Animosity against Populist policies served as a conduit for attacking African Americans. Reflecting on the presidential elections of 1898, Joe Creechley concludes that at least in North Carolina, "the white supremacy campaign of 1898 and the disfranchisement of blacks in 1900 must therefore be understood as an attack on both Populism and blacks."[39]

Evangelicals figured prominently in the routing of the Populist movement and the decade-old inter-racial threat. Their role in North Carolina echoed similar development in the other states. Here, "the Democratic machine enlisted the help of mainline evangelical leaders, most of whom were long-standing opponents of populism, to champion the cause of white supremacy as a means of maintaining God's axioms for race relations."[40] When the Party promised to indefinitely fund Trinity College (a Methodist institution, renamed Duke University in 1924), Josiah Bailey, editor of the *Biblical Recorder*, dropped his former opposition to "state aid" to the state university and advocated franchise qualifications that dispossessed not only African Americans but illiterate whites as well. In a speech delivered at a white supremacist rally in 1898, a trustee of Trinity College welcomed "the supremacy of that race destined not only to rule the country but to carry the Gospel to all nations and maintain Civil and Religious Liberty throughout the world."[41] In 1909, the Nashville *Advocate* declared,

There is no community of Anglo-Saxons on the face of the earth that would submit quietly and permanently to be ruled by a colored race ... We have no trace of ill-will against our colored fellow-citizens ... But we record it as our sober judgement that they will not in a thousand years reach that level of intelligence and that stability of character which will make them equals for man of the white race. They will never again have a controlling influence in the Southern States. That question is settled.[42]

Southern Baptists played a central role in girding white Southerners for a general war against Reconstruction and provided vital sanctification for the specific practice of racial violence. The summary execution of a black man in North Carolina in 1867, a Baptist minister wrote, was perhaps questionable, "but under the excitement of the times" they would "forgive all who were concerned."[43] By the mid-1870s, few ministers questioned the violent tactics of groups such as the Ku Klux Klan, an organization that one minister justified in 1872 as follows: "In a state of society where there is no law, and where men must form temporary organizations for the redress of intolerable grievances and the maintenance of social order, justice itself is perverted by attack on these organizations."[44] J. L. Johnson, a Baptist minister who proudly proclaimed his role in drawing up the "Mississippi Plan" – which used violence and terror to destroy Reconstruction, disfranchise African Americans and set segregationist laws in place in Mississippi – spoke for the Southern majority when he explained that the Ku Klux Klan was "the salvation of whites and segregation the greatest blessing for the Negroes."[45]

Evangelical Populists in the 1880s and 1890s resembled the counter-cultural evangelicals a full century earlier who, without guessing their future impact, initiated religious changes that transformed American society and history. But the evangelical activists of the late nineteenth century fell short of their own mission on an almost equally grand scale – and had an opposite effect on democracy. Early evangelicals had revolted against erudite Episcopalians, decorous congregations and centralized church bureaucracies, replacing these with rough and ready exhorters, homespun hymns enlivened with fiddles and itinerant "circuit riders" who took religion into the backwoods and hollows of the South and wherever else the still unconverted lived. Once the Democratic Party played the race card in the 1880s and 1890s and gained sufficient white support to exile blacks from the political arena, the routing of the Populist movement stripped white religion of its insurgent edge. White Protestantism in the twentieth century would not again accelerate the centrifugal forces of race, class and gender in Southern society, becoming instead an avowed bastion on which the cultural cohesion of the Solid South rested. Only a small minority of evangelical Populists would remain true to the racially egalitarian creeds that had drawn them to the movement.

Evangelical Populists looked upon the wreckage of their movement and asked, "What do you do when Satan wins?"[46] The majority responded by submitting to the siren song of race and blended into the segregated churches that the exodus of African Americans and the racism of white evangelicals had created. A much smaller number hewed to the inter-racial culture of the brief but epochal Populist movement by retreating into pre-millennial dispensationalism and Pentecostalism, inter-racial movements that grew like wildfire across the Southern states in the Third Great Awakening (1900–30). Earlier millennial theology had enjoined individuals to actively prepare the world for the return of Christ. In contrast, pre-millennial dispensationalism dampened social activism by proclaiming that God would achieve this task Himself.[47] The ascent of apolitical Pentecostalism and disabling pre-millennialism was a definitive repudiation of an authority-challenging version of Protestant evangelicalism within white Southern society.

Afrikaners in South Africa also asked the same demoralizing question, "What do you do when Satan wins?" For Afrikaners, the answer was clear, "You embrace the Social Gospel, organize the poor, and compel the government to come to your aid." Recent historians of the American South suggest that the mass of poor whites did not submit meekly to the dominance of forked-tongue employers who preached the "Solid South" but undermined whites by turning them against fellow black workers (see Chapter 3). The weak labor movements that poor whites established as the agricultural South slowly became industrialized in the first half of the twentieth century were in no small measure a function of Populism's defeat. The same may be said of the anemic version of the Social Gospel that white evangelicals came to favor in the New South. More concerned with moral issues than with material progress, this version of the Social Gospel, too, was very much the diminished offspring of a vanquished Populist past.

Civil religion and the Social Gospel in the South

C. Vann Woodward's *Origins of the New South* established the basic view that the Social Gospel never quite took off in the New South. In Woodward's dyspeptic assessment, "one searches in vain for important manifestations" of the Social Gospel in the Southern states.[48] Woodward's thesis contains a powerful truth that seems unavoidable to any attempt to answer why lynching became entrenched in a region noted for its devotion to the Christian faith. Evangelical doctrine in the New South stressed the overriding importance of individual salvation, bearing witness to God and the centrality of the conversion experience – the building blocks of what Wilbur Cash called "the Southern Protestant ethic."[49] Because it discouraged inquiries into issues of social and political power, this theological worldview dissuaded whites from focusing on the relationship between secular culture and their Christian faith. Evangelical leaders inculcated amongst white churchgoers a message of non-involvement with the state, insisting that progress stemmed from individual morality and not from government assistance or political agitation.[50] In the 1890s Southern evangelicals had come down on the side of Redeemers and reactionary Bourbon Democrats in the battle against Populism. Once Populism was defeated, their suspicions of aggressive Social Gospelism in the New South era again strengthened the hand of employers and did little to dull the growing competition between white and black workseekers. The churches' hostility to an active social ministry was therefore pernicious and consequential. It simultaneously weakened white struggles against rapacious employers, focused poor whites' animosities against blacks instead of employers and bestowed on the ensuing racial violence the distinct aura of a Christian sanction.

Not all scholars agree with Woodward's claim that Southern Protestant theology opposed the Social Gospel in either principle or practice. Woodward's critics readily concede that Social Gospelism was relatively stunted in the South but attribute it to the virtual absence in the region of industrialization, the matrix from which Social Gospelism has historically emerged. The extensive urban problems that plagued Northern industrial cities and preoccupied the Benevolent Empire of social Christians there were simply less germane to churches in the agrarian South. Less learned than their Northern counterparts, deeply conservative and therefore unlikely to be the source of radical new doctrines, Southern ministers hewed to the familiar Baptist interpretation of the Scriptures, emphasizing the feudal-like bonds of deference and authority that bound the agrarian social order together. Southern theologians remained largely silent about the systemic causes of social problems and saw no need for the radical solutions – especially trade unions and socialist doctrines – that flourished dangerously in the North.[51] Woodward's critics concur that Southern Protestants rejected the essential premise of the Social Gospel – that people are inherently good and corrupted only by social circumstances – as well as the Northern view that "brotherhood" and solidarity were essential foundations of Christian community. Still, scholars of the South conclude that a "Southern tradition" of Social Gospelism is readily discernable if allowance is made for the virtual absence of industrialization in the region.

While their Northern brethren immersed themselves in urban problems such as homelessness, unemployment and labor movements, Southern Protestants committed themselves to an array of "blue law" issues which, they believed, threatened the agricultural communities of the South: "temperance reform, anti-gambling crusades, campaigns for the elimination of political corruption, and the promotion of public morality, care of orphans and the aged."[52] Moreover, not all evangelical leaders were indifferent to poverty, low wages, the lack of education and the often appalling health of their white congregants. Authors such as John W. Storey, Howard Hopkins, Henry May and Kenneth Bailey therefore all present the case for an active Social Gospel in the South. John Storey, for example, argues that the Social Gospel in the South was not only strong but also self-consciously different from its Northern expression. In Storey's telling, evangelicals in the "Southern Baptist bureaucracy" in Texas "were steady reformers for

issues such as child laws, alcoholism, family life, poor wages, and race relations." Keith Harper's work on "Southern Baptists and Social Christianity"
presents some of the strongest evidence in favor of a dynamic Social Gospel
in the South. Southern Baptists engaged a "broad spectrum of social concerns ... within a distinctly southern context" but "were not reformers in
the traditional Progressive Era sense." Instead, Baptist reformers "avoided
calling for legislative changes to alter social behavior," preferring to subordinate their social work to missions, evangelization and the salvation of
individuals. Because they approached "societal ills through churches and
such social networks as families and communities, Southerners, especially
Baptists, may have camouflaged their Social Christianity to later generations
with differing cultural expectations."[53] Criticism of Woodward's thesis gathered momentum with the publication of works devoted to social movements
around prohibition, temperance and anti-lynching legislation after 1900.
Wayne Flynt showed that Baptists in Alabama, Appalachia and Georgia
championed health care, child labor and educational reform; Southern Presbyterians even explored reunification with Social Gospelers in the Northern
church. John Lee Eighmy found more evidence of a significant social ethic
amongst Protestant churches than Woodward allowed. However, Eighmy
concluded, churches were in "cultural captivity" to the region's conservative traditions; involvement in social issues was a voluntary – but not a proscribed – matter for individual churches.[54] The collective weight of all these
studies leaves little doubt that a Southern variant of the Social Gospel took
root in the decades immediately after the Civil War.

   At best, however, this literature largely qualifies Woodward's uncom-
promising picture of a church establishment without a social mission. For
Samuel Hill, Eighmy's view of churches passively ensnared in "old southern
folkways, social conservatism, and local church autonomy" exonerates the
churches. As Hill shows, Protestant churches were all too energetic in their
opposition to an ethic of social benevolence and were actively complicit in
shaping the conditions that maintained widespread poverty across the region.
Even when they successfully pressed state legislatures to engage in reforms
in a field such as education, evangelical leaders refrained from confronting
head-on the wage and employment policies on which the low-wage Southern economy rested. Social Gospelism, too, often reflected the impact and
commitment of pioneering individuals rather than church denominations.[55]
Thus, the problem was not that Baptist reformers remained cloistered in
theological institutions or that ministers devoted themselves to a narrow
range of "social ills." The deeper problem was that their solutions reflected
a conservative theology that displayed little interest in the social matrix of
poverty, leaving them incapable of confronting the landowners and employers
who prospered at the expense of the working poor. "Progressive activism
clashed with the localist tradition of southern communities," ensuring
that the work of social Christians in the South remained self-limiting and
fundamentally conservative.[56] Robert Martin's study of the Fellowship of

Southern Churchmen, an association of liberal and radical clergymen who championed the cause of workers in the 1940s and 1950s, demonstrates that a radical Social Gospel was a rare and improbable phenomenon in the South, almost certain to succumb to the theological insistence in the region that reforms, when justifiable, should be entrusted to the machinery of local government and prominent elites.[57]

Rufus Spain's observation that "American Protestantism by and large, defended the prevailing economic system" was particularly true in the South. Here, the advent of factories and the culture of industrialization were often viewed as threats to the slow and deeply entrenched rhythms of society. Social Gospelers who saved Southern souls one at a time had little to say about the structural causes of poverty. They had even less to say about altering a social system that was overwhelmingly dominated by oppressive planters and an emerging class of businessmen who defended and benefited from the region's low wage system. Unsurprisingly, employers frequently solicited the churches to coax workers into cooperating with company policies, while clerics met challenges to the hegemony of local elites with suspicion.[58] "Seldom," one source notes, "did well-educated ministers with their scholarly sermons offend the sentiments of the mill management."[59] Many Protestant leaders supported the formal proposition that labor was entitled to "better its condition"; some even supported unions and accepted workers' right to stage strikes. However, ministers generally opposed picketing, supported management's right to bring in scab labor, and insisted that strikes should not threaten public property and public safety – this at a time when management's first response to labor unrest was to summon the police, state militia, army units, "private detective agencies" and strike-breaking goon squads. The clerical editor of the *Religious Herald* (Richmond) clearly had the interests of employers at heart in a labor dispute in his state when he wrote: "If laborers, of any class, without or with cause of complaint, may break up the travel and trade on railroads, or arrest any other kind of business, at their own pleasure and for their own profit, then all right is disregarded, all laws trampled in the dust, all authority is overthrown. We are at the mercy of mobs." The editor of the *Christian Index* (Atlanta) reflected on the same strike and went further. Strikers were "entitled only to the consideration which is accorded public enemies ... Law and order and the rights of property must be maintained whatever the cost. Civilization, Christianity, even while they may weep over the cruel necessity which is forced upon them, have no alternative but to unite in the enforcement of the law." The way to deal with strikers who disrupted the public peace or sought to prevent others from reporting to work, another Baptist newspaper recommended in 1894, was "the bayonet and the bullet, promptly and fearlessly applied."[60]

Church leaders who believed that "Secular reforms [had] no place in the kingdom of heaven" did not hesitate to become "New South boosters" and lavish praise on employers and anti-labor policies of state governments.[61]

Many of their sermons filtered sin, grace and salvation through the promise of industrial progress. In their view, industrialization lay at the root of moral collapse, poverty and the "anti-Christian" antidote – Social Gospelism – that prevailed in the North. In the South, however, industrialization was different. Here, railroads, mines and factories "could become instruments of divine grace." Pastors preached that "it was not the financial system, not the trusts, not any institutional failing" that plagued Southern society but a "decadence of morals" in the individual's heart.[62] Virtually all religious leaders believed that the Populist challenge of the 1890s represented a fundamental threat not only to the political and economic foundation of the South but also to the spiritual fortitude of individuals who were being "tested" by God. Populists and the "godless hotheads" in the movement who railed against "wage slavery" and demanded a clutch of reforms – the printing of more money, the breakup of financial monopolies, the creation of a "subtreasury" to prop up agricultural prices – therefore struck at the heart of the soul-saving mission that Southern churches pursued. With only rare exceptions, the churches turned their backs on labor movements and repudiated labor militancy as violating a divine order. In reply to the accusation, "the church today stands where it has always stood, on the side of human slavery," a Methodist minister blithely declared that the Protestant establishment was "necessarily a conservative power, and therefore an antagonist to all disorder." It could only "align itself with the powers that be, for 'they are ordained of God.'"[63]

Such views rested on Baptists' support for the free market system and a vitriolic antipathy for anything that smacked of socialism. Convinced that capitalism was "natural" and "American capitalism [was] the best of all possible orders," Baptists in particular looked dispassionately upon an economic system that assigned fortune to a small minority and kept the mass of society mired in poverty. Wealth and poverty, for Baptists, were equally signs of God's will on earth, reflected further in the various gradations that separated the rich from the poor. The wealth of a "Mr. Vanderbilt," a Baptist minister observed, was the mark of God's approval and "an indication of providence that he ought to *live* like a rich man." Poverty, in contrast, is "an expression of Divine disfavor" with a man's "faults and follies," and "when it arises from other causes, it may be regarded simply as the schooling of Providence."[64]

With Reconstruction and Populism destroyed and the "race question" finally "settled," evangelical churches scaled down their rapprochement with labor movements in the last quarter of the nineteenth century. Turning inward, they obsessed about the morals of their white congregants. Samuel Hill concludes that evangelism in the New South was a "means of avoiding other matters of importance." Protestant establishments, he muses, could have reasoned more forthrightly: "we must save souls so that we won't have to put the South's house in order."[65] Beginning in 1892 with the publication of Ida B. Wells' pioneering pamphlet, "Southern Horrors," this, in a nutshell, is the essential thesis of the literature on lynching in the New South. Numberless private lynchings that went unpunished and dramatic communal lynchings attended by thousands sounded the same distracting song – "the enemy is race" – even as poverty, unemployment and landlessness dogged poor whites well into the middle of the twentieth century. Meanwhile, preachers reiterated the staple lessons of Southern evangelicalism – duty, guilt, sacrifice – and generally agreed to "stay out of politics." Fiery preachers therefore turned into "stupid foolish men when confronted with questions that ask 'Why?'" "Wherever their answers came from," Lillian Smith continues, "that place did not send them answers to the problems of poverty, of race segregation, unions, wages, illness and ignorance, war ... or answers to the old question of human freedom."[66] A critical theology would have perforated the civil religion of a Solid South that simply demanded allegiance to white supremacy:

> Any semblance of a social-gospel ideology would have upset the balance and rendered impossible mutual support between church and State. Any novel interpretation of the Christian world view with intense focus on the relation of ethical values to social conditions would have constituted a formidable threat to the (white) Southern Way of Life. In the process of challenging, then overturning, traditional social patterns, especially racial, it would have wrought disruption. Southerness, the "God above God", would have been dethroned, and support crumbled.[67]

Whatever their commitment to a social Christianity, white churches actively campaigned for "the Solid South" and rejected the politics of confrontation. As a result, whites' efforts to secure the "second serfdom" of African Americans necessarily reinforced other fundamental pillars of Southern society – the dominance of agrarian elites and industrial employers, the subordination of poor whites to employers and the control that white men sought over women.

Retributive justice: "The Southern rite of human sacrifice"

Violence was as central to Southern Protestantism as Southern Protestantism was to the making of segregation. As Donald Mathews writes: "crucifixion, an act of violence, is at the very core of the Christian paradigm that was so essential a part of Southern culture."[68] Whites may not have been as cognizant as African Americans of the similitude between Christ's crucifixion and Southern lynching, but they were not entirely insensible to the religious aura that communal lynching evoked. For example, scholars have often likened the hushed and cathartic silence that descended on mobs present at a spectacle lynching to the silence that befell Golgotha as Jesus Christ died.[69]

The issue, however, runs deeper than such similarities. Much of Southern Protestantism hinged around an interpretation of Christianity that emphasized retribution and a sanctified view of violence. According to the theory of Atonement, Jesus Christ suffered a violent death to compensate for the sins of Man and open the gates of Heaven for Christians. This view of violence as simultaneously destructive and redemptive is central to the ability of white Southerners to be simultaneously religious and tolerant of lynching. At the very end of *Religion and the Solid South*, Hill ponders why Protestantists who considered themselves already "saved" nevertheless listened to evangelical ministers week after week "when the appeal of the sermon is to repent and be saved." Hill advances several possible explanations, every one of which is also remarkably adept at explaining why lynching could appear as a virtuous activity in the Protestant South.[70] Ritualized sermons, for example, regularly testified to the "differentiation" of the world into "the spiritual haves" and the "spiritual have nots." And, Hill adds, "the evangelistic modality ... resonates to southern experience." Hill's elaboration on this point is so pertinent to the ritual execution of blacks that it requires minimal comment:

> Churchgoers keep on hearing that humanity is differentiated, a fact they have learned from their ordinary experience of distinguishing Southerness from all other cultural identifications. By implication, the evangelistic sermons commend the in-group, those who have undergone conversion, saying to them individually and corporately as Southerners that a comparison of themselves with other persons and societies places them at an advantage.

Lynching, then, dramatized the dominance of the white "in-group," and dramatically "exposed" the inherent sinfulness of the black "out-group." Plain white folk struggling to survive at the margins of Southern society and elites who lorded it over society supported lynching for different reasons. But "individually and corporately," lynching reassured both that they "belonged" to the upper reaches of a differentiated society. Communal lynchings, Hill continues, also evoked a festive and cathartic atmosphere that closely resembled the collective participation of worshippers in the conversion experience. The moment the lynch victim passed from life to death was the mirror image of the convert's passage "from death to life." Both movements – one securing a sacrificial death, the other a personal rebirth – constituted a reassuring fellowship, a righteous sense of whiteness in the case of lynching and the certainty of redemption at evangelical meetings.[71]

However, the most sustained account of the role that Protestant theology played in cultivating the lynch culture is perhaps to be found in "The Southern Rite of Human Sacrifice," in which Donald Mathews underscores the inextricable fusion of religious and secular themes in the world of white Southerners. The Southerner's understanding of racial violence was subsumed under a larger and more encompassing understanding of the role that violence and punishment play in Christianity. At the source of this understanding lay the polarity between God's infinite love and human sin. The inescapable corollary of human sin is "the belief in someone's right to punish you." A belief in just punishment is foundational to all Christian theology but would be fused with the racial binary in the South, first through slavery and then through segregation. Both racial orders upheld whites' "right to punish" African Americans. Religious and secular justifications for segregation combined inextricably, blending religious and secular creeds that enabled white Southerners to normalize lynching as a form of divine retribution. At the core of this moral reasoning lay the idea of atonement through "blood sacrifice," an event that resides at the heart of Christian theology. In Christian dogma, the ritual murder of Christ is the precondition for individual salvation and the event that unlocked the gates of heaven. Christ's own violent execution therefore established the possibility of community in the afterlife.

Mathews is not alone in arguing that lynching reinforced a similar sense of community amongst white Southerners. In making this point, Wilbur J. Cash spoke of the connection between a "primitive frenzy and the blood sacrifice," suggesting that lynching both sprang from and assuaged the irrational savagery of wild mobs. Scholars such as Jacqueline Hall and William Brundage reject the idea of a "primitive frenzy" on the ground that its obscures the eminently rational and sociological determinants of lynching. Mathews concurs but also argues that "the primitive frenzy" embodies the sociological determinants of lynching: "if 'primitive frenzy' is translated as the result of repressed sexuality, challenged patriarchy, and reasoned violence fused in the act of murder, we may be able to understand it in less emotionally freighted ways. But the frenzy remains." Mathews' point about the importance of "blood sacrifice," then, is that lynching emanated from not one but two inextricable "frenzies": from Southern Protestantism and from Southern segregation. Blood sacrifice, he writes, "is at the core of southern white fundamental Protestantism":

> Blood sacrifice is the connection between the purpose of white supremacists, the purity signified in segregation, the magnificence of God's wrath, and the permission granted the culture through the wrath of 'justified' Christians to sacrifice black men on the cross of white solidarity.

Lynching accorded with a religion that unleashed the saving grace of violence against the ineradicable sin of Man. Christ died in *propitiation* (atonement) for human sin and His death was the price of mortal sin. But His death was also an act of expiation which, going further than the mere propitiation ("to make amends"), actually *did* heal the rift between God and Man the Sinner. The sheer generosity of Christ's sacrifice therefore served as a continual reminder of the enormity of human sin. For white congregants who forgot about the essential depravity of Man, any number of "exhortations, prayers, hymns, recitations, scowls, maternal tears, and patriarchal condemnation [all] worked to cry 'guilt', to teach guilt, to instill guilt: to make the offending soul shudder at the enormity of his/her guilt." The polarity between a Wrathful God and guilt-filled Man filled the fire-and-brimstone sermons for which Southern preachers were noted. Guilt demanded punishment, and "the right to punish"– Lillian Smith observed in *Killers of the Dream* (1949) – resided permanently at the core of both Protestantism and segregation. Smith, a white novelist and an early Southern champion of the civil rights movement, once described segregation as "spiritual lynching." The multiple taboos of segregation and Protestantism were so hopelessly entangled in her own childhood in Clayton, Georgia, that "sin and sex and segregation" seemed to form a systemic trinity that was guarded by a phalanx of priests, policemen, and lynchers who were always "ready to punish."[72] White children sensed at an early age that "God so loved the world that he gave His only begotten Son so that we might have segregated churches."[73]

The theory of retributive punishment arrived late in the history of Christianity – fully one thousand years after the death of Christ in fact.[74] At the time when John Calvin set about reinterpreting Christianity in the mid-sixteenth century, the prevailing theory of retributive punishment – that of Anselm of Canterbury – held that Christ's actual death had indeed satisfied Man's debt to God. Calvin, however, contended that it was not the act of death but the *bearing of punishment* that epitomized Christ's agony on earth. Southern Protestantism was powerfully drawn to Calvin's vision of hell on earth. If pastors returned ceaselessly to the image of Man the Sinner, they did so because they possessed a fundamental faith in the cleansing power of punishment. Punishment, like sin, was inevitable and so unavoidable. But punishment was also virtuous: certainly an instrument of wrath but also of salvation. Southern religious leaders looked to the travails of Christ and concluded that he had "suffered legally and righteously for the guilt of sin imputed to him." They spoke of the "punitive providence" of God and warned against the danger of "mere pity" – for pity was no reason not to punish the guilty (or even those to whom guilt was only "imputed"). These themes were central to the theology of Robert Lewis Dabney (1820–98), the influential Calvinist Presbyterian theologian from Virginia. Dabney served as a chaplain in the Virginia regiment in the Confederate army and became a professor of theology in Texas after the war. As a Calvinist, Dabney's theology is crafted around the propositions that human nature is profoundly ruined by sin and that only the stern intervention of God can turn Man from rebellion to willing obedience. God, Dabney writes, rejoiced in punishing the guilty because "retributive punishment is the impartial satisfaction of eternal justice." Dabney therefore refused to apologize for slavery because human bondage was God's "punishment of, and remedy for ... the peculiar moral degradation of a part of the [human] race."[75]

Why, however, was Christ punished when he was incapable of offending God? Dabney's response to this question hinges on the concept of a "penal substitute" and clearly illumines the slippage between religious and racial orders in the South. In an argument that closely resembles René Girard's theory of the "scapegoat mechanism," Dabney observes that Christ was a "substitute."[76] Although God is implacably retributive only against those who are irredeemably "reprobate," he nevertheless deems it acceptable to punish "substitutes." As Dabney wrote in *Christ Our Penal Substitute*: "To secure this end, the punishment of a substitute may be as truly relevant as of the guilty principal, provided the adequate substitute be found, and his own free consent obviates all charge of injustice against him personally." A "penal substitute" fully meets the test of propitiation and expiation, "for now law is satisfied, guilt is duly punished, though the guilty man be pardoned. The penal debt is paid." Equally noteworthy is Dabney's speculation about the generosity of God, who turned over his only Son to violent mortals, and the selfless love of Christ, who suffered violence so that his very tormentors would one day be saved. It is quite conceivable, Dabney concludes, to "effect a substitution by which impartial justice and law are more gloriously satisfied than by the condign punishment of the guilty themselves." For Dabney, therefore, the demands of retributive justice may be fully satisfied by punishing a scapegoat. However, his qualification of this proposition is important: the scapegoat must *voluntarily* agree to suffer on behalf of the genuinely guilty.[77]

It requires little imagination to see how a stern vision of retributive justice in the spiritual sphere readily translates into pitiless punishment in the volatile arena of race relations in the South. Dabney harbored the deepest contempt for those who saw in God only "the delightful attribute of benevolence," and so recoiled from the "awful attribute of vengeance." The ceaseless battle against evil requires "Godly men" to embrace the central fact of vengeance in Christian theology. Dabney's views were therefore dominated by a "theology of vengeance," the appropriate response to the alliance of Godless threats that conspired against the postbellum South: Northern domination; "caviling creatures" who were appalled by the divine wrath of God; and the menace of masterless slaves.[78] In practice, Dabney's Southern compatriots simply set aside Dabney's view that a penal substitute had to voluntarily submit to his punishment. They fastened onto his vision of a "Calvinism driven not by a confession of one's own sin but the draconian punishment of others." The principle of voluntary substitution was duly ejected from Southern theology in the segregation years and "punishment was sacralized as the dominant religion of the American South."[79]

Protestant ministers were not noted for their scholarly skills, and few Southerners could have engaged in or even followed learned exegeses such as those that preoccupied Dabney. However, the theology of vengeance and punishment in the South did not require a grasp of recondite disputes about theodicy, the penal-substitution theory, or the doctrine of atonement. Echoing arguments by Wilbur Cash and Donald Hill, Mathews argues that churchgoers divined the central importance of punishment from the "primitive frenzy" of group worship itself. Sunday sermons and often boisterous camp meetings vividly hammered the essential point home: redemptive violence lay at the core of Christianity. Baptist congregations "heard countless familiar and ritualistic sermons, whether read, exposited or chanted, that described the blood flowing from the Redeemer's head, hands, side, and feet; they felt the terrible jolt against His searing wounds when the cross was plunged into the earth. They could not fail to have been impressed, as was the young Wilbur Cash, with the 'primitive' feelings that would later allow him to understand the 'blood sacrifice' as essential to the Mind of the South."[80]

By Anselm's time, the concept of "satisfaction" was fundamental to the feudal system so that, Millard Erickson notes, "Anselm pictures God as a feudal overlord who, to maintain his honor, insists that there be adequate satisfaction for any encroachment on it."[81] Anselm argued that God may either punish sinners directly or seek satisfaction by requiring offenders to pay a price above and beyond the debt incurred. Like God, society, too, is free to punish crime by pursuing either of these options to ensure that criminals "pay their debt" to the social order. Anselm therefore connected religious and civil law by placing satisfaction at the center of both.[82]

Like the honorific society in which Anselm of Canterbury lived when he developed his "Satisfaction Theory" of retribution, Southerners – elites and commoners alike – were notoriously prickly about perceived offenses to their reputation and social standing. Their attraction to a theology of vengeance mirrored the premium they placed on the region's code of honor. Familiar as they were with *lex talionis*, white Southerners intuitively appreciated the deep connections among satisfaction, punishment, and suffering. (One dissenting theologian has described Satisfaction Theory as tantamount to "cosmic child abuse.")[83] Alternative theological discourses that celebrate reconciliation with God through empathy and forgiveness accordingly played a subordinate role in white Protestantism. In contrast, a theology of compassion immediately became the backbone of the independent evangelical churches that African Americans formed and also echoed powerfully in the gospel of forgiveness that the civil rights movement championed after the Second World War. For white Protestant leaders, qualities such as forgiveness and compassion could not appease a wrathful God. For this God, forgiveness is contingent on propitiation, "a sacrifice or payment which removes wrath."[84] Dabney's theology therefore insistently dismissed the view that punishment should "fit the crime." To the contrary, he argued that the theory of propitiation demands that punishment should *exceed* the crime.[85]

Shorn of the complicated intellectual scaffolding, theological views such as these found their way into countless Southern sermons and provided a virtual *carte blanche* to conceive of lynching as a religiously sanctioned enterprise. Southern Protestantism larded retributive violence with intense symbolic meaning that readily suggested to white men that lynching was a righteous crusade to rid society of the "black-beast rapist." Dabney's theology had insisted that substitutes should voluntarily take on the burden of suffering. Without the element of voluntary cooperation, the selfless generosity of the substitute is replaced with a guilt which is simply imputed to him. Dabney's substitute dissolves and reappears as René Girard's scapegoat. In the mind of the killers, however, the rapist-scapegoat is executed in accordance with Divine Justice.[86]

White lynchers were too racist and indifferent to the victim's suffering to desist from cruelly killing their black victims. Racism and an absence of human compassion no doubt inoculated white Southerners against the horrors of ritual sacrifice. However, Girard argues that emotions such as hatred, contempt and indifference are overshadowed by the more important element in the ritual killing of a scapegoat – the victim's marginality and vulnerability. These two characteristics are essential to the selection of the scapegoat: marginality deprives the scapegoat of communal support and sympathy, while vulnerability ensures that the victim will not retaliate. Marginality and vulnerability therefore make violence against a scapegoat possible, while victimhood transforms the scapegoat into a symbolic representative of the evil that is said to threaten society.[87]

Girard's argument explains why "vagrants" and "itinerant strangers" figured so prominently amongst the 800 white men who were lynched prior to the Civil War. Simply being a "stranger" was a potentially lethal matter in a region where trusting but generally poor locals rarely locked their homes or tied down their property. But when marginality could be systemically connected to sex and race, as the myth of the "black-beast rapist" did so effectively in the postbellum era, the result was an explosive atmosphere that ignited the amorphous connections amongst "sex, sin, and segregation." Southern racial etiquette subjected African Americans to multiple and frequently murky obligations so that the possibility of transgression inhered in all racial interactions. Under these conditions, even blacks who were familiar to local whites could suddenly "take on" marginality by violating any number of taboos which, in the South, were always pregnant with the allegation of rape. Christ was innocent, but he too, so the Bible says, "took on" his fate on Calvary. This, ultimately, was the potent core of the myth of the black-beast rapist: even whites who otherwise distanced themselves from the harshest forms of white supremacy could readily associate themselves with the lynching of a black accused of committing "the unmentionable deed."

Lynching as ritual murder

To view lynching as an act of ritual human sacrifice is to establish a powerful case for the religious nature of lynching. Orlando Patterson observes that lynching shared the essential qualities of human sacrifice associated with primitive societies. For the anthropologists Henri Hubert and Marcel Mauss, ritual murder in primitive societies involved "drama, celebration and play." The rituals began with the taunting of the victim and culminated in the moment of death, "at which point there was usually absolute quiet, often in stark contrast to the mirth and singing, even rowdiness, of preceding and later stages."[88] Frequently, the spot where the sacrifice was carried out was consecrated: beforehand by priests in primitive societies and, in the case of lynching, by the ritual killing itself. Patterson notes that African Americans were usually executed on trees, the closest approximation to the Holy Cross on which Christ died. Blacks were also frequently lynched on bridges; in Patterson's analysis, bridges symbolized the transition from a turbulent world to a more promising afterlife. Anthropologists have long recognized that murder by fire established a connection between the sacred and the secular worlds. Fire symbolically cleansed a sinful world by consuming the embodiment of evil.[89]

It is instructive to pause on the appalling fondness that white Southerners displayed for retaining the charred mementos of a lynching. Grizzly remains were highly prized artifacts of ritual murder. They included branches taken from the tree, faggots blackened by fire and pieces of the ropes used to truss and hang the victim. In primitive societies, either the victims or their remains were held to mediate the relationship between sacrificers and their gods. The remains of the victim were commonly dispatched to the sacred realm, usually by allowing the fires to consume the body entirely. Or the sacrificial remains were retained and dispersed in the secular world in fragments that could be preserved as sacred souvenirs. Absorbing the victim's remains into society – either in one's pockets or, as a horrified W. E. B. Du Bois once witnessed, by displaying fire-blackened remains in a store window – symbolically preserved ritual communication between sacrificers and their gods. Patterson describes this practice as "ritual cannibalism."[90] Whites, of course, did not actually eat the flesh of their victim. However, the literature does record instances of "autocannibalism" in which the victims were forced to consume pieces of themselves. Such was the case of Claude Neal who died at the hands of lynchers in Jackson County in October 1934. For Patterson, Neal's death blurs any categorical distinction between autocannibalism and actual cannibalism.[91] Moreover, at least some white Southerners appear to have sensed the element of cannibalism. In August 1920, two brothers, Irving and Herman Arthur, were chained and dragged through the streets of an African American neighborhood while jubilant whites screamed, "Here come the barbecued niggers!"[92]

Whites acknowledged the central role that Christian symbolism played in human sacrifice. Pastors frequently condoned lynching and clothed the practice in religious language that all Southerners understood. Invoking the Bible, ministers preached about the inferiority of blacks, their capacity for evil and the unremitting threat that "black-beast rapists" posed to white women, that vulnerable gateway to the racial order itself. "The presence of a preacher in the conspiracy was not at all unusual," Howard Smead concluded in his study of Mack Parker's lynching in Mississippi in 1959. "They were men given to extreme violence who invoked the Bible to justify black subordination." Preacher Lee, a Baptist minister from Picayunne, Mississippi, used his own car to summon up the lynch mob that killed Parker. "A wild-eyed fanatic" whose racially invective sermons were his stock in trade,

Lee "fervently believed God had intended blacks to be servants of whites" and frequently spoke out in favor of lynching.[93] A "fiery sermon" delivered by a Presbyterian minister, the Rev. Robert A. Elwood, was blamed for the lynching of George White in Wilmington, Delaware, in June 1903. Elwood railed against the incarceration of the accused, basing his anger on the constitutional provision that "In all criminal prosecutions the accused shall enjoy the right to a speedy and public trial." In a sermon filled with religious metaphors, Elwood complained: "Tonight [a black prisoner] is in jail with armed guards parading about for his protection. Is that speedy? Is that even constitutional?" Elwood declared: "If the judges insist that the trial of the murderer of Miss Bishop be delayed until September, then should he be lynched? I say yes." George White was duly hanged by a mob of several thousand. The Rev. Elwood did not comment on the event. But his congregation did by passing resolutions "expressing firm belief in the pastor's honesty, integrity, and Christian character."[94] In response, the Rev. Montrose W. Thornton, preached to his congregation in the First African Methodist Episcopalian Church, "The white man is a heathen, a fiend, a monstrosity before God." The enraged minister urged his awestruck listeners: "Be a law unto yourself ... Be your own Sheriff, court and jury ... Die in your tracks, perhaps drinking the blood of your pursuers ..."[95]

Powerful evidence that white Southerners understood lynching in religious terms, indeed that they viewed it as an expression and extension of their Christian faith, lies in the popular support that the Ku Klux Klan enjoyed. The ideological growth of the Klan, Nancy Maclean writes, can be explained by "evangelical Protestantism in general, and to fundamentalism in particular."[96] Klan ideology fused sacred messages and political goals and, according to Imperial Wizard Evans, the organization "was more than religion." For Wizard Evans, the movement was "emotional and instinctive"and operated beyond the reach of rational thought. This description aptly summarizes Southern evangelical Protestantism, which Charles Reagan Wilson describes as "a religious tradition that prizes religious experience over liturgy, theology, and other forms of religious life."[97]

Mathews does not argue that "white Christians justified the torture and murder of black men because of their consent to a certain doctrine." He notes that "those who believed the dogma of penal substitutionary atonement could be nauseated by the ghastly rituals enacted in public lynchings."[98] Ample evidence supports this important point. The letter that appeared in the Wesleyan Christian *Advocate* at the turn of the century articulated views that many sincere Christians shared: "The government that winks at lynching is vicious; the government that does not care is foolish; the government that will not put it down is bad, as well as foolish; the government that cannot is weak." In 1892, a Methodist newspaper in Nashville observed that it had suffered a drop in subscriptions after it had condemned the lynching in Texarakana, Texas, of a black man who was suspected of "an unnamable offense." The journal defiantly reiterated its opposition to lynching in clear terms: "We should not change our course by a hair's breadth if 10,000 names were to be dropped tomorrow."[99] Prominent Southern Baptists who believed that the Bible proclaimed "Negro inferiority" and upheld racial slavery nevertheless also bravely opposed lynching. William J. Northen, for example, campaigned against lynching as an "un-Christian" practice while serving as Governor of Georgia from 1887 to 1890, and vice-president of both the Southern Baptist Convention (SBC) and the Georgia Baptist Convention. Appalled by the 1906 Atlanta race riot, Northen organized a Business Men's Gospel Union, a bi-racial coalition of leading Christian laymen and clergy who attempted to organize a network of anti-lynching groups.[100] In tone and in spirit, the views of Christians such as Northen clashed with the intensifying violence used to subjugate and disfranchise "our black brothers in Christ." Impressed by several Methodist ministers who publicly denounced lynching between 1900 and 1914, Hunter Farish therefore concludes that "the outspoken denunciation of lynching by the journals and leaders of the denomination did much to check such violence in the South."[101]

Perhaps. Protestant leaders who rejected "applied Christianity" as a distraction from and betrayal of the church's evangelical mission work and damned as "evil" the very idea that the church should devote resources to the upliftment of poor whites were powerless in the area of race relations. Accordingly, liberals such as William J. Northen could do no more than call for "greater inter-racial cooperation" and "dialog" between white and black Southerners even as the number of lynchings continued to rise.[102]

Conclusion

Orlando Patterson's unsparing assessment of the cultural foundations of lynching is perhaps excessive: "In the Southern religion of the Lost Cause, in the fundamentalist lynch mob's sacrificial feasting on Afro-American blood, and in the negrophobic and supremacist iconoclasm of the burning cross, we find Christianity at its most destructive, its most socially cannibalistic, and its most demonic, on a par with the malevolent distortions of the crusades, the Thirty Years' war, and the Nazi terror."[103] This harsh judgment, unfortunately, is essential to any explanation of lynching in the God-haunted South.

Evangelical Protestantism in the South did not "cause" lynching. It did, however, establish a cultural predisposition that normalized lynching. Because it left unexamined the many social and political asymmetries in Southern society, evangelical Protestantism remained "generally aligned with the causes of conservatism, aesthetic vacuity, anti-intellectualism, provincialism, resistance to new cultural currents."[104] The alignment was never perfect, and many ministers and theologians denounced lynching as fundamentally un-Christian. Still, the organizing creeds of evangelical Protestantism were sufficient to sustain lynching as a religious and specifically *Christian* practice. By uncritically supporting the Democratic Party's grip over the region, Southern Protestantism legitimized the violent methods that landowners used in their attempt to restore the "perfect labor system" when "God watched over humanity; husbands provided for and protected wives and children and received obedience and respect in return; masters provided for and protected slaves and demanded obedience."[105] Still enamored with the vanished past, evangelical churches looked with suspicion and even hostility on the emergence of interest-based politics within white society, damning confrontational politics as a betrayal of the region's God-sanctioned hierarchies.[106]

In this respect, "Anglo-Saxon evangelical faith" in the South contrasted strikingly with the religious worldview that Afrikaners in South Africa developed to make sense of the postbellum racial order in the first decades of the twentieth century. The next chapter shows that Afrikaners developed a theology that fused a virulent racism to a "strong state" which they successfully manipulated to address the "poor white problem." Afrikaners, in other words, sought to protect impoverished whites by making Social Gospelism the very business of the state itself.

6

"The weakness of some ...":
Afrikaner civil religion
and racial paternalism

For white Protestants in the New South, the lineage through which racial violence descended did not begin with slavery but with the theology of Atonement-through-punishment. Southern Protestantism embraced the image of "God as Supreme Hangman" but concentrated his cleansing fire-power on the "black-beast rapist."[1] Especially for poor whites, the virtue of this theological orientation was that it potentially transformed every white man into a rope-carrying footsoldier of Christ.

In sharp contrast, white Christians in South Africa never developed a theology of personal vengeance and did not embrace affirmative notions of sacrificial murder. Their settler colonial experience emphasized communal responses to external threats instead. Communal responses therefore permeated their theological approach to the black majority. Fortified towns, armies and the various mission stations of the Benevolent Society better symbolize the modernizing spirit of the royal British forces and their approach to subjugating African kingdoms. Rugged Boer nomads exacerbated their own vulnerability by regularly hiving off and dispersing ever further northward. Rifle-carrying men and women therefore hitched their fate to the *laager* and *kommando* as they navigated precariously through the African interior.[2] The merger of the royal and the rugged in the wake of the centrifugal forces that the mineral revolution unleashed was reflected in an unstable amalgam of theological approaches to "the Native Question" after 1910. The differences between British and Boer theologies were important and consequential. Nevertheless, both theologies were united in acknowledging the primacy of the state – the supreme expression of communal will – in the field of "race relation." As a result, competing communities of white Christians in South Africa coalesced around a "bureaucratic theory of atonement" that reflected their confidence and dependence on the formal powers of a paternalist state.

Like the Afrikaner farmers and the English-speaking captains of industry who were all bent on manipulating "segregation" to suit their competing interests in black labor, Christian churches also set aside their theological differences in support of segregation. Christian discourses in the first three decades after 1910 were therefore marked by a close engagement with the rash of laws, administrative regulations and bureaucratic institutions that emerged in this period. The infusion of spiritual perspectives – including even those that were hostile to aspects of prevailing government policy – into the emerging bureaucratic framework of white supremacy is further evidence of statism's magnetic power in South Africa.

This churchly cooperation reflected whites' "diffuse and generalized support" for segregation policies. Liberal, conservative and reactionary whites disagreed over the precise meaning of "segregation" but agreed on two minimal premises. They agreed that "assimilation between the races" was impossible because of the "cultural gulf" that separated "tribal" blacks and "civilized" whites. All Christian churches also agreed that modernity corroded the moral world of "tribal" Africans. They therefore championed segregation because it regulated the pace at which Africans were inducted into a fast-moving and baffling modernity. This bedrock paternalist consensus meant that few lines cleanly separated the Christian ideologies that emerged in the first two decades after unification. Indeed, segregationist policies in South Africa were initially championed not by reactionaries but by the most progressive political and Christian circles within the white population. The policy even enjoyed the broad, but incrementally reluctant and critical support of the small African middle class. Distinguishing the "true friend of the Native" from the "anti-Native element" in the inter-War years was therefore a murky enterprise.[3]

A measure of clarity emerged only in the late 1920s and early 1930s as influential liberals criticized the pro-tribal direction of "Native policy" that Prime Minister J. B. M. Hertzog spelled out in his controversial "Native Bills." On the one side of this debate were the members of the "Benevolent Empire," a diverse alliance of English-speaking liberals and Christian Africans who cooperated in a large number of religious and secular bodies. After championing segregationist policies, leading Christian liberals from the mid-1920s onward again turned to the Cape's tradition of "assimilationism." In practice, "assimilationism" meant support for education and missionary policies that would gradually encourage a class of educated, property-owning Africans. However, English-speaking white liberals in Natal challenged the Cape liberal doctrines in the 1920s and 1930s. Whites in Natal pressed for a policy of "retribalizing" Africans, a policy of restoration that dovetailed with Natal's historic reliance on "tribal structures" to generate cheap migrant labor and maintain control over the famously resistant Zulu kingdom. Although relations between "assimilationists" and "tribalist" liberals became strained in the 1930s, the ideological tensions between them did not assume a religious expression, and the two are commonly understood to comprise South Africa's white liberal establishment.

On the other side of the Benevolent Empire stood the vast majority of

Afrikaners in the three "Afrikaner churches," collectively referred to as the Dutch Reformed Church. The DRC was the only church in South Africa to formally segregate congregations on the basis of race. Despite the emphasis it placed on missionary work, and in sharp opposition to the practical work of the Benevolent Empire, the DRC had virtually no formal dealings with Africans. Nor did it possess an official theological approach towards the black majority for at least two decades after unification. A distinct position on the racial question crystallized only in the late 1920s and early 1930s when the first exposition of Apartheid theory emerged; a full-blown theological justification for racial separation would only emerge on the eve of the historic election of 1948.[4]

The overlap between the "explicit racism" of Afrikaners and the "implicit racism" of English-speaking whites signals an important difference in racial theology in South Africa and the American South.[5] On the eve of the Civil War in the South, the Protestant churches split cleanly down the regional divide, enabling Southern Protestants to accommodate and even promote a theology of blood sacrifice. No such regional cleavage emerged in South Africa. Instead, the DRC found itself in stiff post-War competition with the Anglican Church for Afrikaner souls. At the same time, spatial propinquity encouraged a cooperative development that did not emerge in the USA. In South Africa, prominent members in the DRC and the Benevolent Empire actively sought each other out in the 1920s and early 1930s to formulate a common politico-theological policy that would place the nation's "Native policy" on a "Christian basis." The result of this engagement was a brief ecumenical movement in the 1920s and early 1930s. This rapprochement would backfire and the DRC would recoil from its encounter with liberal theologians. The brief period of flirtation, however, left its paternalist mark on the DRC. Even as they explored the ramifications of the new Apartheid theology, DRC leaders continued to oppose gratuitous racial violence just as vehemently as their English-speaking counterparts.

The Benevolent Empire and the DRC

By the time the Union was formed in 1910, the "Benevolent Empire," for all its diffuseness, was a recognizable constituency with a proven track record in "ameliorating the position of the Natives." Scores of segregated hospitals, day schools, mission stations and boarding schools populated the countryside, evidence of the zeal amongst missionaries and administrators to spread Western education and Christianity amongst Africans. In contrast, the DRC's evangelizing work amongst Africans was slight; remarkably, the DRC's mission work within South Africa was only marginally greater than its work in other parts of colonial Africa.[6] This difference between the English-speaking churches and the DRC reflected different approaches to the "Native question." As carriers of the Enlightenment into southern Africa, English-speaking churches and missionaries had played a major role in defining the proper form and content of "race relations" in the Cape colony. These self-styled "friends of the Native" played vanguard roles in destroying racial slavery in the western Cape and linked Western education in the mid-1800s to the expansion of free markets and greater civil liberties amongst Africans. They also hounded the Boer republics for their allegedly "brutal policies" against blacks and so championed the Anglo-Boer war as a necessary episode in the emancipation of blacks from bondage to tyrannical Boer patriarchs.[7] Enlightenment principles about "universal rights of Man," "free trade" or the "civilizing" effects of education that these nineteenth century liberals espoused came at a heavy price for Africans. These modernizing creeds actually broadened the repression of Africans in ways that were inconceivable in the succession of rickety nineteenth-century Boer "republics", where cruder forms of racial oppression prevailed. Still, however much the Benevolent Empire was implicated in maintaining white supremacy in the nineteenth century, capricious violence towards blacks was decidedly not one of the movement's creeds. Instead, the contribution liberals made to the management of race relations was to promote an efficient bureaucracy as the favored means for simultaneously controlling and "civilizing" blacks.[8]

The history of the DRC's involvement in race relations differs significantly from the lengthy and extensive work of the Benevolent Empire in southern Africa. The DRC was marked at an early stage by two conflicting impulses. Soon after their arrival in the Cape, many Dutch settlers gravitated toward "the doctrine of the covenant," coming to believe in both the racial superiority of whites and the doctrine of "internal holiness of children," which held that children of Reformed Christians are already redeemed from the moment of birth. The Reformed Christianity of Dutch settlers therefore established a spiritual and communal boundary that elevated Dutch settlers above the population of indigenous blacks and dark-skinned slaves imported from Malaysia. Scholars who continue to insist that subsequent Boer/Afrikaner identity was molded by the "neo-Calvinist" conception of Afrikaners as a "chosen people" make much of evidence that points to the exclusivist basis of Dutch settlers' religious identity.[9]

However, contrary evidence suggests that Dutch settlers did not turn to religion to justify racial intolerance, especially after the spread of evangelism in the Cape after the 1790s when numerous settlers underwent a "personal conversion." Dutch settlers engaged in missionary work amongst blacks, in the process forging cordial relations with the British and German missionaries laboring amidst black and colored communities in the region. From approximately 1820 onward, the DRC's missionary activities yielded a small number of black converts, who duly began attending "formerly all-white congregations, requesting access to Holy Communion, and the right to hold church weddings." A growing number of Dutch congregants rebelled against multi-racialism, however, and demanded a reversion to an all-white church from 1830 onwards. The seeds of a Christian crisis were thus sown, but would yield its bitter fruit only *after* the Great Trek of 1820 was well under way.[10]

Dutch trekkers in the remote hinterland certainly cited the Bible as an authority for justifying critical developments such as the introduction of slavery and the decision to quit the Cape. Still, it was by no means a consensus amongst the Dutch population that the Bible could be used to justify the emerging patterns of racial domination. Not even the settlers furthest from the urban milieu of Cape Town justified their more oppressive control over blacks in terms of the Bible. Instead, most Dutch settlers viewed the cultural differences that distinguished them from blacks, and from the Khoi Khoi in particular, in the framework of "degeneracy." This perspective embodied two elements that serve as a more accurate account of the role religion played in the development of Afrikaner nationalism. As they trekked into the northern and eastern interior, Dutch settlers feared that the wilderness would deplete their "civilization." Later, as Boers established a precarious mastery over the black populations they encountered, pressing the latter into involuntary servitude whenever they could, they came to look upon menial work as *kaffirwerk.* "Degeneracy" thereafter came to mean avoiding work that was fit only for uncivilized blacks. For André du Toit, practical and material interests, not Biblical arguments, galvanized the emerging racial consciousness of Boer trekkers. Despite the occasional religious justifications that do indeed pepper the writings and observations of Boers and nineteenth-century observers, there is no evidence that doughty and barely literate clans of Boer trekkers ever engaged in a sustained re-articulation of Christian theology in conditions so inhospitable to scholarly labor.[11]

The origin of racial segregation within the DRC illustrates the point. This innovation, the most portentous developments in Boer theology prior to the 1920s, was announced in tones that are strikingly uninspired. After three decades of trekking amidst, warring against and uneasily co-existing with a succession of black communities in the country's northern regions, congregation members repeatedly petitioned the Cape Synod for the right to exclude blacks from common worship. The Synod demurred but eventually agreed to do so in 1857. But to justify this departure from longstanding practice in the Cape, the rationale that church elders proffered is strikingly limp and self-consciously expedient: segregated churches, the Synod of 1857 declared, would be granted as "a concession to the weakness of some ..." No theological innovation lay behind this important departure from a century of religious practice, and the tone of Christian apology, even accusation, is unmistakable. In contrast, Southern intellectuals had spilled vast amounts of ink to root slavery in the Bible and vigorously debated whether blacks possessed souls. For the Boers of South Africa, ecclesiastical segregation was simply the pragmatic complement of an "obvious" cultural hierarchy that assigned whites to the top and blacks to the bottom. Because Boer supremacy was the only end this principle was intended to serve, the handful of Afrikaner *predikante* (who were tutored by theologians imported from the

Netherlands) displayed no further theological interest in blacks. All agreed that blacks were culturally inferior, but none doubted that Africans were part of the human race or that they possessed souls.[12] Africans were simply unimportant to Boer theology.

At the same time, in the aftermath of the 1857 ruling that authorized racially segregated churches, the DRC established "daughter churches" for Africans (in 1881) and Coloreds (1888). By the 1920s, 194 DRC evangelical missionaries were active in black rural communities inside South Africa while a handful of *predikante* were proud of the missions they had established in central Africa and Nigeria. The number was unimpressive – Afrikaner missionaries accounted for less than a tenth of the missionaries attached to South Africa's English-speaking churches – but was still notable in light of the modest financial fortunes of the DRC and the hostility that the laity bore towards missions for Africans. For Africans, the excision of the "daughter churches" from the "mother church" was a grating matter, but not a crucial one since Africans accounted for just 2.8% of the DRC's membership by 1900. In short, the DRC and Africans neglected each other. Political and social upheaval in the last quarter of the nineteenth century all but squelched any interest or capacity the church had to evangelize amongst Africans. Britain stood poised to crush the Transvaal. *Uitlanders* (foreigners) were flooding into the mineral-rich but wobbly Orange Free State and Transvaal republics. More importantly, the DRC had encountered the beginnings of a problem that would dominate its theology and political concentration in the next few decades – the growing population of "poor white" families unable to survive the collapse of agriculture in parts of the Transvaal.[13]

"Poor whiteism" was doubly troubling to the church. First was the phenomenon's sheer novelty among essentially classless bands of Boer nomads. Boer governments and the DRC were accordingly unequipped to play the role of welfare agencies. After the Anglo-Boer War, the DRC was forced to assist a steadily increasing number of failed farmers and *bywoners* driven off their lands by the ruinous combination of drought and stock disease, rising land prices and strong market competition from African peasant production.[14] The sheer discovery of sudden destitution amongst Boers was not all that troubled the DRC. Extreme poverty also threatened to turn poor whites into *kaffirs*, and *verkaffering* ("Africanization") posed a fundamental threat to *all* Afrikaners. Fear of "degeneracy" and *gelykstelling* (equality) with Africans therefore became the church's organizing obsession after 1910.[15]

The DRC developed two responses to the "poor white problem," both of which distinguish the DRC from the social and racial politics of southern Protestantism. The first was the emergence of a strong Social Gospel movement within the church to rescue "poor whites" from the maws of poverty. This orientation squarely aligned the DRC alongside the cause of poor whites and the increasingly radical labor movements that emerged in the gold mining areas of the Transvaal. Unlike Southern white workers who were spurned by employers and harried by state governments, Afrikaner workers enjoyed a privileged place within the Afrikaner republican movement that emerged after the Anglo-Boer war. It was through this fervent embrace of Social Gospelism that the DRC discovered its second calling: solving the "problem" of the urban African. The DRC hit upon a defining insight soon after the First World War: if the fate of Afrikanerdom hinged around the destiny of "poor whites," then the salvation of "poor whites" hinged around "the problem of the urban Native." One year after the 1922 strike had propelled militant white workers onto the national stage, the DRC therefore took another plunge, this time not to save "poor whites" but to commandeer the field of "Native policy." The discovery of the "poor white problem" led to two major theological innovations that would transform the DRC in the inter-War years. It led, firstly, to the emergence of a theology centered around the material upliftment of the Afrikaner working class. Secondly, by cooperating with the Benevolent Society to deal with the "Native question," the church was compelled to finally elaborate a definite theological defense of racial domination. Both developments, we see below, firmly oriented the church to the state and impeded an ideology of vengeance from swamping the political and theological outlook of Afrikaners.

Saving "poor whites": The DRC and the Social Gospel

In a way that seems inconceivable in the American South, the DRC responded to the poor white problem by embracing Social Gospelism and challenging the hegemony of employers in the young, pro-imperial state. Themes that resonated in Protestant churches in the American South – "blue law" issues such as alcoholism, marital infidelity, child neglect, and so on – also echoed in the modest Afrikaner churches that emerged in South Africa's urban areas, especially on the bustling Witwatersrand and its "running sore," the city of Johannesburg.[16] *Predikante* and deacons in the DRC after 1910 were therefore as vexed as Protestant leaders in the South about dangerous moral lapses such as dancing, drinking, illicit sex, indolence and other irresponsibilities that imperiled individual souls and threatened family life.[17] Such concerns, however, were soon subordinated to the extraordinary attention the DRC lavished on the poverty of white workers. After 1910, the DRC came to believe that the key to moral salvation lay in improving the material circumstances in which poor Afrikaners were mired. To salvage souls and save *die volk*, Afrikaner poverty would first have to be eliminated. The Afrikaner poor therefore found in the DRC a firm ally and champion in their battles against mine owners. Already enfranchised by the Act of Union and the beneficiaries of "job color bars" that barred Africans from competing for a range of jobs in the mining industry, white workers in South Africa defined their goals with precision: more employment and higher wages. White workers were no less precise in identifying their enemy: the symbiotic union between mine owners and the increasingly pro-imperial SAP government.[18] Africans were more or less excised from Afrikaners' mobilizing concerns in this period. Neither friend nor enemy, blacks remained on the margins of Afrikaner cultural politics, a blurred presence on the fringes of the white labor movement and almost entirely ignored in the theology of the DRC.

The ascent of the Social Gospel movement within the DRC was a watershed moment in the history of the church. For all practical purpose, Social Gospelism snuffed out the nineteenth-century tradition of pietism and transformed the church into a self-proclaimed *volkskerk*.[19] The previous chapter showed that pietism thrived in the South, drawing from and reinforcing the region's hostility to "big government" and its commitment to the "conversion experience." The pietist strain in South Africa all but disappeared the moment the DRC became a *volkskerk*. True to the movement's founding principles in seventeenth- and eighteenth-century Europe, the pietist tradition which Andrew Murray, the son of DRC missionaries from Scotland, pioneered in South Africa in the 1860s also emphasized revivals, evangelization and a personal relationship with God. Pietism disdained politics, focused on individual salvation and displayed little interest in questions of social welfare – positions that Murray held until his death in 1917. These doctrines clashed with the emerging Afrikaner nationalist movement after the Anglo-Boer war. DRC theologians also opposed the pietist emphasis on emotional "revelation." An experiential approach to religion implied that all "saved" Christians were equal in the eyes of God and so fuelled the twin threats of *gelykstelling* and *verkaffering*. We saw earlier that doctrines that preached self-reliance, the individual's "conversion experience," and their "personal relationship with God" took firm root in the segregated political culture of the American South. In South Africa, these doctrines quickly succumbed to the upwelling of popular Afrikaner opposition to British hegemony. Social Gospelism became the spine of a republican movement that subordinated the individual to *die volk*.

The transformation of the DRC into a *volkskerk* also suppressed a second theological tendency that had arisen in the late nineteenth century. A "neo-Kuyperian" tradition emerged from the theological writings of Adam Kuyper (1837–1920), the Dutch cleric and politician who is frequently cited as the source of Apartheid theology. The aspect of Kuyper's theology that would resonate with Afrikaner intellectuals from the 1920s onward was his view that society was fragmented into a series of discrete "natural spheres" (such as family, education, work). Each sphere enjoyed a "sovereignty" which the state was obliged to preserve. Kuyper therefore insisted on the separation between church and state, writing that "the State may never become an octopus, which stifles the whole of life ... [but] has to honor and maintain every form of life which grows independently in its own sacred autonomy."[20] DRC theologians in South Africa radically distorted Kuyper's views, mining the many ambiguities and contradictions in his works to justify calls for a church-driven ethno-nationalism and a strong state to actively disaggregate

society into separate ethnic and racial "spheres." Kuyper's own goal, however, was to restore God, and *not* the church, as the absolute sovereign
over human affairs. Kuyper also argued that the power of the state had to
be *contained* by an autonomous (but "differentiated") civil society. Rather
than recoil from centralized state power as Kuyper did, Afrikaner nationalists were drawn irresistibly to the state.[21]

However, the Kuyperian sources of Afrikaner theology made their impact
only in the late 1930s and 1940s, by which time Apartheid theology was
already taking form. Prior to this period, the majority of Afrikaner theologians distanced themselves from Kuyper's teachings for the same reason that
pietism in the DRC had died down: neither pietism nor neo-Kuyperianism
offered substantive solutions to the material crisis that gripped the Afrikaner poor.[22]

A strong social orientation was precisely the strength of the *volkskerk*
approach and the reason it became the pivot of Afrikaner politics around
the First World War. The *volkskerk* model originated in the waning days
of the Transvaal republic (1881–1900). [23] After five decades in which they
had grown steadily more estranged from both British influence and the
DRC, Transvaal trekkers who no longer felt bound by loyalty to the DRC
headquartered in the western Cape broke away to form the Nederduitsche
Hervormde Kerk (NHK) in 1853. Ministers in the Transvaal Republic were
the first to embrace the poor white problem when the phenomenon emerged
on the eve of the Anglo-Boer War. They again took up the cause of Afrikaner unemployment and urban poverty after 1910.

Pastoral support for poor whites arose in direct response to the pro-imperial policies of the SAP government, whose major goal at the time of unification was "to assist mining, promote export industries, introduce lower
tariffs, and encourage an efficient agriculture to lower the cost of food."
For Prime Ministers Louis Botha and Jan Smuts, "the poor would benefit
in the rising tide of growth and prosperity."[24] Smuts declared in 1911 that
the rehabilitation of poor whites was "a vital matter" for his government.
For Smuts, however, poor whites would have to advance on their own, even
if this meant competing with non-whites for urban employment. Echoing
the recommendations of the 1908 Transvaal Indigency Commission, the
government refused to implement an extensive system of social assistance
and limited itself to small amounts of "poor relief."[25] Afrikaner nationalists viewed Smuts' "solutions" – industrial training, education, hard work,
patience and a modicum of occasional "relief" – as indifferent bromides.
Confronted by an Afrikaner-dominated government seemingly in the thrall
of British imperialists, the Afrikaner churches set aside their theological differences and collaborated on the common task of saving poor whites.

The churches embraced the Social Gospel with a fervor that dwarfed the
charitable activities of churches in American South. It "involved itself at
every level with the plight of the poor, becoming a major institution of social
assistance," Herman Gioliomee writes:

Wherever there were Afrikaner families in distress, there was the DRC *predikant* doing what he could to encourage and help them. He became the central figure in the life of a demoralized people. The church took the lead in organizing a *volkskongres*, or peoples conference, to devise ways to combat the poor-white problem. It started feeding schemes for the poor, created job opportunities for them, and started Afrikaans schools in the vestries of its churches to establish what it called "Christian-National education." ... Through the intensity of this involvement with the material plight of the Afrikaner people in the cities, the DRC came to be regarded as the *volkskerk*, or people's church ... The *volkskerk* became literally an organ of the people, the theological arm of the emerging *volksbeweging*, or people's movement, which was soon to start mobilizing the Afrikaner people politically for the realization of their nationhood and fulfillment of their calling.[26]

Repelled by the "unmixed evil of bastardization between White and non-White," the church outlined its new mission: "Should we want to save our country from declining into such a bastard country, let every means be implemented to protect the poor-Whites ..."[27] Afrikaans churches and women's organizations collaborated closely to address the needs of poor Afrikaners, becoming pioneers in the area of social welfare policy in South Africa. Elders, ministers and deacons on the local church council took a direct interest in the material and moral life of their members. Deacons played particularly important roles in the grassroots activism of the DRC: "Deacons fulfilled the important function of administering the welfare program of the church. They were required to collect and distribute aid to the needy. In their charge were widows, orphans, the poor and sick. The whole social ministry of the church rested upon its deacons who were in effect voluntary social workers ... In this way the Church performed a role which is now assumed to the duty of the Government."[28]

Church documents that record the importance of the Social Gospel also chronicle the ongoing threats that "degeneration" and "Anglicization" posed to *die volk*. In 1908, for example, the church council in Burgersdorp discovered that a congregant was running a brothel on the strength of services that "a native girl" provided to black and white clients. Confronted by the local *predikant*, the man alternately denied and confessed the deed before claiming that he had done so in a "sin-sleep" induced by the devil. After a painstaking investigation, and still uncertain whether he had fully repented, the Council censured him for an indefinite period. Incidences of inter-racial sex were far from uncommon, as were cases involving "belief in magic" (referring to Afrikaners who used the services of traditional African healers and sorcerers – dreaded evidence of *verkaffering*). Various church councils between 1910 and 1920 investigated complaints of adultery, illegitimate births, drunkenness, illegally selling alcohol, being baptized in other (usually Anglican) churches, occasional incest and "dancing in public halls," and investigated these alongside such misfortunes as bankruptcy, unemployment, indebtedness and imprisonment. DRC ministers also established a number of orphanages such as those in Bethulie (1903) and Rustenburg (1905).[29] Clearly, "blue law" issues were as important to Afrikaner Protestants as they were to the evangelical Protestants of the New South. Moreover, DRC adduced such issues when it demanded administrative measures to disentangle poor whites and blacks and segregate them in separate residential areas.[30]

At the time of the First World War, however, such issues were superseded by Afrikaner theologians' concern with broader questions of state policy. In 1916, the church held an urgent *Volkskongres* to deal with the "poor white" crisis. The conference exemplifies two important points about the DRC at this time: the inextricable relationship between church and state within DRC doctrine and the relative unimportance of Africans in that theology. The two principal speakers at the conference were both clergymen: D. F. Malan was the secretary of the Cape National Party and F. W. Reitz was one of the most prominent leaders of the NP. In addressing the issue of Afrikaner poverty, overwhelming attention was devoted to the colossus of Anglo domination. The connection between urban white poverty and economic competition from cheaper black labor surfaces only as a passing interest. D. F. Malan, for example, identified three "causes" of white poverty in his address to the conference: natural disasters and the outbreak of the Boer War; poor education or illiteracy amongst *bywoners*; and the competition between Afrikaners and English-speaking whites. Competition with black workers is strikingly absent from this list of "causes." Blacks surfaced in Malan's comments only when he discussed "degeneracy" as a *consequence* of Afrikaner poverty. Malan argued that the social plight of poor whites imposed a moral duty on the state:

> I have observed instances in which the children of Afrikaner families were running around as naked as kaffirs in Congoland. We have knowledge today of Afrikaner girls, so poor they work for coolies and Chinese. We know of white men and women who live married or unmarried with Colored. They are all our flesh and blood; they all carry our names; they are Afrikaners all of them; they are the sons and daughters of the Huguenots and the children of [Afrikaner] martyrs.[31]

For Malan, as for most speakers at the conference, the duty of the Afrikaner churches and other Afrikaans institutions such as the *Reddingsdaad* was to prevent the Anglicization of *die volk*.[32]

Speakers at the conference were only mildly concerned with the impact that competition with cheaper African workers had on working-class Afrikaners. Professor A. Marais, for example, articulated the view that would surge to the forefront of Afrikaner discourse in the following decade. "In order to eliminate this unequal competition between black and white, or to limit it to the minimum," the DRC supported "the principle of industrial segregation, insofar as this was possible." Comments by Reitz, the chair of the conference, also echoed the call for "industrial segregation."

These sentiments, however, played second fiddle to the primary obsession at the conference: erasing the gap between Afrikaners and English-speaking whites.[33]

Africans, of course resided at the core of the conference's concerns. Yet Africans appear as little more than a background constant in the genesis of the poor white problem. For most whites at this time, "Blacks were still part of the landscape, like the animals and thorn trees."[34] Recounting his early years growing up in the small town of Kuruman in the Cape Province, the Afrikaner theologian and missiologist David Bosch recalled that Afrikaners in these years assumed that blacks were "hewers of wood and drawers of water ... a part of the scenery but hardly a part of the human community ... They belonged to the category of 'farm implements' rather than to the category 'fellow-human beings.'"[35] Unsurprisingly, Afrikaners who viewed blacks as barely human became notorious for inflicting personal violence on blacks.

With the DRC at the helm of the nationalist cause, the lumpenproletariat – the unemployed and the unskilled Afrikaner who was "forced into kaffir work" – became the pivot of Afrikaner nationalism. Far from being abandoned to the sharp edge of job competition with blacks, as white workers in the American South were, the Afrikaner poor became the *cause célèbre* of ethnic mobilization. Armed with the vote, wooed by religious institutions and wooed by two major political parties – the NP and the Labor Party – poor white workers looked well beyond the "psychological wages of whiteness" and concentrated their growing militancy on the country's political and economic institutions. Afrikaner churches legitimized the collective struggles of poor Afrikaners, imbuing proletarian politics and the combative posture of white workers movements with a theological vindication that never emerged in the South.

Indeed, it is not too much to see a parallel between the church's support for white workers and official support for Afrikaner landowners after the Anglo-Boer war. Milner's land restoration policies during Reconstruction, which placed Afrikaner farmers back in control of their land, prefigured the extensive support that the Union state gave to white farmers, including policies for "keeping as many farmers on the land as possible."[36] White workers were not quite as fortunate. From 1910 to the mid-1920s, government policy was committed to an industrialization strategy that was based on the exploitation of cheap black labor, a policy annunciated in the Report of the Transvaal Indigency Commission of 1908. The report dismissed as a "pernicious theory" demands from white workers for laws that would reserve certain skilled and semi-skilled jobs for whites only.[37] Subsequent theological support for the poor whites' campaign against the alliance between state and capital therefore turned out to be critical.

The church's integration of pastoral and proletarian missions denied a foothold to the appalling violence that Southern poor whites viewed as integral to their competition with black workers. In the Southern states, the combination of individualism, a tendency to accept authority and the region's exaggerated concern with individual "honor" all diluted the likelihood that workers would challenge employers with aggressive labor movements. In South Africa, an anti-imperialist outlook, the sacralization of ethnic mobilization and resolute demands for material solutions to white poverty fused proletarian anger to a religious pursuit of political power. The formation of the NP in 1914 captures this proletarian-driven, theological affinity for state power. The NP was the party of "the small man" par excellence. J. B. M. Hertzog, the founder of the NP in 1914 and Prime Minister of South Africa from 1924 to 1939, never wavered from his commitment to constitutional struggle throughout his political career. Socialist and Calvinist views about the dignity of labor combined in his thought. Shorn of his narrow ethnic worldview, Hertzog's concern for the victims of industrialization resembled the ideas of Calvinist reformers in Europe.[38]

For Hertzog and theologians in the *volkskerk*, solutions to the poor white problem lay in providing decent employment, higher wages and improved living conditions. Hertzog emphasized this view, the bedrock of the Social Gospel, when he broke with the SAP to form the NP. His broadsides against the government's pro-mining policies were redolent of socialist themes. He described Prime Minister Louis Botha as "The Prime Minister of Imperialism and Capital" and attributed the "poor white problem" to the government's "capitalist policies" that denied many poor whites even the possibility of employment and, hence, dignity.[39] D. F. Malan, on the other hand, was less concerned with Calvinist principle of dignified work than with the "pastoral obligation of the church to care for its poor fellow Afrikaners." A son of the western Cape and at first influenced by the Cape's evangelical tradition, his original views ascribed to the principle of "from doctrine to life," the orthodox view in which all revelation arises from the Bible – the predominant framework of Southern Protestantism. After studying in Utrecht, however, Malan embraced the contrary view, the ethical approach known as "from life to doctrine." The later Malan was attracted to arguments advanced by the Irish "empiricist" philosopher George Berkeley (1685–1753), whose views elevated experience and action above thought and reflection, activities that Berkeley argued could not effect change in the material world. In Berkeley's view, "volition without Power" was feckless; in contrast, "Power implyeth Volition."[40] This perspective reinforced Malan's republican and activist goals. The fusion of theology and power in Berkeley's philosophy captures the thrust of the *volkskerk* approach. An ordained minister himself, Malan played a leading role in infusing an explicit concern with political power into the theology of the *volkskerk* movement, placing the church at the epicenter of the republican cause and poor whites at the heart of its social mission.[41] By 1920, the dominance of the *volkskerk* tradition already meant that theological distinctions between social and evangelical theological arguments within the DRC were largely inconsequential, suppressed by the consensus that the poor white problem forced upon Afrikaner leaders.

Clerical alarm over the spiritual decay amongst urban Afrikaners diminished by the late 1920s. "It would seem," Hexham writes, "that the Reformed Church was slowly winning its battle to impose its own high moral standards" on the urban flock.[42] Hexham's assessment may well be correct. However, another explanation seems more plausible. It is more likely that the emergence of segregationist measures such as the Urban Areas Act, the establishment of residential segregation and the implementation of pass laws in the urban areas had begun to allay the fear of "degeneration" amongst the urban Afrikaner poor.

Neither plebeian whites nor the DRC isolated blacks as the dire threat of the day. Yet, even when Africans metastasized into the principal "menace" confronting *die volk* in the 1920s, the Afrikaner religious leaders who formulated Apartheid theology did not embrace a creed of racial violence against the subordinate black majority. To the contrary, their Apartheid solutions were in large measure framed by the church's encounter with paternalist liberals in the Benevolent Empire. This encounter, the second force to transform Afrikaner theology, also encouraged the DRC to view "the native problem" through the prism of state power.

The "problem of the urban Native": The DRC and the Benevolent Society

Unlike the English-speaking churches, the DRC emerged into the twentieth century saddled with a reputation for, at best, neglecting its mission to blacks; at worst, in Dr D.D.T. Jabavu's stinging characterization – which he offered after the DRC came out in support of the 1913 Land Act – the DRC was an "anti-Native church."[43] Repeated criticism by English missionaries had much to do with the DRC's unfavorable reputation. Missionaries spared no ink in vilifying Boers as crude racists and an embarrassing "European" impediment to the civilizing mission, the "worst" of the "unimproved" lumpenproletariat in the empire.[44] Such priggish sentiments reflected the middle-class views of Victorian England and the jingoism that fired up support for the Anglo-Boer War, but they were also responses to the DRC's unstinting support for the oppressive "Native policies" in the Boer republics. For example, in 1848 and 1868 British settlers in Natal successfully brought to light the slave-like condition on Boer farms. Still, harsh labor practices continued well into the 1870s. Hemmed in by the disapproving presence of British imperialism and their own administrative incapacities, Boers in the Transvaal Republic had disguised the system as a form of *inboekseling* (apprenticeship).[45] British missionaries had a field day and gained the attention of the abolition movement at home. Although they were unsuccessful in pressing onto the British government the issue of coerced labor in the recondite Transvaal, missionaries were able to accuse the DRC of a serious moral lapse that reinforced the church's "anti-Native" reputation. The government, meanwhile, had failed to replace the four "Native policies" inherited from the colonial era with a single nationwide "Native policy" as the constitution of 1910 stipulated. The resultant unsettled state of "Native policy" provided the DRC with an opportunity to clarify its relationship to the black majority.

The DRC entered into the languishing field of "Native Affairs" against a background of swelling protest and mobilization by blacks and white working-class communities. Rising black opposition to segregation policies led John Merriman to speculate in 1917 that "the experiment of a white race settling in Africa [was] by no means assured" and that South Africa might "become an African Mexico."[46] Africans who had served in the First World War spread rumors variously predicting the imminent arrival of French, German or American liberators, while strikes and picket lines by black workers in 1918 and 1919 announced the emergence of militant black workers in the industrial arena. The rural areas, too, hummed with persistent talk that Africans would rectify the worsening problem of landlessness by violently reclaiming land from whites. It was against the backdrop of such a rumor that General Smuts' army massacred more than 160 unarmed African members of a religious sect in Bulhoek, near Queenstown in the eastern Cape, in May 1921.[47] The DRC, however, seems to have moved into high gear only after white mine workers staged their epochal strike in 1922, pausing to slaughter dozens of innocent black workers in the process. Alarmed by the sour mood in "race relations," black and white Christians in the Benevolent Empire searched for ways to address the rising militancy of black politics in both the urban and reserve areas. The DRC took its cure from this development. Beginning with cautious steps, DRC leaders acquainted themselves with the liberal veterans of "race relations" in the Benevolent Empire, hoping to cooperate in areas of common concern over the direction of "Native policy."

DRC theologians after the First World War were ill-equipped to exert an authoritative influence over "Native policy." Obsessed with resisting British imperialism in the 1890s and focused on saving "poor whites" after 1910, the DRC had displayed no theological concern with Africans. Meanwhile, the failure of Afrikaner theologians to find in the Bible a single compelling theological reason for ecclesiastical segregation placed the DRC on the defensive. Bald assertions of *baaskap* and *kragdadigheid* were out of place and a cause for apology in the liberal state of 1910. Once Afrikaner theologians became convinced that they needed to influence the debate over African policy, the church may have had no alternative but to enter the field of race relations through the portals of liberalism. Thus, in contrast to Southern Protestant religious leaders who remained autonomous from and hostile to Northern churches who criticized white supremacy, Afrikaner theologians approached the Benevolent Empire to jointly search for a "Christian solution" to South Africa's racial problems.[48]

Liberals in the Benevolent Society at first enthusiastically championed segregation and the administrative structures the policy threw up. By the time they scaled back their enthusiasm for segregation in the late 1920s, they had contributed to the beginnings of an arrogant and modernist culture that believed in large-scale planning involving pass laws, advisory "Native" institutions, segregated legal systems and the creeping army of administrative regulations that began to encircle Africans. They assumed that such bureaucratic paraphernalia were essential to stabilize white supremacy and were therefore also the instruments of the civilizing mission, as beneficial to blacks as to whites. Christian liberals hoped that an enlightened civil service and the selfless work of Christian men and women in civic bodies, and especially the South African Institute of Race Relations (SAIRR, established in 1929), would promote the civilizing mission by steadily improving the bureaucratic juggernaut. Without providing the necessary details, they hinted that sufficient "progress' amongst Africans would one day render the machinery of segregation unnecessary. Many members of the Benevolent Society attacked various government policies with vitriol, sometimes even demanding reforms that were unmistakably socialist in nature.[49] But the most important legacy of liberal white Christians was the legitimacy they bestowed on the bureaucratic approach to the management of race relations.[50]

The DRC was immediately attracted to liberals' orientation to bureaucracy.[51] Like Southerners who fashioned a Religion of the Lost Cause in response to ignominious defeat, Afrikaner views of state power were also decisively shaped by defeat in the Anglo-Boer War. However, the Religion of the Lost Cause in the American South had nurtured a wary and hostile attitude towards the central state. Southerners therefore sought to circumvent and undermine the federal state and would never fully reconcile themselves to "big government." The Afrikaner theologians and nationalists who formulated a Religion of the Lost Cause set course on a very different trajectory.

The involvement of the Afrikaner churches in the "Native question" falls into two broad periods. From 1910 until 1923, the highwater years of the *volkskerk* approach, the DRC displayed scant interest in the black population. Africans assume the form of an "absent presence" in Afrikaner discourse in this period, an ambient threat to the medical, moral and economic well being of Afrikaners, but not the immediate cause of poverty amongst whites. Passing references to Africans at the conference of 1916 reflect the *volkskerk's* secondary interest in racial competition within the industrial working class.

The second phase began in 1923. With growing clarity throughout the 1920s, Afrikaner theologians realized that any solution to white poverty was inextricably bound up with "Native policy" and that any proposal to ameliorate white poverty had inescapable implications for the resolution of the state's racial policy. Having positioned the church as the people's champion, DRC leaders now grasped that only restricting the rights and liberties of blacks could advance the cause of Afrikaner workers. Revelations of the scale of unemployment, poverty and destitution amongst Afrikaners had come as a shock at the church conference of 1916. Church leaders concluded that the combination of charitable relief provided by the government and the strenuous efforts of the *volkskerk* were insufficient to manage the crisis. What was needed, they resolved, was a "civilized labor policy" that would give white workers preferential employment in the mining and manufacturing industries as well as in the civil service, a labor-intensive sector rich with the prospect of sheltered employment for angry poor whites.[52]

Despite unstinting support for the cause of white workers in particular and Afrikaner nationalism in general, church leaders did not embrace the prospect of racial repression with equanimity and were aggrieved by their church's "anti-Native" reputation. As D. F. Malan, a DRC minister in Cape Town, ruefully observed in his 1920 survey of the church's missionary work amongst Africans, "In spite of the good work done by the DRC in the last 30 years, the idea remains in Native minds that this Church is opposed to their upward striving for more knowledge and enlightenment."[53] A genuine concern with framing the church's support for segregation in a framework that would be acceptable to black leaders is a striking feature of Afrikaner theological developments in the 1920s; this spirit waned in the next decade as the sterner logic of Apartheid theology took hold in the 1930s and 1940s, but it never entirely disappeared.

The church's uncertainty about how to proceed after the First World War was reflected in the second conference it called in 1923, this time to discuss the state of race relations in the country. The *volkskerk's* surprising offer to serve as a national broker in the still unresolved field of "Native policy," the traditional domain of Social Christians in the Benevolent Empire, signaled a deepening of the DRC's political and theological ambitions. On the eve of the historic 1923 conference, an article in the *Round Table* observed: "[the event] has caused not a little hope among those who realize that the Dutch Reformed Church is the most influential social and political institution in the country today."[54] The conference was a remarkable event even for the more relaxed political atmosphere of the day, when individuals and organizations with divergent views on "the Native question" kept up cordial relations. Most South Africans at the time did not cleanly distinguish the DRC from other Christian denominations on the issue of "racial discrimination." Although only the Afrikaner churches adopted a strict policy of segregating religious services, in practice English-speaking churches were "also segregated at the local level."[55] Moreover, the DRC's policy of racial exclusion and passionate Social Gospelism amongst poor Afrikaners was counterbalanced, or so church leaders hoped, by the mission churches it had established for Africans and Colored. Missions had even been established in several other colonies in Africa at a time, John de Gruchy notes, when "the English-speaking churches … were often unable and usually unwilling, to act in concert with their African memberships in the struggle for justice and equality."[56] Clements Kadalie, the founder of the ICU, offered an even more scathing rebuke of liberals in the Benevolent Empire. South Africa's

Social Christians, he wrote , had aligned themselves "with the rich against the poor, opposing every effort toward social and economic freedom of the masses."[57] Still, the DRC stood out for strictly enforcing its policy of seg-regated churches. A 1923 article in the *Round Table* described the DRC as "apathetic, if not actually hostile, where the development of the natives [was] concerned."[58]

The very idea that the Southern Baptist Association, the closest counter-part in the American South to the DRC, would host a bi-racial conference "to improve race relations" seems unthinkable in the South, and all the more so because, as we see below, the 1923 conference roundly condemned major aspects of segregation. The DRC would in fact convene another "National European–Bantu Conference" in 1927 and participated in two "European–Bantu Conferences" in 1925 and 1929, called by the Joint Councils Movement.[59] The idea of the 1923 conference was proposed by the Rev. A. F. Louw, a DRC minister from Bloemfontein, and unanimously accepted by the Federal Council of the three Reformed churches. The reso-lution noted: "The object of the conference shall be to get better acquainted with each other, and to confer together concerning the interests of Europeans, colored and Natives … from the viewpoint of a Christian civilization." Claiming "Divine guidance," the Federal Council invited the broad sweep of black and white religious leaders from all Protestant denominations. Black and white ministers from the Dutch Reformed, Anglican, Wesleyan Methodist and Presbyterian Churches sat alongside one another at the con-ference. They were joined by liberal luminaries such as J. D. Rheinallt Jones and Professor W. M. Macmillan (founding members of the SAIRR in 1929) and a clutch of African religious and political leaders such as the Revs A. Mtimkulu and Z. R. Mahabane, D. D. T. Jabavu, Dr S. Molema, H. Selby-Msimang and R. V. Selope Thema. The Moderator of the DRC, D. S. Botha, captured the prevailing spirit of Christian fellowship in his opening speech. Botha's speech was redolent with the paternalism that was standard amongst the most progressive circles but also betrays the bemuse-ment of the newcomer. Reminding the conference that its "chief aim" was "the glory of God and the temporal and spiritual welfare of the whole community," Botha declared:

> Under Divine direction the white and black races are living in this country, and alas it is not clear to all, at least not clear to the vast majority what White and Black owe to one another, what duties they have to perform and what line of conduct they should follow. Instead of cooperating with one another, they look upon each other … with suspicion, antipathy and even enmity … We feel that unless these problems are properly solved the future will be a very dark one for all concerned … The one race does not fully comprehend the aims and aspirations of the other race. Our object at this conference is to teach and be taught by giving and receiving useful informa-tion on the race problems in our country.[60]

The Rev. A. F. Louw followed Botha's sentiments with these words:

> We declare that the only safe and just Native Policy for Europeans and
> Natives to follow is one based on the teaching of Christianity ... What I do
> declare is that the European Christian in this land, who is imbued with the
> spirit of his Master, does not look upon the African black man as an article
> for exploitation, as a mere asset for the gain of filthy lucre, but as a man
> made after God's own image and must be treated by him as such ... Today
> let us take our stand side by side, standing shoulder to shoulder, holding
> high the banner of Jesus Christ.

Before concluding, the conference agreed to "impress upon the Christian
Churches, and other responsible bodies and persons, the urgent need of
employing every means for educating public opinion." To this end delegates
resolved to promote a "Christian Native Policy" and established a "Committee to cooperate with the standing Committee of the South African General Missionary Conference and the Native Welfare Associations to influence
public opinion, inter alia, through the Municipal and Divisional Council
Congresses, and to watch legislative measures, and if necessary to bring to
bear on the Government in order to safeguard the rights of Natives."

Soon after the conference, a bi-racial committee representing the conference did indeed hold a meeting with F. S. Malan, the acting Minister
of Native Affairs. Representing "European views" were the Revs W. Nicol
and D. Theron (DRC), F. B. Bridgman (American Missionary Society),
J. D. Rheinallt Jones and E. H. Brookes. The "Bantu view" was represented
by H. S. Msimang and R. V. Selope Thema. All delegates, the Rev. Theron
assured Malan, "wanted the best for the child race." As was usual for the
period, disagreements were freely expressed. The Rev. Mahabane's criticism
of "territorial segregation" was reprised (Mahabane recommended that the
reserves should be increased from thirteen per cent to fifty per cent of the
country's land surface); Brookes contended that "Compulsory and complete
segregation was an impossible aim, for the day of repression had gone forever." The Acting Prime Minister accepted minor recommendations (such as
Bridgman's proposal that urban administrative regulations should be published in the government *Gazette* so that policy could benefit from public
comment) and parried the more difficult questions (such as "the shortage of
enough land for every European and native").[61]

The conference of 1923 was the DRC's first practical attempt to come to
grips with its racial policies. In 1921, the church had published an anthology,
The Dutch Reformed Church and the Native Problem, consisting of essays
penned by DRC ministers. The editor, Johannes du Plessis, was the undis-
puted doyen of the church's missionary work. His biography captures the
paternalism that would shape the church's approach to race relations until
well into the 1920s. An active participant and office-bearer in the General
Missionary Council and a founding member of the International Missionary Council when the body was established in 1922 at Lake Mohonk in

New York, du Plessis easily qualified as a "liberal," in whose circles he was indeed at home. He had already published the foundational work on the church's missionary program in his *History of Christian Missions in South Africa* (1911), followed by his travelogue, *Thrice Through the Dark Continent* (1917), a record of three trips he made through central and western Africa. *The Dutch Reformed Church and the Native Problem* sought to rebut the perception that the DRC was "anti-Native" by highlighting the extent of the DRC's commitment to evangelization and missionary work amongst Africans.[62]

The surprisingly liberal tilt of *The Dutch Reformed Church and the Native Problem* was more progressive than most liberals of the day. In declaring segregation "a most excellent theory," the DRC ministers merely expressed a universal white consensus. In other matters, however, they upheld sentiments that only the most left-wing progressives among the Benevolent Society espoused. The book advocated a massive increase in the provision of education to blacks and allied strategies to increase the black middle class, a category that the liberal "Cape tradition" viewed as central to "the spread of civilization" among blacks. Surprisingly, the ministers explicitly rejected racial barriers in employment, and so put themselves at odds with Afrikaner workers who would soon be slaughtered during their 1922 strike for a "civilized labor policy." Pass laws should be either "abolished altogether" or applied only to "the raw native" in the reserves. Black workers deserved not only higher wages from all employers but also the legal right to form unions and go on strike. The text also supported Africans' demands that the size of the reserves should be increased, a promise contained in the Native Land Act of 1913. Endorsing a policy of enlarged reserves would have buttressed segregation by keeping as many blacks as possible on "tribal lands" in the reserves. On the other hand, support for this policy placed DRC leaders sharply at odds with sentiment in the white agrarian areas, where farmers were furiously opposed to "giving more land to Natives."[63] It was surprising enough that the DRC supported the views expressed in du Plessis' anthology. Most striking, however, is the absence of any call for "political segregation" in the Conference's recommendations.[64]

The conference of 1923 reinforced the DRC as an emerging redoubt of liberal paternalism and earned glowing praise from black and white Social Christians alike. The liberal educationist Charles Loram, for example, viewed it as "altogether fitting that this, the largest and most important unofficial Conference on Native Affairs ever held in South Africa, should have been called by the oldest, largest and most completely South African Church in the country"; "from that Conference onward," he later informed the DRC, "I date the future of your Church's dealings with Natives."[65] Jabavu agreed, describing the conference as a "milestone" in race relations. The Rev. Z. R. Mahabane, representing the ANC and the Cape Native Voters' Association, enthused that "it had restored the confidence of the Bantu people in the ruling race, and removed the causes of suspicion and mistrust."[66]

South Africa's budding multi-racial ecumenical movement did not last long, however. An upsurge of black mobilization deepened white anxiety and unleashed anxieties about *swaartgevaar* (black peril) amongst Afrikaners. For Afrikaners, General Smuts' decisive assault on striking mine workers in 1922 poisoned the cause of liberalism even further. Two years later, the Labor and National Parties capitalized on popular anger and won the election of 1924. Furthermore, in the midst of the exploratory rapprochement between the Benevolent Empire and the DRC, Prime Minister Hertzog set the cat amongst the pigeons by inviting public discussion on his "Native Bills," a series of inter-related measures intended to comprehensively restructure "Native affairs" along "tribal lines." Many English-speaking liberals recoiled from these harsh "retribalization" measures. By the mid-1930s, leading liberals had become critics of tribal-based segregation and, against declining odds, sought to re-invigorate the Cape's policy of gradualism and assimilationism. Religion, however, was not the preferred battle-field of the stalwart liberals in the Benevolent Society, and they concentrated their efforts on secular institutions such as the Joint Councils Movement, the SAIRR and the various "Native advisory" bodies that had been established for blacks. By 1930, liberals had effectively abandoned the strategy of influencing the racial policies of Hertzog's government by forging alliances with the DRC.[67]

The Apartheid backlash

The DRC, meanwhile, was roiled by an internal rebellion against the liberal position that church leaders had staked out for the church under the guidance of du Plessis. Reaction against the flirtation with "liberals" and "assimilationist" set in and once again, the DRC yielded to "the weakness of some." Angry accusations were leveled at the Church for seeking "reconciliation" with Africans: "Our Church must realize," one outraged congregant wrote, "that her calling in the first instance is to the whites and not to the natives."[68] Another wrote that "it is impossible to fraternize in society: we must be brothers in the spirit. [Blacks] are too far below us in the area of morals. Friendly advances in practical life are impossible, and according to God's will sinful." Under pressure, and also attracted by emerging theological developments within the church, liberal DRC theologians now distanced themselves from their liberal past. Du Plessis, for example, repudiated his editorial position of 1923. Although he continued to insist that racial color bars in employment were unnecessary to protect white workers and in conflict with the free market, he now came out in strong support of segregation, arguing that the policy should be extended from the churches to education and politics as well.[69] When the Federal Council of the DRC convened its second "European–Bantu" conference in Cape Town in 1927, pressure from the laity barred it from using the Church's Hall.

This second conference was notably less "frank" and bold than the earlier one. Delegates from the DRC carefully refrained from engaging the most controversial issues of the day and cautiously concurred with black and white liberals present only over minor aspect of Hertzog's "Native Bills." The dwindling spirit of rapprochement was evident several years later, when the SAIRR convened its fifth "National European–Bantu Conference" in Johannesburg in 1933. By this time, the breach between the DRC and the Social Christians could not be papered over, with liberal after liberal rising only to condemn various aspects of segregationist policy. In response, R. B. Saayman, representing the Nederduitse Gereformeerde Kerk addressed the conference "as a representative of the Afrikaans-speaking section of the population ... that is ... wrongly accused of a lack of sympathy ... to the Native." Saayman disputed Dr Xuma's claim that Afrikaners were "repressionists" and that only the English-speaking churches were "progressives." His speech warmed to the Kuyperian-derived theme that had surfaced within Afrikaner discourse. The desire "to uplift and advance [Africans]" was the "tangible expression of that inner urge [Afrikaners] call race-consciousness." Afrikaners rejected the "repressionist" approach because "the soul of any race [could not] be smothered or repressed for all time." Saayman's exposition "not for equal treatment, but for equality of opportunity," captured the central features of the new ideology that would become known in the United States as the "separate but equal" doctrine:

> If there is any doubt on this point on this point you have merely to look to history for confirmation, and the best and most recent example we find in our own treasured South Africa. The history of my own Afrikaans-speaking race proves that century-long domination, systematic oppression and violation of rights, hostility, contemptuous and unsympathetic treatment, nothing could extinguish or smother this race-consciousness. On the contrary, because of this treatment our race has emerged from the struggle strengthened and purified, and has reached maturity, so that today we can hold our head high and demand our rights if need be ... The soul of the Bantu ... can be repressed just as little [as] that of the European. Repressive methods have never yet answered, and there is no conclusive evidence to show that in this case things will be different.

Liberals and Afrikaners, he concluded, were at "a crossroads, where we begin to flounder between the dangers of Scylla and Charybdis, where we take different paths."[70]

The "liberal phase" that DRC missionaries briefly and unsuccessfully sought to pursue bequeathed two entwined legacies to Afrikaner theology in the 1920s and 1930s. Firstly, the ecclesiastical flirtation with the Benevolent Society provoked a strong backlash among a new generation of theologians. As the literature widely notes, many of these scholars had recently returned from universities in the Netherlands and Germany, brimming with the *volkish* theories of nationalism that flourished there in the inter-War years. These racial doctrines did not directly lead to the formulation of Apartheid theology, as conventional wisdom once assumed.[71] Nevertheless, they undoubtedly squelched the influence of liberals within the DRC. Still, one searches in vain in the profusion of articles, conferences and synods devoted to the church's relations with blacks for any suggestion that violence was an appropriate tool for managing African opposition. Instead, the trajectory of "the idea of Apartheid" in the first three decades after unification ran in the opposite direction. Theological views that transformed the DRC into a narrowly conceived *volkskerk* dedicated exclusively to the salvation of Afrikaners and poor whites in particular were soon broadened to include Africans as well. By recognizing the essential humanity of Africans within its theology, the DRC throughout the inter-War period explicitly repudiated both the most vulgar forms of biological racism and the utility of "repression" as an agent of salvation.

As du Plessis' liberal missionary views went into decline around 1930, other missiologists arose to again grapple with "the Native question." Originating from the Orange Free State, where it became closely identified with the DRC missionary, J. G. Strydom, this new faction of theologians categorically rejected equality with blacks. Strydom described racial "fraternization" as "race degeneration and bastardization" and repugnant to "every right-minded white and native." Such language may have been vulgar, but the basic sentiment against racially mixed sex and marriage was by no means unfamiliar to the "implicit racism" of liberal whites. Moreover, Strydom's "Free State Mission Policy" also incorporated the quintessential liberal idea that whites enjoyed a "stewardship" over blacks. Amongst its first declarations was the following assertion:

> [The DRC] bases its relations with the native on the teaching of God's word that teaches that the native is a human being with similar emotions to ours and that his soul is of equal value in the eyes of God as that of any other human being. He has the same right as we have to lay claim to the rights and privileges that are in principle bound to Christian civilization. Our view is that a sacred responsibility rests with us, as a Christian civilized people ... to raise the native out of poverty and misery of barbarism.

Liberal segregationists may have fiddled with the forthright language but could hardly have disagreed. For example, the idea that segregation was a "sacred responsibility" is the central theme of Charles Loram's book, *The Evangelization of South Africa*.[72]

Where Strydom's views departed from standard liberal rhetoric is his straightforward assertion that "Apartheid" was a permanent project. The liberal claim that segregation was a temporary epoch – a "purgatory," as Adam Ashforth describes it – that would eventually succumb to the civilizing process suggested that "racial assimilation" was far-off but also inevitable.[73] The Free State Mission Policy repudiated this outcome as "psychologically unsound." To square segregation with its own view that all "human beings" had "equal value in the eyes of God," Strydom advanced the opposite outcome: the goal of the civilizing process was to guarantee segregation. Hence, the DRC would civilize Africans on "their own terrain, separated and apart." This sacred obligation would set in place a secular and self-propelling dynamism: the church would "build up the natives into a Christian people that through its own Christian virtue, resourcefulness, and organization shall take care of its economic life apart from, yet, where possible, in cooperation with the white community." The DRC would teach Africans to "know their own language, people and history"; like Afrikaners, Africans would preserve their own, distinctive "racial identity."[74] Thus, the antidote to "equalization" was "equality in separate spheres" – a theological derivative from Adam Kuyper's teachings that also echoed the "separate but equal doctrine" in *Plessey V Ferguson* (1896).

The forthright language of the Mission statement brushed past the liberal sensitivities that had marked the DRC's entry into the "Native question." The document organized a loose assembly of familiar paternalist ideas into a declarative and distinctive statement in a process that the American political scientist George Lakoff describes as "reframing." Reframing works by rearranging familiar concepts into a definite conceptual framework, establishing an internal coherence and resonance amongst loosely associated concepts and implicit claims.[75] At various points, leading liberal segregationists had developed a raft of themes – racial equality in principle, no political rights for whites in "tribal areas," no political rights for blacks outside the reserves in black spheres, unlimited "advancement" for blacks along separate tracks, white stewardship over blacks, and so on – which now also formed the backbone of Strydom's Mission Statement. Far from borrowing from Nazi ideology, as T. Dunbar Moodie once claimed, Strydom's theological vision of race relations sprang from an internal debate within the DRC. Indeed, the Mission Statement may have had a very different provenance: in 1937, while on a tour of the USA, Strydom informed an audience in North Carolina that "Apartheid" resembled segregation in the South and "held up" the American South, with its segregated schools, as his model.[76] Lord Hailey, on a research trip to South Africa in 1934 and 1935 to collect information for *African Survey*, his magisterial summation of colonialism throughout the African continent, was struck by the parallels that white South Africans drew with the American South. He jotted down in his diary that "South Africa regards itself as a USA in the making."[77]

From the mid-1930s onwards, the church's racial policy was again revamped. The changes indicate that the spirit of paternalism remained a defining feature of Apartheid theology, reflecting the success that Cape missionaries enjoyed in influencing NP policy in the 1940s. G. B. H. Gerdener, Professor of Missiology at the University of Stellenbosch, played a key role in this development. An evangelist cut in the liberal mold of du Plessis, Gerdener shared many of du Plessis' liberal leanings but was also more forthright in his commitment to segregationist policies. At least as important as his support for measures such as a ban on racially mixed marriages or his belief that existing segregationist policies needed to be more effectively implemented was his campaign to accentuate the "positive" impact of segregation on blacks. Gerdener made his contribution in the late 1930s and the 1940s, a period marked by heightened racial unrest and numerous contradictions and vacillations in the racial policies of Smuts' government, especially those involving Africans in the country's urban areas.[78] More clearly and forcefully than his Afrikaner contemporaries, Gerdener successfully grasped that "Apartheid" – a word he did his best to avoid – could be presented not only as an institutional continuation of paternalist policies but also as a moral improvement over them.[79]

With Africans daily squeezing into already overcrowded townships and their mobility and employment opportunities subject to ever stricter administrative controls, "justice for the Native" became all the more important for the DRC as it became more illusive in practice. Against this background, the DRC searched for ways to justify on Christian grounds the stepped-up segregationist policies it was calling for. These differed from, but were as paternalist as, the creeds that informed the racial programs of the Benevolent Empire. Afrikaner theology sanctioned neither private violence nor communal retribution against blacks.

Church leaders may therefore be condemned for turning a blind eye to the high levels of violence in the *platteland*. In the matter of communal violence, however, they were indistinguishable from the liberals in the Benevolent Society. Like the latter, they were simply not drawn to disruptive and savage lynch mobs. Ever more cognizant of the threat that a mobilized black majority posed to whites generally and Afrikaners in particular, the *predikante* who surged to the forefront of white politics saw in the organized power of the state a weapon that was unimpeachably modern and morally sound. They therefore leached their theology of venegeance into the legal system in particular and state power generally. "The judicial system never hesitates to confront violence head on," René Girard writes in *Violence and the Sacred*, "because it possesses a monopoly on the means of revenge".[80] Unlike the Protestant clergy in the South who were compromised by their close association with lynching, Apartheid theologists claimed that they promoted racial justice in place of conflict and violence.

Afrikaner theology entered the twentieth century as a resentful Religion of the Lost Cause that Afrikaner nationalists used to challenge their British conquerors. Three turbulent decades later, Afrikaner politician-*predikante* were in a position to plan on burying the hatchet. That they buried the hatchet in the heads of blacks says less of any malevolence that Afrikaners might have had toward blacks than the volumes that it does speak about the Afrikaners' basic faith in the interventionist powers of the modern state and its capacity to transform racial violence into a series of God-sanctioned public works.

7

The nightmare of multiple jurisdictions: States rights and lynching in the South

> The black man asks for justice and is given the theory of government. He asks for protection and is confronted with a scheme of governmental checks and balances. [1]

Rutherford Hayes eventually emerged victorious from the inconclusive election of 1876 but commenced his presidency fatally compromised to Southern planters. In terms of the "Compromise of 1877," Southern Democrats relinquished the presidency in exchange for a promise from Hayes to bring Radical Reconstruction to an end and withdraw Northern troops from across the South.[2] Withdrawing the Northern army from the South was the first of three fateful betrayals that abandoned emancipated blacks to white-hot Southern rage. Two other federal institutions – Congress and the Supreme Court – would also betray blacks.

The violence that hammered segregation into place was patently illegal and anti-constitutional. Congress would not again turn to the spirit that had secured the passage of the "Enforcement Acts," a set of highly effective measures that almost immediately rendered the Ku Klux Klan moribund in the late 1860s and early 1870s. It was the Supreme Court, however, that arguably inflicted the greatest harm on African Americans and the nation. When African Americans responded to Northern betrayal by seeking justice in the courts, they ensured that persistent legal challenges would shadow the emergence of segregation, causing whites to grow anxious and jittery about the Supreme Court. There was, after all, ample constitutional ground for the Supreme Court to imperil segregation with a single, categorical decision. The Supreme Court, however, declined to undo the violent juggernaut in the South. With contorted and bizarre legal logic, it gave repeated succor to exploitative capitalists, fiercely protected property rights while hobbling labor movements, and all but gutted the constitutional rights of African Americans in the South. In the name of states rights, neither Congress nor the Supreme Court moved against white Southerners who viewed "popular justice" as separate from and superior to the US constitution.

Congress and the Supreme Court were the only institutions that could have corrected or seriously ameliorated President Hayes' disastrous withdrawal of the Northern army from the South. In neither branch of government would blacks find allies willing, powerful or skilled enough to press the manifest obviousness of their case. Instead, Congressional foot-dragging and the apathy of the Supreme Court delivered blacks trussed and gagged to white mobs. The fig leaf that concealed the Court's tolerance of racial violence was the doctrine of "states rights."

Segregation and the problem of multiple jurisdictions

On 12 February 1909, on Abraham Lincoln's birthday, Ida B. Wells joined W. E. B. Du Bois and other African American luminaries to establish the NAACP. Two specific events, both violent, had dramatized the need for an organization to protect and, in the South, secure the citizenship rights of African Americans. As the publication of Well's *Red Record* in 1898 had chronicled, lynching in the former Confederacy was on the ascendance with no end in sight, prompting northern African Americans to intercede on behalf of their Southern compatriots by securing a federal law that would target the specific crime of lynching. Then, just as efforts to illegalize lynching were taking off, a "race riot" erupted on 14 August 1908 in Springfield, Illinois, Lincoln's birthplace. Seven African Americans died in the riot and hundreds of thousands of dollars' worth of damage was inflicted on public property. The mayhem erupted after a sheriff transferred two African American prisoners to spare them from a lynch mob outside the city jail. One of the prisoners had murdered a white man; the other was accused of raping a white woman. Seven African American residents of Springfield perished in the riot, including an affluent and influential resident named William Donnegan. The 84-year-old Donnegan, Abraham Lincoln's personal cobbler and reputedly his friend before the Civil War, had been married to a white woman for thirty-two years when the mob seized him from his home, slit his throat, dragged him across the capitol grounds and lynched him on the front lawn of a nearby school.[3]

Forcing Congress to pass anti-lynching legislation became the central focus of the NAACP, black leaders and white liberals in the South. Despite enormous efforts by the NAACP in particular, a federal anti-lynching bill would never emerge from Congress, not even after lynching had all but ceased in the 1950s. Throughout the inter-War period, the NAACP was compelled to rely on a variety of other legal provisions to bring lynchers to justice. These were occasionally successful. Landmark cases such as the "Scottsboro Boys" trial rescued black men from the gallows but were perhaps more important for their success in alerting the nation to the terrorist ends which the criminal justice system was made to serve in the South. The struggle for an anti-lynching bill proceeded with fitful success in Congress, buoyed by occasional press reports about racial outrages in the South. Accounts of bestial ferocity that accompanied many of these lynchings briefly stunned Northerners before indifference and apathy again set in. As the events in the 1950s would make clear, it would take a combination of factors – national and international, economic and political, but most of all, the emergence of irrepressible black grassroots mobilization in the South – before the culture of judicial neglect would finally dissipate, and then, not even decisively.

Until that time, the doctrine of multiple jurisdictions that defined the American democratic system was the elephant in the room. Until the outbreak of the Civil War, the theory of divided government had given sanctuary to slavery in the South under the banner of "states rights." With war over and Reconstruction successfully beaten back, Southern states again asserted the doctrine of states rights to limit the influence of the federal government. For fully eight decades after the 1870s, Southern states returned the theory of divided government to the creature it had been prior to the Civil War. Throughout the inter-War years, no more than a handful of Republicans in Congress and two or three members of the Supreme Court had the courage or simply the human compassion to move against the lynch culture in the South. Again, the antebellum interpretation of states rights was permitted to seep out from the South and dominate the federal government. As before, African Americans were sacrificed to the fiction that the sheer separation of powers in a state marked by co-equal branches of government obstructed racial reform. In Congress, Southern politicians made full use of the legal conundrum they concocted: federal laws that might protect blacks from white violence would usurp the rights of states.[4]

The courts and lynching

The image of blacks had changed dramatically after Reconstruction: in place of the pliant slave there arose the specter of "masterless slaves" prone to crime and corruption in Reconstruction governments and to the "unmentionable deed" in society. United by the fiction of rampant black criminality, whites adopted an attitude of impatience towards the law and rejected constitutionalism. Formal legalities, they argued, limited their ability to eliminate both "crime" and the matrix from which it sprang, black freedom. In particular, planters, hungry for cheap labor, demanded a free hand to "restore order" and so took the lead in sabotaging lawful authorities.

This development was a new turn in planters' history. Slave owners had supported constitutionalism in the antebellum years because the law was designed to protect their property interests. Slave owners, of course, designed the laws and were careful to devise statutes that limited the intrusion of the criminal justice system on their plantations, where the patriarch's discretion was supreme. Subject to this function, however, the law was permitted to bestow on slaves a degree of habeas corpus and a certain measure of due process derived not from the formal legal system – from which virtually all slaves were excluded – but from English common law. Lawyers therefore mined treatises on English common law to defend slaves in court. As a result, "prisoners could not be tortured into confession; defendants had to be tried by a jury and could challenge the prosecution's evidence as well as present their own."[5] Such protections actually strengthened as the market value of slaves increased in the 1850s, so much so that slaves were frequently permitted to challenge prospective juries in the hope of securing a favorable verdict. Although he is careful to note that slave owners viewed plantation law and whippings as the final word in the control of their own slaves, Christopher Waldrep notes that slave owners extended at least some benefits of the law to their black chattel who committed crimes off the plantation.[6]

Nevertheless, the very courts and judges involved in investigating off-plantation crimes favored slave owners. Slaves were brought before "slave courts" when they were accused of any number of off-plantation acts that threatened the public good or affected the well-being of other whites. Because elected judges and members of the landed elite presided over these institutions, slaves were at a decided disadvantage. Not always, however. Timothy Huebner's analysis of "slave justice" in antebellum North Carolina, for example, illustrates how a slave named Caesar was brought before the court, which sentenced him to death for murdering a white man in a brawl provoked by the latter. Caesar's lawyer successfully appealed the case to the North Carolina Supreme Court and secured a new trial. Caesar was again convicted, but this time on the non-capital charge of "felonious assault," sparing him from execution.[7]

Granting slaves access to the courts clearly raised certain problems. Slave owners never embraced the practice, not least because lawyers had pecuniary interests in extending the authority of the courts on to the plantation, thereby challenging the authority of slave owners and complicating the –simplicity of summary punishment. Slave owners' acceptance of constitutionalism was therefore tightly circumscribed, and they never lost their distrust of the formal legal system, drawing comfort from the arrangement that largely restricted the involvement of the courts to off-plantation offenses. When Reconstruction measures destroyed plantation law and extended the formal law to black and white alike, whites turned hostile towards the entire legal system.[8]

Reconstruction and the courts

Most accounts of Reconstruction agree that landowners rejected the criminal justice system in favor of controlling emancipated blacks with outright terror. Based on his close study of the legal system in Mississippi in the 1870s, however, Christopher Waldrep offers a different interpretation. In an argument that may well apply to most Southern states, Waldrep demonstrates that both whites and emancipated blacks in Mississippi pinned their still uncertain fortunes primarily on the formal legal system. With opposite goals in mind, each group looked to the infamous "Black Codes."[9] Waldrep argues that the Black Codes inadvertently widened blacks' access to the courts, by encouraging the hope amongst freedmen that existing laws would protect and promote their freedom. White employers found themselves drawn into the procedural workings of the formal courts, where papers had to be filed, lawyers hired, arguments made and evidence adduced. The high profile of African Americans in office equipped whites with another weapon, however. Although no evidence demonstrated that Reconstruction officials were more corrupt or incompetent than civil servants elsewhere in the country (in a decade when such complaints were legion in every state), these allegations were received as axiomatic truths across the South and cemented whites' growing contempt for constitutional governance.[10]

The constitutional path required whites to submit not only to the Thirteenth, Fourteenth and Fifteenth Amendment Acts[11] but also to the many black faces in public office in city, county and state government. The passage of the three "Ku Klux Klan" or "Enforcement Acts" demonstrated Congress's resolve to compel the region to submit to the law immediately after the Civil War. The first of these was passed in 1866 to "protect all Persons in the United States in their Civil Rights, and furnish the Means of their Vindication." When terrorist violence persisted, Congress responded with another act in 1870 to "enforce the Right of Citizens of the United States to vote in the several States of this Union." This measure, too, failed to stanch Ku Klux Klan violence, prompting a third measure from Congress "to enforce the Provisions of the Fourteenth Amendment to the Constitution of the United States." These measures initiated an important shift in American constitutional law by clarifying the superordinate power of the federal government over the states. They also provided the country with a glimpse of what a strong resolve in the federal government could achieve. Late in 1871, President Grant used the Enforcement Acts of 1866 and 1870 to hound the Ku Klux Klan and stirred a national debate by suspending habeas corpus in nine South Carolina counties. Hundreds of suspected terrorists were detained in roundups and convicted in federal courts. Greatly weakened and cowed by Grant's assault, the Ku Klux Klan in South Carolina crumbled and extra-legal violence virtually ceased within a year.[12]

Planters latched on to the "Enforcement Acts" as an example of an inept federal government that was indifferent to the cherished state rights doctrine. These were Southern-derived attacks on the federal government, but they merged with a nationwide disillusionment over Grant's scandal-plagued presidency (1869–77). In this context, Southern allegations of "black criminality" became a catch-all battle cry that appealed to Southern whites because it attributed the popular stereotypes of rampant corruption and crime by "black-beast rapists" to an undifferentiated black population, fueling the narrative of the "Lost Cause" a decade before the Northern army departed in 1877. A powerful disaffection with Grant's demonstrably inefficient and corrupt administration now added grist to the baleful lament about chivalry and female virtue in a courtly South that had been defeated not by a superior civilization but by overwhelming brute force.[13] Grant's despised administration transformed seething hostility against the North into a fundamental creed of the New South: saving the South meant staving off intrusions by the federal authorities into the region's "affairs". More than just a rallying cry to bolster demoralized whites, the vilification of federal authority gave rise to the electoral strategy known as the "Solid South." Until the 1960s, Southern states would vote as a monolithic bloc on racial and economic policies and were remarkably successful in repelling any scrutiny or legislation deemed unfavorable to the region.[14]

Extra-legal racial violence escalated in the New South because the plantocracy, more than any other actor, saw profit in the practice. However, the war against African Americans also resonated with the tradition of plebeian violence in the South. An antebellum culture that embraced *lex talionis* foregrounded the eruption of extra-legal racial violence in the New South, making it unnecessary for whites to invent from scratch a propensity for retributive violence. Scholars such as Grady McWhiney argue that Scotch–Irish immigrants in the eighteenth and nineteenth centuries brought to the South a ferocious tradition of honorific violence honed in centuries-long rebellion against British occupation.[15] Approximately eighty per cent of white Southerners trace their ancestry to Scotch–Irish immigrants to the region. For scholars such as McWhiney, this common stock explains the region's disinclination to rely on formal courts and its tolerance for interpersonal violence. This antebellum "cultural tolerance" for interpersonal violence in the antebellum period merged with the sweeping disregard for federal authority that arose in the New South. Once whites rejected the courts as the arena for resolving disputes over "race relations," the length and breadth of civil society became a potential battlefield in which any white male could assert his power over blacks.

Emboldened white plebeians were prepared to attack white officials who obstructed "repressive justice" during Reconstruction but reserved the most appalling violence for vulnerable blacks. Accordingly, the traditional divisions amongst white Southerners gave way as men, women, Protestants, Jews, Irishmen, and even former Yankee soldiers closed ranks in violent defiance of the federal state. Few phenomena capture the democratization of violence as well as the Ku Klux Klan, which most visibly transformed the doctrine of personal enforcement into the signature of race relations in the New South. With the ejection of Reconstruction in 1877, "the tension between constitutionalism and extra-legal violence" became the defining contradiction of legal culture in the New South.[16]

More often than not, the racist views of politicians and court officials legitimized the myth of rampant black "criminality." Even state Supreme Court judges could be as scathing and suspicious as ordinary Southerners of the legal system. For the majority of ordinary whites, the legal system was "too good for black beast-rapists and murderers." A chief justice of North Carolina, as well as the president of the Georgia Bar Association, shared this opinion, as did the attorney from Mobile, Alabama, who justified lynching as "the outcry of a conservative and law loving people against the abuses of a system of criminal procedure which has become intolerably inefficient."[17] The claim that the legal system was too inefficient or liberal to adequately deal with black criminality was grossly false. In fact, accused murderers in most Southern states were more likely than their counterparts in the North to be sent to prison.[18] Nevertheless, some judges were as strident as the fire-breathing editorialists who lambasted the courts and concluded that lynching was a reasonable response to the legal nitpicking that allegedly let black criminals free. White Southerners also wrongly assumed that most black lynch victims were rapists and therefore manifestly beyond the domain of the legal courts. Questions of veracity were not central to the outbreak of lynching, and the truth was rarely relevant to the infrequent court cases involving charges of lynching. Judges and jury members knew that lynching was less about punishing specific crimes than symbolic iterations of white supremacy. Extensive connivance amongst the various cogs that comprised the administration of justice virtually guaranteed inaction or the acquittal of accused lynchers. The police routinely intimidated the rare souls who offered to testify against lynchers; juries took a few minutes to return "not guilty" verdicts despite volumes of incontrovertible evidence; lawyers, jury members and the accused would hob-knob jovially in the corridors of the courthouse before reassembling to accept the pre-ordained "not guilty" verdicts; disregarding eyewitness reports, which were frequently recorded in newspaper articles with ample evidence about the identities of the lynchers, coroners unfailingly ascribed deaths to "parties unknown"; and judges came to the accused's defense by ignoring incriminating evidence of guilt before opting for acquittal.

By 1933, fewer than one per cent of lynchings had led to successful convictions. Between 1882 and 1940, only 40 of 5,150 lynchings in the United States led to legal action against accused lynchers. Only four southern states had ever secured convictions, more than half of which took place in a single state (Georgia) "where half of all the persons in the entire country punished for lynching in the first three decades of the twentieth century were prosecuted during Thomas Kilby's 1919–23 gubernatorial term."[19] Lynching and extra-legal violence generally were supported by a veritable cabal in which all rungs and branches involved in the administration of justice were complicit. One authority on the legal systems in Southern states describes the collusion as "near total."[20] Congress and the Supreme Court were the two federal bodies that could have done something about the South's brazen culture of legal subversion. Neither had either the inclination or commitment to do so. As soon as it fell under the control of the Democratic Party, Congress set about diluting the strength of the laws that outlawed racial terror and intimidation. When these laws were consolidated into the *Revised*

Statutes in 1873, Southern Congressmen took the opportunity to dismantle and disperse a series of key provisions. In 1894, Congress dropped from the books provisions that protected suffrage. Similar incursions again were made when federal criminal laws were reformulated in 1909.[21]

The Supreme Court and lynching

Still, the gutting of protective measures had to contend with a number of statutes that continued to vest the nation's courts with powers to protect the political and civil rights of African Americans. Sections 19 and 20 of the penal code, for example, provided omnibus shelter to African Americans. Section 19 made it a federal offense for *two or more persons* to "conspire to injure, oppress, threaten, or intimidate any citizen," to prevent citizens from enjoying "any right or privilege secured to him by the Constitution or laws of the United States," or to persecute him for doing so. In addition, the measure also outlawed the wearing of disguises on public roads or on the private property of another in order to obstruct the latter from exercising any constitutional right. Section 20 underscored the reach of this protection by making it a crime for any *individual* who, acting "under color of any law, statute, ordinance, regulation, or custom," engaged in these same activities.[22] Commenting on the immediate success these measures had in quelling extra-legal violence and anti-Reconstruction agitation, Justice William Strong, speaking from the Third Circuit Court bench, lectured that it was "an exploded heresy that the national government cannot reach all individuals in the states."[23] Unable to undo the constitution, Southern Congressmen were unable to undo all the protections that blacks could appeal to.

Yet the Supreme Court did far more than Congress to entrench *de jure* segregation in the South and tolerate massive extra-legal violence against African Americans. From the 1870s until *Brown v Board of Education* in 1954, the Supreme Court, fastening on to the ambiguities inherent to the federal state, strove to limit the reach of federal authority in the South. A tension within the Ku Klux Klan Acts provided the point of entry. These measures set out to punish private violence, but their "constitutional basis was the Fourteenth Amendment, which forbade only states, not individuals, to deny privileges and immunities, due process, and the equal protection of the laws."[24] Proposers of the Amendment argued that the *failure* of a state to punish private violence in fact also constituted "state action." Legal opinion on the matter subsequently differed, however. Some judicial theorists saw in the law adequate authority for the federal state to intervene wherever private parties threatened blacks' liberties; others argued that federal intervention was only warranted if states failed to protect blacks' rights. The Supreme Court addressed the tension between measures that punished private conduct and constitutional amendments that addressed state actions by repeatedly ruling in favor of "states rights." Morrison Remick Waite, Chief Justice of the Supreme Court (1874–88), even contended that the Fourteenth Amendment was redundant because the political rights of African Americans were already protected elsewhere. Insofar as it addressed criminal matters such as murder, the Fourteenth Amendment therefore could not be invoked because cases involving murder fell under the rubric of states rights. Reasoning that "Sovereignty, for this purpose, rests alone with the States," the Chief Justice refused to consider any situation in which the federal courts could intervene in matters of murder. Waite refused to even consider the goals of the Fourteenth Amendment when he argued against the Enforcement Act, which the Court struck down in *United States v Cruikshank*.[25]

From that point onward until the outbreak of the Second World War, the Supreme Court generally refused to uphold either the spirit or the intent of laws that sought to protect the political rights of blacks in the South. Many of its rulings seemed designed to protect violent white perpetrators instead. The Courts, for example, concluded that inaction on behalf of state officials – refusing or failing to intervene while marauding mobs deprived blacks of their constitutional rights – did not amount to a violation of the constitution; mere inaction, therefore, did not warrant federal intervention. In the Court's opinion, federal intervention applied only in cases where blacks were seized from federal custody before being lynched. The Court therefore permitted cases to be brought against lynchers who had snatched blacks from one or the other form of federal custody, sometimes with the connivance or open support of law enforcement authorities. Almost all lynch victims, however, were *not* federal prisoners and so failed to benefit from even this limited protection. Supreme Court rulings so effectively pared down Section 19 that the only "conspiracies" the Court acted on were those that obstructed blacks from voting in federal elections. Thus, as late as 1945, the Courts ruled in *Screws v United States* that three policemen who had beaten a prisoner to death could not be charged under Section 20 for "willfully" depriving the victim of his life without trial. In this case, the Court ruled, the state had not proven that the officers "willfully" subjected the victim to a "trial by ordeal" with the express intention of eliminating the victim's constitutional right. The reference to "under color of law" in Section 20 was therefore rendered ineffective, protecting police who murdered their prisoners.[26]

But this reading was not inherent to federalism. As numerous commentators observed at the time, the strict interpretation of federalism was not extended to all spheres of governance. Government regulation of alcohol sales in the Prohibition period in the 1920s was a case in point. A Northern Democrat noted in 1922 that "surely if the Federal Government can step in to take a mug of wholesome beer from the hand of a workingman, it can step in to take a murderous halter from the hands of a lyncher."[27] Nor were Southern elites consistent in denying the federal government powers to intervene in certain matters. For example, Southerners who opposed moonshining, including owners of distilleries, gladly collaborated with federal agents in prosecuting moonshiners under federal statutes.[28]

Federalist discourse and whites' desire to reconcile North and South remained as deeply entwined as they were when the country's two-party system emerged to balance and accommodate divergent views over slavery.[29] The resultant doctrine of "state rights" confronted African Americans with a stacked deck from the outset. In Claudine Ferrell's words: "On the state level, 'the law' claimed the power to end lynching, but it made virtually no effort to exercise that power. On the national level, 'the law' made no effort because it claimed no power."[30] Appeal after appeal for a federal anti-lynching law foundered in the first half of the twentieth century, trapped in legalisms about the nature of federal government or sacrificed to other ends in horse-trading between Democrats and Republicans, Northerners and Southerners. Almost immediately after the First World War, the South's near-unanimity over the need for lynching began to erode and Southern editorialists began to support anti-lynching bills in Congress. *The Daily News* (Greensboro, NC) supported a bill in 1922 "because none of the States had made an honest effort to prevent lynching by making examples of those who indulge in them." A Baptist minister from Chattanooga supported the bill in stronger terms: "State Rights are good as far as they work for Justice, Mercy and the Fear of god. Where these are ignored, State Rights is a failure and sin."[31] But the bill petered out by the end of 1922, done in by Congressional anxiety over the rights of states. As federal provisions weakened at the hands of the Congress and the Supreme Court, a conventional argument set in: in the view of a succession of presidents, congressional leaders, and judges, lynching was a "Southern problem" in need of a Southern solution. In 1918, President Wilson did no more than appeal to "the governors of all the states, the law officers of every community and, above all, the men and women of every community in the United States ... to make an end of this disgraceful evil," adding that "it cannot live where the community does not countenance it."[32] Wilson's solution therefore failed to acknowledge either the special horror of lynching or the demonstrated complicity of law-enforcement institutions in the South. The "hands off the South" policy disabled the nation's judicial and political institutions, making them virtual accomplices in legalized terror and lynching in the post-Reconstruction South.

Nothing captures the gutting of the spirit of Reconstruction and the appeasement of Southern whites quite as well as *Plessey v Ferguson*, which gave segregation the force of law in 1896. In his ruling, Justice Brown rejected the argument that white supremacy *ipso facto* "stamps the colored race with the badge of inferiority." ("The colored race," he countered, "*chooses* to put that construction upon it"). The ruling came in the wake of earlier decisions that had whittled down federal protection of blacks' civil rights and invalidated the public accommodation rulings of the 1875 Civil Rights Act. Subsequent rulings in civil rights cases in 1883, specifically the Supreme Court's judgment that the Fourteenth and Fifteenth Amendments had been framed too broadly and that the Civil Rights Act of 1875 was unconstitutional, created the necessary legal room for the proliferation of Jim Crow laws from the 1880s onwards. *Plessey v Ferguson* was widely perceived in the South as a national repudiation of the Reconstruction experiment and a return by the federal government to a policy of appeasement that had made the Dred Scott decision of 1857 possible.[33] In this conservative legal climate, anti-lynching legislation stood no chance in Congress. Although white killers were occasionally convicted and jailed for murdering African Americans, the NAACP concluded that Southern courts either ignored racial violence or actively shielded lynchers.[34]

African Americans and the courts

V. O. Key argues that while the courts did fail to enforce existing legislation, naked terror and intimidation were sufficient to expel blacks from the political arena between 1876 and 1890. However, in the view of J. Morgan Keyser, legal measures were more important in stripping blacks, along with many poor whites, of the right to vote.[35] Some states, such as Alabama, gerrymandered black areas into multiple voting districts to ensure that blacks did not form a majority anywhere. Mississippi devised an opposite strategy by centralizing black votes in one district to limit black influence to just one of several voting districts. Both strategies effectively rendered the black vote useless even in states where blacks voted in large numbers.[36] Poll taxes achieved the same end, and were, Alfred Stone notes, "the most effective bar to negro suffrage ever devised."[37] In response to the Populist movement in the 1890s, several states moved to protect white supremacy by going further than such electoral chicanery to straightforwardly deny the vote on the basis of race. A delegate to Virginia's constitutional convention in 1901 could not have been more candid: the goal of the convention was to "to disfranchise every negro that [they] could disfranchise after 1890 under the Constitution of the United States, and as few white people as possible." Constitutional conventions were held to formally strip blacks of their political rights in five states – Mississippi, South Carolina, Louisiana, Alabama and Virginia. Mississippi's "four-step" strategy confronted prospective voters with the following hurdles: proof that a $2 poll tax had been paid before registering to vote; a literacy test in the presence of a white state election official to prove that the voter could read, understand and interpret any section of the state constitution; proof that the voter had resided for at least two continuous years within the state and one year within the voting district; and permanent disfranchisement for crimes that blacks were more likely to be convicted for. By 1890, most states had adopted the essentials of the "Mississippi Plan."[38]

Still, small numbers of black voters continued to legally cast their votes despite the combination of poll taxes, the quadruple restrictions of the "Mississippi Plan," and grandfather clauses. Much of the racial violence in the decade before and after 1890 was intended to terrorize blacks and their allies in the Populist movement into staying away from the hustings. Dissatisfaction with even small numbers of black voters culminated in the invention of the all-white primary, the final nail in the coffin of the black vote. C. Vann Woodward vividly describes in *Origins of the New South* how white men roamed through towns and countryside "looting, burning, and shooting" to keep blacks and white Populists from voting. The logic of the all-white primary was simple but thoroughly effective: to prevent blacks from voting in the general election, African Americans were first prevented from voting in state primary elections. Since the Solid South was virtually a one-party region, this meant "the effective and complete disfranchisement of the black community."[39]

After the First World War, the ability of a few hundred blacks who still managed to vote in the primary elections to determine electoral outcomes illuminated the ability of corrupt politicians to buy, coerce or manipulate the black vote. Even Populists who had set out to "clean out" the state's corrupt electoral system were persuaded that any wholesome alternative required the elimination of the black vote. In Texas, Democratic Party politicians lobbied the Texas legislature for the final solution, demanding the explicit right to withhold the vote on the basis of race. Around 1920, a number of rulings by the Texas Supreme Court provided the legal opening. In the view of the state Supreme Court, political parties were "private organizations" and therefore fell beyond the jurisdiction of the Fourteenth and Fifteenth Amendments to the constitution which, the Court argued, applied only to "state action." In 1921, the US Supreme Court reached a similar affirmative conclusion in *Newberry v US*, which held that the two amendments did not apply to primary elections. This meant that the highest court in the land had somehow persuaded itself that primary elections were unrelated to the exercise of civil rights. This was all that white Texans needed. Two years after the *Newberry* ruling, an emboldened Texas legislature enacted a law to expressly prohibit all blacks from voting in the state's primary elections: "in no event shall a negro be eligible to participate in a Democratic primary election held in the state of Texas." The all-white primary remained in force until it was finally overturned by *Smith v Allwright* in 1944.[40]

By the outbreak of the First World War, the tide had already shifted in favor of segregation in both North and South, as the eruptions of "race riots" across the country as well as the *Newberry* decision made clear. Accord over *de jure* segregation effectively brought to an end the political disputes that had divided the two regions since the 1850s. Other issues soon dislodged the sectional conflict from the forefront of American political culture: "The new industrialism, the labor movement, agrarian reform movements, the silver and tariff issues, the waves of immigrants, and the new role of the United States as an imperial power captured the attention of the government and citizens alike," leaving African Americans unprotected against the violence of lynchers in the South.[41] Regional rapprochement after 1900 all but extinguished the civil rights issue. After America's entry into the Great War in Europe, the question of civil rights for blacks now surfaced as an unwelcome irritant in national politics.[42] Not a single party that contested the presidential election of 1912 – including the Democratic, Republican, Progressive, Republican, Socialist and "Socialist Labor" parties – so much as referred to the issue of civil rights. Paul Frymer blames the Republican Party for this development. Because blacks were a "captive constituency" of the party, Republicans could safely dispense with courting a vote that had become a major liability in national politics. The Party therefore struck the divisive civil rights from its electoral agenda.[43]

Lynching and "states rights"

It is a disquieting fact of American history that the Constitution itself was adduced as the primary reason for failing to clamp down on lynching. At the root of this inaction was a false god, the doctrine of state rights. The case of *US v Shipp* (1909) illuminates the ability of lynch mobs to tie up the court systems in a tragic conundrum. An examination of the case below establishes two points. Firstly, it indicates that it was not just local elites who looked upon extra-legal violence as essential for "keeping blacks in their place": the extensive participation of ordinary white citizens in racial violence indicates that Southern society as a whole rejected the authority of the legal system in favor of "repressive justice." Secondly, however, *US v Shipp* also shows that whites in the New South engaged in extra-legal violence against African Americans precisely because segregation *was* indeed vulnerable to legal review from above. This legal vulnerability did not spring only from the formal architecture of the legal system but also, and primarily, from the persistent efforts of African Americans to protect themselves by attacking segregation in the courts. Small in itself, each legal victory that blacks achieved reminded Southerners of the sword of Damocles above them: a single major ruling from the Supreme Court could set a legal precedent that could unravel segregation. White Southerners feared that the formal architecture of the federal state meant that the Supreme Court was always pregnant with the possibility of something like *Brown v Board of Education*. Anxiety about an institution the region could not control fueled white Southerners' suspicions of the courts. The ideology of "popular justice" therefore retained its deadly cachet long after segregation had become entrenched.

The lynching of Ed Johnson and US v Shipp (1909)
The lynching of Ed Johnson in Chattanooga in March 1906 is a fitting illustration of the legal confusions in which lynching cases were liable to flounder. The lynching, which was predictably triggered by an allegation of rape, eventually prompted the US Supreme Court to hear a state criminal case involving federal constitutional issues. The case is exceptional because it marked the first and only time that the federal court has intervened in a state criminal trial to enforce its authority.[44]

The legal saga began on the night of 23 January 1906, when a white

woman, Nevada Taylor, was attacked and raped within a hundred yards
of her home. At first, Taylor was unable to identify her attacker or to state
whether he was white or black but then changed her story and said, "He
was a Negro with a soft, kind voice." A full day passed in which no one
could offer any assistance in identifying the assailant. Within hours of its
posting, however, a reward of $375 jolted the memory of a white man who
offered information that led to the arrest of Ed Johnson, a casual worker
with sketchy ties to Chattanooga. Within minutes of Johnson's arrest, a
mob of between 300 and 400 whites assembled outside the jail. Meanwhile,
anticipating precisely such an event, the judge and sheriff had Johnson
quietly removed to Nashville.[45]

Chattanooga, it seemed, was about to relive two earlier lynchings of black
men. In 1893, Alfred Blount had been detained on suspicion of raping an
elderly white woman who was not able to identify her attacker. A mob soon
gathered outside the jail but the sheriff declined to hand Blount over to his
certain fate, partly on the grounds that he was not sure if Blount had committed the crime. The mob received this explanation as an intimation that
Blount would be released. White men quickly stormed the jail and hanged
Blount from a nearby bridge. Almost exactly the same scene was repeated
after a sixteen-year-old white girl had been raped in 1897. A mob again
forcibly extracted one Charles Brown from jail. After unsuccessfully trying
to hang Brown from a bridge, the mob burned him to death.

Although he too would be eventually lynched, Ed Johnson's fate was to
be more complicated and tortuous. Apprised of the danger brewing outside
the jail, the governor dispatched members of the National Guard to the
scene. These young and inexperienced "citizen-soldiers" could not bring
themselves to open fire on fellow whites, who promptly disarmed them. The
city police were next on the scene. They managed to control the mob, which
finally dispersed after searching the jail without finding Johnson. Although
they made no attempt to conceal their identities, none of the would-be
lynchers was arrested. Johnson, meanwhile, insisted on his innocence.
Nevada Taylor's testimony therefore became vital. Taylor identified him as
her assailant based on what she vaguely described as his "soft voice." Unusually, however, she also placed on record her objections to mob law and
denounced the earlier attempt to lynch Johnson. Sheriff Shipp advised Judge
S. D. McReynolds that Johnson was Taylor's attacker. McReynolds immediately empanelled a grand jury and set the case against Johnson in motion,
not knowing that it would eventually culminate in *US v Shipp* (1909).

Speed, McReynolds informed the all-white, all-male jury, was of the
essence: "Such outrages as this must have the immediate attention of the
law, that the law may be preserved. It is the 'law's delay' that brings about
the mob spirit ... And if in the investigation of this most dreadful crime there
is any attempt to interfere with the due process of law, the law shall and will
be preserved at any cost of treasure or human life."[46] Seventeen days later,
in a four-day trial marred by multiple violations of judicial procedure, it

took just one hour for the jury to deliver a guilty verdict. Even the judge and state prosecutor were surprised when Johnson's three state-appointed lawyers declined to appeal the sentence to the state Supreme Court, although Tennessee's capital offense laws automatically invoked Johnson's right to appeal. Johnson's fate took a sudden turn when two black attorneys, Noah Parden and Styles Hutchins, intervened and offered to appeal the case to the Tennessee Supreme Court. Hutchins and Shepherd were undeterred when the state Supreme Court rebuffed the appeal. They immediately filed a petition for writ of habeas corpus before the federal District Judge in Knoxville. The appeal was based on the argument that Johnson had not received a fair trial, had illegally been sentenced to death and had been deprived of his federal constitutional rights. These grounds had been adduced in a handful of earlier lynch cases, but federal judicial authorities had never ruled in the plaintiff's favor and granted a re-trial. However, Parden had changed the course of the case in one critical way: simply by filing the petition, he had immediately converted Johnson from a prisoner of the state of Tennessee into a prisoner of the federal state.

Parden used the appeal process before US District Judge C. D. Clark to reveal the scale of the plot confronting Johnson. McReynolds, the mayor of Chattanooga, and the defense lawyers had conducted secret meetings to settle on a verdict that would satisfy the lynch mobs; a juror had yelled in court "If I could just get at him, I would tear his heart out"; an all-white jury failed to meet the test of "a jury of his peers"; and, finally, Johnson's lawyers had immediately abandoned him after the verdict was announced instead of activating the automatic appeals process as required by law. Judge Clark dismissed all of these grounds. He based his position on the doctrine of states rights: even if Johnson's rights had been violated in the manner described by Parden, these reasons did not warrant federal intrusion into a state criminal case, not even if Johnson's rights under the Fourteenth Amendment had indeed been violated. Only the US Congress or Supreme Court could empower federal authorities to usurp state responsibilities under certain conditions, but neither had done so. Clark therefore refused to delay Johnson's execution. However, he also ruled that Johnson enjoyed the right to have his case heard before the US Supreme Court and granted Parden ten days to prepare his case, effectively delaying Johnson's execution for those ten days. Meanwhile, Sheriff Shipp confidently prepared the gallows. A nervous Parden began assembling the evidence he needed to submit an emergency appeal to the Supreme Court in Washington DC. Parden was well aware that the nation's supreme judicial body had never investigated the overlapping authority that federal and state levels enjoyed in state criminal matters. He knew, too, that a black attorney had never before addressed the Court.

Fortunately for Parden, the Supreme Court Judge for the Sixth Circuit Court of Appeals was Associate Justice John Marshall Harlan. As a young man, Harlan had roundly criticized Lincoln's war against the South as an abuse of executive power and an unwarranted intrusion into state affairs. He changed his views during Reconstruction, however, and came to enjoy a reputation as a liberal Republican strongly committed to the extension and protection of civil rights for blacks (even if, as Daniel Mangis argues, his liberal views on race had more to do with his Presbyterian and federalist views than any sense of racial justice). A critic of segregation – he famously broke with his Supreme Court colleagues in a minority opinion in which he described Plessey *v Ferguson* as a "badge of servitude" on blacks – Harlan was outspoken in his contempt for the Ku Klux Klan. Known as "the Great Dissenter," he cast the lone vote against the Court's decision to overturn the Civil Rights Act of 1875 on the grounds that the Act exceeded Congressional power. Harlan also believed the obvious: the Fourteenth Amendment provided the federal government with ample authority to protect African Americans in the South.[47] Forty-eight hours before the scheduled execution was to take place in Chattanooga, Harlan succeeded in getting the Supreme Court to hear Johnson's case. Johnson's life was again spared, this time by a month.

Johnson would not live to enjoy this brief reprieve, however. As enraged by the ruling of the Supreme Court as they were by the audacity of federal intervention into local "state matters," furious members of a mob in Chattanooga used a sledgehammer to destroy the steel door of the jail. Sheriff Shipp, meanwhile, was anxious. His earlier decision to summon the National Guard had culminated in the Supreme Court's intervention, and the city's white voters had promised to punish him in the elections that were just two weeks off. Shipp would not repeat his error and remained studiously inactive throughout the mob's activities. Brushing aside the jailer and the passive sheriff, members of the mob extracted the terrified Johnson from his cell and paraded him outside where more than 250 men, women and children were baying for his blood. Johnson was marched from the jail, noose around his neck, and lynched from the same bridge span from which a mob had hanged Blount in 1893. His body was shot to ribbons by the delirious mob and his head blown off to make sure that he was dead. A taunting placard was placed on his remnants, proclaiming "To Justice Harlan. Come get your nigger now." Two weeks later, Sheriff Shipp was re-elected to office by an overwhelming majority – a reversal of fortune that was widely acknowledged to be his reward for not interposing the local police and the National Guard between the mob and the prisoner.[48]

Johnson's demise would have been the same as that of thousands of other lynch victims whose names followed their lives into oblivion. There was, however, one crucial difference in Johnson's case: his status as a federal prisoner at the time he was abducted from jail. The fact that a federal prisoner had been lynched provided the deeply offended Supreme Court Justices in Washington with an opening. The US Attorney ordered two Secret Service federal agents to Chattanooga to gather evidence in order to indict those responsible for lynching Johnson. However, in the time-honored tradition of the Solid South, no-one in Chattanooga could recall the name of a single participant in the lynching – including Sheriff Shipp and the jailer, both of whom had conversed with the mob for more than an hour prior to Johnson's murder. Frustrated, the Justice Department settled for filing charges against Sheriff Shipp and eight of his deputies, accusing them of failing to adequately protect Johnson and with complicity in his death. Lawyers recognized that the charges were precedent-setting. According to the US Constitution, states and not the federal government bear the responsibility for dealing with state crimes, including murder. White Southerners saw the matter more broadly and succinctly: they saw in the case an assault on the entire doctrine of states rights and, by extension, on the "Southern way of life." In court, Shipp's attorney was shocked when he realized that the Supreme Court took the view that the Sixth Amendment (which guarantees a fair trial) applied not only to defendants but to the state courts as well. According to the judges, by short-circuiting the legal system the mob had unlawfully deprived the state of Tennessee of its right to conduct a fair trial.

While the Supreme Court was hearing *US v Shipp*, reports arrived of a lynching in Oxford, Mississippi, in which US Senator W. V. Sullivan had played the leading role. As usual, the alleged offense involved an "outrage" against a white woman. Aware that the Supreme Court had just engaged the question of federal versus state jurisdiction over the crime of murder, Senator Sullivan addressed the Court directly by openly admitting to journalists, "I directed every movement of the mob. I wanted him lynched. I saw his body dangling from a tree and I'm glad of it. I aroused the mob and I directed them to storm the jail."[49] Despite this confession, no charges were filed in connection with the lynching. However, the incident emboldened the Supreme Court Justices to act in the Chattanooga lynching. Finding that "this lamentable riot was the direct result of opposition to the administration of the law by this court," on 24 May 1909, by a narrow five-to-four decision the Justices found Shipp and several deputies guilty of contempt and sentenced them to sixty days' imprisonment in a federal penitentiary. After four decades of failing to act in hundreds of lynchings, for the first time officers of the law were found guilty of aiding and abetting the lynching of blacks. This assertion of federal dominance over recalcitrant state public officials met with mixed reactions. Blacks gratefully extolled it. But across the country numerous officials, state judges, prosecutors and law enforcement authorities reviled the principle that the federal government could regulate "local matters," even when state public officials were demonstrably corrupt or violated the constitutional rights of citizens.

Mark Curriden and Leroy Phillips take the view that *US v Shipp* was an historic clarification of the proper relationship between federal and state authorities and credit the ruling with playing a pivotal role in reducing the frequency of lynching. The ruling, they write. launched "one hundred years of federalism" and properly belongs in the company of more illustrious Supreme Court rulings such as *Brown v Board of Education* and *Roe v*

Wade. Lynch law, they note, "presented the first and only direct attack on the nation's judiciary" and *US v Shipp* was "the only proactive step the U.S. Supreme Court has ever taken to combat mob rule directly and demand that the public respect its authority and the authority of the written law."[50] However, the evidence does not support the view that *US v Shipp* was a definitive affirmation of the law. Curriden and Phillips take comfort in the slow decline in the number of lynchings from 82 in 1909 (when *Shipp* was handed down) to 64 in 1918. However, as the Appendix in *Contempt of Court* itself illustrates, the number of recorded lynchings seesawed after that. For example, it was 83 in 1819, 16 in 1924, 30 in 1926, 8 in 1932, and 20 in 1935 before finally remaining in single digits from 1936 onward. In 1914 the Tuskegee Institute refined its database by including for the first time the number of "prevented lynchings." The Institute found that the number of lynchings exceeded that of prevented lynchings by a ratio of two to one between 1914 and 1919; for the year 1918, the figure stood at 3.37 to 1. Prevented lynchings overtook lynchings only in 1920.[51] This erratic, if steadily diminishing, pattern does not support the claim that *US v Shipp* released the federal courts from the fetters of the states rights doctrine, enabling court officials to stanch extra-legal murders in the South. It is quite probable that the pattern of erratic decline was actually unaffected by *US v Shipp*. More plausibly, the NAACP's untiring campaign for anti-lynching legislation in Congress, sporadic reports in the national press that embarrassed Southern communities, the economic modernization of the South after the First World War, the increasing professionalization of law enforcement that this process stimulated, and the advent of the New Deal are a more likely cluster of explanations for this downward trend.[52]

It should be borne in mind, too, that as late as 1945, Section 20 of the criminal code preserved the nebulous distinction between state and federal authority in race-related violence. Section 20 reinforced the "under-color-of law" provisions of Section 19 and so stood ready as a potential weapon that federal authorities could use to monitor and punish private citizens and state officials who violated the constitutional rights of African Americans. These provisions were successfully used in the 1870s to eviscerate the Ku Klux Klan. Then, beginning with *US v Cruikshank* (1875), the Supreme Court issued several rulings that significantly diluted federal protections for blacks and emboldened the Ku Klux Klan. *US v Cruikshank*, the first Supreme Court decision involving the Second Amendment,[53] arose from events in Colfax, Louisiana, when a white mob surrounded and massacred one hundred black soldiers in 1873. Members of the Louisiana Ku Klux Klan, the group responsible for this Reconstruction-era atrocity, were indicted for thirty-two counts of conspiring to deny African Americans the right to assemble, vote, and "the 'right to keep and bear arms for a lawful purpose.'" The decision in *US v Cruikshank* set in place the restrictive view of federal power that would reign for decades to follow. For example, the ruling held that the "conspiracy" to deprive blacks of their civil and political rights was so narrowly construed that "the only significant conspiracies to intimidate that [the federal Criminal Code] could reach were ones to keep them from voting in federal elections." Mob lynchings, therefore, were excluded from the purview of federal authorities.[54] Contrary to Curriden and Phillips' assessment of *US v Shipp*, Johnson's death actually spared the Supreme Court from directly addressing the question: did the trial in Chattanooga violate Johnson's civil rights, as generally set out in the Bill of Rights and more specifically defined in the Fourteenth Amendment Act? *US v Shipp* only went so far as to note that, by agreeing to hear Parden's evidence that Johnson's rights to habeas corpus had been violated, the Court had sufficient ground to make its ruling binding on Shipp and his deputies. Johnson's demise and the consequent dismissal of Parden's case therefore absolved the court from definitively resolving whether or not federal courts enjoyed paramountcy over states in habeas cases. *US v Shipp* was not as sweeping and precedent-setting as Curriden and Phillips argue.

It is in fact quite easy to demonstrate that the nation's highest courts persisted in the late nineteenth-century fallacy concerning the inviolability of states rights whenever lethal violence against blacks was involved. In 1935, a state prosecutor in Columbus, Texas, refused to take action against a lynch mob because lynching was "an expression of the will of the people." This view was by no means atypical in the decades leading up to the Second World War. Arthur Raper reports in *The Tragedy of Lynching* that sheriffs and their deputies – the tandem that permitted Johnson's mob execution – actively facilitated almost half of all lynching between 1930 and 1933.[55] Although the decline of lynching undoubtedly signaled the arrival of change, including the willingness of state and local elites to clamp down on the practice in the South (see below), the details of numerous cases provide evidence of extensive official complicity. Jessie Daniel Ames, for example, isolates no fewer than 80 cases out of a total of 118 lynchings that occurred between 1931 and 1941 in which mobs (defined as "three or more persons") removed blacks who were "in the custody of peace officers" before lynching them; blacks were not seized from law officers in the remaining cases but did perish at the hands of "three or more persons." The details of these cases provide no cause for the optimism of Curriden and Phillips.[56]

No less important than the combined inertia of Congress and the Supreme Court was the complicity by all incumbents of executive authority. Between 1882 and 1951, 281 bills were put before Congress to outlaw "mob action directed against individuals by reason of their race." Not one president in this span threw his weight behind any of these initiatives. Andrew Johnson was an ardent Southerner whose obdurate support for the region provoked Congress to charge him with eleven articles of impeachment. William McKinley (1897–1901), a Republican from Ohio, did not respond when whites in Lake County, SC, lynched the postmaster simply because he was an African American. Theodore Roosevelt (1901–9) claimed to be powerless to stop lynch mobs. His successor, William H. Taft (1909–13), supported a federal investigation by the Justice Department into the cold-blooded mass killing of twenty black plantation workers in Palestine, Texas, in 1910, just months after the founding of the NAACP, but did nothing when the Department claimed that it, too, was powerless because no federal statutes had been broken.[57] US imperialist policies in the late 1890s diminished the chance that the federal government would come to the assistance of African Americans trapped in the Southern states. McKinley's decision to annex Cuba, the Philippines, Puerto Rico, Guam and Hawaii prompted W. E. B. Du Bois' prophecy in *The Souls of Black Folk* that "the problem of the Twentieth Century is the problem of the color-line."

The struggle for an anti-lynching bill

The founding fathers had looked to a federal system of government partly to unify the several states and depoliticize the slave question at a time when the central administration was still too weak to impose its will on restless communities hundreds of miles from the new capital.[58] When the moment for racial reform in the postbellum South arrived, the regional compromise over slavery degenerated even further by evolving into a quagmire that swallowed the embryonic and vulnerable rights of freedmen. From her review of lynching, Jessie Daniel Ames, the white suffragist and civil rights activist who led the campaign in the South against lynching, correctly predicted that the federal government would not join the campaign against lynching with a "flashing sword of vengeance."[59] With no more than a handful of congressional representatives who were interested in an anti-lynching bill, aid unexpectedly came to the NAACP in the form of Leonidas Dyer, a Republican congressman from Missouri.

Alarmed at the worsening condition in race relations after the First World War, Dyer committed himself to the NAACP's battle for a federal anti-lynching law and re-submitted a slightly modified version of a Bill he had unsuccessfully brought to the Congress's attention in 1918. The Dyer Bill proposed to make lynching a felony and prescribed the following punishments:

> (a) A maximum of 5 years in prison, $5000 fine, or both, for any state or city official who failed to protect any person in the area of jurisdiction or who failed prosecute those responsible;
> (b) A minimum of 5 years in prison for any citizen or public official who participated in a lynching;
> (c) a $10,000 fine to be paid by the county in which the lynching took place. The fine would be given to the victim's family. Furthermore, in the case of a victim who was abducted in one county and killed in another, each county would pay the fine.

To the jubilation of the NAACP, Dyer's Bill passed the House of Representatives on 26 January 1922; the Senate Committee responsible for the

Bill subsequently endorsed the measure. But Southern Democrats deftly managed to delay the Bill and it was held over to the next session of Congress. Never strong, Republican support wilted as soon as Oscar Underwood, the Senate Minority Leader the Democratic Senator from Alabama, threatened that the "Solid South" would oppose any federal anti-lynching law by blocking all business in the Senate. The comments of Benjamin Tillman from South Carolina reflected the Southern view that the Dyer Bill was an unconstitutional attack against states rights. The Bill, he argued, proposed to displace the states and "substitute for the starry banner of the Republic, a black flag of tyrannical centralized government ... black as the face and heart of the rapist ... who deflowered and killed Margaret Lear."[60] Underwood's threatened filibuster succeeded. On 2 December 1922, the Republican leadership agreed to withdraw the Bill, bringing the saga of the "Dyer Bill" to a close. In the fortnight after the Bill's demise, lynch mobs in the South executed four blacks.[61]

The sheer fact that the frequency of lynching was decreasing was a double-edged sword to the anti-lynching campaign. As fewer blacks met their deaths "at the hands of persons unknown," Southerners argued that the downward trend proved that federal intervention was unnecessary and that the states had already begun to act against the practice. According to James Elbert Cutler, several post-Reconstruction states did indeed enact either "anti-lynching legislation" or laws that targeted violent "mobs" before the First World War, reflecting the gradual abatement of support for extra-legal violence. Georgia and Virginia, it appears were among the first to do so in 1893 and 1894 respectively – just as Ida B. Wells launched her anti-lynching campaign in England, stirring both fury and anxiety across the Southern states. Georgia strengthened its anti-lynching law in 1895. North Carolina also enacted an anti-lynch law in 1893, followed by a similar law in South Carolina two years later. The legislatures of Tennessee, Kentucky and Texas adopted anti-lynching laws in 1897, and West Virginia did so in 1903. Arkansas soon had a law providing for a special term of court to deal with lynch cases.[62] Seeking to balance the rights of a prisoner under state custody against the rights of policemen who preferred not to risk their lives "protecting a nigger," Governor Atkinson of Georgia, advanced a startling recommendation. The officer "should be required to unshackle the prisoner, arm him, and give him an opportunity to defend himself."[63] Quintessentially Southern, this recommendation managed to preserve the right of both the mob and victim to resort to violence.

The problem, of course, was not the law: lynching took place in each of these states, just as they did in states without anti-lynching legislation. The problem was that, without officials willing to enforce existing legislation, state legislation was moribund. Even when lynchers were indicted, any willingness to convict rapidly dissipated as juries, sheriffs, witnesses and coroners lied, lost their memories or winked their way through "trials" whose outcomes were a foregone conclusion. Justice only occasionally managed to defeat this stacked deck. In 1902, for example, for the first time in the history of Alabama, several white men were sentenced to jail for lynching a black man. In Joplin, Missouri, a white man named Samuel Mitchell was sent to jail for ten years for participating in the lynching of a black man, Thomas Gilyard.[64] It is not known how many such cases there were in which white lynchers were sent to jail, but it is certain that no white person was ever sentenced to death for lynching a black man. Most Southerners demanded nothing less than precisely this degree of control of their local courts. Since federal authorities threatened the corruption and implicit violence that were inherent to racial justice, Southerners could not take comfort in their control over local state bodies. Time and again, their representatives in Washington DC forestalled any attempt to involve federal bodies in matters they claimed fell under state rights.

Until 1930, Southern anti-federalism remained defiantly on the offensive. A reactionary Supreme Court, a pliant Congress (in which the seniority system placed the majority of standing committees in the hands of Southern politicians) and an indifferent national audience presented few threats to the suffocating violence that blanketed the region. Soon after the First World War, however, after the "Red Summer" riots of 1919 had alarmed urban officials and white property-owners, the South's near-unanimity over extra-legal murder began to erode and Southern editorialists began to support anti-lynching bills in Congress. The *Daily News* in Greensboro, NC, wrote in 1922 "none of the States had made an honest effort to prevent lynching by making examples of those who indulge in them." In that same year, a white Baptist minister identified a fundamental pillar of the lynch culture with precision: "State Rights are good as far as they work for Justice, Mercy and the Fear of god. Where these are ignored, State Rights is a failure and sin."[65] Around 1930, Jessie Daniel Ames could write: "Formerly, a community not only made no effort to hide the criminal conduct of either the respectable or the hoodlum element of its population, but actually boasted of it ... But communities nowadays that permit a lynching for no reason other than a 'service to the tradition and races' sees to it that no local correspondent is present..."[66] As local elites slowly withdrew their support for racial terror and the practice came to be increasingly associated (at least in the popular mind) with "poor whites of the lower type," scholars noticed that law enforcement and judicial authorities were increasingly willing to clamp down on the practice.

The changes that were coming to the New South boded well for the campaign to extract an anti-lynching law from Congress and "spread the word against lynching" in white communities. Although it ultimately failed, the near success of the Dyer Bill in 1922 convinced the NAACP of the correctness of a legal approach to the "race problem"; furthermore, it was not lost on the Southern politicians in the US Congress that parliamentary tactics, not a clear vote, had defeated the Bill. Southern politicians who understood the vagaries of horse dealing in Congress remained anxious. W. E. B. Du

Bois derided the NAACP's cautious strategy as a "legalism" that did not promote "the essential need" of African Americans "to earn a living, safeguard their income, and raise the level of their employment." While Du Bois contended that "legalism" left the masses out of the politics, Southern politicians fretted over the possibility of unfavorable rulings from the Supreme Court or pro-federalist legislation in Congress.[67]

In 1934, another anti-lynching bill – the Costigan–Wagner Bill – was again before Congress. Southerners were less alarmed by Franklin Delano Roosevelt, who had assumed the presidency in 1933, than by his wife who quickly established herself as a champion of civil rights and other liberal causes at home and abroad. Eleanor Roosevelt quickly reassured the NAACP of her support for the Costigan–Wagner Bill and promised to lobby her husband. The president eventually decided not to support the Bill in deference to voters in the South, but his liberal sympathies, like the New Deal policies he unveiled in 1934 and began implementing from 1937 onwards, were clearly tilted toward an energetic federal authority. Southerners feared that the tide was changing. The Costigan–Wagner Bill proposed no direct action against lynchers themselves, concentrating the weight of federal authority on law officers who were either negligent or complicit in lynching that took place in their area of jurisdiction. As its predecessor had, the Bill sailed through Congress, and its sponsors again easily secured a positive review from a Senate judicial committee. Again, however, Congress adjourned without acting. Concerned that Southern voter might destroy his re-election prospects, Roosevelt refused to throw his weight behind the Bill. Walter White, however, counted the exercise a partial success. He had persuaded the Senate committee to broadcast its proceedings on radio, capitalizing on this milestone in American broadcast history to reach a national audience of millions.[68]

In 1938 Jessie Daniel Ames attributed the decline of popular support for lynching to two factors: the success of anti-lynching organizations and, more importantly, the sense of hope that the New Deal programs stimulated in the Southern economy. Apart from the NAACP's quest for a federal anti-lynching law, the separate labors of the Southern Commission on the Study of Lynching; the Committee on Interracial Cooperation (these two bodies fused in 1944); and the Association of Southern Women for the Prevention of Lynching had also begun to pay fruit. New Deal programs accelerated the process. According to Ames' research, poor whites had featured more prominently in lynch mobs after the First World War. But by 1938, "Work relief from the Federal and State Governments put these people to work and reduced idleness and boredom and … gave them a little cash money to spend with white merchants," which contributed to the declining number of lynchings. Southern whites still looked upon white supremacy as a "sacred and inherent trust" but were more concerned with "the more pressing and important problem of living and earning and spending … than with finding a Negro to lynch to prove their supremacy."[69] To the extent that the New Deal

did indeed concentrate the attention of Southerners on matters of employment, as Ames argues, this development echoes the situation of whites in
South Africa in the inter-War period. As Chapter 3 argued, South African
whites who were focused on obtaining state recognition of their claims were
also much less inclined to commit ritual murder against blacks.

There was another factor at work: the emergence of a "civil rights culture"
within the Justice Department in the late 1930s. Robert K. Carr argues that
the federal reluctance to clamp down on extra-legal violence was the regret-
table but unsurprising outcome of a federal arrangement that intentionally
hobbles national government. Neither the Bill of Rights nor the rest of the
constitution bestows the federal government with express powers to protect
civil liberties. These powers, Carr notes, are "found in the interstices of the
Constitution with the aid of the implied power doctrine." The American
constitution is consequently better at defending people against the abuse of
government power than it is at protecting individuals from private actions
in society. Private actions, meanwhile, weigh disproportionately on people
who have little economic power and social standing, while the most powerful sections of the community are asked to frame and implement laws that
inevitably benefit themselves. Carr concludes that the American legal system is designed to frustrate reliance on the federal government as a means
of redressing civil rights violations. As the anti-lynching movement learned
throughout the inter-War period, the result was a legal culture that was pitted against the civil liberties of ethnic minorities and the nation's poor. The
establishment of a "Civil Liberties Unit" within the Department of Justice in
February 1939 therefore signaled a promising departure from the legal culture that had diluted the federal enforcement of civil rights laws. For Carr,
establishing a Civil Liberties Unit signaled a firmer grasp within the federal
system of the double-headed threat to the civil liberties of African Americans. Government alone was not "the villain in the civil rights drama":
ideological currents and movements within civil society posed a more pressing danger to African Americans. *Brown v Board of Education* took up this
point when it enshrined what would become a foundational principle in the
post Second World War era: when the security and rights of African Americans were persistently violated, the inescapable legal obligation of federal
authority was to support the struggle against racial oppression.[70]

Yet even after Attorney General Frank Murphy took it upon himself to
establish a Civil Rights Unit in 1939, federal attempts to prosecute lynchers remained essentially cautious. In 1945, the Supreme Court actually
weakened legislation that sought to check police brutality. The case became
known as *Screws v US*. The defendants – a policeman, a special deputy and
a sheriff in Baker County, Georgia – had beaten a black prisoner to death.
A federal prosecutor charged the officials with violating the prisoner's Section 20 rights because, "under color of law," they had willfully trampled the
victim's right not to be deprived of his life without a fair trial. The defendants appealed their convictions all the way to the Supreme Court, which

ruled that there was insufficient evidence to prove that the defendants had "willfully" violated that specific right. This ruling gutted the effectiveness of Section 20, ensuring that Southern law enforcement officers could again kill prisoners in their charge with little fear of reprisal from federal authorities. In effect, *Screws v US* exposed murderous law enforcement officers to the possibility – remote at best – that a local state judge and a local jury might charge and convict them.[71]

Still, just three years later in 1942, the federal government moved for the first time to charge white citizens (as opposed to state officials) who had taken part in a lynching in the small town of Sikeston, Missouri. Policemen in Sikeston had sought to arrest Cleo Wright, a black man, for the rape and near-murder of a white woman named Grace Sturgeon. Wright, who was almost certainly guilty of the rape, was shot four times while resisting arrest, but not before almost fatally slashing a police officer with the same knife he had used to disembowel Sturgeon. The mob that assembled was doubly predictable: Wright had violently assaulted a white woman and nearly killed an officer of the law. Brushing aside a state trooper and Sikeston's local prosecutor, the lynchers attached the barely conscious Wright to an automobile and dragged him through the streets of the black residential area, followed by a boisterous caravan. Wright was then incinerated in a street where his remains were left to smolder for several hours after the mob departed.[72]

The local and national chapters of the NAACP sprang into action. The Department of Justice, which that same year had instituted a policy of launching a federal investigation of all lynchings,[73] compiled a dossier that it turned over to the governor of Missouri, who duly empanelled a state grand jury. Predictably, the jury refused to issue any indictments.[74] The Civil Rights Section then proceeded with a federal grand jury, which also refused to indict any of the lynchers. According to the members of the federal grand jury, Wright's murder was indeed a crime, but it was not a federal offense. This was clearly a fig leaf. Mob behavior that prevented state officials from providing prisoners with due process of law was clearly a federal offense under the Fourteenth Amendment, and that would have been sufficient ground to accept the matter as a federal case. As Dominic Capeci notes in his study of Wright's lynching, the obstructionism of both juries was as predictable in this case as it was in so many others, and for the same reason: the all-white, all-male juries were selected from the same "autonomous, provincial community that functioned through face to face relations, mutual dependence, and local pride." Roughly the same sequence of events ensued in the federal government's second attempt to prosecute a lyncher. Several months after juries had stymied the Wright case, a black prisoner who had been convicted for murdering a white man in Laurel, Mississippi, was seized and lynched by a mob. This time a grand jury returned indictments against four white men and a jailer who had handed over the prisoner to the mob. The jailer was charged with violating Sections 51 and 52 of the Fourteenth Amendment; the lynchers were charged with violating Section 51 and with participating in a conspiracy to deprive the prisoner of his right to a fair trial before being legally deprived of his life. The case was again turned over to a state jury, which refused to issue any indictments although one of the men had earlier confessed to his role in executing Wright.[75]

Such exercises in federal futility against lynching suggest that little had changed in the South over the decades. On the other hand, the simultaneous occurrence of two trends indicates otherwise: federal authorities were increasingly aggressive in prosecuting lynchers, and lynching was in fact declining.[76] Were the two trends related, and if so, how exactly? No case can be made for any causal connection between the two because the downward trend preceded stepped-up federal investigations by decades. A more robust federal interest may have accelerated the decline of lynching to some unknown degree. Assuming that federal enforcement of existing laws was a negligible contribution to the precipitous drop in lynching after the 1920s, what does this decline say about changes in the legal system of Southern states? The answer is not that Southern courts were losing their commitment to white supremacy. Instead, the answer involved a change in the manner in which these institutions defended white supremacy. Reflecting the unease with which an increasing number of white Southerners looked upon violence in the inter-War years, law enforcement institutions in the South had gradually modernized their continuing assault on blacks. The clearest expression of this change involved the administration of the death sentence. Capital punishment, we see in the final section below, took off as lynching declined with each successive decade in the twentieth century.

"Legal lynching"

"The death penalty," observes Stephen Bright of the Southern Center for Human Rights, "is a direct descendent of lynching and other forms of racial violence and racial oppression in America."[77] Another source concurs: "lynching came from the early modern death penalty, and the modern death penalty came from lynching."[78] The historical relationship between capital punishment and white supremacy had early roots and is easily established by the differential treatment of the race and gender of the victim and defendant. Already in the colonial period, most states directly used race to impose different penalties. Georgia, for example, expressly stated that the rape of a white woman by a black man "shall be" be punishable by death, but reserved a sentence of between two and twenty years if the rapist was not black. If a black woman was raped, punishment varied between a "fine and imprisonment," a minor matter that was left to "the discretion of the court."[79] In the years up to 1900, the death sentence played second fiddle to the terrorist violence of lynch mobs. Once black challenges to white supremacy were effectively checked and mechanisms such as the all-white primary began to reliably keep blacks out of the political arena, the calculus of extra-legal violence began to change.

Gunnar Myrdal argues in *An American Dilemma* that the perception that "lower class whites" were principally responsible for extra-legal violence became widespread in the 1920s.[80] Elite support for lynching may even have begun to decline as early as the 1890s, when the frequency of lynching reached its zenith. More than 100 lynchings took place each year between 1822 and 1901. The figure declined to around 62 per annum between 1905 and 1919 and then declined significantly after 1923; the number stood at 24 in 1933.

Lynching then became infrequent in the 1930s – an average of ten per year – and rare by the 1940s, when the figure stood at three per annum. This decline charts the decreasing salience that white southerners attached to lynching. Once they viewed lynching as impeding their best interests, elites grew increasingly discomforted with the monster they had spawned. While the reasons for this are not clear, they no doubt center on the gradual modernization of the South in this period. According to Robert Gibson, "There has been much speculation about this matter, but several logical reasons have been considered responsible for this steady decline in lynchings. Some have suggested the growing distaste of Southern elites for anti-Negro violence, particularly Southern women and businessmen. Others mention the increasing urbanization of the South during the 1930s and 1940s. Moreover, statewide police systems were developed which were willing to oppose local mobs, and the National Guard was increasingly called to stop lynchings. Also, Southern newspapers began frequently to denounce lynchings."[81] Sensational stories, usually reported in lurid and damning detail in the northern newspapers, drove home to Southerners that "lynchings were untidy and created a bad press."[82] "Bad press," furthermore, was distinctly counter-productive when Southern blacks fought back against lynch mobs by packing up and migrating to the North, depleting the local pool of cheap labor. While numerous opinion makers and regional elites did indeed declaim the virtues of lynching well into the 1940s, by 1930 it was clear that the tide had already swung.[83] Not rope or fire, but the gallows became the preferred means for exercising lethal violence against blacks.

James Cutler's 1905 book, *Lynch Law*, was perhaps the first to argue that legal executions became a substitute for lynching.[84] Cutler extracted two conclusions from the graph he compiled (overleaf). Between 1882 and 1900 variations in the number of legal executions mirrored the frequency of lynching: legal executions increased when lynchings increased and decreased when lynchings decreased. This pattern held true until 1900, when legal executions began to increase as lynching began to decrease. From this, Cutler concluded in 1905, "the punishment of crimes by law may tend to make recourse to lynching less frequent."[85] Many scholars have subsequently underscored the inverse relationship between legal and illegal executions and agree on the essential point: white Southerners had discovered in the state-sanctioned death penalty a more orderly and more defensible method of killing blacks.[86] By 1930 the emerging businessmen and middle class in an

Number lynched (solid line) compared with number legally executed (dashed line), 1882–1903

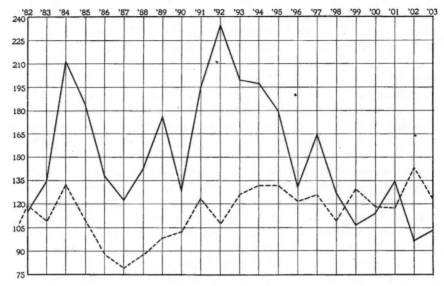

Source: James Elbert Cutler, *Lynch-law: An Investigation into the History of Lynching in the United States*, 183.

increasingly urbanized and industrial New South viewed the Satanic rituals that Northerners tended to associate with all lynching as an embarrassing and counter-productive institution that threatened to provoke federal intervention. "The integrative forces of the market led a growing southern white middle class to disavow lynching" and entrust the state with the task of killing blacks.[87] Official executions carried out behind prison walls, as we see in the next chapter, brought the South more into alignment with the administration of justice in South Africa.

Still, although the inverse movement of lynching and legal executions is incontrovertible, several statistical studies find little or no support for Cutler's "substitution thesis."[88] Partly for this reason, William Brundage rejects the view that the escalation in legal executions after 1900 was "the continuation of lynching under another guise."[89] Mostly, however, Brundage argues that legal and illegal executions are sharply distinguished by the contrasting rituals each embodied. The rituals associated with lynching were unique, preventing them from being "substituted" with the rituals involved in the legal capture, trial and execution of a prisoner. Precisely because capital punishment exemplified "restraint, discipline, control, and order" – values that had become important to the New South – Brundage concludes that the cloistered killing of blacks in officially designated execution centers was too much of an individual, recondite and bloodless affair. The clinical administration of the death sentence could not substitute for the riotous ecstasy and collective catharsis that only a public lynching could deliver. Moreover, the legal script provided a crucial point of access for black attorneys such as Noah Parden and Styles Hutchins to easily expose the multiple violations that routinely occurred when blacks were accused of capital crimes. In Brundage's view, all that legal and illegal executions had in common was an outcome that most white Southerners continued to prize – the death of a black man. But the two institutions marched to different drummers, appealed to different sensibilities of whiteness and were not, in the end, "substitutable."[90] Instead, they co-existed for a while, one gaining strength as the South modernized, the other exiting the stage with grudging and somewhat unpredictable steps.

Still, the dominant trend in the inter-War years pointed to the consolidation of capital punishment and more formal processes for securing the death of black men. In other words, around the outbreak of the Second World War, the New South gradually accepted a judicial philosophy that white South Africans had already embraced as early as 1910.

8

Racial violence and
the legal system in South Africa

> "Without these statutory borders and
> boundaries one would have lynch law in
> South Africa."[1]

Caught between the democratic promises of the American constitution and
the violence of "repressive justice," the law in the South was quite easily
made to serve the ends of the latter and, in the end, was permitted to function as an instrument of terror itself. The legal system in South Africa's
centralized system presents a somewhat different picture. State makers at
the time of unification recoiled from federalism, fearing that a fractured
form of government would inflame ethnic and regional animosities amongst
whites and complicate the business of controlling Africans. They feared that
a federal system would ensure that "inter-racial and quasi-political cases ...
were likely to become more frequent."[2] The courts were therefore vested
with minimal powers of judicial review and were restricted to implementing the will of lawmakers. The problem of multiple jurisdictions, the bane
of attempts to end racial violence in the Southern states, was irrelevant in
South Africa's centralized state. Control over the government, and hence
over the legislature, was the critical issue.

It mattered a great deal, therefore, that benevolent paternalism and constitutionalism served as umbrella ideologies for all governments in the inter-
War years. The Afrikaner Rebellion of 1914, the strike of 1922 and the
response of Smuts' government to the strike were rare extra-constitutional
moments that confirmed this basic trend. It was also important that all
political parties and the vast majority of whites in South Africa looked to
the law, formal procedures and the civil service to manage "race relations."
Explosive exceptions such as the massacre of Africans by striking white
workers in 1922 only confirmed this basic trend. Furthermore, to bury
the divisive past, English-speaking whites and Afrikaners searched for "a
new South Africanism" in the decades after 1910 and therefore studiously
looked to impartial courts to resolve divisive issues and consummate "closer
union" between Afrikaners and English-speaking whites.[3] The drive for this

"new South Africanism" – essentially a search for a depoliticized whiteness – survived the severest challenges confronting the country. This was reflected in the fact that between 1910 and 1950 the courts would not hear a single case that questioned the constitutional basis of racial domination.[4] Even as racially oppressive legislation multiplied, the South African judicial system continued to enjoy an extremely favorable reputation at home and abroad in the inter-War period. No less an opponent of segregation than Eddie Roux, a communist who acquired first-hand knowledge of the legal system, observed that "Throughout the history of race relations in South Africa the judges of the Supreme Court, with very few exceptions, have shown themselves more liberal than either the Government or the local magistrates."[5] Roux' assessment raises a point that places in context how the courts in South Africa dealt with racial violence.

At its upper echelons, white men who are readily described as liberal managed the legal system. A few were products of a liberal legal education in the Cape, but the majority had received their training in England at a time when a "positivist" approach to the law was gaining strength. Their very training discouraged judicial activism and encouraged them to uncritically accept the constitutional subordination of judges to parliament. Under the influential direction of Lord de Villiers, the Union's first Chief Justice, senior liberal judges in South Africa set the tone for the judiciary as a whole. The legal system largely owed its prestige to the tradition of dispassionate and impartial deliberation established by stalwart liberal jurists such as Lord de Villiers and Sir James Rose Innes. The hackneyed epigram, "the rule of law" was as important to South African jurists as it was to the esteemed constitutionalists, legal practitioners and administrators who serviced the sprawling imperial machine. It meant, Sir Arthur Keith wrote in 1924, "the absolute supremacy" of "regular law" over "arbitrary power" and the "equal subjection of all classes to the ordinary law of the land administered by the ordinary courts."[6] There was accordingly nothing in judges' training or personal views that would lead them to encourage lawlessness by either civil servants or the populace at large. Although they construed their task narrowly – as one of interpreting, not making, the law – courts in South Africa gained a strong reputation for holding governments to the spirit and the letter of laws enacted in parliament. Informed by these sensibilities, the highest reaches of the legal system in South Africa provided little sanctuary for official lawlessness. In the view of the most senior legal men, official violence should be justified by clearly defined and codified procedures, failing which the courts should punish it.[7]

But these judges were also very much the products of a ruling race that employed the legal system to support a social order that was inherently discriminatory towards blacks. If their training predisposed them to vigilantly ensure that justice was impartially applied to all in society, their upbringing in a white supremacist culture also ensured that they were cut off from the lived experiences of blacks. Because their rulings were formalistic and honed by a "positivist" approach to the law, judges were disinclined to explore systemic interconnections that lay beneath the circumstances examined in court. As a result, liberal judges who hewed closely to "the facts" appeared unconcerned with "substantive justice." They rarely challenged laws that blacks and a small but prominent coterie of white liberals damned as obviously unjust and oppressive and were incapable of condemning a system that bestowed great honor on its legal establishment. A recent study of the legal system therefore concludes with an impression of a judiciary that was "willing to carry out legislative and electoral opinion in matters of race to the full," there being "no apparent attempt by the court to mitigate the harsh effects of oppressive laws, or to criticize their substance and application."[8] Nevertheless, as recent scholars such as Don Chanock and Rob Turrell have shown, the highly formalistic approach of judges in the Supreme Court and the Appellate Division also meant that senior jurists could ensure that a measure of justice was done – but only if they were convinced that racially oppressive laws specifically provided the statutory grounds for justice.[9]

Lower down the rarified legal atmosphere of the Supreme Court and the Appellate Division, the legal system was a much more organic reflection of white racism. Indeed, the legal system was itself cleaved along the racial divide, reflected in the distinction between "Native courts" and what were collectively known as "the normal courts of the land." The two legal systems were governed by radically different legal principles (see below). If the upper reaches of the judiciary at least aimed at impartiality, the lower courts were all too often transparently biased. Racism was rampant in virtually every aspect of the lower courts system, clearly visible in the racist pronouncements of judges, the biased recommendations of corrupt juries, the virtual absence of adequate legal representation for blacks and the racial disparities in sentences handed down for similar crimes. Judges frequently adduced racial considerations to justify the sentences they handed down. In many cases white defendants were told to look upon their light sentences as "a warning"; blacks were left in no doubt that they received heavier sentences because they "had to be punished."[10] The transparent bias in the lower courts was particularly important in cases involving racial violence. In many instances the courts afforded violent whites with a sympathetic mechanism within the system of institutional segregation. Although whites could not always assume that the courts would rule in their favor or that they would avoid jail time for charges of serious violence, the torrent of "assaults against Native" cases suggests that many of them were sufficiently confident to game the system.

What impact did the legal system in South Africa have on racial violence? This chapter argues that the impact of the courts registered in two ways. Firstly, the paternalist sensibilities and a commitment to the "rule of law" within the bench firmly shut the door on public and communal violence against blacks. Although the Supreme Court largely overlooked the lethal "pogrom" that striking mine workers unleashed against innocent blacks during the 1922 strike, sentencing to death just one of the men who murdered innocent black bystanders, South Africa's legal system was strongly opposed to the quasi-legal ideology of "repressive justice" that prevailed in the Southern states. To illustrate the jaundiced view that authorities maintained about "repressive justice," this chapter explores the "Port Elizabeth incident" of 1920, when policemen and white vigilantes collaborated in the gunning down of seventeen unarmed blacks.

Secondly, courts in South Africa were quite willing to accommodate *private* racial violence. Whether in the form of serious assaults or murder, private racial violence became an ingrained feature of race relations in South Africa. Records suggest that private racial violence first took hold in the gold mining industry before it became the hallmark of labor relations in the white farming areas from the late 1920s onward. From that point, the bulk of private violence occurred in the farming areas, although it was by no means uncommon in the urban areas as well. Cases involving private violence were tried in the "normal courts of the land," where the courts could have stanched the bloodletting with commensurate punishment, had judges and juries been so inclined. In the vast majority of cases, they were not.

These trends contributed to the broad pattern of racial violence that informs this study: in South Africa, the legal system firmly clamped down on extra-legal communal racial violence but sported a porous legal approach that enabled white citizens to engage in high levels of private violence with little fear of punishment. This broad pattern, furthermore, transpired in a context of high levels of bureaucratic violence which, insofar as they were permitted by law, were supported by the courts. Lynching and its ideological correlate, the doctrine of "repressive justice," therefore did not take hold in South Africa. Nevertheless, blacks were trapped by extensive private violence from below and lawful but often lethal "policing" methods from above.

Repressive justice, private violence and the legal system

The pattern of racial violence in South Africa owes much to the racially segregated legal system that became entrenched after the First World War. The Native Administration Act of 1927 was the apotheosis of legal segregation. More so than any other measure enacted in the first two decades after unification, the Act entrenched the paternalist view that the different cultural conditions of blacks and whites justified different legal procedures and institutions. The measure consolidated two contrasting, racially based systems of governance: a modern system for whites and "tribal government" for blacks. While whites remained subject to "the normal courts of the land," the Act centralized enormous powers in the Minister of Native Affairs by defining him as the "Supreme Chief of all Natives" throughout the country (except for the Cape Province where it was stymied by the persistence of the vote for Africans until 1936).[11] These vast powers could be devolved to any official of the Department's officials. "Native law and custom" became the legal medium for resolving disputes in which "the interests of Natives predominated." A segregated system of Native Commissioner Courts was set up for this purpose. Serious crimes such as rape and murder, however, as well as all cases involving whites, were assigned to the "normal courts" where "Western" civil and criminal codes prevailed.[12]

The Native Administration Act and the official activities it sanctioned brightly illuminate the different roles that the courts and racial violence played in Southern and South African segregation. The establishment of a parallel system of "Native courts" and "Native law" reassured whites in South Africa that blacks were governed in accordance with "the rule of law," providing whites with "an assurance that the white law contained the core of historical rationality, not simply the commands of the advantaged."[13] The English-speaking whites who dominated the ranks of the Department of Native Affairs and the Department of Justice took seriously the claim that their paternalist labors represented a "half-way house between barbarism and civilization."[14] White South Africans therefore looked upon the law in radically different ways from their white counterparts in the American South: in sharp contrast to Southern hostility to the courts, white South Africans took distinct pride in a legal system that underscored and preserved racial differences by subjecting blacks to extraordinarily undemocratic forms of administration that whites would never have tolerated.

A bifurcated legal system performed more than just ideological service to a population convinced of its moral and cultural superiority. It also served very definite material interests in ways that the federal legal system in the United States made impossible. For example, studies of racial violence in the South have shown that violence against blacks was frequently motivated by economic rivalry and jealousy. Southern elites in the period from 1880 to the Second World War frequently fomented a generalized atmosphere of terror and used lethal violence to eliminate prosperous black farmers by seizing their property; after the First World War, plain whites in the South used racial violence to exclude blacks from the emerging factories of the New South, especially when blacks were used as strike breakers or became successful as tenant farmers in depressed rural areas.[15] Constitutional and territorial segregation in South Africa rendered such extra-legal violence unnecessary. In the three decades after unification, whites looked to the state and the legal system to eliminate or counterbalance any economic rivalry that blacks posed.[16] South Africa therefore did not undergo the sort of traumas that befell the black communities of Rosewood, Florida (in January 1923), or Tulsa, Oklahoma (in May 1921), when envious white citizens incinerated the black quarters, killed dozens of blacks, expelled hundreds more and then laid claim to the assets they left behind. Segregation in South Africa obviated the needs for racial terror of this sort. By the simple convenience of issuing a proclamation, the Minister of Native Affairs in his capacity as "Supreme Chief" could simply strip Africans of their land and require them to quit the area, in the process converting them into either wage labor or tenants on nearby white farms. The structural violence that was embodied in South African laws and routinely upheld by the courts transformed the drama of Southern racial violence into a mere administrative banality.

Laws and the slew of administrative regulations that emerged from the 1920s onward elevated a growing array of national and municipal police, Native administrators and magistrates into a corps of official oppressors. Most of these men were liberals whose duties were spelt out in documents bearing ponderous titles such as "Regulations for the Planning and Siting of Native Urban Locations" and "Procedures to be Used in Native Commissioner Courts." Throughout the segregation period, liberal hegemony within the state persuaded civil servants that such powers should be wielded with restraint, even munificence. In practice, many Native Administrators ruled over the rural districts "like little kings."[17] Regardless of the personal characteristics of individual administrators, a prominent feature of the administration of racial justice in South Africa was its dull, quotidian character. However, routine administration and trigger-happy law enforcement were not conflicting displays of state power. For the majority of whites, both were legitimate dimensions of "the rule of law" simply because they bore the imprimatur of parliament.

Yet it was precisely for reasons to do with "the rule of law" that the courts frequently refused to countenance violence committed either by law-enforcement officials or white citizens. This was especially the case for the urban areas. The powers that police wielded were broad and sweeping, but they were not unchecked, as several court rulings made clear. In 1933, for example, one Herzer, a white policeman, was charged with common assault for shooting and killing an African he had atempted to arrest for a pass violation. Herzer claimed that Section 44(1) of the Criminal Procedure Act of 1917 justified the killing because the African man had resisted arrest and attempted to flee. The Appellate Division of the Supreme Court rejected Herzer's argument, all three judges concurring that "a policeman cannot shoot at a person arrested merely because he runs away." That the courts took a dim view of the excessive use of force was again made clear in 1949. Britz, a private citizen, claimed that he had attempted to make a citizen's arrest by detaining an African man. When the man resisted, Britz shot and killed him with a shotgun. A court subsequently found him guilty of culpable homicide. In rejecting Britz' appeal against his conviction, Judge Schreiner referred to the "emphasis which our law and customs have for the sanctity of human life" and ruled that Britz had not shown that the circumstances justified the use of deadly force. On other occasions, the courts were exacting in scrutinizing the conditions that, numberless policemen claimed before the courts, justified the use of force to arrest blacks. It was not unusual for courts to rule against the police on the grounds that the circumstances were sufficiently dubious or ambiguous. In *Herzer* above, for example, two judges rejected the policeman's subsequent appeal against conviction partly because, in their view, it was not clear that Herzer had in fact arrested the man before shooting him. On many occasions, Africans arrested on "beer raids" argued that the police had not produced search warrants before entering their premises. When they upheld such arguments, Hugh Corder writes, "the judges of appeal took decisive action to correct what they saw as excessive use of power by individual police officers."[18]

Scholars dispute whether white Southerners were generally more or less dismissive of the law than other Americans.[19] But none dispute that Southern contempt for the courts was highest in the area of race relations, race being the only issue that regularly inflamed communal violence against the law. Whites in South Africa resigned themselves to the supremacy of formal law because, as the very organization of the bifurcated legal system illustrates, the law was set up to serve their collective interests in oppressing and exploiting black labor. With only rare and dramatic exceptions, white citizens therefore accepted the legitimacy of the legal system they established to regulate "race relations." The state would not face a rival in the administration of racial justice, and its monopoly over the means of violence remained intact. But the logic that effectively suppressed communal violence by no means precluded whites from regularly committing serious and lethal private violence against blacks.

The courts and private racial violence

Racial domination left ample room for whites to routinely attack and kill blacks and for the courts to trivialize or wink at such violence. Systemic patterns in the way courts treated private racial violence were therefore as visible in the South African legal system as they were in the South. To begin with, the racist views that most South African whites held also saturated and informed the everyday work of the courts. At its most general level, racist ideology prompted court officials to devalue the worth of black life. This may be gauged by the paltry sentences that the courts invariably imposed on violent whites.. The "mitigating circumstances" that judges manufactured to justify lenient sentences on white killers could easily be dismissed as risible – such as the farmer who was fined 5 shillings for severely whipping and maiming a twelve-year old "picannin" in 1937 – if they did not amount to transparent miscarriages of justice.[20] Sometimes, however, judges were themselves astonished when juries smugly returned "not guilty" verdicts. Although juries were more likely to decide against white assailants in minor cases, the same reasons that prevailed upon the Southern juries' decisions – a principled racism and, frequently, personal familiarity with the accused – ensured that juries regularly discounted the more serious crimes of violence with which white defendants were charged. Racism also preceded the courtroom stage. Because state prosecutors determined which crime a defendant would be charged with, they were far more likely to opt for lesser charges such as manslaughter when the victim was black and the defendant white; conversely, they preferred the most serious charges when blacks stood accused of assaulting whites.

"Native administrators" also played a role that devalued the security and sanctity of black life. Located as they were between the "formal courts of the land" and "Native law and custom," Native administrators were well placed to influence the administration of justice even in the urban areas. For example, records indicate that in the period between 1910 and 1930, the heyday of racial violence on the gold mines, Native administrators regularly resorted to their sweeping powers to arbitrarily settle serious crimes of violence involving white assailants against African miners. Archival files bulge with complaints that Africans lodged against white overseers. In 1919, for example, an official letter sent out to District Commandants of the SAP recommended a policy that a newspaper summarized as "No marks – no pain." According to the circular letter, African complainants first had to display physical evidence of assault before laying a charge against white assailants, failing which "the time of the Court would be wasted."[21] The DNA recommended that such cases should be settled out of court and white assailants should be pressured to pay "a small sum of money which will not be construed as an admission of guilt."

Such arbitrary interventions were by no means in conflict with prevailing views about the relationship between blacks and the courts. Officials within the DNA and the Department of Justice welcomed such informal settlements precisely because they short-circuited the legal process and kept lawyers at bay. Officials were particularly skeptical of lawyers with clients in the reserves, the very profession being viewed as inimical to "the inherent African belief in unchallenged despotic power."[22] Especially in the reserves, where the application of customary law converted Native Administrators into judge and jury, officials complained that the intervention of lawyers threatened to confound the distinction between the country's two legal systems by skirting or challenging the "efficient" system of rule by proclamation. In the urban areas, lawyers rarely agreed to take up "Native cases." As a rule, lawyers who represented Africans in the urban areas fell into two categories: those who specialized in "Native cases" because they were unable to obtain white clients and the handful of liberal and progressives who opposed racial segregation by representing African clients. As a result, inadequate legal representation often hobbled blacks in the courts, depriving them of procedural opportunities that white clients regularly used.[23]

An inherently biased juridico-political system established a permissive culture that white citizens regularly abused. Whites frequently savaged blacks, torturing and murdering them with cavalier indifference. Father Rand, an Anglican priest based in the northern Transvaal, lamented in 1924 that racial murder had become "a national pastime." His ire encompassed the courts and he blamed the "Department of Justice for its laxity in failing to inflict adequate penalties on those guilty of these crimes."[24] Others asserted that "for every case that made it to the courts, many more outrages against innocent natives take place on the farms and go unreported." An exasperated judge found the frequency of court cases involving racial

violence and murder "depressing" and expressed his frustration with all-
white juries who failed to convict despite "overwhelming evidence placed
at their disposal."[25] Although historical studies of racial violence in South
Africa are not as extensive as those for the American South, these and other
observations by judges, journalists and the black and white members of the
Benevolent Society make it clear that interpersonal violence ran rampant
across the country and was chiefly concentrated in the *platteland* areas.

White citizens were not alone in committing violence against blacks.
Numerous studies of the evolution of racial domination have chronicled
the extent to which policemen were systemically implicated in the culture of
violence, a role that flowed ineluctably from the bureaucratic incarnation of
white supremacy in South Africa. After 1910, a flood of racially discriminatory laws and regulations gradually specified a maze of conditions that
regulated the lives and private behavior of blacks. Many of these laws were
intended to obtain and control cheap black labor. They formally integrated
the respective labors of the South African Police, a growing army of municipal inspectors, "Native Administrators," and court officials. Regulations
framed in terms of the Native Administration Act also incorporated African
chiefs, headmen, and household patriarchs into the system of "local government" established in the reserves. White administrators, the representatives
of the "Supreme Chief" in the reserves, controlled the "Native courts" in
their districts. But they also relied on these "tribal leaders" to resolve local
disputes, allocate land, and collect poll and other taxes – the central pillars
of the migrant labor system. The administrative structure therefore created
a blurred continuum of authority between white administrators and prominent black men in the reserves.[26]

Measures such as the Mines and Works Act, the Native Labor Regulation Act and the Native Service Contract Act sought to deliver various
forms of cheap labor in ways that suited different employers. They therefore
stipulated a host of conditions and obligations that greatly expanded the
category of possible offenses blacks could commit. In the end, measures
that were designed to control blacks as *workers* seamlessly evolved into a
gridwork that controlled blacks as *blacks*. Policemen were authorized to
monitor the most innocuous behavior of black people – regulations issued
under the Urban Areas Act, for example, listed "peeping into motor cars"
as sufficient evidence to charge blacks with being "idle or dissolute," a con-
travention of the "Stallard doctrine" that could get Africans evicted from
the urban areas. If a pretext for doing so was required, the relentless concern
with the "pass" provided an omnibus reason for police to sweep blacks off
the street and invade a town's black quarters, where something as minor as
the hunt for "illegally brewed beer" regularly culminated in the shooting of
black men and women.[27]

Judges and juries in the lower courts regularly accepted the policeman's
account or levied paltry sentences that trivialized the value of black life.
John Brewer has described the activities of law enforcement in the segrega-

tion years as "political policing" because, as in the colonial period, policing was overtly intended to maintain white supremacy. The South African Party would "never transcend its origins as a colonial police force ... it was centralized and under political control, acted as the servant of the state in suppressing part of the populace, performed several non-police duties on behalf of government, and its methods relied on brute force as the first resort."[28] Indeed, policing cohered so intimately with blacks' everyday life that what actually amounted to a fundamental assault on blacks was indistiguishable from, and was accepted by whites as little more than, "administration," even when routine operations led to the killing of men, women and children. Blacks were still incapable of challenging the racial state in this period, and the ANC hewed closely to the politics of moderation, seeking any white allies it could find. Because it fell to state-created bodies to convey black dissatisfaction with policing methods, complaints about police violence were lost in the catalog of "Native grievances" that African leaders drew up in the inter-War years. The Native Affairs Commission, for example, "passed no comment on the poor relations between the police and blacks" throughout the segregation period.[29]

Ambiguities in the legal system

Without doubt, constitutional segregation and the proliferation of discriminatory legislation after 1910 confronted Africans with a deck that was stacked against them. Compared with their counterparts in the American South, however, racist courts in South Africa were models of legal decorum. Black South Africans were much more likely to obtain relatively benign rulings and sentences from judges who prided both racial paternalism and legal professionalism. Charges that were *ipso facto* death sentences in the South wound their way through South Africa's legal system and sometimes yielded outcomes that would have outraged white Southerners. Several cases discussed below illuminate this difference.

Consider the case of *Rex v David and Philemon*.[30] On the evening of 22 August 1923, a German immigrant, Kathe Schmid, was sleeping in her bedroom in an area near Johannesburg. The owners of the property were away and had asked a Mr Grundle, a white neighbor, to sleep in the house in their absence. On the evening of 22 August 1923, two men entered Schmid's bedroom and assaulted her, each man committing "nameless indecencies" before taking turns to each rape her twice. In "terror of possible conception," Schmid drew on her experience as a former nurse in Germany and "thoroughly washed and cleansed herself." All the evidence pointed to two men who resided on the farm. In his summary, the Minister of Justice described the case as "extraordinarily audacious" for reasons that resonated with the fears of all white home owners: Schmid's alleged assailants were "houseboys." David, aged twenty-six, was a "houseboy" who, Schmid claimed in her affidavit, had taken advantage of the home owners' absence to behave in a sexually inappropriate manner; Philemon, also twenty-six, was "the kitchen boy and garden boy." Furthermore, the attack took place while Grundle was asleep in an upstairs bedroom, which, the state prosecutor reasoned, was why the perpetrators had taken the time to disable the electrical alarm. The absence of evidence of a break-in suggested that a key must have been used to gain entry to the house, and a missing key was indeed found in David's pillowcase in the outroom he shared with Philemon. A reliable watchdog had also failed to bark, indicating a familiarity that strengthened the case against David and Philemon. A third man named Philip who was described as a "frequent guest" of David and Philemon claimed to have slept throughout the night. Since only two men had attacked Schmid, no charges were brought against Philip and he was not investigated at all. The accumulation of evidence – the sexually suggestive behavior towards Schmid, the key concealed in his pillowcase, the tampered alarm, the dog that did not bark – all pointed to "David, the houseboy" as the "mastermind behind the crime." Although both men were found guilty in the subsequent trial, only David was given the death sentence. Philemon was sentenced to ten lashes and eight years with hard labor.

However, in a petition it submitted to the court, the Transvaal Native Congress Political Association challenged Schmid's account of the assault on the grounds that no evidence of any sort had been found to confirm that a rape had taken place: "whatever Miss Schmid suffered, she was not actually outraged, it being urged that this part of her evidence is an afterthought." The District Surgeon's report had not found evidence of a forced sexual assault or even that sex had taken place. No physical bruises had been found on Schmid's body and she had not screamed out although she knew that Grundle was in an upstairs bedroom. Schmid's response to these points was that she had been too scared to resist in any way. The defense pointed out that the detective who was summoned to the scene of the assault made no reference to rape in his notes. Rape was first mentioned the following morning when a "medical examination of the boys" was undertaken. In the words of the Minister of Justice, N. J. de Wet, the gravamen of the petition submitted by the Transvaal Native Congress Political Association was that "the whole story of the rape was an invention of an hysterical and erotic, if not vindictive woman."

Justice de Wet carefully considered the evidence for this claim before dismissing the Transvaal Native Congress Political Association's petition and upholding the sentences handed out. Why, de Wet pondered, would two black men truss and gag a white woman and *not* rape her? He was "unable to believe that if two natives had her at their mercy, they would have stopped short at violation." After all, " No woman, with a spark of decency, would falsely confess that she had been the victim of a rape by a black man." De Wet admitted that it had not been proven that it was David indeed who had planned and set the scene for the assault but was prepared to accept the "supposition" that he had done so. This, however, was not the only reason why David would meet his end at the gallows in the Pretoria

Central Prison. What sealed his fate was Schmid's claim that "on various occasions David brushed against her purposely." The Minister made much of this and his remarks clearly convey that more than a sexual assault was involved: David's crime was not "one only of pure lust, but was based on a desire to show his contempt for and to heap shame and indignity upon the white woman placed in authority over him." In the mind of the Minister, David deserved the death sentence not because he had raped a white woman, the same crime for which Philemon had received a non-capital sentence. Instead, merely by sidling up against Schmid, David had dared to challenge the racial hierarchy on which segregation rested. What had tipped the scales against David's life was the fact that he had unnecessarily "brushed against [Schmid] when he could have easily avoided doing so."

This was a distinction that Southerners would not have countenanced. Indeed, other aspects of de Wet's reasoning constituted exactly the sort of legal nitpicking that fueled white's antipathy for the legal process in the American South. De Wet concurred with the assessment of the trial judge that Philemon was "less guilty" than David, although neither doubted that Philemon had also twice raped Schmid. Philemon's crime was "little, if at all, worse than David's, since the reward of his help was the gratification of his lust" and "he was fortunate in escaping with a moderate sentence." Had the Minister dared to suggest to a Southern audience that the violent "gratification of lust" in a black-on-white rape merited no more than a "moderate sentence" of ten lashes and eight years in jail, it is likely that he would have been driven from the county, if not lynched. It also seems inconceivable that a Southern court would have paused to exonerate Philip, a "frequent guest" who often slept in the room of the accused and who claimed that he had slept through the nocturnal coming and goings of his two hosts. Almost anywhere in the South, Philip would have been equally implicated in the assault, and the likely end of all three would have been death, either seated at the gallows or swinging at the end of a rope in full view of a raucous crowd. This was the fate that befell Bob Burton in 1891 in the mining town of Clifton Forge, Virginia. White miners hunted down and lynched three of Burton's friends after the latter had gotten into a minor confrontation with a local policeman. Sensing trouble, the three men had left the town and were captured in the nearby woods. Bob Burton, however, had been jailed well before the disturbance occurred. Still, he was seized from his cell and lynched alongside his three friends; hundreds of bullets were poured into the four corpses swinging from a tree limb.[31]

The relatively restrained approach that the courts adopted in cases involving serious violations of the racial hierarchy persisted throughout the inter-War years. Gabriel Motaung did not deny the charges brought before him in March 1940. Motaung was walking along a road when he came across a stalled car being pushed by a "European man" and his wife. Motaung first agreed to help push the stalled vehicle but then knocked the unsuspecting man unconscious, inflicting multiple fractures on his skull. The screaming woman attempted to escape but Motaung knocked her down and ripped off her clothes. Only a passing car forced him to flee, but not before stealing her handbag and her husband's wallet. Fingerprints left at the scene led to the arrest of Motaung the next day. A jury returned a unanimous guilty verdict, prompting him to finally admit to the crime and plead for a suspended sentence. Justice Solomon, unmoved, suspected that Motaung did not "realise the gravity of the case." For criminal assault, theft and attempted rape, Motaung was sentenced to seven lashes and five years with hard labor.[32] Sam Butelezi received a similar sentence in 1945 after a jury found him guilty of criminal assault and robbery. Pretending to buy a bottle of lemonade in a store run by a white woman, Butelezi used an iron bar to beat the woman to the ground before fleeing into the street clutching a till containing £1. 11s. Butelezi received a sentence of five lashes and five years with hard labor.[33]

Sentences such as these were typical in cases involving black assaults on white civilians. Such a sentence was harsher than most of the sentences handed down when whites violently attacked blacks. However, the sentence was much lighter than the sentences blacks received for commiting the most trivial offenses. For example, in the same year that Sam Butelezi was sent off to jail, Wilson Dhlamini was charged with stealing a hat that belonged to a white man. "It is not that the thing you took is of much value, but it is the principle of the thing. The public must be protected from crimes such as these," lectured the sentencing judge. For an unsuccessful theft of a small article of clothing, Dhlamini received a sentence of three years with hard labor.[34]

A more remarkable example of relative leniency involves an African man's "attempt to murder master and mistress." The Hon. Mr Justice Ward in the Criminal Session of the Orange Free State Supreme Court heard the case in 1934. For reasons that are not recorded in the surviving records, an African "servant" named Hendrik Wills set out to poison his employers, Johannes Petrus Maree and his wife. Departing from domestic routine, Wills had taken charge of making coffee and carefully pointed out to another "servant" which cups should be served to the two employers. From the evidence presented in court, it was found that Wills "put 17½ grains of strychnine in the coffee cups [whereas] one-sixth of a grain is sufficient to cause death and that enough poison had been found to kill a hundred people. The anxiety to poison his master and mistress had been their savior, the coffee being so bitter that they could not drink it." Easily convinced that "the deed had been done deliberately and that there were no extenuating circumstances," Justice Ward sentenced Wills to ten years' imprisonment.[35]

Another case, *Rex v Jack Mathlala and Johannes Mormana*, in which two African men were found guilty of raping a sixteen-year-old white girl near Springs Township in 1934, confirms the impression that the wheels of justice in South Africa ground more predictably and formally than in the American South. Hendrika Koch and her nineteen-year-old brother,

Johannes, were returning home under the bright moonlight on the evening of 25 July 1934. Taking a shortcut across an open field, they were accosted by Mathlala (twenty-four years old) and Mormana (aged twenty) and a "third native" who was not charged with any crime. Johannes was knocked to the ground but managed to chase the third man away. Mathlala drove Johannes off with bricks and a belt and joined the attack on the young girl. Mormana, however, was unable to subdue the struggling girl and failed to penetrate her. An angry Mathlala pushed Mormana aside and raped her. Upon completion, he kicked and swore at her. Both men were found guilty, and the judge, accepting the jury's recommendation, passed the death sentence on both of them. As in all capital cases, the dossier was sent up for review to the Minister of Justice, J. C. Smuts, then also the Prime Minister. Smuts reviewed the evidence and upheld the death sentence for Mathlala. In Mormana's case, however, he found sufficient cause to commute the sentence to eight lashes and fifteen years' imprisonment:

> In the first place ... there is nothing to suggest that he was the ringleader in this atrocious crime – the probabilities are that the second prisoner was the moving spirit ... [T]he preparatory examination ... shows that the second prisoner was more brutal and actually used a belt upon her and threw a brick at her. In the second place, ... it appears that in fact he did not complete his purpose ... Legally and morally he is guilty of the full offence, since he was aiding and assisting the second prisoner ... Still, in considering whether the extreme penalty should be exacted, it seems to me it is legitimate to take into consideration the fact that, according to the evidence, he in fact was not successful in his purpose.[36]

This case illustrates a significant and interesting trend in the management of the death sentence in South Africa: a judge in the lower courts had sentenced an African man to death for the attempted rape of a white woman but was thwarted by the Minister of Justice who reprieved the convict. In this case, Mormana owed his life to the "positivist" underpinnings of legal discourse in South Africa.

A few years later, the Governor-General's office would consider a particularly brutal capital punishment case in which an African man named Mpikwe Mkize was found guilty of raping an African woman, Gertrude, as well as her daughter before unsuccessfully attempting to murder both of them. Unusually in cases of black on black violence, the judge sentenced Mkize to death for two charges of rape and two charges of attempted murder. The Minister of Justice, however, commuted the sentence to a life sentence in jail. His reasons for doing so are revealing. Because Gertrude was an African woman, "there should have been no question of the death sentence." Adding the second rape to the fact that Mkize had used a knife in his attempt to kill his two victims did not change the fact that a murder had not in fact been committed. "The correct way to regard the whole case is to treat it as one involving two rape convictions and two very serious attempts to commit murder" – hence the commuted sentence.[37]

A comparison of the commuted sentences in *Rex v Jack Mormana* and *Rex v Mkize* suggests a certain logical symmetry. After all, careful legal reasoning plucked both men from the gallows. Embodied in these cases, therefore, is the "positivist" and "strictly impartial approach" approach to the law that earned the South African judiciary its reputation for professionalism and racial impartiality.[38] The same legal formalism that led the courts to accept their subordinate role to the government also encouraged them to "weigh the facts" without regard to race. It is therefore easy to ignore a central difference between the cases of Mormana and Mkize: In Mormana's case, an African man had been sentenced to death for the *attempted* rape of a white woman. In Mkize's case, as the Minister freely admitted, "there should have been no question of the death sentence" when two *actual* rape victims were African.

Racial bias in the application of the death sentence in fact began immediately after the Anglo-Boer War, when "Black Peril" scares rippled through white society. It may well have been the case that the early and vigorous policy of prosecuting and executing the black rapists of white women assuaged whites' fears and obtained the loyalty of white men to the legal system. This development dampened whites' ardor for spectacular extralegal violence such as communal lynchings. All thirteen death sentences that were passed in this period were carried out, erasing the pre-war regional differences that had distinguished how the four pre-war territories treated inter-racial sex. Of the four territories, only in the Transvaal had inter-racial sex been specifically outlawed. This meant that the reconstruction-era Transvaal, the only territory where inter-racial sex and marriage were constitutionally outlawed, already possessed the legal means and the legal culture to execute black rapists before 1910. Rob Turrell has shown that the eight black men in the Transvaal who were executed for raping white women during reconstruction were the harbinger of a national trend after unification. Executions began to take place in the other three provinces once the law was changed in 1903 to permit death sentences for rape.

Still, the trend was not as firm as Turrell suggests. By Turrells' own account, the pattern for the period 1901–10 was as follows. In the Cape, where inter-racial sex and marriage between black men and white women was legal, two blacks were sentenced to death for raping white women. Natal, which tolerated inter-racial sex only within the confines of a Christian marriage, did not hand down death sentences for rape. No death sentences were passed in the Orange Free State, which had legislated against inter-racial sex and marriage. Thus, only in the Transvaal, the most important region of the new country, did judges vigorously implement the death sentence in the decade before 1910.[39] Such concerted judicial vengeance, however, may well have been enough to project the state within the national consciousness as the protector and savior of white women and, by extension, of white masculinity as well. As Chapter 2 illustrated, the postbellum image of white women as the victim of black sexual predators was as novel in South Africa as it was in the postbellum South. Yet fears of Black Peril did not culminate in the lynching of African men. The difference in South Africa, it appears, was the more energetic role the courts played in retaining the exclusive right to deal with the "black-beast rapist."

On the other hand, courts in South Africa also refrained from meting out the severest forms of punishment at their disposal. Turrell's own findings concerning racial rape for the period 1901–10 prefigure the careful legal reasoning judges tended to employ. Thus, more striking than the turn to a policy of executing blacks found guilty of raping white women is the number of blacks who were *not* sentenced to death for the same crime. In the Cape, of the thirty-one black men convicted of raping white women between 1901 and 1910, only two (six per cent) were executed. The Transvaal, predictably, was less sparing. Still, of the sixteen blacks convicted of raping whites, fully fifty per cent were given sentences that stopped short of capital punishment.[40] These statistics signal a dramatic difference between the Southern lynch culture and the bureaucratic framework that white South Africans relied on to exact racial vengeance against black men.

Lynching and near-lynching

It is understandable, but nevertheless surprising, that South African historiography has all but ignored private racial violence in the segregation years in favor of a sustained concern with the evolution of broad racial and economic changes. Evidence indicates that the entire country was in the grip of a quiet but relentless carnage. Of the scores of blacks who perished at the hands of violent whites, the great majority suffered lonely deaths, usually – although not only – on remote farms in rural districts sporting one or two small *dorpe* where white supremacy gradually became a law unto itself as the twentieth century wore on. Here, the smothering control of landowners fused with racist policing and sometimes scandalously biased court officials to leave the country in the dark about the true incidence of private racial violence.

It was always broadly assumed, and frequently asserted in the editorial pages of liberal newspapers, that the farming areas were dangerous places for blacks. Afrikaner institutions maintained an unbroken silence about farm violence, content to speak broadly about the need for a "more Christian spirit in the treatment of the Native," but ready to denounce any suggestion that racial violence was systemically related to evolving Afrikaner political culture. The English-speaking white world fares better compared to this record of moral complicity. Still, none of the liberal institutions, not even the SAIRR, devoted sustained attention to the issue, occupied as they were by state policy and black mobilization in the urban areas. For their part, blacks appreciated the summary violence that white men used to intimidate black men and women. But the attention of black political organizations lay elsewhere in the decades after unfication. Momentous developments – such as disenfranchisement, sharp restrictions on blacks' access to land, the consolidation of "pass laws" and the quandaries that attended participating in or boycotting the official segregated "advisory" institutions in the rural and urban areas – dwarfed the persistent but unspectacular bloodletting that blacks were compelled to endure. In contrast, the NAACP in the United States was born out of the specific attempt to secure an anti-lynching bill and racial violence would remain at the forefront of the organization's mission for the next half century. If racial violence was seared into the founding marrow of the NAACP, the issue was only episodically examined in South Africa.

Articles that appeared in liberal newspapers – chiefly in the *Rand Daily Mail*, the *Star,* and the *Cape Argus* – sporadically compelled the nation to ponder the issue. In a vain effort to create a national debate about racial murder, newspaper articles achieved two things. Firstly, they exposed the extent of violence in the farm areas. Occasionally, the effect was similar to disturbing an anthill. Accustomed to absolute control on their farmlands, farmers were sent scurrying in search of lawyers, "mitigating evidence" and character testimonials that won them either outright acquittals or light sentences in court. Secondly, public exposures of racial violence shone a light on the legal system itself, providing editors and readers with ample evidence of the travesties in the nation's "civilized" courts. These two accomplishments were important simply because they punctured the national silence about racial murder.

Court reporters and editors were perhaps the most important vehicle for exposing racial violence and institutionalized injustice. Yet they could not bring themselves to damn white supremacy *tout court*. Like the learned Justices whose commitment to legal formalism restrained them from questioning the justice of laws enacted in parliament, editors could not conclude that racial murder flowed ineluctably from white supremacy itself and that the phenomenon was in effect ineradicable. Instead, they fell back on standard refrains. Not all whites were violent. Not all cops were corrupt. Not all judges bent the rules to let white killers off the hook. In short, as the *Cape Times* editorialized in 1938, "a few bad apples" threatened to "undermine public confidence in the legal system."[41] Yet commentators at the time persistently reduced the South African judiciary to the solid reputations that liberal jurists and legal practitioners enjoyed. In interviews they regularly gave to the British press to dismiss reports of legal injustice in South Africa, prominent politicians such as Dennis Reitz and General Smuts upheld the "few bad apples" theory and attributed legal travesties to the "lack of education among certain sections of the rural European population." Even as they criticized these sanguine views, the liberal press echoed the central idea that the "courts of law … have the support of a growing body of public opinion in the effort to vindicate the principles of morality and justice in the relations between White and Black."[42]

Private violence and near-lynching

Much of the racial violence that occurred in the 1920s and 1930s is not readily classified as lynching under the restrictive definition that the Tuskegee Institute and the NAACP settled on in 1940: "there must be legal evidence that a person has been killed, and that he met his death illegally at the hands of a group acting under the pretext of service to justice, race, or tradition." Whites who were legally accused of racial violence in South Africa did not generally claim that they acted in the name of "justice, race, or tradition." While many white defendants peppered their accounts with references to "cheeky Natives" who had to be "taught a lesson," the most common explanation they offered the courts was that they acted in self-defense. Perhaps more appropriate to the pattern of racial violence in South Africa is a stipulation that all anti-lynching bills included in the US: "Any assemblage of three or more persons which shall exercise or attempt to exercise by physical violence and without authority of law any power of correction or punishment over any citizen ... within the meaning of this act."[43] Still, two aspects of this definition prevent its application to the South African context. Not all racial murders involved "three or more" white assailants. Furthermore, the requirement that a victim had to have been illegally removed from "the custody of any peace officer" addressed the circumstances of Southern-style lynching but is irrelevant to South Africa, where no prisoners were seized from jail and executed by a mob.

Two characteristics distinguished private racial violence in South Africa. Firstly, almost all racial killing took the form of "murders" in which whites, usually in their capacity as employers, inflicted severe and often lethal punitive violence on black employees. This meant that the rituals that attended lynching in the South were absent in South Africa. Secondly, while South African courts were much more likely than Southern courts to charge and convict violent whites, they were all too willing to downplay the severity of racial violence. More often than not, violent whites were convicted of lesser charges such as culpable homicide or "grievous bodily harm" and, even for these lesser charges, the sentences imposed were light.

The discussion below of a number of racial killings that occurred in the 1930s suggests that many cases of racial killing should be treated as murder. Although the cases are quite typical, the discussion that follows does not aim to provide an exhaustive account of racial murder. It suggests only the extent of the phenomenon and assesses how the courts dealt with the culture of private racial violence in South Africa. From the daily parade of court cases involving "the shooting of Natives," newspaper editors and judges themselves were amongst the contemporary observers who concluded that racial murder in South Africa was a "national shame."[44]

On 23 January 1935, Gert Olifant, an African worker on a farm near Kimberley, was overseeing a gas engine used to divert water from a river when his employee, a farmer named Pieter Jacobson Momsen, arrived and accused him of shirking and mismanaging the water pump. Momsen claimed that he took Gert into the pump house and reprimanded him for wasting water, whereupon Olifant replied "in any angry and impudent way." According to his evidence in court, Momsen said, "I lost my temper and grabbed him by the throat with both hands" and demanded "*Waarom luister jy nie?*" ("Why do you not listen?") before leaving in his truck. When he returned ten minutes later, Olifant was dead. There were no witnesses to corroborate or dispute his story. At his trial, Momsen was held responsible for Olifant's death, convicted of culpable homicide and charged £20. The judge, A. Fraser, noted that that the sentence was influenced by the district surgeon who noted in his report that Olifant's death "had been due to choking from mielie meal which he found in the deceased's mouth" and that "gas from the engine might have caused the boy to become worse while unconscious, thereby choking him." Fraser accepted the jury's recommendation of mercy and permitted Momsen to pay his fine in four installments.[45]

Medical reports were often misused to mitigate sentences, providing judges with a fig leaf for imposing light sentences. Richard Lees, a farmer from Bethlehem, benefited from the exculpatory report that Dr. J. Loubser submitted to the court in September 1937. Lees was offended by the sight of "two natives standing talking on the pavement in front of [his] house." Witnesses described how he had rushed out armed with a pick handle and felled one of the men with a blow to the head. The man died five days later in hospital. Lees claimed that he had used a belt with a heavy buckle but did not deny the charge of culpable homicide. The district surgeon, however, saw matters differently. He found that "the Native's skull was extraordinarily thin at the place where the fracture appeared" and that "the native was suffering from pneumonia." Although he admitted that "the native would have succumbed to the injury even in the absence of pneumonia ... he considered it dangerous to fix the injury to the head as the cause of death." After a twenty-minute recess, the judge, F. E. T. Krause, reduced the charge to "assault with intent to do grievous bodily harm," accepted the jury's mercy recommendation and sentenced Lees to six months in jail or a fine of £15, which could be paid off in installments.[46] Cases in which judges reduced charges at the moment of sentencing occurred frequently. Many of these suggest that judges went to some lengths to justify light sentences.[47]

Even judges with solid reputations as liberal "friends of the Natives" almost never handed down the maximum sentence on white murderers. Justice Ramsbottom was one such judge. Widely respected for his impartial rulings and legal skill, Ramsbottom dealt with the case in which two brothers were accused of stabbing to death a newspaper seller, Jacob Sekaone. The killing took place in 1938 in broad daylight on the corner of Kerk and Smal Streets, in the heart of Pretoria. John and Leonard Chalmers were by all accounts a quirky pair, and their lawyers made much of their erratic behavior to win the court's sympathy. According to the Rev. E. G. Patterson, the assistant director of the DRC's "native mission" in Potschefstroom, both men were "gifted artists." John admitted that he "disliked natives."

His rage boiled over on 24 September, when Jacob Sekaone, preoccupied with selling newspapers, accidentally bumped into him on the sidewalk. For this "trivial matter," the two brothers chased Sekaone down the street. While John fought with Sekaone, Leonard plunged a hand-made dagger into the latter's heart. Both men were charged with culpable homicide. The jury upheld the charge against Leonard, but in an eight-to-one vote reduced John's to one of assault with intent to do grievous bodily harm.[48]

This case illustrates the situation that arose when liberals judges such as Ramsbottom had to deal with racial murder. Ramsbottom pointedly dismissed the race of the parties – "I regard this case entirely from the point of view, that one citizen who was going about his work was killed by another man" – and portrayed the case as purely one of law and order: "This is a grave offense and it must be punished. Citizens must be protected from lawless men who walk the streets carrying knives ready to attack those who cause them some trivial annoyance ... I cannot shut my eyes to the facts of this tragedy ..." He described Leonard as "a violent man willing to strike on the least provocation and a man who is in danger to his fellow human beings." In sentencing Leonard to seven years with hard labor for committing an unprovoked and cold-blooded murder, Ramsbottom justified the relatively stiff sentence by observing that at least one jury member had found Leonard guilty of murder. John received eighteen months' imprisonment with hard labor. Race, however, clearly saved Leonard from either the gallows or a life sentence.

This conclusion is borne out by another murder case that Ramsbottom presided over a few years later. However, this case (on which Alan Paton based his best-selling novel, *Cry the Beloved Country*) may also be read as an example of how legal formalism could either promote the impartiality that judges prized or underscore their subordination to parliament.[49] In November 1945, three African men were accused of murdering Dorothy Campbell-Gilchrist in an affluent Johannesburg suburb. Two of the men, Samuel Sikepe and Joseph Ndwakulu, were arrested for possessing items stolen from the deceased's home. Sikepe was wearing clothing taken from the home. Although he had attempted to hide a gun that had also been stolen from the home, Ndwakulu denied that he had stolen the weapon. A third man, Jack Sheshonga, also in possession of stolen clothing from the house, was arrested several days later in a town more than a hundred miles from Johannesburg. The all-white jury decided that the doctrine of "common purpose" bound all three men and recommended the death sentence. Ramsbottom, however, suspected a hierarchy of guilt. He found the evidence against Sikepe, who had been a "houseboy" in the victim's home, to be strong. He was less certain about Sheshonga's guilt, but decided that the jury had correctly found him to be an "active participant" in the murder. In Ndwakulu's case, the evidence struck the judge as too weak to warrant a sentence of capital punishment. Two of the nine jurors had not been persuaded by the evidence against Ndwakulu and had recommended acquittal.

Moreover, the strongest evidence against Ndwakulu was the word of the other two condemned men, and Ramsbottom had cautioned the jury that they could not consider the evidence these men had given against Ndwakulu. Had the matter ended there, Joseph Ndwakulu's life would have been spared. Instead, his life was lost when the case reached the desk of the Minister of Justice. For, in the privacy of his office, the Minister himself relied on the evidence that Sheshonga and Sikepe had given. On the strength of evidence that the jury had been instructed to ignore, the Minister of Justice over-ruled Ramsbottom and sentenced Ndwakulu to death. All three men were duly hanged.

The devil being in the details, it is not easy to answer why Ramsbottom meted out such different punishment to the Chalmers brothers and to Sheshonga and Sikepe, all of whom were convicted of first-degree murder. It is more than likely that the Chalmers were spared the gallows because they were white while the African men met the gallows because they were not. The Chalmers' verdicts therefore conform to the racial outcome of capital cases in the South, where whites were never hanged for murdering African Americans. Still, a number of factors distinguish the two judicial systems and underscore the ambiguities of legal formalism in South Africa. Not only had the jury split seven–two (coming close to a mistrial), but a judge had accepted the doubts of the two dissenting jurors. Ramsbottom had refrained from imposing the death sentence on Ndwakulu in a case in which the victim was an upper-class white woman. Such restraint would have been a most unlikely, indeed an impossible outcome, in any commu-nity in the New South, even after "legal lynchings" became more common from the 1930s onward. Legal formalism, however, came with a sting in its tail. The Minister of Justice, after all, was well within his rights when he overturned Ramsbottom, even when he availed himself of the testimony that jurors were warned to ignore. He therefore secured Ndwakulu's execu-tion in conformity with the law. Availing himself of the broad factors he was entitled to take into consideration, the Minister reasoned that he sensed "the barometer of white popular feeling" and had to respond to the fears of Johannesburg's affluent white burghers.[50] No less faithful to his training in legal formalism, Ramsbottom was more attentive to deficiencies in the doctrine of "common purpose." Legal formalism, in short, cut both ways: the same legal framework that could spare blacks from the death sentence could also be invoked to overturn "lenient" sentences and impose capital punishment.

Seven years with hard labor for a white killer of a black man was a some-what stiff sentence, suggesting that amongst the factors influencing senten-cing, the attitude of liberal judges made some contribution to racial justice. Conversely, conservative *platteland* judges and juries could short-circuit justice. Many cases in which barely any mitigating circumstances were adduced routinely concluded with the acquittal of white killers. In 1939, three farmers appeared before the Circuit Court in Bethlehem charged with flogging to death a black man named Strooi Makoba. J. H. du Plessis and T. E. Serfontein had pinioned Makoba while J. N. du Plessis administered the lethal whipping. So routine were such incidents that this story, like so many others, warranted no more than a brief 102-word mention deep in the pages of the *Rand Daily Mail*. The article did not bother to mention the reason for the flogging but observed that "Mr. P. H. Van Rooyen, a neighbor, gave evidence of the good character of the accused." All three men pleaded guilty to culpable homicide and were found guilty. Makoba's executioner received a suspended jail sentence (three years' hard labor, suspended for three years) and a fine of £250. His accomplices were each fined £150. All three were given time to pay their fines.[51]

Whether by design of the editor or by accident, the same page on which this travesty was reported records another criminal case that captures the relative value that many whites attached to blacks and farm animals. Two white men were respectively sentenced to four years and nine months with hard labor and two years with hard labor for stealing a total of 246 sheep in Somerset East in the eastern Cape. The editor of the *Rand Daily Mail* was struck by the disparity of the sentences in the death of Makoba and the theft of stock but thought it inappropriate to comment on the "full facts and circumstances which often move the courts to the merciful view in the imposition of penalties."[52] In another case, a judge found no "facts and circumstances" to explain why a fifteen-year-old Afrikaner boy in Kroonstad, affronted by an African bricklayer who asked him to stop kicking his brick pile, "lay in wait for the native ... and shot him in the jaw, the pellets carrying away his lower jaw." The Magistrate, C. L. Botha, warned the boy that "the law allows me to pass the highest punishment, but naturally that I cannot do." In keeping with the "terrible and cruel crime," Botha sentenced the youth to five years at a boys' Reformatory School.[53]

Whites frequently threw themselves at the mercy of the courts by claiming that the violence they inflicted, including murder, was either unintended or the result of "fun" gone awry. "I was feeling jolly" was the only explanation an Afrikaner railway worker, Joachim Johannes Strydom, could come up with to explain why, standing on a moving train, he had fired at a pregnant African woman sitting outside her hut near Bethal on 30 November 1939. Triffina Mavusa gave birth to a stillborn son before dying on the operating table. Supported by a unanimous guilty verdict from the jury, Justice Schreiner "regretted that the sentence would have to be a heavy one." Although "I appreciate the fact that many sentences in somewhat similar cases had been extremely light, I have to look at the matter from the point of view of the Crown." For taking the lives of two people, Strydom was sent to jail for three years with hard labor.[54] A 21-year-old Afrikaner was fined £30 for firing at point-blank range into the abdomen of "Piet, a 12-year native boy."[55] In 1939, A. Gouws, an Afrikaner farmer, grinned at one of his farm workers, Johannes, and said, "I am going to shoot you" before doing so for no reason at all, other than, as he quipped in court, "I often play the fool."

His charge was reduced from attempted murder to "pointing a firearm and in being possession of an unlicensed one," for which he was fined £10 and £5 respectively.[56]

Newspapers also reported several cases of what Southerners would have recognized as near-lynchings. The year 1939 alone sported three cases in which policemen or white farmers were charged with attempting to hang Africans. In one case, a white policeman charged with attempting to murder an African man was acquitted in a Durban court. In another case, two white citizens in Johannesburg were sentenced to three and six months with hard labor for attempting to hang an African woman in a garage. In this case, too, the presiding judge had reduced the sentence from attempted murder to assault with intent to do grievous bodily harm. It is unclear whether either man was actually jailed, however. As often occurred when whites were given prison time, lawyers for the two men immediately appealed the sentence.[57]

Racial murders in white farming areas were also triggered by romantic and sexual encounters between white men and black women. At least three such cases reached the courts in 1937 and 1938 alone. In the case of *Rex v Handley*, a white farmer near Port St. John was accused of murdering one of his workers, a man named Barney Mbob. It was so widely known that Handley was sexually intimate with Mbob's wife Jane that an embittered Mrs Handley had fired Jane who worked as her domestic employee. Handley, however, overruled his wife and asked Barney to persuade Jane into resuming her duties. Barney refused, "owing to their relationship." Handley and Jane, however, continued their clandestine relationship. On the day he was killed, Barney saw Handley, mounted and armed, enter a forest and beckon Jane to follow. Barney waited a minute before accosting the couple deep in the woods. What happened next is unclear. According to another farm worker who witnessed the encounter, Mbob demanded that the lovers end their relationship, seized his wife at the throat and beat her with a stick. He then led Handley's horse away "saying he was keeping the horse as he had found Handley with his wife." A struggle ensued in which a shot was fired and Handley galloped away. Charged in court with culpable murder, Handley denied Jane's confession that the two were lovers and asserted that the gun went off accidentally after he and Mbob had struggled over the horse. He had entered the forest either to "shoot monkeys or protect the woman from assault by her husband." With the assistance of W. J. G. Mears and C. Lever, two senior officials in the Department of Native Affairs who served as assessors for the Court, Justice Fischer declared that the evidence given by the African witnesses "impressed favorably." Still, he ruled that there was insufficient evidence to convict on any charge and Handley was discharged a free man.[58]

Poison was the means of murder in the two other cases, one of which injected a sensational legal drama into the lives of the sleepy hamlet of Graaf-Reinet in the eastern Cape. On 23 August 1938, Johannes Diederichs

Slabbert Blom appeared before the Graaf-Reinet Circuit Court on a charge of murdering an African woman, Elsie Yolola. The courts had some difficulty determining exactly how Yolola died because her battered body was first discovered alongside a railway track, 220 yards from a cottage where she had worked as a "domestic servant." An autopsy revealed two surprises. Yolola was pregnant and had most probably died of chloroform before her body was placed on the railway tracks. A check with a local pharmacy indicated that Blom had recently purchased chloroform under a false name. The case was solved when inquiries revealed that Blom and Yolola had been lovers for several months. The tragedy became clear: "With the idea of not bringing shame and disgrace on to [his] parents, [Blom] endeavored to hide his association with the girl." Still ashamed, Blom did not give testimony in his own defense and left it to his attorney to make the case for extenuating circumstances. "The whole life of Blom constituted extenuating circumstances. Blom, cut off from association with [white] females of his own age, committed the great indiscretion of intercourse with a colored woman." The packed court was stunned when Justice Pittman handed down the death sentence – the first and only time in South Africa that a white man was sentenced to death for murdering a black woman. The case was then automatically sent up to the Appellate Division of the Supreme Court in Cape Town, where Chief Justice Stratford and Justices Watermeyer, Tindall and Centrelevres boiled the case down to three narrow questions: Was there sufficient evidence on which any reasonable man would convict? Were there any extenuating circumstances? Should new evidence be allowed? Ruling for the Crown on all three scores, the Justices upheld the death sentence.[59]

Communal violence and the law: The "Port Elizabeth incident" of 1920
Several episodes of communal violence involving armed white citizens who attacked unarmed blacks scarred the early years of the young state. Two of these were discussed in Chapter 3. The first was the racial "progrom" that occurred in the early stages of the 1922 strike by white mine workers. This tragedy demonstrated the secondary role that racial hostility played in the course of white working-class mobilization. The second episode of communal violence involved the riotous events in Umvoti in 1928, when an enraged mob of white men stopped just short of lynching an African union organizer. Chapter 3 argued that, in different ways, both of these events underscore the limited role that communal violence and lynching played in the establishment of segregation in South Africa, a stark departure from trends in the American South. A third episode of white communal violence is discussed in this final section. Like the other episodes, this event was also a riot in which armed white civilians shot and killed a sizable number of unarmed blacks. The discussion of this event below illustrates how South Africa's "positivist" legal system contended with what was unquestionably a massacre in which white civilians played the leading role.

The extraordinary massacre that took place in the city of Port Elizabeth in October 1920 underscores how the performance and management of racial murder in South Africa differed from similar events in the South.[60] "The Port Elizabeth incident," as the event came to be known, differs from the private violence of the sort discussed above in three ways. It involved a *mob* of white vigilantes who acted *in tandem* with the local police and were *not formally charged* for the mass killing of seventeen unarmed blacks. In this sense, the incident resembles the communal violence of Southern lynch mobs, where white mobs frequently orchestrated mass killings with the collusion of law enforcement authorities. The active collaboration between police and white civilians in the course of the "Port Elizabeth incident," however, appears to have been a unique event in the segregation era. The massacre was doubly troubling to the state: it called official paternalism into question and raised the fear of retaliatory violence by blacks. Thus, the same policy of official segregation that explains why policemen and white civilians would collaborate in the course of the massacre also explains why the government sought to distance itself from the event.

Samuel Masabalala, a popular labor organizer in the ICU, unwittingly became the centerpiece of the impending drama in the course of a drive by the Port Elizabeth branch of Industrial Conciliation Union (PEICU) for a minimum wage. After the First World War, wage demands galvanized black labor movements across the country and led to some of the first strikes by black workers in the country's major cities and, with the aid of the ICU, spread into the countryside as well. Police files for this period are thick with breathless accounts and warnings about the "spread of Bolshevism amongst Natives," testimony to the mounting fear of black labor radicalism after the First World War. White civilians across the country warned Police Commandants and Native Administrators that "Something is about to happen," while officials themselves sought clarification on distinctions such as "Bolsheviks as opposed to Mensheviks, Communists as opposed to Socialists."[61]

The emergence of an increasingly assertive black labor movement in Port Elizabeth had much to do with the PEICU and with Masabalala's fiery approach in particular. Soon after his return from an ICU conference in Bloemfontein to discuss the issue of minimum wages in July 1920, Masabalala met with the white mayor of the city and unsuccessfully pressed the case for a minimum wage of ten shillings. Masabalala did nothing to quell increasingly excited rumors of a citywide strike by black workers, a move that was condemned by Dr Rubusana, a conservative African religious leader who rejected Masabalala's confrontational tactics. Rubusana was physically attacked after speaking out against a proposed strike at a public meeting in Korsten on Sunday 17 September and pressed charges against Masabalala, whom he held personally responsible for the incident. Masabalala was duly arrested and detained at the Baakens Street Police Station, ensuring that a jail would serve, as it so often did in the South, as the focal point of the ensuing violence.

The crowd that converged on the jail, however, was not white. Instead, several hundred black workers peacefully marched from Korsten and New Brighton, two quarters in Port Elizabeth, and assembled outside the prison complex in the city to demand Masabalala's release. PEICU leaders offered to "deposit a substantial sum" to secure Masabalala's release. Within an hour, twenty-two policemen were anxiously staring at a crowd 2,000 to 4,000 strong. Many "coloreds" and a handful of white passersby were present in the curious crowd, some of whom even competed on elevations to get a better view of the scene. This, together with evidence from multiple witnesses, confirms that the crowd was not "bent on violence" as the police would later allege.

Captain Halse, the district commandant in charge of the police station and the person most blamed for the violence, played the leading role in portraying the crowd as an imminent threat. Yet, even after stones and bricks were thrown at the police, the police responded not with weapons but with an unsuccessful blast from a water hose. Indeed, uncharacteristically for situations in which policemen were faced with a hostile crowd of blacks, the members of the Port Elizabeth Police Department did not initiate the day's lethal violence, not even after one of their number fell from his horse and emerged from the throng, revolver in hand and fending off blows from *knobkerries*. The report of the commission that investigated the incident commented favorably on the non-violent crowd-control measures that the police stuck to for two and half hours. It found that "the conduct of the officers, and especially that of Inspector Hart and the two sergeants who occupied the most exposed position in front of the assailants, was most patient and exemplary" and congratulated them for "doing their utmost to disperse the mob without bloodshed."

Although it was not conclusively proved who fired the first shots, strong evidence suggested that a group of white vigilantes accounted for the majority of the seventeen Africans killed. How white civilians came to be in a position to mow down scores of blacks in a furious fusillade became a matter of controversy. Eyewitnesses testified that, either singly or in small groups, whites had dribbled into the police station throughout the afternoon and remained there until the shooting began. Captain Halse claimed that they "had congregated on the side walk close to the Police; had several times requested to be allowed in and had been refused." He accepted their "proffered assistance" only when "it was seen that the charge of the four mounted men had failed and that the natives were rushing back." In his account, he distributed arms to approximately thirty "volunteers" at the last moment and "ordered" them not to fire unless he "instructed" them to. Again, his evidence was contradicted by witnesses, including several of the vigilantes who could not recall being issued any "orders," "command," or "instructions" to hold their fire after each man was given a rifle and had helped themselves to 50–60 rounds of ammunition from an open crate. Halse had positioned the vigilantes on the upper floor where a balcony provided a clear view of the scene outside. Halse and several policemen also claimed that the first shot emanated from the crowd, after a mounted charge by four officers led to the unhorsing of two officers and a near-accident between a third officer and a passing tram. In their depositions, police witnesses claimed that "one or two shots" were fired from the crowd as soon as the two mounted officers fell off their horses. A ricochet from a bullet knocked one of the officers unconscious. Because no other witnesses could verify Halse's claim that someone in the crowd had fired the first shots, the official report treated the claim with the greatest suspicion. Wherever the first shot came from, it was almost immediately followed by a burst of gunfire from two sources: the officers positioned on the steps of the police station and the unsupervised vigilantes on the balcony. Halse would testify that he immediately ordered the policemen to cease firing, but, "unfortunately, those on the balcony did not hear the order and firing continued from that point."

Seventeen people, none of them policemen, were killed in the course of the tragedy. One white man, an onlooker perched on a balcony across the street, was amongst the dead. In addition to the official count of seventeen dead, a white woman who was not felled in the actual shooting, a bystander named Louisa van Rensburg, suffered a death that seems rich with metaphor. Mortally wounded by a bullet himself, a black man fleeing from the gunfire staggered up to her and clubbed her on the sidewalk. One of six whites attacked in the chaotic flight from the gunshots, van Rensburg died shortly thereafter; later, approximately thirty whites claimed that they had been assaulted by members of the fleeing mob. The death of an innocent white woman cast a long shadow over the tragedy, making it appear "a more heinous crime in the eyes of whites than the indiscriminate shooting of the crowd by the police and vigilantes."[62] Although van Rensburg was killed after the violence erupted, many whites, and especially the police, touted her death as evidence of the crowd's violent intentions from the outset of its march on the jail. Her death seemed to give substance, too, to anxious rumors coursing through the eastern Cape's jittery white communities in the years after the First World War, a time when irritated police were regularly called to investigate phantom "surly Natives" said to be skulking about isolated white farms.

The massacre was over within minutes. Apart from the civilians who opened fire on the fleeing crowd, no other whites joined the melee. As evidence of black anger surfaced, the city settled into to a tense mood. Police kept a close eye on New Brighton and Korsten, Port Elizabeth's two black residential areas. Rumors had it that blacks were cutting telephone wires, "sabotaging the Power Station and destroying the petrol depot" as a prelude to attacking the darkened city itself. The fact that the police had in fact fired upon a group of blacks near a petroleum depot either ignited or confirmed the worst fears of white residents. Police shots continued throughout the night, prompting between 800 and 1,300 Africans to flee New Brighton "for their homes in Kaffirland."[63]

Port Elizabeth's white population blamed the tragedy on "outside agitators" allegedly brought in by the PEICU. Whites who were still bemused by the thought that "their" black employees could concoct a sophisticated scheme to paralyze the city's infrastructure in order to destroy the city itself fingered white socialists, a view rejected by none other than the commissioner of the South African Police.[64]

Still, the law had been broken and someone had to explain all those deaths. The response to the tragedy is instructive. Smuts' SAP government did not want to be seen as supporting the activities of the PEICU but also did not want to alienate the small but strategically significant number of African voters in the Cape. Nor could it simply dismiss the killing of unarmed citizens by an unprecedented combination of vigilante and police action.

The government's response took four forms. A judicial inquest was held to accumulate information about the shooting but not to comment on the question of culpability. At the same time, ten blacks were charged and fined for "incitement to violence" in terms of the Riotous Assembles Act, a draconian measure the government had passed to deal with militant white strikers in 1914. None of the vigilantes was charged with any offense. The SAP had hoped that the trials and a judicial inquest would lay the matter to rest. But, beleaguered by demands from blacks and whites to find out what had gone so badly wrong in Port Elizabeth, Smuts agreed to appoint a formal Commission of Enquiry.

The broad terms of reference of this Commission were noteworthy in one respect. They instructed the Commission to approach the shooting "against the general economic conditions as they affected the colored and native population, especially (a) in regard to the rates of wages of and (b) the cost of living." Instead of approaching the incident as a narrowly defined "law and order" matter, the Commission was free to investigate quality of life issues in Port Elizabeth's black population. Whites feared that this view implicitly attributed the shootings to socio-economic conditions and not to "agitators" and "lawlessness amongst the Natives." Those who suspected that liberals within the state had influenced the Commission even before it began its work grew even more suspicious once the names of the three commissioners were announced. Two of them, C. A. Schweitzer and Dr A. W. Roberts, were liberals steeped in the Cape's "assimilationist" tradition. The third, Dr A. Abdurahmin, was not only a Cape liberal but also a "colored" politician and president of the African Political Association (the APO), a moderate, generally pro-SAP organization based in the western Cape. He advised Smuts that the Port Elizabeth incident was "being discussed throughout the country by non-Europeans and [would] seriously affect the political outlook as far as the elections [were] concerned."[65] Seeking to expand support for government beyond its white Unionist base, Smuts may well have agreed to a Commission of Enquiry to appease black voters in the eastern Cape.[66]

The report of the Commission duly criticized the confrontational tactics of the crowd, but its major focus emphatically lay elsewhere. Strongly disputing the claim that the crowd was in a dangerously threatening mood from the outset, the report isolated three immediate causes of the violence: Halse's obdurate refusal to grant bail; the arming of unsupervised vigilantes; and shooting against the standing orders of the police. Paragraphs 71 and 74 of the Report were clear in assigning blame:

> 71 For some time after the firing ceased on the steps it was kept up on the balcony. Indeed, the firing did not cease until the officer in command reached them from downstairs. Had there been an officer in command on the balcony the Commission is of the opinion that firing would have ceased sooner; that it would have ceased immediately the crowd began to scatter; or indeed, that it would never have started at all without an order from such an officer ...

> 74 ... that all the firing which took place after the mob broke away was directed against fugitives; that it was unnecessary, indiscriminate, and it was moreover brutal in its callousness, resulting in a terrible toll of killed and wounded without any sufficient reason or justification.

If the SAP government had hoped to capitalize on a report that was sympathetic to blacks, the irate response from Port Elizabeth's white community, and from a livid Captain Halse in particular, now raised the unhappy prospect of white disaffection at the polls at the next general election, scheduled to take place a few months later in February 1921. The whiff of electoral losses chastened the government and it moved to mollify white opposition to the report. To signal its own "neutral" stance towards a Report which it had commissioned, Smuts' government agreed to include Captain Halse's written riposte as part of the Report itself. Whether or not this decision appeased whites, the three commissioners angrily accused the government of a breach of faith. The issue of compensation to the victims of the shooting provided the government with another opportunity to strike a "neutral" pose. With the Department of Justice opposed to and the Department of Native Affairs pressing for a monetary recognition of the government's culpability, the government accepted what it considered to be a compromise. Following a precedent set in 1913, when the government agreed to pay a compensation after troops fired on white strikers, F. S. Malan, the acting Minister of Native Affairs, excluded "participants" and "willing spectators" from any settlement. In this way, blacks filed only five of the twenty compensation claims that were submitted.[67]

The massacre in Port Elizabeth illustrates the contradictory and ambiguous role that "the Law" played in upholding white supremacy in South Africa. Several elements of the episode reveal a laggard legal system that failed to act despite the enormity of the crime committed against defenseless blacks. Most importantly, the failure to charge either the white vigilantes or the police for shooting down unarmed civilians in cold blood underscores the low value of black life in the racial order. The massacre also suggests how little it took for the distinction between white civil society and the state to rapidly blur when black crowds appeared to threaten the racial order. In this sense, the law enforcement system behaved much as the police and legal system did in the American South. But other aspects of the incident also distinguish the official response in South Africa and suggest the contradictory tensions that were pulling Smuts' government in different directions.

The government's attempt to reinforce its legitimacy with an impartial commission stands in absolute contrast to law-enforcement authorities in the South, none of which would have tolerated black crowds who clubbed policeman in the heart of the city. In South Africa, appointing a commission of inquiry conformed to a "Grand Tradition" in which South African governments discursively elaborated and legitimated their rule.[68] The commission failed to satisfy the contending constituencies but usefully illustrates the legal formalism that informed South Africa's judicial establishment in the segregation era. With a deft legal stipulation that exuded "impartiality" but was actually designed to punish blacks, more whites than blacks eventually received monetary compensation. The official response to the massacre was thus procedural but also highly equivocal – a fitting illustration of the different way the legal system functioned to legitimate and protect racial privilege in South Africa.

9

Conclusion

Most of this book has been devoted to explaining the role that three major institutions – labor controls, the legal system and religion – played in the genesis of distinctive cultures of racial violence in South Africa and the New South in the era that Stanley Greenberg calls the period of "racial intensification." Unofficial violence was clearly endemic to racial segregation in both places. Nevertheless, violence against blacks assumed quite different "styles," captured by the distinction between "private" and "communal" violence around which this book is organized.

The racial orders were most alike in the area of private violence but differed sharply in the matter of communal violence against blacks. Many white citizens in both contexts viewed it as axiomatic that they had the "right" to brutalize individual blacks, especially when the latter fell under their immediate control. This assumption ensured that the work environment – particularly in the primary extractive industries, farming and mining – harbored the greatest danger for blacks. Here, capricious violence that ranged from humiliating beatings to the sadistic and unprovoked killing of sharecroppers in particular were commonplace.

In contrast, the racial orders diverged sharply in the area of unofficial communal violence. In South Africa, communal attacks on blacks did occur, but always in the context of exceptional and rare moments of crisis which, furthermore, were generally rooted in class and ethnic disputes amongst whites: the Anglo-Boer War, the 1914 Afrikaner Rebellion and the crippling strike of 1922. Lethal communal attacks on blacks accordingly ceased in tandem with these crises, presenting the most striking contrast with patterns in the New South. Although they accounted for only one-third of all recorded lynchings, ritual communal lynchings persisted in the New South, certainly declining in frequency with the passage of time but not in their capacity to terrorize African Americans. Notwithstanding the broad similarities that have inspired much of the comparative literature dealing with the two countries, different patterns of unofficial violence also reflected the specificities of the respective contexts in which they arose.

The explicit statist foundations of white supremacy in South Africa led to the emergence of a bureaucratic culture with ambivalent consequences on unofficial violence. On the one hand, the extensive interventions that the centralized state undertook to manage "race relations" effectively inter-posed the state between blacks and whites. Because it remained concerned that black uprisings and counter-violence would imperil the evolving system of racial and industrial relations, the state actively discouraged whites from launching provocative communal attacks. Whenever it occurred, popular white violence invariably tended to fizzle out, leaving its legacy not in tor-tured memories of lynching but in the administrative adjustments that state mangers made to improve the racial regimentation of state and society. On the other hand, state officials and institutions – themselves organized to maintain and expand the racially repressive labor market – tolerated less disruptive private violence against blacks. Over time, an assaultive culture of racial violence took hold and complemented the structural violence that was built into the bureaucratic juggernaut. It is this tradition of low-level but ceaseless racial violence that George Fredrickson's otherwise sound characterization of racial violence in South Africa greatly underplays.

The lynch culture that emerged in the postbellum South was an organic outgrowth of the region's proclivity for interpersonal violence, and its insti-tutionalization in the era of the New South is incomprehensible outside of the complicity of the US state. Still, the Hydra-headed structure of the federal state was not the central issue. Federal power could have been easily invoked to prevent the lynch culture from metastasizing, just as federal power was used to deal with other problems in the first half of the twentieth century. Instead, the ideology of "states rights" became a justification for national indifference and Northern disengagement from white supremacy in the South. Federal neglect enabled white Southerners to redirect the overt political terror they had used to destroy Reconstruction into a latent menace that could erupt with unnerving unpredictability against African Americans. Although communal lynching usually occurred only under cer-tain conditions, the coalescence of these conditions could also be a volatile and unpredictable affair. Because mere allegation carried as much weight as incontrovertible evidence, whites were free to escalate any issue into an incendiary accusation that dissolved restraints against ritual killing and legitimized the savage destruction of black lives. "Festivals of violence" therefore periodically broke out across the New South.

It is not surprising that both contexts sported similar patterns of private violence. Violence is the frequent outcome whenever expropriative relation-ships are paired with the asymmetrical power relationships that mark all racial orders. For example, the regular physical beatings and private killing that abounded in South Africa and the New South were also prominent in most colonial situations.[1] Yet, despite a shared tradition of private and fur-tive violence, South Africa and the New South were also somewhat different even on this score. It is significant that private violence in South Africa was more perfunctory and generally bereft of the ritual and symbolic parapher-nalia, chiefly ropes and fire, which white Southerners often employed to execute African Americans even when no audience was assembled. Whites in South Africa almost never deviated from the standard use of prosaic weapons such as guns, fists and nearby farm implements. Not only are guns more efficient, but they also maintain a cold distance between the killer and his victim, and their frequent use suggests whites' unwillingness to either engage in or celebrate tactile forms of extra-legal killing. Accordingly, most cases of private violence in South Africa are examples of what Mary Jackman calls "instrumental violence."[2] In contrast, the more frequent use of highly symbolic instruments of death, such as the noose, even in cases of private violence in the South reveals not only a greater callousness but also the desire to transform a private killing into a brazen public statement.

However, it is the ritualized violence of communal lynching that most sharply distinguishes South Africa's bureaucratic culture of violence from the lynch culture of the American South. One way to account for this difference is to draw upon Sheila McCoy Smith's concept of "ululation," the sequence of steps that culminated in white collective violence.[3] A communal lynching was a choreographed spectacle that was staged by ordinary citizens in the transparency of civil society. It commenced with an opening incident, progressed through stages that incrementally drew in a widening circle of participants and quickly imposed a shared frame that turned an assembly of citizens into an orderly mob, ready to gleefully participate in rituals that incrementally contributed to the victim's death. When the popular will of white society clashed with conscientious officials who attempted to forestall a public lynching, it was more likely that white citizens would emerge triumphant. In such instances, the full measure of white citizens' ability to intimidate the local state became most clear after the lynching had been carried out. Too beholden to the popular will, too fearful of white rage and as loyal as lynchers were to the "Solid South," state officials only rarely dared to act professionally and prosecute lynchers whose identities were widely known. Public servants often played an active role in the lynching or milled about as the lynchers tortured and executed their victim. Whatever the role of public servants, communal lynchings revealed the supremacy of "popular justice" in the regulation of race regulations in the lynch culture of the New South. In South Africa, communal forms of "popular justice" wilted before the timely intervention of law enforcement authorities.

The three institutions that this book has examined may not provide an exhaustive explanation of these differences, but they do demonstrate that traditions of violence did not grow from the irrational and inscrutable impulses of "a few bad apples" in the dominant population. They show that the bureaucratic and lynch tradition reflected the systemic interweaving of dynamics in the respective racial systems in which they emerged. The rest of this chapter draws out a number of implications that flow from the preceding chapters. The first section explores the differential contribution of *dominant actors* to racial violence, drawing attention to certain structural conditions that either promote or constrain tendencies towards unofficial racial violence. The second section underscores the importance of a *transcendent ideology* and argues that systemic cultures of violence invoke predispositions that make reiterated violence not only acceptable but also righteous. A final section returns to the central role that *the state* played in the two cultures of violence.

Racial violence and dominant class actors

The end of two military conflicts – the American Civil War and the Anglo-Boer War – marked the beginnings of capitalist development and, simultaneously, the transformation of blacks into a vulnerable pool of cheap labor. In each context, whites sought to incorporate familiar patterns of racial domination – racial slavery and colonial despotism – into the emerging capitalist economy. The racial violence that this process entailed and later institutionalized was therefore inseparable from the integration of racial motivations and class interests in the segregation era. Blacks contributed to this process in complex ways, either by trying to wrest political and material advantages from emerging developments or, more importantly, by attempting to stave off the new restrictions and hardships that began to encircle them. Black challenges contributed to the racial state principally by galvanizing whites to attend more closely to the way race and class intersected. At issue was not only how blacks could be simultaneously dominated as a "race" and exploited as a class. These desiderata also had intertwined implications for the class and gender divisions within the white population. As a result, the prospect of racial democracy that briefly emerged on the heels of the two military conflicts profoundly politicized the internal unity of whites. Intra-white divisions made an automatic white consensus over the "race question" impossible and meant that a solution would have to be actively forged. Near-universal racism amongst whites certainly facilitated this quest, but it was also important that not all whites shared the same capacity to influence the emerging segregationist state.

Two power asymmetries amongst whites emerge as particularly salient: the dominance of the farmers and miners in the extractive industries over industrial manufacturers and the weakness of white workers relative to all employers. These asymmetries were common to both orders, ensuring that employers, chiefly those in the extractive industries, were disproportionately responsible for shaping the traditions of racial violence in each context. Agrarian and mining dominance also structured the politics of white labor. In both racial orders, employers created sufficient incentives for already-racist white workers to resist racial cooperation with black workers, but they did so in ways that determined how poor whites would participate in unofficial racial violence.

South Africa

Scholars conventionally ground the emergence of formal segregation in South Africa in the relatively speedy desegregation of the economy into three major sectors – mining, capitalist agriculture and manufacturing industry – and the state's subsequent interventions to mediate the conflicts over cheap black labor. The contrast with developments in the American South suggests another interpretation: these same developments also limited whites' propensity to commit unofficial violence. By engaging itself so extensively in the emerging labor market, the South African state elaborated its own distinct interests in stability into a cornerstone on which white supremacy came to rest. Resistance and counter-violence from the black majority were not the state's overriding concern in the segregation era. Nevertheless, successive governments were vitally aware that the state was vulnerable to a concerted black challenge. Fears of this "Black Peril" therefore peaked whenever intra-white discord broke out into open violence in this period. Thus, the same interventions that whites developed to secure the racially repressive labor market may also be read another way, as limiting the ability of white citizens to imperil a state that had not yet found its feet.

Employers in the three major sectors demanded divergent forms of labor control that precluded all employers from rallying to an overtly violent regime of labor regulation. Mine owners cherished a system of circulatory migrant labor; industrialists favored a settled urban population; while the majority of farmers pinned their fortunes to a system of labor tenancy. These angular demands were incorporated into the bureaucratic culture that emerged after 1910. With the state formally in control over "race relations," whites settled for a modus vivendi that precluded inflammatory communal violence but tolerated private violence against blacks. This arrangement reinforced the racial state as the embodiment of the "universal will" of all whites while still preserving the sense of individual mastery and personal domination that whites viewed as a racial birthright. As a result, the state retained a substantive claim on its monopoly over the means of racial violence.

Employers who linked the success of their operations to the ability of the state to exert control over race relations were hardly likely to permit white workers to imperil the country by unleashing disruptive extra-legal violence against blacks. The "racial pogrom" that white workers inflicted on innocent blacks in the 1922 strike was not only extraordinary but is also instructive: mine owners, army units, the South African Police and even white members of the gawking public rushed to protect blacks. If only as a symbolic display of its paternalist "stewardship" over blacks, Smuts' government ensured that one of the white lynchers was sentenced to death and hanged. White workers, for their part, displayed no sustained interest in imposing communal justice on blacks and, like whites generally, limited themselves to uncoordinated individual assaults on blacks. The thrust of white proletarian politics lay resolutely elsewhere. Nurtured by a burgeoning Afrikaner nationalist movement, militant white workers struck hard bargains with employers who, in turn, solicited the support and intervention of the government to institutionalize a concordat amongst capital, white labor and the state. It is beside the point that white workers remained a junior partner in this pact and never succeeded in obtaining all their demands, although they did receive a great deal more than their counterparts in the South.[4] What mattered for this book was that the statist orientations of aggressive white unions displaced blacks from the crosshairs of their mobilization and occasional rage. The industrial conciliation apparatus that emerged in the wake of the 1922 strike and a range of other benefits simultaneously consolidated the emerging bureaucratic culture and elevated white workers above the black majority. In South Africa, proletarian militancy begat proletarian mobility, and both dissuaded the white worker from fomenting a culture of communal violence against blacks.

The South

The ascent of farmers and the end of Reconstruction in the South were rooted in racial violence. The relatively straightforward dominance of the agrarian class here thus surfaces as the most critical determinant of racial violence. Farmers' specific preferences – to establish labor repressive policies that resembled slavery as closely as possible – were initially masked by the ferocious assault on Reconstruction. By placing its imprimatur on this attack on established government, the agrarian elite legitimized extra constitutional violence and virtually deputized ordinary white civilians, initiating a trend in which ordinary white men could murder African Americans with little fear of punishment. It is impossible to determine with any precision when the elite-driven political terror that brought down Reconstruction evolved into racial terror in the New South. By the 1880s, however, farmers who had been compelled to re-start their operations by experimenting with devices they reviled, such as improving wages and working conditions, were already positioned to concoct an amalgam of legal devices and lethal violence to subjugate emancipated African Americans. Lynching of all sorts took its place alongside convict leases, debt peonage, crop liens and measures against "vagrancy" to inaugurate a system that transformed African Americans into dependent sharecroppers. When they emerged, neither the mining nor textile industries challenged the hegemony of King Cotton. Instead, they incorporated into their operations the basic premises that governed rural labor controls. Aided by their disproportionate influence within the various states, landowners were free to project their own interests in a terrorized and vulnerable black peasantry onto all of Southern society. As all white Southerners knew, this development effectively declared open season on African Americans.

Nowhere were the violent sensibilities that agrarian hegemony fostered more apparent than in the Black Belt states. Escape from sharecropping, summary violence and crushing poverty here was almost impossible for African Americans. Although racial violence was appreciably lower in the region's mining and urban centers, African Americans could not assume that they were safe from extra-legal violence. As a rule, unofficial violence was highest wherever King Cotton ruled.

White workers, the people Idus Newby calls "the plain folk of the South," were not the instigators of unofficial violence in the New South. Growing evidence suggests that their active participation in the lynch culture was by no means foreordained by the combination of racism and their "fear of displacement" by more vulnerable African American workers. Instead, employers who had an interest in a weak and divided working class set the tone that made violence acceptable in the New South. This they did in two ways: they made liberal use of lethal violence to defeat all labor movements and fanned the flames of racial hatred by threatening to displace non-compliant white workers by introducing African American (and immigrant European) workers. In response, droves of poor whites and African Americans turned to inter-racial unions and threw their support behind the Populist Party, threatening the reactionary Bourbons Democrats who dominated the South after Reconstruction. Riven by its complex and unsustainable internal tensions, the Populist movement was defeated in the mid-1890s by a combination of electoral fraud and violence fomented by the Democratic Party. Poor whites henceforth dealt with African Americans as rivals and competitors in the labor market.

The crushing of the inter-racial Populist movement was therefore critical in shaping plebeian violence against African Americans. Defeated and demoralized white workers defected *en masse* from the South's brief experiment with radical proletarian politics. Plebeian whites therefore commenced the twentieth century as a highly vulnerable class, prone to the racial blandishments and divisive class strategies of employers. William Cash's pithy equation[5] exaggerates the subsequent docility and conservatism of white labor but still captures the crippling associations that deprived the region of a militant proletarian culture:

$$\text{Labor unions} + \text{Strikers} = \text{Communists} + \text{Atheism} + \text{Social equality with the Negro}$$

Poor whites participated in racial violence to underscore their marginal but crucial advantages over African Americans. Civil society became the arena of their racial politics and unofficial violence a prized badge of their whiteness. Still, if white workers celebrated the lynch culture partly because they were indeed racist, their racism was in no small measure engineered and amplified by landowners and industrial employers, the actors who were responsible for inaugurating the Southern lynch culture.

Evidence for the claim that racial violence correlated with the relative simplicity of elite domination may be found in Southern states with diverse economies. One Southern state, the Commonwealth of Virginia, illustrates this point. Virginia's diversified economy more closely resembled South Africa than it did essentially monocrop states such as Alabama, Mississippi or Georgia. Productive activities, by themselves, did not determine lynch patterns. Nevertheless, the correlations that arose in diversified Virginia are instructive. Lynchings were fewest and disappeared fastest in Commonwealth regions that were more industrial and economically diverse, and where the wage system was most entrenched. In contrast, lynchings were highest, most persistent and most cruel in the sharecropping regions where King Cotton prevailed. Likewise, communal lynchings were widespread in the state's monocrop areas but infrequent in the diverse and modern economic centers of the state. These patterns suggest that economic differentiation complicates the ability of elites to consolidate a single regime of violence. Employers generally acquire a distaste for disruptive forms of violence in modern, efficiency-driven operations where stable labor markets, the productivity of workers and industrial skills are critical to profitability. Certainly, Virginia gained its reputation for racial moderation largely because race relations in the Black Belt states were more violent and degrading to American Americans. Still, the less violent approach to race relations in the most modernized parts of the Old Dominion also resembled patterns of racial violence in Northern states, where lynching occurred only occasionally. This pattern mirrored trends in South Africa's diverse economy, where whites also avoided the most extreme forms of extra-legal violence.

Racial violence as symbolic power

"Dirt," Mary Douglas argues, "is matter out of place." In this view, objects are not inherently "dirty" but only perceived to be so because they stand outside a prevailing system of classification. Objects become "dirty" when they threaten a consensus. Much as Emile Durkheim does in *The Elementary Forms of Religious Life*, Douglas argues that societies develop rituals, taboos and laws to ward off and expel the threatening pollutant.[6] No less than dangerous objects, people who are "out of place" are also subject to practices that are intended to strip them of their power to threaten a reigning consensus. Douglas' conclusion that the function of ritual (rites of passage) is to renew social order by re-clarifying categories provides a useful way to contrast the symbolic thrust of religion in the bureaucratic and lynch cultures that this book has examined.

Focusing on a durable tradition of lynching and murder instead of the more cataclysmic and episodic phenomenon of race riots underscores the indispensable role that a supportive and coherent ideology plays in sustaining cultures of violence. Two issues have been germane to this study: the general role of ideology and the specific importance of symbolic and ritual violence.

Unsurprisingly, the ideologies that South African and Southern whites generated to legitimize racial domination shared numerous similarities, but, because they were rooted in different historical contexts, the racial ideologies differed even on issues that were common to both. How ideological elements of white supremacy differed and buttressed the distinct cultures

of violence may be illustrated by examining three themes that were common to the origins of segregation in South Africa and the New South: "Lost
Causism"; government intervention in the economy; and paternalism. These
were not the only, and perhaps not even the most important, elements of
segregationist ideology, but they suffice to convey the contrasting ideological meanings that marked the bureaucratic and lynch cultures of violence.

South Africa

Continuing its colonial-era pattern of excising and subsequently neglecting Africans, the DRC remained generally indifferent to the precise way in
which Afrikaner and African lives intersected in postbellum South Africa.
Social Gospelism amongst "poor whites" and Afrikaner equality with
English-speaking whites were the entwined themes that dominated Afrikaner
theology in the first two decades after 1910. Despite the DRC's unique history of exclusionary racism, these concerns effectively dissuaded Afrikaner
theologians from elaborating a theology of racial vengeance against blacks.
The DRC church remained essentially indifferent to blacks and left the control of "race relations" to the state, which was then actively promoting
"closer union" amongst English-speaking whites and Afrikaners. The DRC
neither vilified blacks as irredeemably evil nor fingered them as the principal
cause of the Afrikaner crisis; instead, it actively cooperated with the black
and white Social Christians in the Benevolent Empire to establish a racial
order that it could defend on Christian and moral grounds. Driven by its
republican mission and a "Christian paternalist" approach to race relations,
the Afrikaner version of Lost Causism exuded none of the virulent hatred
that marked Southern Protestantism. By refusing to sanctify the physical
violence that marked farmers' relations with blacks in the *platteland*, the
DRC undermined propensities which, had theologians embraced them,
would have placed blacks in greater mortal danger.

Constitutional segregation bestowed immediate political equality on
Afrikaners and English-speaking whites and rendered anti-reconstruction
violence unnecessary. Lost Causism was instead powerfully shaped by two
developments that were central to state policy after 1910. The first was
the government's commitment to the principle of limited government and
its consequent disinclination to subsidize the living standards of "poor
whites." The second was the paternalist principle on which the state's
"Native policies" were based. Both of these ideological commitments influenced the evolution of the DRC's theology and inhibited Lost Causism from
degenerating into a theology of racial violence.

In response to the *laissez faire* policies of the pro-imperial governments of
Louis Botha and Jan Christiaan Smuts, the DRC courted "poor whites" and
enthusiastically embraced Social Gospelism. Escalating social hardship and
fears that Afrikaners were "degenerating into natives" in the Union's towns
radicalized a generation of Afrikaner theologians and quickly alerted the
DRC to the limits of pastoral charity. After the First World War, the church

championed a "strong" version of the state and embraced the political arena as an extension of its religious work on the behalf of *die volk*. As a result, Lost Causism in South Africa did not simmer and boil in regional isolation as it did in the South; instead, DRC theology became enmeshed with institutional politics. Lost Causism in South Africa rapidly transcended the gloom of defeat. Under the aegis of a nationalist movement and a political party that accepted it as the spiritual guide of Afrikaners, the DRC played the leading role in welding together a class alliance of Afrikaner intellectuals, farmers, workers and emerging businessmen, and helped focus the movement on achieving political power.

A broadly defined racial paternalism was the second ideological force that shaped Lost Causism in South Africa. Even as its *predikante* ran and occupied political office in the 1920s and 1930s, the DRC's racial solutions remained self-consciously within the broad and flexible parameters of segregationist ideology of the inter-War years. The church never embraced the assimilationist ideology of the liberal Cape. At the same time, its racial theology was virtually indistinguishable from the pro-tribalist "liberal" tradition that prevailed in the English-speaking province of Natal. Well into the 1940s, the DRC remained proud of its paternalist orientation towards Africans and incorporated this principle into theological arguments that justified racial and ethnic domination.

In the end, Afrikaner theologians repudiated extra-legal violence and embraced statism because the latter could be made to benefit even the poorest members of the white working class. D. F. Malan, a theologian who became a politician in the 1920s before becoming the first Prime Minister of the Apartheid-era NP, declared in 1943 that his party stood for "state interference and state control on a large scale." This vision emanated as much from a theological worldview as it did from a secular approach to state building.[7] Imperfectly executed in practice and persistently challenged by blacks, bureaucratic authoritarianism nevertheless established a formal system of racial repression that demobilized white civil society and enabled whites to develop rituals that were only vicariously connected to the black majority. While the state ensured that blacks were not "out of place," Afrikaner rituals concentrated on cementing an "internal" class alliance and aimed at gaining political power. The most stirring Afrikaner public rituals of the inter-War years – the Afrikaans language movement, the emotional "*ossewa trek*" in 1938 and the construction of the Voortrekker monument later that year – were decidedly non-violent events.[8] Such rituals harkened to Biblical images of a "lost tribe" beset on all sides by danger, seductive impurity and divine tribulation. Embodied in hymns, sermons and songs, Afrikaner religious rituals imagined an arduous history of trial and privation, a period of testing by God. But these rituals also envisaged the moment when God's blessing would be made clear. The reward for submission to God's will was the discovery and preservation of "nationhood" through the power of the modern state.

If South African whites tended to view Africans as polluting the social body, they also romanticized the reserves as an Eden that restored the health and vigor of a people who were "out of place" in the urban areas. Restoring "order" therefore had a distinct spatial connotation. It meant keeping blacks "in their place" – in the reserves. Afrikaner rituals therefore celebrated the physical extrication and administrative banishment, not the destruction, of Africans in accordance with God's will. The rites of passage that this process entailed were accordingly secular and administrative and centered unavoidably around the paraphernalia of influx control, the crucial apparatus that would regulate the transference of Africans from one state to another, from corrupted urban dwellers to wholesome tribes happily ensconced in the reserves. Afrikaner theologians believed that Apartheid was the full measure of their virtuous intentions and that the proof was in the eventual denouement: like the Afrikaners who came bearing the gift, tribal Africans would one day also exult in their own "nationhood" in their segregated "ancestral homes." Before the realities set in after 1948, the theoreticians in the DRC's missions section viewed the transferal to Africans of the Afrikaners' historic discovery – a God-mandated "ethnic pride" – as a first-order theological principle that confirmed the essential humanity of Africans.[9]

The South

Protestantism, segregation and ritual violence against African Americans were insverably connected in the Southern states. Protestantism did not invent a tradition of lawlessness that included lynching – white mobbism, violence seemingly of all kinds and the lynching of white men had also been rampant in the antebellum era. What Southern Protestantism bequeathed to the twentieth century was a moral justification for concentrating subsequent violence on African Americans. Like the revamped theology of Afrikaners after 1910, Lost Causism in the South provided the glue to hold together a demoralized white community that was divided by class, anxious about its women, and fearful of the social and political equality that would flow from the emancipation of African Americans.

In sharp contrast to the DRC, Protestant leaders disdained political power and provided theological justification for opposing government intervention in the economy, an approach they damned as "communist" and, hence, evil. Social Gospelism in the South did attempt to alleviate the poverty of poor whites, but only rarely challenged the hegemony of employers who were firmly wedded to the low-wage system in the South. This meant three specific things: Southern Protestantism reinforced the dominance of employers, justified the subordination of poor whites and transformed the defense of racial segregation into a popular religious crusade. Lost Causism in the one-party South was therefore profoundly conservative, lacking entirely the confidence that Afrikaners developed to challenge and transform the imperial state after 1910. Because it portrayed established authority as legitimate, Southern Protestantism uncritically embraced the region's social hierarchy.

Women were subordinate to men; men were honor-bound to defend their women and children; the rich were rich because God blessed them; and blacks, who were both inferior and evil, deserved both the "social death" of segregation and the measures that preserved it. White Southerners grasped or intuited the inescapable conclusion: race trumped God. More accurately, they understood that serving God meant expelling evil. And because the "black-beast rapist" was evil incarnate in the white imaginary, white Southern Protestants embraced all forms of violence when they sacrificed black lives on the alter of "sex, sin and segregation".

Purification, and not the "punishment of specific offenders," was the primary goal of religiously sanctioned racial murder. The frequent presence of pastors at lynchings sanctified the shaming, mutilation and execution of black victims and blessed the white consensus that the "proper place" of blacks was outside the community of virtuous humanity. Emile Durkheim famously argued that "religious feeling is the individual's awareness of the group." He may just as well have written that "Southern lynching is the individual's awareness of the group."[10]

The symbolic functions of lynching in the New South afford a dramatic contrast to the non-violent rituals of state formation in South Africa. Mary Douglas' observation that "Holiness means keeping distinct the categories of creation" certainly resonates in the enforced ethnicity policies of Apartheid.[11] Applied to the South, however, the claim almost automatically invokes the specter of retributive violence whenever blacks stepped "out of place." Because an offense against the holy segregationist order was tantamount to, or could easily be portrayed as, an offense against God, blacks who stepped "out of place" triggered a systemic violence that whites readily recast as Bible-derived themes of "punishment" and "atonement." In the Protestantism of the South, sin demands, "someone has to pay." Hymns and sermons in camp meetings and churches circled endlessly around this theme and unfailingly adduced the ultimate proof – the sacrificial death of Christ – that violence is a cleansing agent: "Christ, the Lamb of God, was slain / He tasted death for me."[12] Communal lynching certainly reinforced the economic exploitation of African Americans, but even this cardinal fact was subordinate to the role that lynching played in welding together the white folk of the South and the men whom the "black-beast rapist" transformed into guardians of white women's "honor." One reason why white men in South Africa did not fuse together white femininity and religion quite as zealously as their Southern counterparts did may have to do with the dispersal of more than half of the black majority in recondite reserves, the spuriously "authentic" home of "tribal people." White Southerners, in contrast, lived in unavoidable proximity, even intimacy with African Americans. Here, "the essence of segregation was not geographical or even spatial but was rather an effort to maintain hierarchical social distance between racial groups that were too much involved with each other to be separated by sharply drawn territorial, cultural, or economic boundaries."[13] To forestall or to eliminate the consequences of "pollution," whites placed a greater premium on the regulation of contact, particularly sexual contact with white women. The indissoluble connections that white Southerners established amongst "sin, sex, and segregation" therefore greatly exceeded similar connections within Afrikaner theological discourse, providing an always-present pretext to disgorge into the open all the tension and discord that undermined the image of the "Solid South."

The symbolic content of lynch rituals in the South revealed the cul de sac in which segregation found itself in the twentieth century. Neatly embodied in George Wallace's 1968 electoral battle cry – "segregation today ... segregation tomorrow ... segregation forever" – Southern segregation was utterly devoid of any promissory rationales.[14] Unable to "legitimate the illegitimate," as whites in South Africa did, Southern Protestantism sanctified the only means by which whites could keep blacks "in their place." While private lynchings were easily dismissed at the pulpit as the work of "ignorant poor whites of the lower type," the aura of "holiness" in communal lynchings erased such blemishes on the honor of the New South and underscored the fundamental division that kept all whites and all blacks "in their place": one white and virtuous, the other black and irredeemably tainted with evil. A communal lynching was a liturgy that froze time by preserving the present, a check on the forces that were chipping away at white supremacy. The rites of passage that human sacrifice entailed suppressed the inequalities that divided whites and guided the frenzied but strangely worshipful mob through a choreography that culminated in the supreme suspension of time, the ritual death of a sacrificial and vulnerable victim. A communal lynching, in short, was akin to the crucifixion of Christ on Golgotha. The implications of this symmetry were so awesome, Donald Mathews writes, that, like most scholars of lynching, the hushed lynch mobs of the South did not recognize "in the ritual of lynching a communal transference to the subject of violence all of the violence implicit in community itself; or, if it [saw] the transference, [did] not understand its religious ambience."[15]

Racial violence and healing: The role of the state

Institutional violence was a common feature of both racial orders in the period of racial intensification and accounts for many of the similarities in the comparative literature. Nevertheless, institutional violence was a component of the overall culture and so also reflected the *different* thrusts of state formation in the two societies. The ascent and the decline of unofficial violence in the twentieth century are only explicable in light of these broader patterns. However remorseless they seemed at the time, patterns of racial violence were in fact unstable, subject to complex challenge from below, from above, and from changes in the international environment.[16] Similar themes between the two racial orders certainly persist into the present, providing fertile ground for comparativists to examine important developments in areas such as residential segregation, the desegregation of education, affirmative action policies, the changing relationship between race and class, and the changing meaning of "whiteness." Future comparative work on these and other themes will almost certainly hinge around the critical difference that the state played in the decades following the Second World War.

In South Africa, the NP government reorganized the state into an authoritarian behemoth that preserved white prosperity and unapologetically escalated the repression of the black majority. This development represented a massive increase in the tradition of bureaucratic violence established in the segregation era. The government's refusal to accommodate black opposition polarized the relationship between the racial state and black civil society and severely limited its ability to capitalize on the class distinctions that gradually began to emerge within the African population. Instead, bureaucratic violence associated with labor controls, the *differentia specifica* of racial domination and capitalist development in South Africa, evolved into the garden-variety terror of juntas and police states. Unable to use the courts to dismantle Apartheid, blacks forged a revolutionary climate that finally cracked the disorganized Apartheid state. Although the legacies of racial domination continue to persist in contemporary South Africa, the "miracle" of 1994 successfully terminated the horrors that the TRC so painfully exposed.

In the South, a combative civil rights movement provoked a national crisis that forced a showdown between the federal government and defiant Southern states in the 1950s and 1960s. The result was a constitutional crisis which, had it arisen at any point in the preceding half century, might have been sufficient to dismantle segregation. Perhaps remarkably, the Southern lynch culture was not the primary target of legislative and political reform in the "Second Reconstruction" of the South. A federal anti-lynching bill, the goal that had led to the formation of the NAACP, would never see the light of day in the US, depriving African Americans of even a symbolic act of national contrition.[17] Segregation would instead unravel on the legal rock of desegregating schools. Tragedy and farce again reappeared, just as they had when the violence of Reconstruction mutated into the lynch culture of segregation. In reaction to federal intervention into "state affairs" in the South, Southern whites again discovered in the legal framework of the federal system the means to repel the specter of racial integration.

South Africa

The bureaucratic culture in South Africa was to reach its terrifying zenith after the 1950s, when the NP had all but abandoned the optimistic paternalism of the DRC missiologists who had developed the Apartheid theology of the late 1920s and 1930s. The NP ruled with an iron fist by making full use of a Westminster-style parliament that placed all power in the hands of the party in power and a constitution that provided little effective power of judicial review. Government policies placed Afrikaner interests at the top of the agenda. Farmers, Afrikaner businessmen and white unskilled workers became the primary beneficiaries of Apartheid policies even as the NP attempted to meet the conflicting demands of established manufacturers and mine owners, the redoubts of the English-speaking white world.[18] The Apartheid project rested on an unparalleled degree of state involvement in the reproduction, distribution and employment of black workers in a massive attempt to "rationally" allocate labor at the cheapest rates possible. The NP hoped that Apartheid policies would end the chaos of the 1940s. Its growing intervention in society, however, produced the opposite effect. The 1950s were a tumultuous decade, roiled by ceaseless protests, strikes, anti-pass campaigns, and rent and consumer boycotts, as well as demonstrations organized by women in the urban and rural areas. Peasant opposition in the reserves illustrated how Africans' consciousness and organizations spanned the very divide between the rural and urban areas that Apartheid policies sought to deepen. The ANC also shed its conservative politics in the course of the Second World War and went on to wage an "armed struggle" against an unyielding Apartheid regime. Militant black nationalism and grassroots challenges never came close to destabilizing the state. Nevertheless, mass resistance was sufficiently threatening to discourage the NP government from imposing the full range of Apartheid policies.[19]

A commitment to white prosperity on such a scale inevitably fomented a permissive culture of violence in which the distinctions between official repression and private violence blurred, generally with the blessings of the state. With the government pouring resources into expanding and coordinating a series of state-building activities such as the "development" of the reserves into "Bantustans," the construction of a labor control apparatus to manage the expanded pass system, and the expansion and integration of the police and army, white citizens grew emboldened and became more brazen in their assaults on blacks. A comparison of archival files devoted to "Native assaults" before and after the 1940s suggests that random killings, unprovoked murders and lethal forms of labor control in the farming areas all escalated, matching a surge in complaints about lethal police violence against Africans.[20] Officials in the Native Affairs bureaucracies and the Department of Justice had frequently intervened on the behalf of farm workers in the 1920s and 1930s, reflecting three entwined phenomena in the inter-War years: the lingering paternalist sensibilities of public officials; white farmers' vulnerabilities to the vagaries of the era's "free market"; and the willingness of blacks to make use of the courts. All three diminished sharply after 1948. South Africa's expanding civil service became rapidly "Afrikanerized" in the 1950s, a policy that served as the foundation of the proletarian perks that led to the rapid reduction of white poverty after the Second World War. Personnel who dealt directly with Africans – particularly those in the "Bantu Affairs" bureaucracies that controlled matters such as

African education, the labor bureau system and the administration of the "Bantu Courts" system – soon acquired a fearsome reputation for crude racism and uncritical support for Apartheid policies. Coupling the modernization of agriculture to the Afrikanerization of an authoritarian state apparatus effectively trapped blacks and severely restricted their ability to seek relief in the courts. However, one source observes, the gradual displacement of labor tenancy by impersonal capitalist relations in the rural areas weakened whites' ability to manipulate and control black workers and "opened the way for reactive violence."[21] The days of "reactive violence," however, were a long way off – until the 1970s, black workers in the mines and rural areas remained vulnerable to capricious and occasionally deadly violence.

Nevertheless, unofficial violence in the post-Second World War era adhered to the foundational pattern examined in this book. Institutional violence and private violence escalated, yet communal and spectacle violence did not emerge. Given the racist religious socialization that saturated Afrikaner community, it is conceivable that the use of private violence to exert control and assert a violent white masculinity over Africans could have become *de rigueur* in the most reactionary *platteland* regions. An American cleric who visited South Africa in 2005 recounted a conversation with a contrite Afrikaner theologian: "When I visited apartheid South Africa sixteen years ago, an Afrikaner Christian told me he remembered sermons from his childhood in which the Zulus were compared with Amalekites, with the same implied divine mandate of extermination."[22] To South Africa's good fortune, such theological views about racial violence did not seize the popular imagination. Afrikaners were socialized to submit to the authority of the Apartheid state. Lacking either a sacred or a profane "mandate of extermination," the Apartheid bureaucracy labored to "rationally" displace millions of Africans from inside "white South Africa" to "Bantustans" where all the elements of "structural violence" – poverty, landlessness, unemployment, malnourishment and easily preventable disease – exacted an immense toll on the rural population.

It was only after the Sharpeville massacre in March 1960 that the bureaucratic culture of violence reached its full dimensions. By this time, the National Party government had broadened its appeal within the white population and, having purged liberal ideology and Afrikaner nay-sayers from the civil service, unleashed the full repressive potential of the state it controlled. Its former obsession with perfecting the machinery of labor control broadened and merged with "internal security," the rallying cry that so transformed the regime in the 1960s and 1970s that many scholars have described Apartheid in this period as a "police" or "totalitarian" state.[23] In response to the popular black insurrection after June 1976, the security apparatus definitively eclipsed the labor control specialists within the state. In the 1980s, the ascent of "securocrats" spawned a complex bureaucratic apparatus, effectively a shadow government, that sought with increasing desperation and confusion to counterbalance "repression" with political and administrative "reforms" that were designed to simultaneously preserve white supremacy and fracture mass opposition to Apartheid. New phenomena underscored the extensive transformation of the bureaucratic state: death squads, political assassinations and sinister "third forces" furtively emerged to sow death and confound the regime's opponents. These agents of death enjoyed the support of the state until the historic elections that finally terminated Apartheid in 1994. The bulk of the TRC's work would be devoted to exposing and documenting how violent civil servants had killed, maimed and tortured in the name of Apartheid.

The South

Dramatic events in the 1950s and 1960s would confirm that the NAACP's "legalist" strategy had found a vital chink in the segregation fortress. Yet, in the course of breaking the Solid South in the nation's courts, the NAACP also inadvertently handed white Southerners a strategy for defending the resilient remains of white supremacy. Die-hard segregationists borrowed the NAACP's legal strategy but turned it on its head: because the NAACP's strategy hinged around judicial activism and social engineering, white Southerners set out to hobble the state. This strategy would become known as "starving the beast" during the presidency of Ronald Reagan.[24] White Southerners incubated this strategy in the course of the ten years it took for conflict over the desegregation of schools to subside. This development underscored the contrast between the resolutely statist orientations that defined racial domination in South Africa and the ambiguous relationship of state and civil society in the United States. In South Africa, the state intensified the oppression of blacks after the Second World War but, from 1994 onward, would become the central player in redressing the legacies of Apartheid. In the United States, an activist court in the late 1950s and 1960s tilted the scales in favor of African Americans before a conservative reaction set in. Beginning with the election of Ronald Reagan in the presidential election of 1980, government policies gradually acceded to Southern pressure by steadily returning racial matters to the realm of "local government" and civil society. Buried within the victory of the civil rights movement, therefore, were the seeds of a conservative revolt that would obscure the systemic structure of racial domination and transform it into a matter of individual "discrimination" and "prejudice."

That revolt began with *Brown v Board of Education*. By ordering racial desegregation in public schools, *Brown v Board of Education* made the resocialization of white children the centerpiece of the attack on segregation, striking a vital nerve amongst virtually all Southern whites. By the mid-1950s, however, the manufacturers and commercial businessmen who now dominated the Southern economy feared the economic and political consequences of the region's lynch culture. Lynching had virtually ceased by this time. Gone were the festive ceremonies and gruesome rituals of human sacrifice. As in South Africa, it was now difficult to distinguish between private lynching and common murder, and even these now aroused strong public criticism in the press. Employers hastened to condemn them because leaders in the civil rights and labor movements latched on to every suspicious death "at the hands of persons unknown" as fodder for their increasingly united cause. The federal government, too, was increasingly willing to investigate the murder of African Americans, sending a chill down killers who feared the costs and adverse publicity of a federal trial. Meanwhile, as lynching disappeared, capital punishment began to increase. Whether or not capital punishment served as a "substitute" for racial lynching, the development clearly transferred the killing of African Americans from civil society to the state.[25] The bacchanalian rituals of lynching were displaced by the clinical procedures used to administer death within the confines of the state prison – historically the preferred means for exacting racial vengeance against blacks in South Africa. At the same time, suspicious murders and the mass lynching in 1946 of four African Americans near Monroe, Georgia, revealed that at least some whites were still prepared to lynch African Americans.[26]

Court-ordered desegregation exposed the fissures that marked the South after the Second World War.[27] On the one hand, the new hegemonic elites feared that "violence was bad for business" and unveiled non-violent movements to challenge or delay desegregation for as long as possible. Prominent members of white society – local plantation owners, bankers, doctors, lawyers, legislators, preachers, teachers and merchants – responded to desegregation by establishing reactionary "White Citizens Councils" (WCC) across the South in 1954. Two years later, US Senator Harry F. Byrd sparked the "massive resistance" campaign against the desegregation of Virginia's schools. In Mississippi, Governor J.P. Coleman established the Mississippi State Sovereignty Commission to ferret out and publicize information, including innuendo and outright falsehoods, about "race agitators" and "subversives." These responses to the *Brown* ruling were self-consciously middle-class and non-violent. For example, one WCC leader advised whites to "keep and pitch our battle on a high plane ... keep our ranks free from the demagogue, the renegade, the lawless and the violent ..."[28] In practice, however, these representatives of the white middle class either participated in or turned a blind eye to an explosion of Klan violence. In just the five years after *Brown v Board of Education*, no fewer than 530 suspected cases of Klan violence against African Americans in eleven Southern states were recorded, including twenty-seven bombings in 1959 alone.[29] In effect, a symbiosis emerged amongst a slew of institutions and movements, blurring the differences between the "manicured Kluxism" of the WCCs and the crudity of terrorist violence.[30]

The South, it seemed, had reverted to the violence of the Reconstruction era when leading citizens had taken charge of popular violence. This was only partly the case, however. The terrorist violence of the 1950s and 1960s bore none of the public brazenness of the earlier period when, for example, Ben "Pitchfork" Tillman, governor of South Carolina (1890–94) and later

US Senator (1895–1918), could publically admit, "We have done our level best [to prevent blacks from voting] ... we have scratched our heads to find out how we could eliminate the last one of them. We stuffed ballot boxes. We shot them. We are not ashamed of it."[31] The *Brown* decision triggered a paroxysm of terror from the symbiotic union of white citizens and state officials, but not again would extra-legal violence exude such bravado.

To African Americans, *Brown* indisputably confirmed that the "Second Reconstruction" which the insouciant mood of the 1940s had sparked was underway. However, in deference to popular white opinion in the South, the Supreme Court had carefully stipulated that desegregation should be undertaken "with all deliberate speed" instead of "forthwith," as Thurmond Marshall, the NAACP attorney, had unsuccessfully sought to insert in the Court's decision. White Southerners understood the legal implications of the difference and exploited every opportunity to retard the desegregation of schools. Reed Sarratt writes in *The Ordeal of Desegregation* that Southern states adopted almost 500 measures to get around *Brown*.[32] Desegregation slowed down to a crawl in most Southern school districts, denying the *Brown* ruling a clear and resounding encore. Something more tangible and immediate than *Brown* was needed to harness the energy and optimism that the ruling had stoked.[33]

Perhaps appropriately, the spark came with a particularly poignant lynching. On 27 August 1955, one year after the *Brown* ruling, Emmett Till, a fourteen-year-old boy from Chicago on vacation in Money, Mississippi, was mutilated and shot to death by two white men, J. W. Milam and Roy Bryant, who then threw his corpse into a river. Emmett Till was murdered for "talking sassy" to, and perhaps whistling at, a white woman named Carolyn Bryant, the wife of Roy Bryant. The lynching, the dignified rage of Mamie Till Bradley, Emmett's mother – who insisted on an open-casket funeral so that the world could witness her son's grotesque disfigurement – and the subsequent acquittal of Milam and Bryant provoked a sense of national mourning that placed Southern white apologists on the defensive. As Clenora Hudson-Weems has convincingly argued, more than any other single event, the lynching of Emmett Till "was the real catalytic event" that unleashed the modern civil rights movement.[34]

By insisting on displaying to the public her son's pulverized face, which she insisted the mortician should leave untouched, Mamie Till Bradley overturned the historic meaning that leapt from photographs of lynch victims – "niggers should stay in their place." One of Emmett Till's killers used exactly that phrase in a confessional interview he sold to a newspaper for $4,000 once the all-white jury had safely acquitted him. Roy Bryant said, "I'm no bully; I never hurt a nigger in my life. I like niggers in their place. I know how to work 'em. But I just decided it was time to put a few people on notice. As long as I live and can do anything about it, niggers are going to stay in their place."[35] In the end, Emmett Till would not stay in his place in the muddy waters of the Tallahatchie River. Photographs of his face were published widely in the African American press until it became the single most riveting image and a searing emblem of what black Southerners continued to endure in the 1950s. Mamie Till Bradley, a headline in an African American newspaper summarized, "had opened a casket and opened our eyes."[36]

Southern resistance to desegregation provoked a dramatic constitutional crisis with long-lasting consequences. In 1957, the recalcitrant governor of Arkansas opposed school desegregation by mobilizing the state's National Guard. In response, President Eisenhower dispatched units of the 101st Airborne Division to Little Rock, federalized the Arkansas National Guard and ordered its troops to their barracks. Rather than comply with federal authority, Southern states established "segregation academies" (private schools for whites only) and starved public schools of funds. The logic behind this early response to *Brown* was prophetic and presaged the fate of contemporary race relations in the United States. Southern whites contended that because *Brown v Board of Education* applied only to state schools, whites were free to pursue their racist goals in private institutions they established in civil society. Perhaps remarkably, but in light of similar developments in the first half of the century, not surprisingly, working-class white families willingly agreed to impose a voluntary tax on themselves to avoid racial integration.[37]

Long opposed to "government meddling" in their "private affairs," white Southerners in the era of the Cold War had found another Cause. Religious arguments had once sustained the lynching of the "black-beast rapist." They now came to focus on "big government," a new menace that only a return to "local rule" and "states rights" could combat. The new discourse broadened the conservative attack on *Brown* to include a comprehensive assault on the very principle of judicial activism and interventionist government on the grounds that these, too, were "part of a Soviet-sponsored plan to foment social, economic and political upheaval in the region."[38] What began as a movement against the narrow issue of desegregation expanded into a broad assault on seemingly unrelated issues: bans on school prayer, affirmative action, land-use policies, property rights, reproductive rights, environmental policies, and so on. Wherever the hand of the federal government was, conservative opposition was sure to follow, forcing the issue out of federal control and placing it in the hands of local government officials. By the 1980s, race – the issue that had generated "massive resistance" in the 1950s – was lost in the sweep of issues that conservatives targeted.

In 1980, Ronald Reagan rode to victory in the presidential election and won the support of white Southerners largely on the promise that he would "starve the beast" of big government. For many white Southerners who had been reared in households haunted by the bogeyman of the "black-beast rapist," the racial subtext was clear: in practice, "starve the beast" was another way to prolong whiteness.

***

The legacies of South Africa's bureaucratic culture of violence and the Southern lynch culture therefore seem paradoxical. South Africa's bureaucratic tradition inflated a state that a mass movement would eventually "capture," hold accountable for the violent past and use to broaden democracy. In the United States, a federal state that had tolerated a lynch tradition would resist such "capture" by the African American minority. By transforming a fundamental fault line in American society into just another "interest group" issue, white Southerners denied the nation as a whole the opportunity to reconcile with the violent past.

Notes

Chapter 1

1 James Allen (ed.), *Without Sanctuary: Lynching Photography in America* (Twin Palms, 2000).
2 "A Senate apology for history on lynching," *New York Times* (14 June 2005).
3 Elliot Gorn, "Professing history: Distinguishing between memory and past," *Chronicle of Higher Education* (28 April 2000), B4–5.
4 Bill Nasson, *Abraham Esau's War: A Black South African War in the Cape, 1899–1902* (Cambridge University Press, 2003).
5 Ivan Evans, *Bureaucracy and Race: Native Administration in South Africa* (California University Press, 1996), 13.
6 The TRC has spawned a barrage of scholarly analysis. One of the more acclaimed of these studies is Antjie Krog's *Country of My Skull: Guilt, Sorrow, and the Limits of Forgiveness in the New South Africa* (Times Books, 1999).
7 The word "segregation" has somewhat different connotations in the USA and South Africa. Segregation in the American South originated in the 1870s and 1880s and lasted until the 1960s. By convention, scholars agree that "segregation" in South Africa began in 1910, when British and Boer (Afrikaner) territories were joined to form the Union of South Africa, and ended in 1948, when the period known as Apartheid began. This book focuses on the formative decades of segregation in both racial orders and therefore covers the period between the 1870s and 1940.
8 Donald Horowitz, *The Deadly Ethnic Riot* (University of California Press, 2001), 17–28.
9 For excellent reviews of the voluminous literature on lynching see William Brundage, *Lynching in the New South: Georgia and Virginia 1890–1930* (University of Illinois Press, 1993), 1–17; and William Brundage (ed.), *Under Sentence of Death: Lynching in the South* (University of North Carolina Press, 1997), 1–20. For the impact that lynching continues to have on American politics and culture, see Joel Williamson, "Wounds Not Scars: Lynching, the National Conscience, and the American Historian," *The Journal of American History*, 83/4 (March, 1997), and Jonathan Markovitz, *Legacies of Lynching: Racial Violence and Memory* (University of Minnesota Press, 2004).
10 Albie Sachs, *Justice in South Africa* (University of California Press, 1973), 71. The "Steynsdorp affairs" may be the only documented case of an iconic, Southern-style spectacle lynching in colonial South Africa. In 1910, an African was arrested for allegedly murdering his employer and his wife in the eastern Transvaal. A mob of white men broke into the prison and lynched the man

from a tree. Seven men were arrested but were found not guilty by a judge who accepted their story that "the nigger must have hanged himself, and then carted down his own body and buried it of his own free will." (Neville Edwards, *The Transvaal in War and Peace* [H. Virtue, 1900], 251–252).

11 Brundage, *Lynching in the New South*, 17–48.

12 Christopher Waldrep, "War of words: The controversy over the definition of lynching, 1899–1940," *Journal of Southern History*, 66/1 (February 2000), 75–77.

13 Sachs, *Justice in South Africa*, 173.

14 Brundage, *Lynching in the New South*, 15.

15 The massacre of unarmed members of a religious sect at Bulhoek is examined in Robert Edgar, *Because They Chose the Plan of God: The Story of the Bulhoek Massacre* (Ravan Press, 1988).

16 Ralph Ellison, *Going to the Territory* (Random House, 1986), 107.

17 These anthropological sources are ably summarized in Orlando Patterson, *Rituals of Blood: Consequences of Slavery in Two American Centuries* (Basic Civitas Books, 1998), 171–174.

18 John H. Moore, *Carnival of Blood: Dueling, Lynching, and Murder in South Carolina, 1880–1920* (University of South Carolina Press, 2006), 56.

19 Nigel Worden and Clifton Crais, "Introduction," in Worden and Crais (eds), *Breaking the Chains: Slavery and its Legacy in the Nineteenth-Century Cape Colony* (Witwatersrand University Press, 1994).

20 Brundage, *Lynching in the New South*, 51.

21 Philip Dray, "The killing season: A history of lynching in America," *The New Crisis*, 109/1 (January–February 2002), 41; James Elbert Cutler, *Lynch-law: An Investigation into the History of Lynching in the United States* (Negro Universities Press, 1969), 12.

22 Eugene Genovese, *The Slaveholders' Dilemma: Freedom and Progress in Southern Conservative Thought, 1820–1860* (University of South Carolina Press, 1992), 53. Also see James Messerschmidt, "Men victimizing men: The case of lynching, 1865–1900," in Lee H. Bowker (ed.) *Masculinities and Violence* (Sage, 1998), 125–151.

23 William D. Carrigan. *The Making of a Lynching Culture: Violence and Vigilantism in Central Texas, 1836–1916* (University of Illinois Press, 2004).

24 Jeremy Krikler, *White Rising: The 1922 Insurrection and Racial Killing in South Africa* (Manchester University Press, 2005). Also see Jeremy Krikler, "The inner mechanics of a South African racial massacre," *The Historical Journal*, 42/14 (1999).

25 Southern Commission on the Study of Lynching, *Lynchings and What They Mean* (Atlanta, Ga., 1931), 10.

26 For more on the distinction between lynching and race riots, see Horowitz, *The Deadly Ethnic Riot*, 90–91 and 479–482. Jeremy Krikler presents an excellent analysis of the 1922 "racial pogrom" in *White Rising*, 130–152.

27 Clifford Geertz, quoted in Theda Skocpol and Margaret Somers, "The uses of comparative history in macrosocial inquiry," *Comparative Studies in Society and History*, 22/3 (April 1980), 179. For a study that explores the self-conscious cultural "conversation" between the two countries, see Rob Nixon, *Homelands, Harlem, and Hollywood: South African Culture and the World Beyond* (Routledge, 1994).

28 James Campbell, "Models and metaphors: Industrial education in the United

States and South Africa," in Ran Greenstein (ed.), *Comparative Perspectives on South Africa* (Basingstoke, 1998), 90; also cited in Shula Marks, "*White Supremacy.* A review article," *Comparative Studies in Society and History*, 29/2 (April 1987).

29 George Fredrickson, *White Supremacy. A Comparative Study in American and South African History* (Oxford University Press, 1981), 251–252.

30 Stanley Greenberg, *Race and State in Capitalist Development: Comparative Perspectives* (Yale University Press, 1980).

31 Anthony Marx, *Making Race and Nation: A Comparison of South Africa, the United States and Brazil* (Cambridge University Press, 1998), 141–143 and passim.

32 Maurice Evans, *Black and White in the Southern States: A Study of the Race Problem in the United States from a South African Point of View* (University of South Carolina Press, [1915], 2001).

33 John Cell, *The Highest Stage of Supremacy: The Origins of Segregation in South Africa and the American South* (Cambridge University Press, 1982), 118. Also see Kenneth Vickery, "'Herrenvolk' democracy and egalitarianism in South Africa and the U.S. South," *Comparative Studies in Society and History*, 16/3 (June 1974).

34 Ian Ochiltree, "'A just and self-respecting system?' Black independence, share-cropping, and paternalistic relations in the American South and South Africa," *Agricultural History*, 72/2 (Spring 1998). Also see Charles van Onselen, "Paternalism and Violence on the Maize Farms of the South-Western Transvaal, 1900–1950," in Alan Jeeves and Jonathan Crush (eds), *White Farms, Black Labor: The State and Agrarian Change in Southern Africa* (Heinemann, 1997).

35 John Higginson, "Hell in small places: Agrarian elites and collective violence in the western Transvaal, 1900–1907," *Journal of Social History*, 35/1 (Fall 2001); John Higginson, "Upending the century of wrong: Agrarian elites, collective violence, and the transformation of state power in the American South and South Africa, 1865–1914," *Social Identities*, 4/3 (October 1998); John Higginson and Christoph Strobel, "The instrument of terror: Some thoughts on comparative historiography, white rural unofficial violence, and segregation in South Africa and the American South," *Safundi*, 11 (July 2003); and C. Strobel, "We are all armed and ready: Reactionary insurgency movements and the formation of segregated states in the American South and in South Africa," *North Carolina Historical Review*, 80/4 (October 2003), 430–452. Also see Sheila Smith McKoy, *When Whites Riot: Writing and Violence in American and South African Cultures* (University of Wisconsin, 2001).

36 George Fredrickson, "Reflections on the twenty-fifth anniversary of the publication of *White Supremacy*," *Safundi*, 21 (January 2006), 4.

37 Martin Murray, "'The natives are always stealing': White vigilantes and the 'reign of terror' in the Orange Free State, 1918–24," *The Journal of African History*, 30/1 (1989).

38 Rob Turrell, *White Mercy: A Study of the Death Penalty in South Africa* (Praeger, 2004).

39 Smith, *When Whites Riot*, passim.

40 Krikler, *White Rising*, 147.

41 Brundage, *Lynching in the New South*, 7.

42 Glenn Feldman, *The Disfranchisement Myth: Poor Whites and Suffrage Restric-

tion in Alabama (University of Georgia Press, 2004).

43 In economics, a resource is considered rivalrous if its consumption by one party prevents other parties from gaining access to it.

44 David Yudelman, *The Emergence of Modern South Africa: State, Capital and the Incorporation of Organized Labor on the South African Goldfleids, 1902–1939* (Greenwood Press, 1983).

45 Ken Luckhardt and Brenda Wall, *Organize Or Starve! The History of the South African Congress of Trade Unions* (International Publishers, 1980), 32.

46 Edna Bonacich, "Capitalism and race relations in South Africa: A split labor market analysis," *Political Power and Social Theory*, 2 (1981), 239–277.

47 Anthony D. Smith, *Chosen Peoples: Sacred Sources of National Identity* (Oxford University Press, 2003).

48 David Goldfield, *Still Fighting the Civil War: The American South and Southern History* (Louisina State University, 2002), 43.

49 Charles R. Wilson, *Baptized in Blood: The Religion of the Lost Cause, 1865–1920* (University of Georgia Press, 1980).

50 The poem "Strange Fruit" was written by Abel Meeropol but became the signature song of the great singer Billie Holiday after she first recorded it in 1939 (David Margolick, *Strange Fruit. Billie Holiday, Café Society and an Early Cry for Civil Rights* [Running Press, 2000], 15).

51 Smith, *Chosen Peoples*, 78–85.

52 The high levels of violence in Southern states have been extensively analysed in the literature. For example, see Edgar L. Ayers, *Vengeance and Justice: Crime and Punishment in the 19th-Century South* (Oxford University Press, 1984); Bertram Wyatt-Brown, *Southern Honor: Ethics and Behavior in the Old South* (Oxford University Press, 1984); Kenneth S. Greenberg, *Honor and Slavery. Lies, Duels, Noses, Masks, Dressing as a Woman, Gifts, Strangers, Humanitarianism, Death, Slave Rebellions, the Proslavery Argument, Baseball, Hunting, and Gambling in the Old South* (Princeton University Press, 1996).

53 Max Gluckman, "Inter-hierarchical roles," in Marc J. Swartz (ed.), *Local-Level Politics: Social and Cultural Perspectives* (University of London Press, 1969).

54 For a review of comparative methods, see Skocpol and Somers, "The uses of comparative history in macrosocial inquiry."

55 Two opposite trends confirm this observation. On the one hand, the earlier importance attributed to ideological differences between Afrikaner liberals in the Cape and reactionaries in the Northern provinces has gradually lost its cachet amongst scholars, who invariably locate the political center of gravity in gold mining areas of the Transvaal. On the other hand, the discovery of important differences within the "black box" of the state by the "Poulantzian school" in the 1980s was heralded as a major theoretical contribution to the field. John Lazar discusses the Cape/Northern conflict in Afrikaner politics in "Verwoerd versus the 'visionaries': The South African Bureau of Racial Affairs (Sabra), 1948–1962," in Phil Bonner, Peter Delius and Debora Posel (eds), *Apartheid's Genesis, 1935–1962* (Witwatersrand University Press, 1993). For a review of the "Poulantzian school" in South African historiography, see David Yudelman, *The Emergence of Modern South Africa*, 30–32.

56 Brundage, *Lynching in the New South*, Chapter 1.

57 All references beginning with the following abbreviations are located at the National Archives Repository, 24 Hamilton Street, Pretoria: BAO, GG, GNLB, GOV, JUS, LD, PMO, PM, URU. All newspaper clippings with references that

include "Box 444, A1913 (JPL)" are located at the William Cullen Library, University of the Witswatersrand.

58 Shula Marks, "*White Supremacy*: A review article"; John Breuilly, *Labour and Liberalism in Nineteenth-Century Europe. Essays in Comparative History* (Manchester university Press, 1992), "Introduction."

59 This study does not address "black on white" violence. There is a sturdy body of work written in the "repression and resistance" mold for the South African case. For example, see Anthony Marx, *Lessons of Struggle: South African Internal Opposition, 1960–1990* (Oxford University Press, 1992). For the American case, Steven Hahn excels in illustrating how African Americans occasionally resisted lynch mobs. See Steven Hahn, *A Nation Under Our Feet: Black Political Struggles in the Rural South, From Slavery to the Great Migration* (Belknap Press of Harvard University Press, 2003).

60 Brundage, *Lynching in the New South*, 5.

61 Ronald Takaki, *Regeneration Through Violence: The Mythology of the American Frontier, 1600–1860* (Wesleyan University Press, 1973). Also see Allen D. Grimshaw, "Lawlessness and violence in America and their special manifestations in changing Negro–White relationships," *Journal of Negro History*, 44/1 (1959).

62 Richard Hofstadter, "Reflections on violence in the United States," in Richard Hofstadter and Michael Wallace (eds), *American Violence: A Documentary History* (Vintage Books, 1971), 5–6.

63 William Beinart, "Political and collective violence in Southern African historiography," *Journal of Southern African Studies*, 18/3 (September 1992).

64 Fanon, cited in Beinart, "Political and collective violence in Southern African historiography," 482.

65 Randall Kennedy, "Martin Luther King's constitution: A legal history of the Montgomery Bus Boycott," *Yale Law Journal*, 98 (April 1989).

66 Tony Dunbar and Linda Kravitz, *Hard Traveling: Migrant Farm Workers in America* (Ballinger Publishing Co., 1976), 261; Rodolfo Acuna, *Occupied America: The Chicano's Struggle Toward Liberation* (Canfield Press, 1972), 54.

67 William D. Carrigan and Clive Webb, "The lynching of persons of Mexican origin or descent in the US, 1848–1929," *The Journal of Social History*, 37/2 (Winter 2003).

68 Clive Webb, "The lynching of Sicilian immigrants in the American South, 1886–1910," *American Nineteenth Century History*, 3/1 (Spring 2002), 45–46.

69 Webb, "The lynching of Sicilian immigrants," 45.

70 Noel Ignatiev, *How the Irish Became White* (Routledge, 1995).

71 Milton Shain, *The Roots of Antisemitism in South Africa* (University Press of Virginia, 1994).

Chapter 2

1 For evidence that whites did not view black sexuality as a threat in the antebellum period in both contexts see Dianne Miller Sommerville, *Race and Race in the Nineteenth-Century South* (University of North Carolina Press, 2004), and J. C. Martens, "Settler homes, manhood and 'houseboys': An analysis of Natal's rape scare of 1886," *Journal of Southern African Studies*, 28, 2 (June 2002).

2 Forrest Wood, cited in Patterson, *Rituals of Blood*, 174. F. Wood, *Black Scare: The Racist Response to Emancipation and Reconstruction* (University of California Press, 1970).

3 Patterson, *Rituals of Blood*, 183.

4 Stewart Tolnay and E. M. Beck, *A Festival of Violence: An Analysis of Southern Lynchings, 1882–1930* (University of Illinois Press, 1995) and "The killing fields of the Deep South: The market for cotton and the lynching of Blacks, 1882–1930," *American Sociological Review*, 55 (August 1990).

5 Howard Odum, *Race and Rumors of Race: The American South in the Early Forties* (Johns Hopkins University Press, 1997), 5. For a study that confirms the importance of rumor in racial violence in South Africa, see Jeremy Krikler, "Social neurosis and hysterical pre-cognition in South Africa: A case-study and reflections," *Journal of Social History* (1995).

6 Ann Stoler, "Making empire respectable: The politics of race and sexual morality in 20th-century colonial cultures," *American Ethnologist*, 16/4 (November 1989), 634–660.

7 Elizabeth Hale, *Making Whiteness: The Culture of Segregation in the South, 1890-1940* (Pantheon Books, 1998), 112.

8 Jacquelyn Dowd Hall, "The mind that burns in each body: Women, rape and racial violence." In Anne Snitow, Christine Stansell, and Sharon Thompson (eds), *Powers of Desire: The Politics of Sexuality* (Monthly Review Press, 1983); Gareth Cornwall, "George Hardy's *Black Peril* and the meaning of the 'Black Peril' in 20th century South Africa," *Journal of Southern African Studies*, 22/3 (1996).

9 Jock McCullough, *Black Peril, White Virtue: Sexual Crime in Southern Rhodesia, 1902–1935* (Indiana University Press, 2000), 11.

10 Ann Stoler, "Carnal knowledge and imperial power: Gender, race and morality in colonial Asia." In Micaela di Leonardo (ed.), *Gender At The Crossroads: Feminist Anthropology in the Postmodern Era* (University of California Press, 1991), 51–101; McCulloch, *Black Peril, White Virtue*, 11.

11 See Pamela Scully, "Rape, race, and colonial culture: The sexual politics of identity in the nineteenth-century Cape Colony, South Africa," *The American Historical Review* (1995).

12 Michelle Brittain, *The Politics of Whiteness: Race, Workers and Culture in the Modern South* (Princeton University Press, 2001); Jonathan Hyslop, "White working-class women and the invention of Apartheid: 'Purified' Afrikaner Nationalist agitation for legislation against 'Mixed' Marriages, 1934–9," *The Journal of African History*, 36 (1995).

13 This theme is explored in Chapter 7.

14 Hall, "The mind that burns in each body," 9.

15 Ida B. Wells, *On Lynchings: Southern Horrors, A Red Record, Mob Rule in New Orleans* (Arno Press, 1969), 45–48.

16 Wells, *Red Record*, 45–48.

17 Wells, *Red Record*, 2–11.

18 Brundage, *Lynching in the New South*, 64.

19 Reprinted in Joe W. Trotter and Earl Lewis (eds), *African Americans in the Industrial Age: A Documentary History, 1915–1945* (Northeastern University Press, 1996), 209–217.

20 McCullough, *Black Peril, White Virtue*, 31.

21 "Kaffir outrages on white women" were a rare but widely-feared and incendi-

ary preoccupation in colonial Natal. It was an article of faith among white settlers that many (perhaps a majority of) assault cases did not reach the courts because of the ineradicable odium attached to the very notion of any form of sexual contact with blacks. Colonial records indicate that very few attacks reached the courts: a total of 17 cases were recorded between 1866 and 1873. In fact, most sex attack cases were recorded under different categories, making it difficult to distinguish such attacks from other criminal offences in colonial law: vagrancy, attempted housebreaking, or breaking and entering. Vagrancy laws were used to convict Africans "found outside a female's bedroom window", while another was sentenced to jail for "breaking with unlawful intent", although he was strongly suspected of planning a rape. African domestic servants posed a problem for a society that simultanesouly demanded cheap labor but feared the bodies of Africans. The law was vigilant and elastic on this score. Domestic employees were expected to keep their distance from the bedroom and persons of white females and were taught to avoid any ambiguous encounters. "Touching" a white female or merely looking at her with impropriety was enough to obtain a jail sentence with hard labor, while entering a bedroom was sufficient evidence of intention to rape. See Norman Etherington, "Natal's black rape scare of the 1870s," *Journal of Southern African Studies*, 15 (1988); Jeremy Martens, "Settler homes, manhood and 'houseboys.'" Also see John Pape, "Black and white: The perils of sex in southern Rhodesia," *Journal of Southern African Studies*, 16 (1990).

22 This summary and much of the discussion that follows is taken from material in the following files: LD1448 1957/07, LD1448 1957/369/369 and NA181 1/1912/F472. All archival material cited in this chapter is located in the National Archives Repository, 24 Hamilton Street, Pretoria, South Africa.

23 Clipping from *Leader*, 22 January 1903 in LD263 73/03. The *Leader* kept the Commissioner of Police busy with a series of similar articles in the years after the war. A number of alarmist articles that appeared in the newspaper may have contributed to the growing concern about sexual attacks by blacks, but left the Commissioner increasingly skeptical. For example, the newspaper reported on 22 January 1903 that a black man accused of assaulting a white woman had been lynched by a "Vigilance Committee" in Johannesburg. Investigations initiated by the Commissioner established that the death was a "confirmed suicide." See Commissioner of Police to The Secretary, Law Department, 6 January 1905, in LD263 73/920.

24 Dozens of letters landed on the desks of the Department of Justice, Native Affairs, members of parliament and the South African Police. In addition, private individuals collected signatures and dispatched these to the authority most likely to heed warnings about Black Peril. Since all of these communications are gathered in one fat folder, it suffices to reference that folder: LD263 73/920.

25 James Henderson to SNA, 14 October 1908, in LD14487 1957/07.

26 The Districts Bestuur 'Het Volk' Witwatersrand, 21 January 1907, in LD14487 1957/07.

27 Transvaal Farmers' Association to the Attorney General of the Transvaal, 24 October 1908 in LD14487 1957/07.

28 Guild of Loyal Women of South Africa to Governor-General, 10 February 1911, in LD14487 1957/07. Persistent evidence indicates that vengeance was not the primary motivation behind the formation of the Vigilance Society or its activi-

ties. The motive was more utilitarian – what the citizens of the Turffontein area desired was a stepped-up police presence to protect them from the black areas. After interviewing the local police and residents in the area, the *Leader* concluded that "the [police] force is fully 50 percent under the requirements of the district": "During the past few years suburbs have sprung up like mushrooms, and the fact is that the police authorities have not kept pace with the times …" Wyndham, the member of parliament for the Turffontein who had apprised the police and Minister of Justice of the rape and death of the woman, levelled such criticism against the police for neglecting his constituency that the police responded by comparing the police-to-population ratio of the southern suburbs not only to the metropolitan areas of Johannesburg and Cape Town but to the London metropolitan area as well. The early arrest of Jacobs did not entirely mollify the men of Turffontein. Because of the quick arrest of the man responsible for the Black Peril scare, the Vigilance Society downgraded its *raison d'être*. Formed to protect women against Black Peril, the Society directed its energies towards much less urgent tasks – chasing off members of the Amalaita gang and ferreting out pass law violators.

29 For a summation of this correspondence dealing with these issues, see Acting Secretary, Native Affairs, to the Private Secretary to the Attorney General, 29 June 1908, in LD14487 1957/07.

30 Gladstone's role in Black Peril cases in Rhodesia is well analyzed by McCullough in *Black Peril, White Virtue*. Gladstone was painfully aware that Labour Party parliament members in England were prone to seize on any report of injustice towards Africans and were quick to fire off letters demanding clarifications and confirmations about allegations of assaults against Africans. Complaining privately that these allegations were "tiresome and expensive to substantiate," Gladstone reassured the English Parliament that whites found guilty of attacking Africans would be prosecuted "to the fullest extent of the law."

31 James Thompson (Mayor of Johannesburg) to Secretary of the Rand Pioneers, 26 September 1908, in LD14487 1957/07. Also see "Record of Business transaction at a Meeting of the Representatives of the Various Municipalities on the Rand and the Rand Pioneers," 4 October 1908, and "Resolution of the Presbyterian Branch of the Pretoria Mothers' Union, June 1907," in Ibid.

32 Secretary of the Transvaal Municipal Association to Assistant Colonial Secretary, 18/5/1908, in LD1370 5288/05.

33 "Outrages on white women and girls during March, April and May 1908," in LD1370 5288/06.

34 Turrell, *White Mercy*, 94.

35 For the correspondence between the Secretary of State, London, and Governor Gladstone, see "Lynching – Report re," GOV790 Ps. 81 Vol, 3.

36 This point was made in an exchange of telegrams between the Secretary of the South African Police and "Unicompol" concerning the Southern Suburbs Vigilance Society, Turffontein." See files in LD447 1957/07.

37 Acting Commissioner, South African Police, "Black Peril cases," in LD447 1957/07. The memorandum was prepared for a presentation in parliament by the Minister of Justice.

38 These details are reconstructed from several files and memoranda in LD447 1957/07.

39 "Additional police for Southern Suburbs, Johannesburg," May 1912, in JUS143 3/582/12.

40 Secretary of South Africa Police to Unicompol, 1 May 1912, in JUS143 3/582/11.

41 "Southern Suburbs Vigilance Society, Turffontein," in JUS143 3/582/12.

42 Compol to Minister of Justice, 1 May 1912, in JUS143 3/582/12.

43 "The Turffontein Vigilants – incidents of a recent 'drive,'" *Cape Times*, 3 June 1912, JUS143 3/582/12.

44 This information is taken from documents by John William McDonagh and William Ban Goldsmith, a letter from the Secretary of the Transvaal Police to the The Deputy Commissioner of the Transvaal Police, 7 June 1912, and the *Cape Times* article on "The Turffontein vigilants," all in JUS143 3/582/12.

45 J. S. G. Dougles to The Secretary for the Transvaal Police, 7 June 1912, in LD447 1957/07.

46 J. S. G. Dougles to South Africa Police, 20 June 1912, in LD447 1957/07.

47 H. J. Trent to Resident Magistrate, Pretoria, 13 April 1907 in LD439 1709/07.

48 "A Father," "Shocking crime," Clipping from *The Advertiser*, 19 November 1906, in LD1370 5288/06.

49 See Chapter 8 for a discussion of the legal system in South Africa.

50 Report of the Commission Appointed to Enquire into Assaults on Women (Cape Town, Government Printers, 1913). A draft copy of the report, titled "Commission on Black Peril – Galley One," may also be found in LD1448 1957/07.

51 The 281 witnesses who appeared before the all-white, eight-member Commissioners represented a broad spectrum of society drawn from across racial, class, ideological and religious camps. The majority were white; forty-six were African men, fifteen were white women, and no further mention in the report is made of the several African women "who were also separately examined by the lady members of the commission."

52 This Return is located in a file titled "Drafts and Statistics. Black Peril Commission," in LD447 1599/23. Detailed breakdowns correlate the incidence of the three forms of sexual assaults with race and province.

53 The return reports data under three headings – charges, convictions and sentences. In South Africa, as elsewhere, official data on sexual assaults may be assumed to be unreliable. The number of actual assaults almost always exceeds the numbers recorded in official books, principally because of the victim's reluctance to expose the assault to the public. The predictable inaccuracy of official sexual assault data is heightened by numerous unexplained and dubious fluctuations in the 1913 return. The number of charges brought against white males is a case in point. In 1910, the returns reflect that nine white males were charged with assaults against white women, while twenty-three men were charged with assaults on non-white women. Apparently, a steady reversal took place in the next nine years, for in 1910, eighteen white males were charged with assaults on white women, while only seven were charged with assaulting black women. The most likely explanation is that the data were suspect from the outset and compounded thereafter by changing circumstances. In the case above, it may well be that a double standard came to the fore: white males were more likely to be prosecuted for attacking white women. (Turrell, *White Mercy*, 33.)

54 See Dubow, *Racial Segregation and the Origins of Apartheid in South Africa, 1919–36* (Macmillan, 1988), passim.

55 Brian Willan (ed.), *Sol Plaatje: Selected Writings* (Ohio University Press, 1997), 274–283. A section of the essay, cleverly sub-titled "The Modern Mrs. Potiphar," provided a vignette that would have been the equivalent of a death

certificate in the South. According to the Book of Genesis, Joseph was bought as a household slave by Potiphar. When Potiphar's wife attempted to seduce him, Joseph demurred. The spurned woman falsely accused him of molesting her and had Joseph thrown into prison. The parallel that *The Mote and the Beam* drew between Joseph and a Zulu "domestic servant" employed on a white farm added a twist to the Biblical story. When the farmer's wife tried to seduce him, the Zulu employee confided the matter to the farmer. The farmer then devised a strategem that successfully caught his wife in the act of tempting the black worker. A grateful husband paid the young Zulu man the sum of £5 as a reward. Yet no harm appears to have befallen Plaatje for holding up this story as representative of bedroom antics on white farms.

56 Report of the Commission on Assaults on Women, p. 32, and evidence in Transcripts Assault on Women Commission, K373 1, p. 9.
57 Tolnay and Beck, *Festival of Violence*, 18–19.
58 R. M. Brown, *Strain of Violence: Historical Studies of American Violence and Vigilantism* (Oxford University Press, 1975), 2.

Chapter 3

1 David M. Oshinsky *Worse Than Slavery: Parchman Farm and the Ordeal of Jim Crow Justice* (Free Press, 1996).
2 George Tindall, *The Emergence of the New South, 1913–1945* (Louisiana State University Press, 1967), 521.
3 Greenberg, *Race and State in Capitalist Development*, 216.
4 Greenberg, *Race and State in Capitalist Development*, 215.
5 H. Bond, *Negro Education in Alabama*, quoted in Greenberg, *Race and State in Capitalist Development*, 116.
6 Pete Daniels, *The Shadow of Slavery: Peonage in the South, 1901–1969* (University of Illinois Press, 1972), 82; Kenneth R. Bailey, "A temptation to lawlessness: Peonage in West Virginia, 1903–1908," *West Virginia History*, 50 (1991); Ronald Lewis, "African American convicts in the coal mines of Southern Appalachia." In J. Inscoe (ed.), *Appalachian and Race: The Mountain South from Slavery to Segregation* (University Press of Kentucky, 2001), 263; and Alex Lichtenstein, *Twice the Work of Free Labor: The Political Economy of Convict Labor in the New South* (Verso, 1996).
7 Greenberg, *Race and State in Capitalist Development*, 117.
8 Daniels, *The Shadow of Slavery*, passim.
9 Brundage, *Lynching in the New South*, 257; Hahn, *A Nation Under Our Feet*.
10 Also, as Chapter 4 illustrates, small victories in the Supreme Court seemed to chip away at the Jim Crow Laws around 1915, when the NAACP's campaign for a federal anti-lynch brought national attention to racial violence in the South. In *Guinn v United States* (1915), the Supreme Court alarmed the South by declaring the "grandfather clause" in Oklahoma to be unconstitutional (The Oklahoma law had witheld the vote from any citizen whose ancestors had not been enfranchised in 1860.) In *Buchanan v Worley* (1917), the Court also struck down a Kentucky law that made residential segregation mandatory in urban areas. Powerless to reverse such rulings, Southerners knew that, for all the region's bravado and aggressive posturing, segregation was in fact hostage to the pronouncements of the Supreme Court. Fear that an unsympa-

thetic Court might peer critically into the doctrine of "states right" escalated in the 1930s when the Court began to move "at an ever-accerating pace toward making the negro more and more of a *free man* and less a *freedman*." (Loren Miller, *The Petitioners: The Supreme Court of the Unites States and the Negro* [Pantheon Books, 1966], 433.)

11 Greenberg, *Race and State in Capitalist Development*, 118.

12 Du Bois, *Black Reconstruction: An Essay Toward a History of the Part Which Black Folk Played in the Attempt to Reconstruct Democracy in America* (Atheneum, 1970), 175; Greenberg, *Race and State in Capitalist Development*, 225.

13 Jacquelyn Dowd Hall, *Revolt Against Chivalry: Jessie Daniel Ames and the Women's Campaign Against Lynching* (Columbia University Press, 1979).

14 Jeffrey Goldhagen, *Hitler's Willing Executioners: Ordinary Germans and the Holocaust* (Alfred A. Knopf, 1996).

15 For a discussion of the "growth," "accommodationist" and "Neo-Marxist" approaches to the relationship between industrial development and racial domination, see Greenberg, *Race and State in Capitalist Development*, 131–133, and Gavin Wright, *Old South, New South: Revolutions in the Southern Economy Since the Civil War* (Basic Books, 1986), 50–53.

16 Wright, *Old South, New South*, 58.

17 Greenberg, *Race and State in Capitalist Development*, 215.

18 Sterling D. Spero and Aram L. Harris, *The Black Worker: The Negro and the Labor Movement* (Kennikat Press, 1959), 186.

19 Jay R. Mandle, *The Roots of Black Poverty: The Southern Plantation Economy After the Civil War* (Duke University Press, 1978), 23; W. Levernier, "The determinants of poverty in Georgia's plantation belt: Explaining the differences in measured poverty rates," *The American Journal of Economics and Sociology*, 57/1 (January 1998).

20 Robert D. Ward and William W. Rogers, *Labor Revolt in Alabama: The Great Strike of 1894* (University of Alabama Press, 1965), 22.

21 Idus Newby, *Plain Folk in the New South: Social Change and Cultural Persistence, 1880–1915* (Louisiana State University Press, 1989), 463.

22 This discussion is taken from Brundage, *Lynching in the New South*, passim, but especially 28–30.

23 For more on the differences between the two states, see Figure 1 in Brundage, *Lynching in the New South*, 20.

24 Brundage, *Lynching in the New South*, 141.

25 Brundage, *Lynching in the New South*, 155.

26 See Ralph Ginzberg, *100 Years of Lynching* (Black Classic Press, 1988).

27 Walter White, *Rope and Faggot: A Biography of Judge Lynch* (A. A. Knopf, 1929).

28 Brundage, *Lynching in the New South*, passim.

29 E. Thompson, *Plantation Societies*, cited in Brundage, *Lynching in the New South*, 109.

30 Brundage, *Lynching in the New South*, 110.

31 This point is explored below.

32 Fredrickson, *White Supremacy*, 235.

33 William Cooper and Thomas Terrill, *The American South: A History* (Alfred A. Knopf, 1990), 487. F. Tannenberg, *Darker Phases of the South* (Negro University Press, 1924).

34 White, *Rope and Faggot*, 104–105.

35 Brundage, *Lynching in the New South*, 108.

36 Scott Ellsworth, *Death in a Promised Land: The Tulsa Race Riot of 1921* (Louisiana State University Press, 1982).

37 Taken from Brundage, *Lynching in the New South*, 112–113.

38 Daniels, *The Shadow of Slavery*, 179.

39 Daniels, *The Shadow of Slavery*, 181–182.

40 Daniels, *The Shadow of Slavery*, 184.

41 "a place of residence and work where a large number of like-situated individuals, cut off from the wider society for an appreciable period of time, together lead an enclosed, formally administered round of life." Erving Goffman, *Asylums: Essays on the Social Situation of Mental Patients and Other Inmates* (Anchor Books, 1961), 23.

42 Daniels, *The Shadow of Slavery*, 181–182.

43 Cited in Ginzburg, *100 Years of Lynching*, 10.

44 "Negro burned alive in Florida [sic]; Second Negro then hanged," in Ginzburg, *100 Years of Lynching*, 12.

45 Tolnay and Beck, *Festival of Violence*, 25.

46 "Negro Burned Alive," in Ginzburg, *100 Years of Lynching*, 15; "The Georgia Exhibition," in Ginzburg, *100 Years of Lynching*, 20.

47 Fredrickson, *White Supremacy*, 236; Brian Kelly, *Race, Class and Power in the Alabama Coalfields, 1908–1921* (University of Illinois, Press, 2001), 34; Ronald D. Eller, *Miners, Millhands and Mountaineers: The Industrialization of the Appalachian South, 1889–1930* (University of Tennesse, 1982), 178.

48 David Roediger, *The Wages of Whiteness: Race and the Making of the American Working Class* (Verso, 1991), 13.

49 "Living on the level of the blacks, doing the same work, being treated in much the same way by the landlord, the poor-white tenant has felt even more degraded than he did during slavery times; for then he could stay in the backlands away from humiliation." Shields McIlvaney, *The Southern Poor White: From Lubberland to Tobacco Road* (University of Oklahoma Press, 1939), 167.

50 Displaced black tenants were invariably driven into becoming sharecroppers on plantation lands "where they can be more easily controlled and supervised by managers." Gunnar Myrdal, "The cropper's dilemma," in Allen Weinstein and Frank Gatell, *The Segregation Era, 1863–1954: A Modern Reader* (Oxford University Press, 1970), 205–207.

51 Roediger, *The Wages of Whiteness*, passim.

52 Brittain, *The Politics of Whiteness*, 24. For another view of the material basis of whiteness in the USA, see George Lipsitz, *The Possessive Investment in Whiteness: How White People Profit from Identity Politics* (Temple University Press, 1998). Extensive critiques of "whiteness studies" may be found in Eric Arnesen, "Whiteness and the Historians' Imagination," *International Labor and Working-Class History,* 60 (2001); Peter Kolchin, "Whiteness Studies, "The new history of race in America," *Journal of American History,* 89/1 (2002), 154–173; and Andrew Hartman, "The rise and fall of whiteness studies," *Race and Class,* 46/2 (2004).

53 Du Bois, cited in Donald Nonini, "Du Bois and radical theory and practice," *Critique of Anthropology,* 12/3 (1992), 297.

54 Because the Southern Farmers' Alliance refused to admit them, blacks formed the Colored Farmers' National Alliance and Cooperative Union and the

National Colored Alliance in the late 1880s. A merger between the two groups in 1890 resulted in the formation of the Colored Alliance, boasting a membership of 1,200,000. The two groups cooperated only occasionally, however. The Colored Alliance disappeared after calling for a strike in 1891 that failed to gain support. William F. Holmes, "The Demise of the Colored Farmers' Alliance," *Journal of Southern History*, 41 (May 1975).

55 Michael Kazin, *The Populist Persuasion: An American History* (Basic Books, 1995), 186.

56 Robert A. Margo, *Race and Schooling in the South, 1880–1950* (University of Chicago Press, 1990), 38.

57 J. Morgan Kousser, *The Shaping of Southern Politics: Suffrage Restriction and the Establishment of the One-Party South* (Yale University Press, 1974), 28.

58 Robert Miller, "A Centennial Historiography of American Populism,"*Kansas History: A Journal of the Central Plains* 16/1 (Spring 1993). Miller nevertheless notes that Populism did influence social movements that arose later in the twentieth century.

59 C. Vann Woodward, *Origins of the New South: 1877–1913* (Louisiana State University Press, 1951), 203.

60 Across the South, a forest of state laws and municipal ordinances meticulously identified and defined the precise nooks and crannies where inter-racial contact was proscribed. Public transportation, mental hospitals, barbershops, burial grounds, circus tickets, housing, schools, prisons, telephone booths, child custody arrangements, and "Fishing, Boating and Bathing" were just a few of the concerns written into the Jim Crow laws. See the "Introduction" in J. Dailey, G. Gilmore, and B. Simon (eds), *Jumpin' Jim Crow: Southern Politics from Civil War to Civil Rights* (Princeton University Press, 2000).

61 Glenn Feldman, *The Disfranchisement Myth: Poor Whites and Suffrage Restriction in Alabama* (University of Georgia Press, 2004). Also see C. Vann Woodward, *Origins of the New South, 1877–1913* and *The Strange Career of Jim Crow*, 3rd ed (Oxford University Press, 1974); Kousser, *The Shaping of Southern Politics*; Michael Perman, *Struggle for Mastery: Disfranchisement in the South, 1888–1908* (University of North Carolina Press, 2001). Also see L. Reece, "The poisoned chalice: Electoral reform in post disfranchisement South Carolina." Paper presented at The Citadel Conference on Civil Rights in South Carolina, Charleston, SC, 8 March 2000.

62 Newby, *Plain Folk in the New South*, 463. Even Brittain qualifies her insistence that white workers benefited materially from segregation. White workers did successfully demand that blacks should be excluded from the mills as early as the 1890s but never attempted to enshrine the principle in law. Moreover, Brittain notes that the benefits of racial exclusion emerged only in the 1930s, when "the pairing of whiteness and work had created a new category of racial identity ... that ... intensified distinctions between black and white workers." (Brittain, *The Politics of Whiteness*, 48).

63 Edna Bonacich, "A Theory of Ethnic Antagonism: The split labor market," *American Sociological Review*, 41 (February, 1976), 34–51. For a critique of Bonacich's claim that white workers engineered the exclusion of blacks from industrial employment in the South and South Africa, see Michael Burawoy, "The capitalist state in South Africa: Marxist and sociological perspectives on race and class," in Maurice Zeitlin (ed.), *Political Power and Social Theory*, *Vol. 2* (JAI Press, 1981).

64 For critical reviews of the "exceptionalism" thesis, see Deborah L. Madsen, *American Exceptionalism* (University Press of Mississippi, 1998) and Sean Wilentz, "Against Exceptionalism: Class consciousness and the American Labor Movement, 1790–1820," *26th International Labor & Working Class History*, 1 (1984).

65 By the 1880s, the federal government and eleven states had established machinery to mediate industrial conflicts; by 1905, fourteen more states had followed suit. In virtually, every instance, however, Glenn Feldman concludes that these measures amounted to no more than a "dead letter." Glenn Feldman, "Labour repression in the American South: Corporation, state, and race in Alabama's coal fields, 1917–1921," *Journal of Southern History* 63/3 (August, 1997), 14.

66 Gerald Friedman, "Strike success and union ideology: The United States and France, 1880–1914," *The Journal of economic History*, 48/1 (March 1988), 14.

67 Stephen Norwood, *Strikebreaking and Intimidation: Mercenaries and Masculinity in Twentieth-Century America* (University of North Carolina Press, 2002), 13.

68 Frankfurther and Greene, quoted in Friedman, "Strike success," 15.

69 Philip Taft and Philip Ross, "American labor violence: Its causes, character, and outcome," in Hugh D. Graham and Ted R. Gurr (eds), *Violence in America: Historical and Comparative Perspectives* (Sage Publications, 1979), 187.

70 Allen H. Stokes, "Black and White Labor and the Development of the Southern Textile Industry 1800–1920" (Ph.D. at University of South Carolina, 1977), 177.

71 Writing about black and white workers who lived in the "company houses" in "company towns," Glenn Feldman notes: "Usually black quarters were located at the tops of hills; whites preferred the lower slopes because water had to be carried uphill" (Glenn Feldman, "Labour repression in the American South," 344).

72 Stokes, "Black and White Labor," 178. For a more sympathetic account of white workers' "conservatism," see Christopher Waldrep, *Southern Workers and the Search for Community: Spartanburg County, South Carolina* (University of illinois Press, 2000).

73 For example, see David Letwin, *The Challenge of Interracial Unionism: Alabama Coal Miners, 1878–1921* (University of North Carolina Press, 1998); Greenberg, *Race and State in Capitalist Development*; and Marilyn D. Rhinehart's review of Letwin's book in *The American Historical Review*, 104/4 (October 1999), 58.

74 Cited, in Leon Litwack, *Trouble in Mind: Black Southerners in the Age of Jim Crow* (Vintage Books, 1999), 371.

75 W. E. B Du Bois, "Georgia, Invisible Empire State," *Nation*, 120 (21 January 1925), 64.

76 The following discussion is taken from Newby, *Plain Folk in the New South*, 474–475.

77 Newby, *Plain Folk in the New South*.

78 Wright, *Old South, New South*, 114; Newby, *Plain Folk in the New South*, 404.

79 Newby, *Plain Folk in the New South*, 477.

80 Newby, *Plain Folk in the New South*, 480.

81 Brittain, *The Politics of Whiteness*, 9.
82 William Brundage, "Racial violence, lynchings and modernization," in James Incoe (ed.), *Appalachians and Race: The Mountain South from Slavery to Segregation* (University of Kentucky Press, 2001), 311.
83 Newby, *Plain Folk in the New South*, 491.
84 Brundage, *Lynching in the New South*, 55–56.
85 Brundage, *Lynching in the New South*, 57.
86 Brundage, *Lynching in the New South*, 84.
87 Litwack, *Trouble in Mind*, 291.
88 Woodward, cited in Shawn M. Smith, *Blood Talk: American Race Melodrama and the Culture of the Occult* (University of Chicago Press, 2003), 112.
89 Taken from Dan T. Carter, *Scottsboro: A Tragedy of the American South* (Louisiana State University Press, 1969).
90 Carter, *Scottsboro*, 203.
91 The frequency of communal lynching – which accounted for one-third of all known lynchings – casts strong doubt on Edna Bonacich's "split labor market" theory. The upshot of Bonacich's argument is that higher-priced white laborers attempted to preserve their favorable position by ensuring that blacks would not undercut white workers by agreeing to work for lower wages. By implication (Bonacich does not specifically address the issue of racial violence), white workers developed strategies to restrict economic competition with blacks by violently excluding them from the labor market. Bonacich is not alone is suggesting, therefore, that lynching was primarily perpetrated by white workers. But this theory fails to address the strenuous efforts that *employers* made to fuel and even generate the white worker's "fear of competition." Moreover, according to her split labor market theory, employers who maximize profits by seeking to employ cheaper black labor should have little interest in conniving with mobs of white workers intent on driving off blacks with violence and terror. Yet such cooperation occurred frequently even when evidence confirmed that thousands of blacks were fleeing racial terror in the South – between 1900 and 1930, more than one million blacks departed for the North. Also, because Bonacich's rigidly economic explanation sheds little light on the links between the industrial workplace and the social milieu of white workers, it does not comprehend lynching as a cultural phenomenon that transcended the "rational" pursuit of labor market objectives. For a critique of Bonacich's theory, see Michael Burawoy, "State and social revolution in South Africa," *Kapitalistate*, 9 (December 1981). Newpapers often noted that lynchings were followed by the mass flights of blacks in the area. For example, see Tolnay and Beck, *Festival of Violence*, 240, and "Negro Haters Fire Town" in Ginzburg, *100 Years of Lynching*, 65.
92 "Nearly dead strike-breaker seized from hospital, hanged," in Ginzburg, *100 Years of Lynching*, 157–158.
93 Ginzburg, *100 Years of Lynching*, 163.
94 Ginzburg, *100 Years of Lynching*, 193.
95 Ginzburg, *100 Years of Lynching*, 201–202.
96 Ginzburg, *100 Years of Lynching*, 229.
97 Ginzburg, *100 Years of Lynching*, 107.
98 Ginzburg, *100 Years of Lynching*, 125.
99 Still, rare convictions of lynchers illustrate that law enforcement authorities could, and sometimes did, challenge "mob justice," perhaps because the lynch-

ers were "poor whites." No furore appears to have followed the conviction of George Hall, a worker in a cotton mill, who received a sentence of fifteen years in August of 1902. Hall was convicted on the basis of evidence given by a deputy sheriff (Newby, *Plain Folk in the New South*, 491).

100 James Cameron (until his death in 2006, "the only still-living survivor of a lynching") was amongst the few such fortunate men who were saved from being lynched on the strength of such a testimonial. A noose had already been placed around Cameron's neck when an unknown white person in the crowd insisted that Cameron was innocent, leading to Cameron's reprieve. In 1998 Cameron opened and ran a non-profit museum devoted to preserving the history of lynching in the United States. Cameron's account is narrated in the documentary *Lynching: The Heinous Past* (New York: Filmakers Library; directed by Rolf Porseryd and Jacek Machula, 2001).

Chapter 4

1 Reinhold F. Hoernlé, *South African Native Policy and the Liberal Spirit* (Negro University Press, 1939), 123.

2 Leonard M. Thompson, *The Unification of South Africa. 1902–1910* (Oxford, 1960), 239.

3 Bonacich, "A theory of ethnic antagonism," 34.

4 Other researchers have also shown that efficiency considerations influenced the degree of violence African American workerss in different part of the New South. See Lee Alston and Joseph P. Ferrie, *Southern Paternalism and the American Welfare State* (Cambridge University Press, 1999), 22.

5 Evans, *Bureaucracy and Race*, Chapter 3.

6 Greenberg, *Race and State in Capitalist Development*, passim.

7 The use of the concept "labor effort" is influenced by the argument of Lee J. Alston, "Race etiquette in the South: The role of tenancy," *Research in Economic History*, 10 (1986).

8 The literature on the economic foundations of segregation in South Africa is extensive. For a discussion of some of these works, see Evans, *Bureaucracy and Race;* Doug Hindson, *Pass Controls and the Urban African Proletariat in South Africa* (Ravan Press, 1987); and Debora Posel, *The Making of Apartheid, 1948–1961: Conflict and Compromise* (Clarendon Press, 1991).

9 The Chamber of Mines itself established two labor recruiting organizations: the NRC dragooned labor domiciled in Native reserves within the Union, while the Employment Bureau of Africa (TEBA) was established to recruit migrants throughout southern Africa.

10 Evans, *Bureaucracy and Race*, Chapter 2.

11 Evans, *Bureaucracy and Race*, Chapter 2.

12 Doug Hindson notes that the state itself was a major employer of African workers. Hindson, *Pass Controls*, 23.

13 Cited in Evans, *Bureaucracy and Race*, 29.

14 Johan Galtung, "Violence, peace and peace research," *Journal of Peace Research*, 6/3 (1969), 167–191. For a discussion of the limitations of the concept "structural violence," see Jean-Pierre Derriannic, "Theory and ideologies of violence," *Journal of Peace Research*, 9/4 (1972).

15 Mary Jackman, "Violence in social life," *Annual Review of Sociology*, 28

(2002), 387–415.

16 Jane Yawitch, *Betterment: The Myth of Homeland Agriculture* (Johannesburg, 1981).

17 Randall Packard, *White Plague, Black Labor: Tuberculosis and the Political Economy of Health and Disease in South Africa* (University of California Press, 1989).

18 Daniel J. Christie *et al.*, "Introduction," in Daniel J. Christie, Richard Wagner, and Deborah Winter (eds), *Peace, Conflict, and Violence: Peace Psychology for the 21st Century* (Prentice Hall, 2001), 7. The claim that the worst forms of violence are often instituonalized and depoliticized within hegemonic systems is also the central claim of Mary Jackman's "generic theory of violence." See Mary Jackman, "Violence in social life" and "Gender, violence and harrassment," in Janet Chefetz (ed.) *Handbook of the Sociology of Gender* (Kluwer Academic/ Plenum Publishers, 1999). For a discussion of "invisible" rural poverty in the Transkei, see Clifton Crais, *The Politics of Evil: Magic, State Power and the Political Imagination in South Africa* (Cambridge University Press, 2002).

19 Christie, Wagner and Winter, "Introduction," in *Peace, Conflict, and Violence*, 9.

20 Christie, Wagner and Winter, "Introduction," in *Peace, Conflict, and Violence*, 10. This point is elaborated in Chapter 8.

21 These themes are analyzed at length in Evans, *Bureaucracy and Race*, Chapter 3.

22 Yudelman, *The Emergence of Modern South Africa*.

23 Johnathan Crush, *South Africa's Labor Empire: A History of Black Migrancy to the Gold Mines* (David Philip, 1991); Peter Alexander, "South African and US labor in the era of the Second World War: Similar trends and underlying differences," in Rick Helpern and Jonathan Morris (eds), *American Exceptionalism? Working Class Formation in an International Context* (Basingstoke, 1997); Keith Breckenridge, "The allure of violence: Men, race and masculinity on the South African goldmines, 1900–1950," *Journal of Southern African Studies*, 24/4 (December 1998).

24 Steven Friedman, *Building Tomorrow Today: African Workers in Trade Unions, 1970–1984* (Ravan Press, 1987), 23.

25 Denis MacShane, Martin Plaut and David Ward, *Power! Black Workers, Their Unions and the Struggle for Freedom in South Africa* (Spokesman Press, 1984), 7.

26 Breckenridge, "The allure of violence"; T. Dunbar Moodie, *Going For Gold: Men, Mines, and Migration* (University of California Press, 1994).

27 G. J. (signature illegible) to DNL, "Assault on three natives by miner A. Wood," 15 June 1914, in GNLB151 213/14/D9(6).

28 Breckenridge, "The allure of violence."

29 I would like to thank Keith Breckenridge for this personal communication.

30 Inspector (name illegible) to General manager, NRC, "Assault on Native Jelliconise," 23 September 1926, in GNLB151 213/14/9/(30).

31 H. G. Falwasser to the SNA, "Assaults on Natives," 27 June 1926, in GNLB151 213/12/9(29).

32 Cited in Breckenridge, "The allure of violence," 674.

33 Inspector (NAD) to DNL, "Rex versus John Barker, shift boss, for assault," in GNLB151 213/14/99.

34 "Précis of correspondence. Assault on Native William by miner G.T. v.d. Nest,

Simmer and Jack," in GNLB151 213/14/9/(18).

35 See Acting DNL to Deputy Commissioner of Police, 6 October 1920, in GNLB151 213/14/9(19).

36 General manager of the NRC to the Acting Director of Native Labor, "Assaults on Native mine employees," 28 June 1926, and Inspector J. Edmonton to DNL, "Assaults committed upon native by J. F. de Vries, miner at New Heriot," both in GNLB151 213/14/9(11).

37 H. G. Falwasser to the SNA, 6 October 1926, in GNLB151 213/12/9(29).

38 H. G. Falwasser to the SNA, 6 October 1926, in GNLB151 213/12/9(29).

39 Breckenridge, "The allure of violence," 680.

40 T. Dunbar Moodie, "Maximum average violence: Underground assaults on the South African goldmines, 1913–1965," (Unpublished paper, 2005). Also see his "Ethnic violence on South African gold mines," in Fernando Coronil (ed.), *States of Violence* (University of Michigan Press, 2006).

41 Moodie, "Maximum average violence," 14; Michael Burawoy, *Manufacturing Consent: Changes in the Labor Process Under Monopoly Capitalism* (University of Chicago Press, 1979).

42 Horowitz, *The Deadly Ethnic Riot*, 22.

43 Horowitz, *The Deadly Ethnic Riot*, 556–557.

44 Krikler, *White Rising*, 146.

45 Krikler, *White Rising*, 130.

46 Neil Smelser, *A Theory of Collective Behavior* (Free Press of Glencoe, 1963).

47 Krikler, *White Rising*, 143. For a similar discussion of the role of rumor in the rural areas of the South, see Steven Hahn, "'Extravagant expectations' of freedom: Rumor, political struggle, and the Christmas insurrection scare of 1865 in the American South," *Past & Present*, 157 (November 1997).

48 Horowitz, *The Deadly Ethnic Riot*, 524.

49 Krikler, *White Rising*, passim.

50 Brittain, *The Politics of Whiteness*, 85.

51 Worsening disputes between mine employers and white workers about the reach of the "job color bars," however, detract attention from the broad consensus both parties shared over the *principle* of reserving jobs on the basis of race. See Yudelman, *The Emergence of Modern South Africa*, 100. Also see Belinda Bozzoli, *The Political Nature of a Ruling Class: Capital and Ideology in South Africa, 1890–1933* (Routledge and Kegan Paul, 1981), 94.

52 Krikler, *White Rising*, 291.

53 Higginson, "Hell in small places," 95.

54 Greenberg, *Race and State in Capitalist Development*, 75.

55 Ritual violence could boomerang, however. After Kruger had Chief Kgamananyane whipped for rejecting Kruger's demands for forced labor, the chief decamped with half of his people – a common response to flogging. Bernard Mbenga, "Forced labor in the Pilansberg: The flogging of Chief Kgamanyane by Commandant Paul Kruger, Saulspoort, April 1870," *Journal of South African Studies*, 23/1 (March 1997), 129.

56 When they reappeared in the course of Afrikaner insurrections in 1922, *kommandos* were mobilized against imperial British interests (Krikler, *White Rising*, 170).

57 Jeremy Krikler, *Revolution from Above, Rebellion from Below: The Agrarian Transvaal at the Turn of the Century* (Clarendon Press, 1993).

58 Major H. Walton to P. M., A. H. Q., "Several natives murdered," in PMO80 16/02.

59 "The Boers and Natives," Undated newspaper clipping titled "Lord Kitchener's Dispatch" in PMO80 16/02.

60 V/C M. du Plessis," 10 June 1902, in PMO80 MC 16/02.

61 "Copy of Evidence re the outrage committed by Boers on Kaffirs and Sand-spruit on 1.10.01" (stamped 24 October 1901) and "Mr. FB Arendorf and J. de Beer murdered," in PM81 MC 22/02.

62 J. C. Lyttleton to Sir Henry Rildyard, 5 October 1907, in GOV81 136/1907.

63 In terms of the treaty, Boers were permitted to regain their land and retain livestock they had seized from Africans in the course of the war. Lord Milner's reconstruction government encouraged Africans to voluntarily return livestock to Boers by reimbursing them for the value of the animals and successfully dis-armed Africans by purchasing their weapons. To maintain rural peace, Milner also permitted Africans to be paid in full for all animals that they could show had been appropriated and retained by Boers. Africans, however, remained intensely hostile to the restoration of Boer landowners (Krikler, *Revolution from Above*, 190).

64 Stefan Schirmer, "Motives for mechanisation in South African agriculture, c1940–1980," *African Studies*, 63 (July 2004), 4.

65 Evans, *Bureaucracy and Race*, Chapter 2.

66 Lacey, *Working for Boroko: The Origins of a Coercive Labour System in South Africa* (Ravan Press, 1981), 22. Tim Keegan also provides a lucid summation of the Land Act's impact on African in his "Introduction" to R.W. Msimang's *Natives Land Act 1913: Specific Cases of Evictions, Hardship, etc* (Friends of South African Library, 1996), v–ix.

67 Evans, *Bureaucracy and Race*, 30.

68 According to the historian de Kiewiet, "There is the same exchange of labor services for the permission to cultivate the land and graze on the common, the same right to cut wood for fuel or building, the same tendency for the tenant's entire family to be bound by his 'contract'." Cited in Greenberg, *Race and State in Capitalist Development*, 51.

69 van Onselen, *The Seed Is Mine: The life of Kas Maine, a South African Share-cropper, 1894-1985* (Hill and Wang, 1996), 336.

70 Alan Jeeves and Jonathan Crush, "Introduction," in Jeeves and Crush (eds), *White Farms, Black Labor*, 25–26.

71 Helen Bradford, *A Taste of Freedom: The ICU in Rural South Africa, 1924–1930* (Yale University Press, 1987).

72 Charles van Onselen, "The social and economic underpinning of paternalism and violence on the maize farms of the south western Transvaal, 1900–1950," *Journal of Historical Sociology* 5 (June 1992). Rob Morrell's research on labor relations in Natal argues that the paternalist ethic in agriculture was strongest in areas where "progressive" farmers predominated. Although "physical violence in the form of assaults and murders – was not uncommon," Morrell concludes that severe violence was in fact infrequent. Even more rare was the capricious use of violence against blacks who were employed by other farmers. When it was invoked, violence conformed to the code of authority that bound men who were connected by the formal and informal ties of the work relation. "Given the school experience of farmers, the administration of corporal punishment was likely to have been relatively infrequent, serving generally, with the household

head's consent, to discipline the men who actually did the work. It operated therefore largely in symbolic ways, reinforcing the authority of the white farm owner and black household head, respectively, and reminding the victim of his obligation to the system ... And the corporal punishment was delivered by the person charged with the responsibility of ensuring good order and the spiritual well-being of his subordinates. In this context, farm violence should be distinguished from anonymous violence." (Rob Morrell, "'Synonymous with gentlemen?' White farmers, schools and labor in Natal, c.1880–1920," in Jeeves and Crush (eds), *White Farms, Black Labor*, 189, and Rob Morrell, "Competition and cooperation in Middleburg, 1900–1930," in William Beinart, Peter Delius and Stanley Trapido (eds), *Putting a Plough to the Ground: Accumulation and Dispossession in Rural South Africa, 1850–1930* (Ravan Press, 1986). Also see Jonathan Crush, "'The colour of civilization': White farming in colonial Swaziland, 1910–1940," in Jeeves and Crush (eds), *White Farms, Black Labor*, 225.

73 Ian Ochiltree, "Sharecropping, and paternalistic relations in the American South and South Africa," *Agricultural History*, 72/2 (1998).

74 Ian Ochiltree, "'A just and self-respecting system?' Black independence, the evolution of sharecropping, and paternalistic relations in the American South and South Africa," in Peter Alexander, Rick Halpern, Shula Marks and Hilary Sapire (eds), *Beyond White Supremacy: Towards a New Agenda for the Comparative Histories of South Africa and the United States* (University of London School of Advanced Study/Institute of Commonwealth Studies, 1997), 54–55; van Onselen, *The Seed Is Mine*, passim.

75 van Onselen, *The Seed Is Mine*, 288.

76 Lacey, *Working for Boroko*, 47. Also see Ian Ochiltree, "Mastering the sharecroppers: Land, labor and the search for independence in the US South and South Africa," *Journal of Southern African Studies*, 30/1 (March 2004).

77 Ochiltree, "A just and self-respecting system?", 55.

78 Cited in Schirmer, "Motives for mechanization in South African agriculture," 8.

79 See Evans, *Bureaucracy and Race*, 89.

80 After the Anglo-Boer War, returning Boer farmers often discovered that their lands had been re-appropriated by Africans. Too weak to expel the new occupants with violence, they appealed to the British Administration for assistance. See Krikler, *Revolution from Above*, Chapter 3.

81 Bradford, *A Taste of Freedom*, 50.

82 Farmers' complaints are discussed in Evans, *Bureaucracy and Race*, 30–31.

83 Charles Mather, "Wage workers and labor tenants in Barberton, 1920–1950," in Jeeves and Crush (eds), *White Farms, Black Labour*. Supremely confident in his survival skills in the agrarian world, the plucky Kas Maine was no doubt exceptional when he responded to the thrashing his son received at the hands of a white farmer by packing his belongings and departing from the farm. For the vast majority of blacks, it was more politic to endure humiliation at the hands of these feared managers. Many farm managers were poor Afrikaners – often failed farmers themselves – who were unable to secure positions in the urban economy at a time of mass white unemployment in the inter-War years. Indeed, Kas Maine noted that farm managers in the southwestern Transvaal were called "*knegte*"– "servants" in Afrikaans – and recalled occasions when he had lent money to a farm manager. Many of these white *knegte* were known for their violent reputations and, like the "plain folk of the South," also for the

non-negotiable premium they placed on racial etiquette. A farm worker in the Barberton district observed: "You know those white employees we used to call them *malala pipe* [no place to live], that is why they used to beat us," and "they kicked you very hard, and when they asked you why they said they didn't talk to kaffirs." (van Onselen, *The Seed Is Mine*, 280.)

84 "Justice for Natives. The Reitz assault case," Clipping from *The Cape Mercury*, n.d. but marked 17 July 1932 in BAO6648 103/331.

85 The "Standerton flogging case" is discussed in a document (marked "Very Secret") in High Commissioner to J. H. Thomas, Colonial Office, 7 November 1924 in GG1558 50/1143.

86 *Star,* 24 March 1936, in GG1558 50/1143.

87 "Allegation of murder, Native found dead," Clipping from *Star*, 6 January 1938, in Box 444 A1913 (JPL).

88 Clipping from *Sunday Times*, 16 October 1938; "Shot a Native," Clipping from *Star*, 16 November 1936; and "Rawsonville farmer fined," Clipping from *Cape Times*, 23 March 1923, all in Box 444 A1913 (JPL).

89 David Courtwright, *Violent Land: Single Men and Social Disorder from the Frontier to the Inner City* (Harvard University Press 1996), 27.

90 "Assault on a native teacher; a conversation in English," Clipping from *Star*, 20 June 1934, in Box 444 A1913 (JPL).

91 Martin Murray, "'The natives are always stealing': White vigilantes and the 'reign of terror' in the Orange Free State, 1918–1924," *Journal of African History*, 30/1 (1989), 116. Farm violence is also discussed in several contributions in Jeeves and Crush (eds), *White Farms, Black Labor*. For example, see the essays by Stefan Schirmer, "Land, legislation and labor tenants: Resistance in Lydenburg, 1938," and Martin J. Murray, "Factories in the fields: Capitalist farming in the Bethal District, c.1910–1950."

92 "The shame of the sjambok," Clipping from *Cape Times*, 7 August 1935, in Box 444 A1913 (JPL).

93 "A prosecutor's indiscretion," Clipping from *Cape Times*, 10 January 1941, 24, in Box 444 A1913 (JPL).

94 Murray, "The natives are always stealing," 120.

95 Helen Bradford, "Lynch law and laborers: The ICU in Umvoti, 1927–1928," *Journal of Southern African Studies*, 11/1 (October 1984), 145.

96 Bradford, "Lynch law," 145–146.

97 Bradford, "Lynch law," 146.

98 Ben Turok, "The African on the farms," *Africa South*, 4/1 (October–December 1959), 27.

99 Ruth First, "Bethel case-book," *Africa South*, 2/3 (1958).

Chapter 5

1 Martin Luther King, Jr, quoted in Richard O. Emerson and Christian Smith, *Divided by Faith: Evangelical Religion and the Problem of Race in America* (Oxford University Press, 2000), 47.

2 Sam Hill, "Fundamentalism in recent Southern culture: Has it done what the Civil Rights movement couldn't do?" *Journal of Southern Religion,* 1/1 (1998), http://jsr.as.wvu.edu/essay.htm; Wilbur Cash, *The Mind of the South* (Vintage Books, 1991).

3 Patterson, *Rituals of Blood*.

4 Gwendolyn Brooks, *Selected Poems* (Harper Perennial Modern Classics, 1999). For a discussion of lynching in African American aesthetics, see: Kimberly Banks, "'Like a violin for the wind to play': Lyrical approaches to lynching by Hughes, Du Bois, and Toomer," *African American Review* 38/3 (Fall 2004), 451–466; Kathy A. Perkins, and Judith L. Stephens (eds), *Strange Fruit: Plays on Lynching by American Women* (Indiana University Press, 1998); Jeff Webb, "Literature and lynching: Identity in Jean Toomer's cane," *English Literary History*, 67 (2000), 205–228; Trudier Harris, *Exorcising Blackness: Historical and Literary Lynching and Burning Rituals* (Indiana University Press, 1984); Phyllis R. Klotman, "'Tearing a hole in history": Lynching as theme and motif,"*Black American Literature Forum*, 19/2 (Summer, 1985), 55–63; Judith L. Stephens, Racial violence and representation: Performance strategies in lynching dramas of the 1920s, *African American Review*, 33 (1999); and Steven Weisenburger, "The shudder and the silence: James Baldwin on white terror," *American Notes and Queries*, 15/3 (Summer 2002), 3–14.

5 Donald Mathews, "'We have left undone those things which we ought to have done': Southern religious history in retrospect and prospect," *Church History*, 67/2 (June 1998), 308.

6 C. C. Goen, *Revivalism and Separatism in New England, 1740–1800: Strict Congregationalists and Separate Baptists in the Great Awakening* (Wesleyan University Press, 1987); C. C. Goen, "Scenario for secession: Denominationalism schisms and the coming of the Civil War," in Sam Hill (ed.), *Varieties of Southern Religious Experience* (Louisiana State University Press, 1988), 11.

7 Goen, "Scenario for secession," 13.

8 Hill, "Conclusion," in Hill (ed.), *Varieties of Southern Religious Experience*, 212.

9 Hill, "Conclusion," in Hill (ed.), *Varieties of Southern Religious Experience*, 98.

10 Paul Harvey, *Redeeming the South: Religious Cultures and Racial Identities Among Southern Baptists, 1865–1925* (University of North Carolina Press, 1997), 3. See John B. Boles, "Slaves in biracial Protestant churches," in Hill (ed.), *Varieties of Southern Religious Experience*, 101.

11 David E. Harrell, Jr, "The evolution of plain-folk religion in the South, 1835–1920," in Hill (ed.), *Varieties of Southern Religious Experience*, 24.

12 John Eighmy, *Churches in Cultural Captivity: A History of the Social Attitudes of Southern Baptists* (University of Tennessee Press, 1972); Neil Semple, *The Lord's Dominion: The History of Canadian Methodism* (McGill-Queen's University Press, 1996). Northern and Southern Methodists reunited in 1939 and Presbyterians did so in 1983. The SBC remains a distinct organization.

13 Sam Hill, "Introduction," in S. Hill (ed.), *Religion in the Southern States: A Historical Study* (Mercer University Press, 1983), 1.

14 Ted Ownby, *Subduing Satan: Religion, Recreation and Manhood in the Rural South, 1865–1920* (UNC Press, 1990), 128. Also see Mark Newman, *Getting Right With God: Southern Baptists and Desegregation, 1945–1995* (University of Alabama Press, 2001).

15 Gary Wills, *Democratic Religion: Freedom, Authority, and Church Discipline in the Baptist South, 1785–1900* (Oxford University Press, 1997), 51.

16 Edward R. Crowther, *Southern Evangelicals and the Coming of the Civil War* (The Edwin Mellen Press, 2000), 223.

17 The Southern version of the Social Gospel is discussed in the next section.

18 Paul Harvey, *Redeeming the South*, 93–95.

19 Katherine Dvorak, *An African American Exodus: The Segregation of the Southern Churches* (Carlson Publishing, 1991), 2.

20 Dvorak, *An African American Exodus*, 4.

21 Paul Harvey, *Freedom's Coming: Religious Culture and the Shaping of the South from the Civil War through the Civil Rights Era* (University of North Carolina Press, 2005), 42.

22 Cited in Dvorak, *An African American Exodus*, 186.

23 Cited in Dvorak, *An African American Exodus*, 185.

24 For example see Winthrop D. Jordan, *White Over Black: American Attitudes Toward the Negro, 1550–1812* (Chapel Hill, 1968), 214–215; Eugene Genovese, *Roll Jordan Roll: The World the Slaves Made* (Pantheon Books, 1974), 183–184; Donald Mathews, *Religion in the Old South* (University of Chicago Press, 1977), 70–71; and Dvorak, *An African American Exodus*, 14–15.

25 Dvorak, *An African American Exodus*, 20–21.

26 This point is well made by Cecil W. Cone, *The Identity Crisis in Black Theology* (AMEC, 1975), 49.

27 Harvey, *Freedom's Coming*, 41. For a study of the failure of white religious paternalism after the Civil War, see Glenn T. Eskew, "Black elitism and the failure of paternalism in postbellum Georgia: The case of Bishop Lucius Henry Holsey," *The Journal of Southern History*, 68/4 (1992).

28 By 1900, too, most moderate and conservative African American ministers gave up on the paternalists in the white churches. The latter insisted on extending "assistance" to the independent churches on conditions that all African Americans rejected as servile and insulting. See Harvey, *Freedom's Coming*, 14.

29 Harvey, *Redeeming the South*, 55.

30 This discussion is based on Harvey, *Redeeming the South*, 57–58. Also see Harvey, *Freedom's Coming*, 34–35.

31 Harvey, *Freedom's Coming*, 36–37. For anti-Reconstruction violence in the state, see Richard L. Zuber, *North Carolina During Reconstruction* (North Carolina Division of Archives & History, 1996).

32 C. Vann Woodward, *Tom Watson Agrarian Rebel* (Oxford University Press, 1938), 138–139.

33 Harvey, *Freedom's Coming*, 36. For an examination of Populism's appeal among white mill workers, see Julia Walsh, "'Horny-handed sons of toil': Mill workers, Populists and the press in Augusta, 1886–1894," *Georgia Historical Quarterly*, 81/2 (1997), 311–344.

34 Joe Creechly, *Righteous Indignation: Religion and the Populist Movement* (University of Illinois Press, 2006), xx–xxi. Also see Keith King, *Religious Dimensions of the Agrarian Protest in Texas, 1870–1908* (Ph.D. dissertation, University of Illinois at Urbana-Champaign, 1985) and Robert McGrath, "Populist base communities: The Evangelical roots of farm protest in Texas," *Locus*, 1/1 (1988), 53–63.

35 Creechly, *Righteous Indignation*, 152.

36 Robert C. McMath, *Populist Vanguard: A History of the Southern Farmers' Alliance* (University of North Carolina Press, 1975), 65.

37 Creechly, *Righteous Indignation*, "Conclusion."

38 Lawrence Goodwyn, *The Populist Moment: A Short History of the Agrarian Revolt in America* (Oxford University Press, 1978), 237; C. Stock, *Rural*

Radicals: Righteous Rage in the American Grain (Cornell University Press, 1996).

39 Creechly, *Righteous Indignation,* 168–169.

40 Creechly, *Righteous Indignation,* 170.

41 Creechly, *Righteous Indignation,* 171.

42 Hunter Farish, *A Social History of Southern Methodism, 1865–1900* (The Dietz Press, 1938), 222.

43 Cited in Harvey, *Redeeming the South,* 42.

44 Harvey, *Redeeming the South,* 42.

45 Harvey, *Redeeming the South,* 43.

46 Creechly, *Righteous Indignation,* 177.

47 God would cleanse the world of evil in an apocalyptic Battle of Armageddon that would first lead to the return of Christ and only subsequently inaugurate the new millennium. Christ would therefore return *before* this new age began – hence the term "*premillennium.*" See Creechly, *Righteous Indignation,* 170; Randall Stephens, "The Convergence of Populism, religion, and the Holiness-Pentecostal Movements," *Fides et Historia,* 32/1 (2000), 51–64; and Paul S. Raybon, "Stick by the old paths: An inquiry into the Southern Baptist response to Populism." *American Baptist Quarterly,* 11/3 (1992), 231–245.

48 Woodward, *Origins of the New South,* 450.

49 Cash, *The Mind of the South.* Also see Charles Reagan Wilson, *Baptized in Blood: The Religion of the Lost Cause, 1865–1920* (University of Georgia Press, 1980); Frederick A. Bode, "Religion and class hegemony: A Populist critique in North Carolina," *The Journal of Southern History,* 37/3 (August 1971), 417–438.

50 Harvey, *Freedom's Coming,* 252.

51 Rufus Spain, *At Ease in Zion: Social History of Southern Baptists, 1865–1900* (Vanderbilt University Press, 1967), 209.

52 Spain, *At Ease in Zion,* 129. For a concise discussion of these points, see Harper, *The Quality of Mercy: Southern Baptists and Social Christianity, 1890–1920.* University of Alabama Press, 1996), Chapter 1. Wayne Flynt examines Baptists' campaign for public education for whites in Alabama but ultimately concludes that their commitment to Progressivist causes "fell on shallow soil" (*Alabama Baptists: Southern Baptists in the Heart of Dixie* [University of Alabama Press, 2005], 7).

53 Harper, *The Quality of Mercy,* 115; Howard Hopkins, *The Rise of the Social Gospel in American Protestantism* (Oxford University Press, 1940); Henry May, *Protestant Churches in Industrial America* (Octagon Books, 1963); Kenneth Bailey, *Southern White Protestantism in the Twentieth Century* (Harper & Row, 1964).

54 Flynt, *Alabama Baptists*; Andrew Manis, *Southern religions in Conflict: Civil Rights and the Culture Wars* (Mercer University Press), 162.

55 Hence the prominent focus devoted to visionary reformers in the literature. For example, see D. E. Soden, "The Social Gospel in Tennessee: Mark Allison Mathews," *Tennessee Historical Quarterly,* 41/1 (1982), 159–170.

56 Harvey, *Redeeming the South,* 198.

57 Robert F. Martin, "Critique of Southern society and vision of a new order: The fellowship of Southern churchmen, 1934–1957," *Church History,* 52/1 (1983), 66–77.

58 Liston Pope, *Millhands and Preachers: A study of Gastonia* (New Haven, 1942), 24.

59 Kenneth Cauthen, *"I Don't Care What the Bible Says"*: *An Interpretation of the South* (Mercer University Press, 2003), 56.

60 Spain, *At Ease in Zion*, 139.

61 *The North Carolina Christian Advocate*, cited in Bode, "Religion and class hegemony," 426.

62 Bode, "Religion and class hegemony," 424.

63 Cited in Bode, "Religion and class hegemony," 424–425.

64 Bode, "Religion and class hegemony," 424.

65 Samuel Hill, *Religion and the Solid South* (Abingdon Press, 1972), 199–200.

66 Lillian Smith, *Killers of the Dream* (Norton, 1961), 105.

67 Hill, *Religion and the Solid South*, 47–50.

68 Mathews, "The Southern rite of human sacrifice," *Journal of Southern Religion*, http://jsr.fsu.edu/mathews.htm.

69 Patterson, *Rituals of Blood*, 237.

70 Hill, *Religion and the Solid South*, 199–200.

71 Lillian Smith wrote that only three things offered small rural towns a "blessed respite from monotony": revival meetings, a "political race-hate campaign" and a lynching. It was not an easy matter to disentangle these three acts of communal catharsis, so deeply were they conjoined in the mind and experience of every white Southerner (Smith, *Killers of the Dream*, 101).

72 Smith, *Killers of the Dream*, 107.

73 Smith, *Killers of the Dream*, 28.

74 Mathews, "The Southern rite of human sacrifice."

75 Robert Dabney, quoted in Stephen R. Haynes, "Original dishonor: Noah's curse and the Southern defense of slavery," *Journal of Southern Religion*, http://jsr.as.wvu.edu/honor.htm#21n.

76 René Girard, *The Scapegoat* (Johns Hopkins University Press, 1986).

77 Roger L. Dabney, *Christ Our Penal Substitute* (Presbyterian Committee of Publication, 1898).

78 Dabney, *Christ Our Penal Substitute*, 67.

79 Mathews, "The Southern rite of human sacrifice."

80 Mathews, "The Southern rite of human sacrifice."

81 M. Erickson, *Christian Theology* (Baker Book House, 1985), 790.

82 As Donald Mathews notes in "The Southern rite of human sacrifice," "Once the devil had held mankind to ransom, but now it was God; the God Who Paul believed had liberated Christians from bondage to the Law had become Law itself."

83 Steve Chalke, *The Lost Message of Jesus* (Zondervan, 2003), 182.

84 Brian Anderson, "Overwhelmed by His Grace," http://www.solidrock.net/library/anderson/books/overwhelmed/chapter_4.php.

85 Dabney, *Christ Our Penal Substitute*, 15. An example culled from the web site of Brian Anderson, the evangelical preacher cited above, clearly illustrates how complex theological creeds come to echo in popular religious discourse. Although he does not discuss Dabney's theology, Anderson's document makes Dabney's theory of propitiation very clear with the following example:

> Let us suppose that you have been shopping, and having finished up, walk out to your car to put your groceries away. As you approach, you notice a large dent in

the passenger door, as well as a car nearby with a large dent in its front bumper. I happen to be in the front seat of the other car. I jump quickly out of the car, run over to where you are and exclaim, "I'm so sorry! It all happened so fast! I'll pay for the damages. Here – is this enough?" All the time I am talking, I am putting $100 bills in your hand. Now, your car is only worth $1,000, but I have already placed $2,000 dollars in your hands. At this, you turn to me and say, "Yes, that's enough. I'm satisfied! I'm happy! Don't worry about that old dent – this will do just fine!"

In this illustration I have propitiated you. I offered a payment which satisfied you and made you happy. In the same way, Jesus Christ offered a sacrifice to His Father which satisfied His justice and removes His wrath from sinners who turn to Christ in faith. The death of Jesus Christ turns away God's righteous indignation so that He can accept the believing sinner without violating His holy nature. (Brian Anderson, "Overwhelmed by His Grace")

86 René Girard, *Violence and the Sacred* (Johns Hopkins University Press, 1977).
87 Girard, *Violence and the Sacred*, passim.
88 Patterson, *Rituals of Blood*, 182.
89 Patterson, *Rituals of Blood*, 184.
90 Patterson, *Rituals of Blood*, 187.
91 According to Patterson, scientific evidence demonstrates that "taste and smell stimulants add up to the same sensation and that their effects are not perceived differently by the brain." In the end, therefore, "The experience of being suffused with the odor of the lynch victim's roasting body amounted literally to the cannibalistic devouring of his body."
92 Patterson, *Rituals of Blood*, 197–199.
93 H. Smead, *Blood Justice: The Lynching of Mack Charles Parker* (New York and Oxford, 1986).
94 Ginzburg, *100 Years of Lynching*, 69.
95 "Wants Negroes to fight. Wilmington pastor tells them to drink blood of Whites," *New York Times* (28 June 1903).
96 Maclean, *Behind the Mask of Chivalry: Gender, Race, and Class in the Making of the Ku Klux Klan of the 1920s in Georgia* (Oxford University Press), 137.
97 Charles Reagan Wilson, "Religion and the American South, 1830–1940,"*Southern Spaces*, http://www.southernspaces.org/contents/2004/wilson/print/1d.htm.
98 Mathews, "The Southern rite of human sacrifice."
99 Farish, *The Circuit Rider Dismounts: A Social History of Southern Methodism, 1865–1900* (Da Capo Press, 1969), 226–227.
100 James F. Cook, *The Governors of Georgia, 1754–2004* (Mercer University Press, 2005), 284.
101 This discussion and quotes are taken from Farish, *The Circuit Rider Dismounts*, 226–227. Also see C. Owen, *The Sacred Flame of Love: Methodism and Society in Nineteenth-Century Georgia* (University of Georgia Press, 1998), for a history of Methodism in one state.
102 Kevin Gaines, *Uplifting the Race: Black Leadership, Politics and Culture in the Twentieth Century* (Chapel Hill, 1996), 45.
103 Patterson, *Rituals of Blood*, 171.
104 Hill, *Religion and the Solid South*, 182.
105 Harvey, *Redeeming the South*, 9.
106 Local reaction to the celebrated "Scopes Monkey Trial" of 1925, which featured a riveting clash between William Jennings Bryan and Clarence Darrow over the teaching of the theory of evolution in schools, reflected the broad tap-

estry of Southern conservatism. The Ku Klux Klan, the first major organization to urge that creationism and evolution should be given equal time in public schools, expediently ignored Bryan's earlier support for Progressive Populist ideals. For his spirited attempt to debunk Darwin's theory in favor of a literalist interpretation of the Bible, the organization adopted Bryan as "one of our own." When a dejected Bryan unexpectedly died a few days after the trial, the Klan hailed him as "the greatest Klansman of our time" and set crosses ablaze in his honor (Edward J. Larson, *Summer for the Gods: The Scopes Trial and America's Continuing Debate Over Science and Religion* [Harvard University Press, 1997]; Wyn C. Wade, *The Fiery Cross: The Ku Klux Klan in America* [Simon and Schuster, 1987], 287–288).

Chapter 6

1 Mathews, "The Southern rite of human sacrifice."
2 A *laager* is a camp that nineteenth-century Boer trekkers created by forming a circle of wagons. The formation became a symbol of either the obduracy or, for Afrikaners, the gritty determination of Afrikaners in the twentieth century.
3 Dubow, *Racial Segregation,* 13.
4 Johann Kinghorn, "On the theology of Church and society in the DRC," *Journal of Theology for Southern Africa* 70 (March 1990), 22.
5 The distinction is taken from George Fredrickson, *The Arrogance of Race: Historical Perspectives on Slavery, Racism, and Social Inequality* (Wesleyan University Press, 1988), 189–190.
6 Johan du Plessis, *History of Christian Missions in South Africa* (C. Struik, 1965), 6.
7 Tim Keegan, *Colonial South Africa and the Origins of the Racial Order* (University Press of Virginia, 1996), 87.
8 Keegan, *Colonial South Africa,* 97.
9 Jonathan Gerstner, "A Christian monopoly: The Reformed Church and colonial society under Dutch rule," in R. Elphick and R. Davenport (eds), *Christianity in South Africa: A Political, Social, and Cultural History* (University of California Press, 1997), 2–3.
10 André du Toit, "Puritans in Africa? Afrikaner Calvinism and Kuyperian Neo-Calvinism in late nineteenth century South Africa," *Comparative Studies in Society and History,* 27/2 (1985), 233.
11 Giliomee, *The Afrikaners: A Biography of a People* (C. Hurst and Company, 2003), 450.
12 Giliomee, *The Afrikaners,* 208. Also see Susan Ritner, "The Dutch Reformed Church and Apartheid," *The Journal of Contemporary History,* 2/4 (October 1967).
13 Francis Wilson, "Farming, 1866–1966," in Monica Wilson and Leonard M. Thompson (eds), *The Oxford History of South Africa* (Oxford University Press, 1969).
14 Giliomee, *The Afrikaners,* 206.
15 Giliomee, *The Afrikaners,* 210.
16 Martin Chanock, "Criminological science and the criminal law on the colonial periphery: Perception, fantasy, and realities in South Africa, 1900–1930," *Law and Social Inquiry,* 20/4 (Autumn, 1995), 930.
17 Irving Hexham, *The Irony of Apartheid: The Struggle for National Independ-*

ence of Afrikaner Calvinism Against British Imperialism (Edwin Mellen Press, 1981), 37.

18 Yudelman, *The Emergence of Modern South Africa,* passim.

19 T. Dunbar Moodie, *The Rise of Afrikanerdom: Power, Apartheid, and the Afrikaner Civil Religion* (University of California Press, 1975), 69.

20 Abraham Kuyper, *Calvinism: Six Stone Foundation Lectures* (William B. Eerdmans, 1943), 96–97.

21 Evans, *Bureaucracy and Race,* 225–227.

22 Moodie, *The Rise of Afrikanerdom,* 68.

23 Kruger's government had initially rejected the principle that government was bound to intercede on behalf of its poorest subjects. But when growing numbers of Boers began responding to the missionary work of Anglican ministers by joining their churches and schools, Kruger changed course and opened up the Republic's meager resources to a small but growing number of impoverished Boers in desperate need of "relief funds." John Bottomly, *Public Policy and White Rural Policy in South Africa, 1881–1924* (Ph.D. thesis, Queens University, 1990), 96–99.

24 Giliomee, *The Afrikaners,* 326.

25 Bottomly, *Public Policy and White Rural Policy in South Africa,* 94.

26 Allister Sparks, *The Mind of South Africa* (Heinemann, 1990), 155.

27 Quoted in Johan A. Loubser, *A Critical Review of Racial Theology in South Africa* (Edwin Mellen Press, 1987), 16.

28 Hexham, *The Irony of Apartheid,* 74.

29 Hexham, *The Irony of Apartheid,* 70.

30 Liz Lange, *White, Poor and Angry: White Working Class Families in Johannesburg* (Ashgate Publishing, 2003), Chapter 6.

31 Cited in Ritner, *Salvation Through Separation,* 100.

32 Dutch Reformed Church, *Het Armen Blanken Vraagstuk. Verslag van Het Kerklijk Kongres, Gehouden te Cradock op 22 en 23 November, 1916.* Also see E. O. du Plessis, *'n Volk Staan Op: Die Ekonomiese Volkskongres En Daarna. 'n Opdrag van die Ekonomiese Instituut van doe F.A.K.* (Cape Town, 1964).

33 Dutch Reformed Church, *Het Armen Blanken Vraagstuk,* 13.

34 Sparks, *The Mind of South Africa,* 151.

35 Cited in J. Kevin Livingston, "Bosch, David Jacobus 1929 to 1992, Dutch Reformed Church, South Africa," www.dacb.org/stories/southafrica/legacy_bosch.html.

36 Schirmer, "Motives for mechanization in South African agriculture," 4.

37 Cited in Lange, *White, Poor and Angry,* 146.

38 For example, the Rev. Thomas Chalmers of Scotland (1780–1847), drew on Calvin's writings to campaign on behalf of the poor and destitute, the victims of "the Satanic mills" of early industrialization. Like Chalmers, Hertzog also looked to legislation to protect Afrikaner workers from the predations of capitalism. Alexander C. Cheyne, *The Practical and the Pious: Essays on Thomas Chalmers* (Saint Andrew Press, 1985), 107.

39 Giliomee, *The Afrikaners,* 319.

40 John Daniel Wild, *George Berkeley: A Study of his Life and Philosophy* (Russell & Russell, 1962), 111.

41 Giliomee, *The Afrikaners,* 295.

42 Hexham, *The Irony of Apartheid,* 99.

43 Jabavu, cited in Rick Elphick, "The Benevolent Empire and the Social Gospel:

Missionaries and South African Christians in the age of segregation," in Elphick and Davenport (eds), *Christianity in South Africa*, 360. Sol Plaatje, *Native Life in South Africa: Before and Since the European War and the Boer Rebellion* (Negro Universities Press, 1969), 148.

44 John L. Comaroff, "Images of Empire, contests of conscience: Models of colonial domination in South Africa," in Frederick Cooper and Ann Laura Stoler (eds), *Tensions of Empire: Colonial Cultures in a Bourgeous World* (California University Press, 1997), 184.

45 *Inboekselings* were "the unfree servants" of Boer households in the South African Republic. They were acquired "either as a result of being taken captive by Boer commandos, or they were handed over by settlers or by some African societies ..." Peter Delius and Stanley Trapido, "*Inboekselings* and *oorlams*: The creation of and transformation of a servile class," *Journal of Southern African Studies*, 8/2 (April 1982).

46 John Meriman, cited in B. Hirson, "The general strike of 1922," www.revolutionary-history.co.uk/supplem/Hirson/1922.html.

47 Eddie Roux, *Time Longer Than Rope: A History of the Black Man's Struggle for Freedom in South Africa* (University of Wisconsin Press, 1964), 217. The massacre is analyzed in Edgar, *Because they Chose the Plan of God: The Story of the Bulhoek Massacre* (Ravan Press, 1989).

48 Elphick, "The Benevolent Empire," 362; Giliomee, *The Afrikaners*, 97.

49 Elphick, "The Benevolent Empire," 361–362.

50 This theme is discussed in Evans, *Bureaucracy and Race*, passim.

51 The church's attraction was no doubt also influenced South Africa's colonial pattern in which imperial armies and Boer paramilitary *komandos* assumed responsibility for hammering home the realities of white supremacy on resistant African communities.

52 Yudelman, *The Emergence of Modern South Africa*, 118.

53 Quoted in Rick Elphick, "Missions and Afrikaner nationalism: Soundings in the prehistory of Apartheid," in Brian Stanley (ed.), *Missions, Nationalism and the End of Empire* (William B. Eerdmans, 2003) 58.

54 Ritner, *Salvation Through Separation*, 118.

55 John de Gruchy, "Grappling with a colonial heritage: The English-speaking churches under imperialism and Apartheid," in Elphick and Davenport (eds), *Christianity in South Africa*, 156; Allan A. Anderson and Gerald J. Pillay, "The segregated spirit: The Pentecostals," in Elphick and Davenport (eds), *Christianity in South Africa*, 232.

56 de Gruchy, "Grappling with a colonial heritage," 157. Johan du Plessis, the controversial Afrikaner theologian and nationalist, criticized the DRC's Federal Council for spending money on missions in central Africa at the expense of poor whites in South Africa. See Johan du Plessis, *De arme blanke en de heidensending: Open brief aan den redacteur van De Volkstem* (Zuid Afrika Bijbel Vereeninging, 1917). Also see Enrico N. Casaleggio, "*En die land sal sy vrug gee*": *Vyftig jaar van sendingwerk in die Soedan* (Die Algemene Sendingkommissie van die N.G. Kerk, 1965).

57 Kadalie, cited in Elphick, "The Benevolent Empire," 359.

58 Cited in Ritner, *Salvation Through Separation*, 94.

59 The church's inter-racial conferences continued sporadically into the 1950s before they were eliminated. These conferences are described in Ritner, "The Dutch Reformed Church and Apartheid," 22–24.

60 D. D. Botha, "Opening Address," in Federal Council of the DRC, *European and Bantu: Papers and Addresses read at the Conference on Native Affairs* (DRC, 1923), 7–8.

61 Federal Council of the DRC, *European and Bantu*, 27.

62 For a discussion of du Plessis' work, see David J. Bosch, "Johannes du Plessis as sendingkundige," *Theologica Evangelica*, 19/1 (March 1986). In the introduction to *The Dutch Reformed Church and the Native Problem*, the missionaries candidly conceded that a "large amount of deep prejudice" amongst the laity impeded these goals, but also reminded readers that the DRC was the only church to sustain missionary work entirely on individual donations from church members.

63 The Beaumont Commission was appointed in 1916 to demarcate land that would be added to the existing reserves. Agrarian hostility led to the subversion of the Commission's work for more than a decade, until the issue was finally resolved by the passage of the Native Lands and Trust Act of 1936. Agrarian hostility to the "scheduled reserves" is discussed in Lacey, *Working for Boroko*, and Chapter 2.

64 Giliomee, *The Afrikaners*, 458.

65 Federal Council of the DRC, *European and Bantu*, 5. For a discussion of the impact that American educational ideas had on Loram, see R. H. Davis, "Charles T. Loram and an American model for African education in South Africa," *African Studies Reviews*, 19/2 (September 1976), 87–99.

66 Cited, in Elphick, "Missions and Afrikaner Nationalism," 60.

67 du Toit, "Puritans in Africa?," 227.

68 Cited in Ritner, "The Dutch Reformed Church and Apartheid," 31.

69 Elphick, "Missions and Afrikaner Nationalism," 65.

70 Elphick, "Missions and Afrikaner Nationalism," 65.

71 Giliomee, *The Afrikaners*, 375.

72 C. Loram, *The Evangelization of South Africa: Missionary Conference* (Die Nasionale Pers, Cape Town, 1925).

73 Ashforth, *The Politics of Official Discourse in Twentieth century South Africa* (Clarendon Press, 1990), 23.

74 Elphick, "Missions and Afrikaner Nationalism," 67–69.

75 George Lakoff, *Moral Politics: How Liberals and Conservatives Think* (University of Chicago Press, 2002).

76 Elphick, "The Benevolent Empire," 355.

77 Lord Hailey, quoted in Roberta B. Miller, "Science and society in the early career of Dr. HF Verwoerd," *Journal of Southern African Studies*, 19/4 (December 1993), 646.

78 In 1942, upon returning from a meeting of the United Nations in New York where he had endured hostile interrogation over racial policies he had done much to set in place, a dour Prime Minister Smuts declared that "Segregation has fallen on evil days." The baleful remark also captured the SAP government's half-hearted commitment to segregation and liberal paternalism. Paul Rich, *White Power and the Liberal Conscience: Racial Segregation and South African Liberalism, 1921–60* (Manchester University Press, 1984), 33–34.

79 Herman Giliomee, "Making of the Apartheid Plan, 1929–1948," *Journal of Southern African Studies*, 29/2 (June 2003), 392.

80 Elphick, "The Benevolent Empire," 363.

Chapter 7

1 Claudine Ferrel, *Nightmare and Dream: Antilynching in Congress, 1917–1921* (Garland, 1986), 1.

2 William J. Cooper, and Thomas Terrill, *The American South: A History. Vol. II* (McGraw Hill, 2002), 396.

3 Roberta Senechal, *The Sociogenesis of a Race Riot: Springfield, Illinois, in 1908* (University of Illinois Press, 1990).

4 Christopher Waldrep, *Racial Violence on Trial: A Handbook with Cases, Laws, and Documents* (ABC-CLIO Ltd., 2001); Goldfield, *Still Fighting the Civil War*.

5 Waldrep, *Roots of Disorder: Race and Criminal Justice in the American South, 1817–80* (University of Illinois Press, c1998), 45. Also see T. D. Morris, "Slaves and the rule of evidence in criminal trials," in Paul Finkelman (ed.), *Slavery and the law* (Madison House, 1997).

6 Christopher Waldrep, "Substituting law for the lash: Emancipation and legal formalism in a Mississippi County Court," *The Journal of American History*, 82/4 (March 1996).

7 Timothy Huebner, "The roots of fairness: *State v Caesar* and slave justice in antebellum North Carolina," in Christopher Waldrep (ed.), *Local Matters: Race, Crime and Justice in the Nineteenth-Century South* (University of Georgia, 2001).

8 Waldrep, *Roots of Disorder*, 14.

9 Mark Curriden and Leroy Phillips, *Contempt of Court: The Turn-of-the-Century Lynching that Launched 100 years of Federalism* (Faber and Faber, 1999), 22. In Mississippi, the Black Codes severely restricted the rights of blacks to bear firearms, ammunition or knives; they also prevented black farm workers from leaving the service of their employer before the expiration of their term of service without good cause. Criminal statutes were singled out blacks. In Tennessee, laws stipulated that any black person convicted of commiting an assault on a white woman, impersonating a white woman for carnal purposes, or stealing a horse, mule or bales of cotton would automatically be given the death sentence.

10 Du Bois, *Black Reconstruction in America*, 239.

11 The Thirteenth Amendment abolished slavery in 1856; the Fourteenth granted civil rights to all blacks in 1868; in 1850, the Fifteenth granted the right to vote to all regardless of race, color or previous condition of servitude.

12 Lou Faulkner Williams, *The Great South Carolina Ku Klux Klan Trials, 1871–1872* (University of Georgia Press, 1996), 44–50.

13 Wilson, *The Religion of the Lost Cause*, 12.

14 Dewey W. Grantham, *The Life and Death of the Solid South: A Political History* (University Press of Kentucky, 1988); Courtwright, *Violent Land*. Also see F. Butterfield, *All God's Children: The Bosket Family and the American Tradition of Violence* (Knopf, 1995).

15 Grady McWhiney, *Cracker Culture: Celtic Ways in the Old South* (University of Alabama Press, 1988), and *Attack and Die: Civil War Military Tactics and the Southern Heritage* (University of Alabama Press, 1982).

16 Waldrep, "Substituting law for the lash," 15.

17 Quoted in Michael Belknap, *Federal Law and Southern Order: Racial Conflict and Constitutional Conflict in the Post-Brown South* (University of Georgia

Press, 1987), 6.

18 James Chadbourn, *Lynching and the Law* (University of North Carolina Press, 1933), 96.

19 Belknap, *Federal Law and Southern Order*, 9.

20 Belknap, *Federal Law and Southern Order*, 9.

21 Belknap, *Federal Law and Southern Order*, 14.

22 Belknap, *Federal Law and Southern Order*, 13.

23 Quoted in Ferrel, *Nightmare and Dream*, 16.

24 Belknap, *Federal Law and Southern Order*, 11.

25 Belknap, *Federal Law and Southern Order*, 12.

26 Philip Dray, *At the Hands of Persons Unknown: The Lynching of Black America* (Random House, 2002), 112.

27 Quoted in Ferrel, *Nightmare and Dream*, 229.

28 Brundage, *Lynching in the New South*, 14.

29 Paul Frymer, *Uneasy Alliances: Race and Party Competition in America* (Princeton University Press, 1999).

30 Ferrel, *Nightmare and Dream*, 1.

31 Quoted in Ferrel, *Nightmare and Dream*, 5.

32 NAACP, *Thirty Years of Lynching in the United States, 1898–1918* (Negro University Press, 1919), 5.

33 In March of 1857, seven of nine Justices on the Supreme Court declared that, being property, no slave or descendant of a slave could be a US citizen. Dred Scott therefore had no rights, could not sue in a Federal Court and therefore should be kept in enslavement.

34 NAACP, *Thirty Years of Lynching in the United States*, 5.

35 Valdimer O. Key, *Southern Politics in State and Nation* (Vintage Books 1949), 534–536; J. Morgan Keyser, *The Shaping of Southern Politics: Suffrage Restriction and the Establishment of the One-Party South, 1880–1910* (University Press, 1974), 244.

36 Charles L. Zelden, *The Battle for the Black Ballot: Smith v Allwright and the Defeat of the Texas All-White Primary* (University Press of Kansas, 2004), 15.

37 Cited in Zelden, *The Battle for the Black Ballot*, 17.

38 Cited in Zelden, *The Battle for the Black Ballot*, 17. Each restriction is described in Derrick Bell, "The racial imperative in American law," in Robert Haws (ed.), *The Age of Segregation: Race Relations in the South, 1890–1945* (University Press of Mississippi, 1978), 13–15, and Kousser, *The Shaping of Southern Politics*, 91–138 and 182–223. Also see Albert Kirwin, *The Revolt of the Rednecks: Mississippi Politics: 1876–1925* (P. Smith, 1951), 25–35. The new suffrage restrictions also disenfranchised some poor whites as well. As Stetson Kennedy noted in 1946: "A number of white primary states require the ability to read or write 'any' section of the Constitution. In practice, the registrars apply the test almost exclusively to negroes, although it is increasingly being directed against white union members." (Stetson Kennedy, *Southern Exposure* [Doubleday, 1946], 46.) The reverse was true in South Africa, where no "poor whites" were ever disenfranchised. White women in South Africa were given the vote in 1930 to offset the small numbers of African voters in the Cape Province. See Lacey, *Working for Boroko*, 86.

39 Zeldin, *The Battle for the Black Ballot*, 40.

40 Zeldin, *The Battle for the Black Ballot*, 44.

41 Mary Frances Berry, "Repression of Blacks in the South 1890–1945: Enforc-

ing the system of segregation," in Haws (ed.), *The Age of Segregation*, 96; and Brundage, *Lynching in the New South*, 26.

42 Alice Fahs and Joan Waugh, "Introduction," in Alice Fahs and Joan Waugh (eds), *The Memory of the Civil War in American Culture* (University of North Carolina Press, 2004), 13.

43 Frymer, *Uneasy Alliances*, 54.

44 Curriden and Phillips, *Contempt of Court*.

45 The details of this case are taken from Curriden and Phillips, *Contempt of Court*, passim.

46 Curriden and Phillips, *Contempt of Court*, 58–67.

47 Daniel Mangis, "Dissent as prophecy: Justice John Marshall Harlan's dissent in Plessy v Ferguson as the religious rhetoric of law," in Clarke Rountree (ed.), *Brown v Board of Education at Fifty: A Rhetorical Perspective*. (Lexington Books, 2004), 26. Also see Linda Przybyszewski, *The Republic According to John Marshall Harlan* (University of North Carolina Press, 1999).

48 Curriden and Phillips, *Contempt of Court*, 320.

49 Curriden and Phillips, *Contempt of Court*, 329.

50 Curriden and Phillips, *Contempt of Court*, 329.

51 *Tuskegee Year Book*, 9th edition.

52 Numan V. Bartley, "In search of the New South: Southern politics after Reconstruction," in S. Kutler and S. N. Katz (eds), *The Promise of American History* (University Press, 1982), 159–160.

53 "A well regulated militia, being necessary to the security of a free state, the right of the people to keep and bear arms, shall not be infringed."

54 Belknap, *Federal Law and Southern Order*, 15.

55 Raper, *The Tragedy of Lynching*, 20.

56 For example, see Ames, *The Changing Character of Lynching. Review of Lynching, 1931–1941, With a Discussion of Recent Developments in This Field.* (AMS Press, 1973), 44; and Ginzburg, *100 Years of Lynchings*, 100 and 212. The size of several lynch mobs exceeded 15,000 in 1930 alone, swarming mobs that officials could not overlook. Nor did they. In Honey Grove, Texas, the sheriff boasted that "he saw to it" that the lynchers executed the right man while another responded to researchers with a rhetorical question: "Do you think I am going to risk my life protecting a 'nigger'?" (Southern Commission on the Study of Lynching, *Lynchings and What They Mean: General Findings of the Southern Commission on the Study of Lynching* [Atlanta, 1931], 36.)

57 Belknap, *Federal Law and Southern Order*, 17–23.

58 Frymer, *Uneasy Alliances*, passim.

59 Ames, *The Changing Character of Lynching*, 61.

60 Quoted in B. Holden-Smith, "Lynching, federalism, and the intersection of race and gender in the progressive era," *Yale Journal of Law and Feminism*, 8 (1996), 34. Margaret Lear was a young white girl who had earlier been raped.

61 Zagrando, *The NAACP Crusade: The NAACP Crusade Against Lynching, 1909–1950* (Temple University Press, 1980), 66–68.

62 Cutler, *Lynch-law*, 227–266; Belknap, *Federal Law and Southern Order*, 22.

63 Cutler, *Lynch-law*, 235.

64 Cutler, *Lynch-law*, 254.

65 Quoted in Ferrel, *Nightmare and Dream*, 5. On the other hand, Jessie Daniel Ames surveyed editors of Southern newspapers in 1938 and concluded at that late date that the number who dared to editorialize against lynching were "so

few, in fact, that they d[id] not make up even a respectable minority." Jessie Daniel Ames, "Editorial treatment of lynchings," *The Public Opinion Quarterly*, 2/1 (January 1938), 78.

66 Ames, *The Changing Character of Lynching*, 7.

67 Du Bois, cited in Steve Redding, "Portrait of W. E. Burghardt Du Bois," *American Scholar*, 18 (Winter, 1948–1949), 94.

68 Zagrando, *The NAACP Crusade*; Robert K. Carr, *Federal Protection of Civil Rights: Quest for a Sword* (Cornell University Press: 1947), 164.

69 The Association of Southern Women for the Prevention of Lynching remained neutral on the struggle for an anti-lynching law because the body pinned its hopes on "applying pressure to southern sheriffs" and did not want to alientate them (Ames, *The Changing Character of Lynching*, 62–63).

70 Robert K Carr, *Federal Protection of Civil Rights*, 23.

71 Belknap, *Federal Law and Southern Order*, 17.

72 Dominic J. Capeci, *The Lynching of Cleo Wright* (University Press of Kentucky, 1998).

73 Carr, *Federal Protection of Civil Rights*, 169.

74 Capeci, *The Lynching of Cleo Wright*, 109.

75 Carr, *Federal Protection of Civil Rights*, 171.

76 The records of the Tuskegee Institute confirmed the latter trend: there were five lynch victims in 1940; four in 1941; five in 1942; three in 1943; two in 1944; one in 1945 and six in 1946. The 1946 figure includes the two couples who were lynched in Monroe, Georgia. The quadruple, execution-style murders are examined in Laura Wexler's book, *Fire in the Canebreak: The Last Mass Lynching in America* (Scribner, 2003).

77 Steven Bright, "Discrimination, death and denial: The tolerance of racial discrimination in infliction of the death penalty," *Santa Clara Law Review*, 35/2 (1995), 1. Also see The Southern Center for Human Rights, "A preference for vengeance: The death penalty and the treatment of prisoners in Georgia. A report on human rights violations in Georgia," (June 1996). This report is available at www.schr.org/reports/index.htm.

78 Michael J. Pfeifer, *Rough Justice: Lynching and American Society, 1874–1947* (University of Illinois Press, 2004).

79 Cited in Bright, "Discrimination, death and denial," 7.

80 Myrdal, *An American Dilemma*, 560–561.

81 Gibson, "The Negro Holocaust: Lynching and Race Riots in the United States,1880–1950," (Yale-New Haven Teachers Institute, 1979). Found at www.yale.edu/ynhti/curriculum/units/1979/2/79.02.04.x.html. Also see Ames, "Editorial treatment of lynchings."

82 Cited in Bright, "Discrimination, death and denial," 8.

83 Brundage, *Lynching in the New South*, "Epilogue."

84 Cutler, *Lynch-law*, 163.

85 Cutler, *Lynch-law*, 164.

86 For example, see George W. Wright, *Racial Violence in Kentucky, 1865–1940: Lynchings, Mob Rule and "Legal Lynchings"* (Louisiana State Univerity Press, 1990).

87 Pfeifer, *Rough Justice*, 122–123.

88 See James L. Massey and Martha Ayers, "Patterns of repressive social control in post-Reconstruction Georgia, 1882–1935," *Social Forces*, 68/2 (December 1989), 458–488; C. David Philipps, "Exploring relations among forms of social

control: The lynching and execution of blacks in North Carolina, 1889–1918," *Law and Society*, 21/3 (1987).
89 Brundage, *Lynching in the New South*, 255.
90 Brundage, *Lynching in the New South*, 257.

Chapter 8

1 Piet Cillié, quoted in Giliomee, *The Afrikaners*, 498.
2 Quoted in Martin Chanock, *The Making of South African Legal Culture, 1902–36: Fear, Favour and Prejudice* (Cambridge University Press, 2001), 37. Also see Thompson, *The Unification of South Africa*, 54.
3 Saul Dubow, "Colonial Nationalism, the Milner Kindergarten and the rise of 'South Africanism,' 1902–1910," *History Workshop Journal*, 43 (1997).
4 Hugh Corder, *Judges at Work: The Role and Attitudes of the South African Appellate Judiciary, 1910–50* (Juta, 1984), 5.
5 Roux, cited in Corder, *Judges at Work*, 6.
6 Chanock, *The Making of South African Legal Culture*, 470.
7 Corder, *Judges at Work*, 23.
8 Corder, *Judges at Work*, 167.
9 Chanock, *The Making of South African Legal Culture*, 30; Turrell, *White Mercy*, 9.
10 Turrell, *White Mercy*, 89.
11 For example, the law empowered the "Supreme Chief" to declare pass areas, amalgamate or dissolve whole "tribes," banish individual Africans or entire tribes from an area, and impose a variety of discretionary sanctions on Africans suspected of disturbing the peace through criminal or political acts. Not only did it authorize the department to do all this by simply issuing a proclamation, but it also pointedly prevented "the normal courts of the land" from counter-manding "any utterance ... of the Supreme Chief." Cited in Evans, *Bureaucracy and Race*, 170.
12 For a full discussion of the system of "Native courts," see Evans, *Bureaucracy and Race*, 163–189.
13 Chanock, *The Making of South African Legal Culture*, 52.
14 Dubow, *Racial Segregation*, 22.
15 Feldman, *The Disfranchisement Myth*, 157.
16 Marian Lacey illustrates how industrialists, farmers and mine owners collabo-rated to establish legislation and specific state bodies to regulate their compet-ing land and labor policies. For example, the commercialization of agriculture inevitably made white farmers covetous of land that remained under African occupation throughout the inter-War years. In such cases, the intervention of formal bodies made it unnecessary for White farmers to resort to violence. See *Working for Boroko*, 167.
17 Govan Mbeki, *The Peasant's Revolt* (Harmondsworth, 1964), 67.
18 The cases discussed here are taken from Corder, *Judges at Work*, 63.
19 See Christopher G. Ellison, "An Eye for an Eye? A Note on the Southern Sub-culture of Violence Thesis," *Social Forces*, 69/4 (June 1991).
20 "Blow costs farmer 5s.," *Sunday Times* (18 June 1937), Newspaper clipping in "Assaults on Natives," Box 444, A1913, JPL. These newspapers clippings are located at the William Cullen Library, University of the Witswatersrand.

21 See "No marks – no pain," *Star* (27 September 1921), Newspaper clipping and Sgt. M.J. Sharp (SAP) to The District Commandant, SAP, Krugersdorp, 8 August 1921, both in GNLB151 213/14/9(24).

22 Chanock, *The Making of South African Legal Culture* 234.

23 Chanock, *The Making of South African Legal Culture*, 234.

24 Quoted in Turrell, *White Mercy*, 142.

25 "Spotlight on justice," *Rand Daily Mail* (3 October 1926), in Box 444 A1913, JPL.

26 Evans, *Bureaucracy and Race*, 208–210.

27 Evans, *Bureaucracy and Race*, 31–34.

28 John Brewer, *Black and Blue: Policing in South Africa* (Clarendon Press, 1994), 333.

29 Brewer, *Black and Blue*, 99.

30 This discussion is based on a lengthy memorandum in which the Minister of Justice summarizes his reasons for upholding the sentences meted out in *Rex v David and Philemon*. See N. J. de Wet (Minister of Justice) to His Excellency, the Officer Administering the Government, January 1924, "Rex versus David and Philemon," in GG1740 51/6972.

31 William Brundage, "Racial violence, lynchings and modernization," 310–311.

32 "Assaulted man and wife: Lashes for Native," *Rand Daily Mail* (5 March 1940), Newspaper clipping in "Crime, 1933–1940," in Box 444 A1913, JPL.

33 "Five years for attack on woman: crowd wanted to manhandle Native," *Rand Daily Mail* (17 May 1945), in "Crime, 1933–1940," in Box 444 A1913, JPL.

34 "Three years for stealing a hat," *Rand Daily Mail* (5 March 1940), in "Crime, 1933–1940," in Box 444 A1913, JPL.

35 "Native's attempt to murder master and mistress," JUS116 1/438/11.

36 J. C Smuts (Minister of Justice) to the Governor-General, "Rex versus (1) Jack Mathlala and (2) Johannes Mormana: Rape," 9 November 1934, in URU1476 2824 (1934).

37 Minister of Justice to the Governor-General, 6 October 1944, "Rex versus Mpikwe Mkize," in URU2181 2188 (1944).

38 Corder, *Judges at Work*, 18.

39 Turrell, *White Mercy,* 59–60.

40 Turrell, *White Mercy*, 60.

41 "A prosecutor's indiscretion," Editorial in the *Cape Times* (10 January 1941), Newspaper clipping in "Assaults on Natives," Box 444, A1913 (JPL).

42 D. Reitz, "Bad treatment of Natives 'isolated,'" *Rand Daily Mail* 20/10/1935, Newspaper clipping in Box 444, A1913 (JPL). "Assaults on Natives," *The Friend* (25 October 1935), Newspaper clipping in "Assaults on Natives," Box 444, A1913 (JPL).

43 Both definitions are cited in Ames, *The Changing Character of Lynching*, 29.

44 "Sheep versus men" and "Life versus property," *Rand Daily Mail*, n.d.; "He was feeling jolly," *The Star* (13 March 1939), 24.

45 "£20 for causing Native's death," *Rand Daily Mail* (30 April 1936), in Box 444, A1913.

46 "Sequel to death of Native," *The Star* (21 September 1937), in Box 444, A1913.

47 One such case involved the death of "a colored servant named Meidje" in Uppington in October 1936. Evidence given before Justice Sutton of the Circuit Court recounted that a white woman, Aletta White, had severely flogged

Meidje on two successive days. With H. A. Fagan serving as her attorney, White disowned any knowledge of the bag that two witnesses had seen been placed in car and denied driving in the direction of the river in which Meidje's body was found. Despite the evidence of four eye-witnesses, Justice Sutton accepted White's version and ruled that there was "insufficient evidence" to convict her either for murder or for culpable homicide. After admonishing her for beating Meidje, he fined her £50 or three months for common assault. In South African terms, a £50 fine was a severe fine for common assault and suggests that Sutton may have been out to assuage his own conscience. "Woman on murder charge: Story of girl flogged for an hour," *Rand Daily Mail* (23 september 1936); "Murder charge agianst woman fails," *Rand Daily Mail* (4 september 1936), in Box 444, A1913.

48 "Sentence on brothers," *Star* (5 December 1938), Box 443, A1913.

49 This discussion is taken from Turrell, *White Mercy*, 204–207.

50 Turrell, *White Mercy*, 205.

51 "Farmer fined for flogging Native to death – gaol sentence suspended," *Star* (12 April 1939).

52 "Prison for stealing sheep" and "Sheep versus men," in *Rand Daily Mail* (11 April 1939) and (13 April 1939) in Box 443, A1913.

53 "Youth kills Native – Found Guilty of Murder," *Natal Mercury*, 27 April 1937 in Box 443, A1913.

54 "Woman shot from train," *Rand Daily Mail* (13 March 1939), in Box 443, A1913.

55 "Set light to Native's head," *Rand Daily Mail* (24 September 1936), in Box 443, A1913.

56 "I often play the fool," *Rand Daily Mail* (15 March 1939), in Box 443, A1913.

57 "Constable now charged with assault" and "Assaulted native woman," *Rand Daily Mail* (2 and 5 April 1935), in Box 443, A1913.

58 Farmer acquitted at Umtata – story of struggle in forest," *The Star* (15 September 1938), in Box 443, A1913.

59 "Native girl's body found on railway line," *Star* (24 August 1938), and "Death sentence to stand," *Cape Times* (11 November 1938), in Box 443, A1913.

60 The discussion of the shootings in Port Elizabeth is taken from the *Report of the Commisioners Appointed to Enquire into the Causes of, and Occurrences at, the Native Disturbances at Port Elizabeth on 23 October, 1920, and the General Economic Conditions as They Affect the Native and Coloured Population* (U.G. 1921). Gary Baines, "The Port Elizabeth disturbances of October 1920" (M.A. thesis at Rhodes University, South Africa, 1988), 121, and Peter Wickens, *The Industrial and Commercial Workers' Union of Africa* (Oxford University Press, 1978). Documents relating to the incident in the Carter-Karis Collection were also used. See Reel 4 in MF 3652 in the CAMP Collection, Northwestern University Library.

61 Sgt H. Fowle to the Provost Marshall of the Union, "Bolshevism in the Union of South Africa," 2 May 1919; L.W. Quicke (SAP) to District Commandant, SAP, Rustenberg, 29 September 1917 in "Inquest re Shooting of people during Native Riots, Port Elizabeth, 1920," in Vol. 275 File 2/950/19.

62 Baines, "The Port Elizabeth disturbances," 121.

63 Baines, "The Port Elizabeth disturbances," 126.

64 Baines, "The Port Elizabeth disturbances," 137.

65 Dr. A. Abdurahmin, cited in Baines, "The Port Elizabeth disturbances," 145.
66 Wickens, *The ICU in South Africa*, 162.
67 Baines, "The Port Elizabeth disturbances," 163.
68 Ashforth, *The Politics of Official Discourse*, 17.

Chapter 9

1 Fred Cooper, "Race, ideology and the perils of comparative history," *The American Historical Review*, 101/4 (October 1996), 11–20.
2 Mary Jackman, "License to kill: Violence and legitimacy in expropriative intergroup relationships," in John T. Jost (ed.), *The Psychology of Legitimacy: Emerging Perspectives on Ideology, Justice and Intergroup Relations* (Cambridge University Press, 2001).
3 Smith, *When Whites Riot*, 7.
4 Yudelman, *The Emergence of Modern South Africa*, 227; Debora Posel, "Whiteness and power in the South African civil service: Paradoxes of the Apartheid state," *Journal of Southern African Studies*, 25/1 (March 1999).
5 Cash, *The Mind of the South*, 362.
6 Mary Douglas, *Purity and Danger: An Analysis of Concepts of Pollution and Taboo* (Routledge and Keegan Paul, 1978); Emile Durkheim, *The Elementary Forms of Religious Life* (Free Press, 1965).
7 Cited in Greenberg, *Race and State in Capitalist Development*, 385.
8 For a discussion of these events, see Moodie, *The Rise of Afrikanerdom*, passim.
9 For a discussion of the clash between Apartheid "idealists" and "pragmatists" in the 1950s, see Posel, *The Making of Apartheid*, passim.
10 Bertram Wyatt-Brown, "*The Making of a Lynch Culture: Violence and Vigilantism in Central Texas, 1836–1916*" [Review essay], *H-Law* (March 2005).
11 Douglas, *Purity and Danger*, 54.
12 Cited in Mathews, "The Southern rite of human sacrifice."
13 Fredrickson, *White Supremacy*, 254.
14 Dan T. Carter, *George Wallace, Richard Nixon, and the Transformation of American Politics* (Markham Press Fund, 1992), 78.
15 Mathews, "The Southern rite of human sacrifice."
16 Greenberg, *Race and State in Capitalist Development*; Robert Price, *The Apartheid State in Crisis: Political Transformation in South Africa, 1975–1990* (Oxford University Press, 1991); Frances Fox Piven and Richard Cloward, *Poor Peoples Movements* (Vintage Books, 1979); John Skrentny, *The Ironies of Affirmative Action: Politics, Culture, and Justice in America* (University of Chicago Press, 1996).
17 Zagrando, *The NAACP Crusade Against Lynching*, 145.
18 Posel, *The Making of Apartheid*, 202.
19 Evans, *Bureaucracy and Race*, 301.
20 For example see the newspaper reports of increasing white-on-black murders in *The Argus*: "'Murder' for the following periods: 1936–48, 1959–60 and 1962–63," in the National Library of South Africa. Also see the newspaper clippings in JPL A1913, Box 350 and JPL AD1912, Box 1962.
21 William Beinart, "Political and collective violence in South African historiography," *Journal of Southern African Studies*, 18/3 (September 1992), 463.

22 Rosemary R. Ruether, "Nations built by ethnic cleansing: The US and Israel," *Catholic New Times* (30 January 2005), 12.

23 Bernard Magubane, *The Political Economy of Race and Class in South Africa* (Monthly Review Press, 1979), 167. For a critique of this view, see Herbert Adam, "South Africa's search for legitimacy," *Telos*, 59 (1984).

24 *Blueprint Magazine* (30 June, 2003). www.ppionline.org/ndol/print.cfm?contentid=251788.

25 Cooper and Terrill, *The American South*, 671–673; Brundage, *Lynching in the New South*, 251.

26 The episode is analysed in Laura Wexler, *Fire in the Canebreak: The Last Mass Lynching in America* (Scribner, 2003). Also see Brundage, *Lynching in the New South*, 252–257.

27 Greenberg, *Race and State in Capitalist Development*, 404.

28 Cited in Wade, *The Fiery Cross*, 299.

29 Wade, *The Fiery Cross*, 300.

30 In Mississippi, for example, evidence would later confirm that the symbiosis incorporated the state legislature, the state executive, the WCCs, the Ku Klux Klan, and the State Sovereignty Commission. Neil McMillan, *The Citizens' Council: Organized Resistance to the Second Reconstruction 1954–1964* (University of Illinois Press, 1971).

31 Rayford Logan, *The Betrayal of the Negro from Rutherford B. Hayes to Woodrow Wilson* (Da Capo Press, 1997), 91.

32 Reed Sarratt, *The Ordeal of Desegregation: The First Decade* (New York, 1966), 357–58; Also cited in Webb, "A continuity of conservatism: The limitations of Brown v Board of Education," *Journal of Southern History* 70/2 (May 2004), 330.

33 Clenora Hudson-Weems, "Resurrecting Emmett Till: The catalyst of the modern Civil Rights Movement," *Journal of Black Studies*, 29/2 (November 1990), 175; Michael J. Klarman, *Jim Crow to Civil Rights: The Supreme Court and the Struggle for Racial Equality* (Oxford University Press, 2004), 235; and Webb, "A continuity of conservatism," 331.

34 Hudson-Weems, "Resurrecting Emmett Till," 179. Also see her book, *Emmett Till: The Sacrificial lamb of the Civil Rights Movement* (Bedford, 1994). "If the men who killed Emmett Till had known his body would free a people," Jesse Jackson Jr. observed, "they would have let him live." Cited in Christine Harold and Kevin Michael De Luca, "Behold the Corpse: Violent Images and the Case of Emmett Till," *Rhetoric and Public Affairs*, 8/2 (2005), 279.

35 Quoted in Harold and De Luca, "Behold the Corpse," 280.

36 Quoted in Harold and De Luca, "Behold the Corpse," 280.

37 Carla Crowder, "Private white academies struggle in changing world," *Birmingham News* (10 October 2002), 1.

38 George Lewis, *The White South and the Red Menace: Segregationists, Anti-communism, and Massive Resistance, 1945–1965* (University Press of Florida, 2004), 12.

Index